THE PUNISHMENT OF VIRTUE

MODERN AFGHANISTAN

KAZAKHSTAN

KYRGYZSTAN

ZBEKISTAN

TAJIKISTAN

u Darya

Mazar-i Sherif •   • Qunduz

F G H A N I S T A N

CHINA

★ Kabul

Ghazni •

in Kot

Kandahar

kar

PAKISTAN

Indus

NEPAL

Ganges

I N D I A

Arabian Sea

0   Miles   500
0   Kilometers   500

THE PUNISHMENT
OF VIRTUE

INSIDE AFGHANISTAN AFTER

THE TALIBAN

SARAH CHAYES

THE PENGUIN PRESS

NEW YORK

2006

THE PENGUIN PRESS
Published by the Penguin Group
Penguin Group (USA) Inc., 375 Hudson Street, New York, New York 10014, U.S.A. •
Penguin Group (Canada), 90 Eglinton Avenue East, Suite 700, Toronto, Ontario, Canada
M4P 2Y3 (a division of Pearson Penguin Canada Inc.) • Penguin Books Ltd, 80 Strand,
London WC2R 0RL, England • Penguin Ireland, 25 St. Stephen's Green, Dublin 2,
Ireland (a division of Penguin Books Ltd) • Penguin Books Australia Ltd,
250 Camberwell Road, Camberwell, Victoria 3124, Australia (a division of Pearson
Australia Group Pty Ltd) • Penguin Books India Pvt Ltd, 11 Community Centre,
Panchsheel Park, New Delhi – 110 017, India • Penguin Group (NZ), Cnr Airborne
and Rosedale Roads, Albany, Auckland 1310, New Zealand (a division of Pearson
New Zealand Ltd) • Penguin Books (South Africa) (Pty) Ltd, 24 Sturdee Avenue,
Rosebank, Johannesburg 2196, South Africa

Penguin Books Ltd, Registered Offices:
80 Strand, London WC2R 0RL, England

First published in 2006 by The Penguin Press,
a member of Penguin Group (USA) Inc.

Copyright © Sarah Chayes, 2006
All rights reserved

LIBRARY OF CONGRESS CATALOGING IN PUBLICATION DATA

Chayes, Sarah, 1962–
The punishment of virtue : inside Afghanistan after the Taliban /Sarah Chayes.
p. cm.
Includes index.
ISBN 1-59420-096-3
1. Afghanistan—History—2001–. 2. Afghan war, 2001–. 3. Kandahar (Afghanistan)—
History—21st century. 4. War correspondents—Afghanistan. 5. Chayes, Sarah, 1962–.
I. Title.
DS371.4.C43 2006
958.104'7—dc22   2006043499
Printed in the United States of America
1   3   5   7   9   10   8   6   4   2

Designed by Marysarah Quinn
Maps by Jeffrey L. Ward

IN HONOR OF ABRAM CHAYES, MY FATHER

AND

MUHAMMAD AKREM KHAKREZWAL,

WHO DIED TRYING

CONTENTS

THE PUNISHMENT OF VIRTUE

CHAPTER 1
SUICIDE BOMBING

JUNE 2005

THE ROAD TO KHAKREZ is graveled now, a hard right turn off cement thick enough to bear the weight of Soviet tanks. It passes behind Elephant Rock and the stony crests that form the northern bulwark of the city of Kandahar. It crosses the Arghandab plain, leaving behind its shock of leafy, mud-walled orchards, then climbs through another range of rocky hills to a plateau, with more mountains bulking in the distance. It is a beautiful road, profoundly peaceful—though once the scene of violent battles against the Soviets.

We drive in a convoy, lights and blinkers on, Toyota Land Cruisers mostly, and white-and-green police pickup trucks flanking the black van that bears the body of Muhammad Akrem Khakrezwal. I am in one of these.

A few hours earlier I sat in that van, keeping him company for a little while. Afghans don't do that. They don't sit with the bodies of their dead. But I couldn't keep myself away. "There he is, your friend!" his brother had cried at me hoarsely as he pulled back the blanket to show me his face. It was perfect, come to rest in that stern, almost brooding expression of his. Only a nick, a bit of a bruise, and a scrape above the right eye marred his features. *Then what killed him?*

A few minutes later, we loaded him, limp and heavy, into the black van. People were flocking to the disused school building near his house, requisitioned for the purpose of receiving them: his brothers serving as hosts, his heartbroken bodyguards and tribal elders weeping silently, raising the long tails of their turbans to their eyes, police officers in uniform, squeezing down to sit cross-legged on the broad veranda. Two men wrestled great blocks of ice to the ground in front of a bank of rose bushes, and left them there. Someone talked about lunch. "What do we want with lunch?" a voice assuaged him. There was obsessive speculation, punctuated by the lament of Akrem's older brother—questions flung at the sky—and by pauses for prayers murmured in unison with hands spread wide. But he was alone in there. And after a time I went to sit with him. I could feel the heat radiating up from the floor of the van, despite the air-conditioning that drew on the motor in pulses like long painful breaths. He seemed so alone, and so small, under his blanket. He who, alive, had been so much the opposite. I sat there with him, a little steadied by his presence beside me. I sat there to stave off my own sudden aloneness, in this impossible place.

It was a suicide bombing. That's what I had heard on the radio, and Akrem's name. And I had dropped everything. A suicide bombing—scourge of our young twenty-first century—words with the alchemy to terrify, to paralyze, wherever they are heard on this earth. It was a suicide bombing in a mosque, no less, my favorite mosque in Kandahar: the ancient one made of mud plaster in the middle of the bazaar, with the four towers leaning a little jauntily into the sky.

An Arab had done it, the governor's thick-lipped voice had lisped on the radio. Documents had been found to prove it, he said. An image was making the rounds, of a young man in a soldier's uniform who had bent down in front of Akrem, as though to reach for his hand to kiss, right before the explosion. That would be the Arab, the implication was. And then, an instant later, the pandemonium so familiar by now from television footage, or worse. The sobs, the smoke, the broken glass, the chunks of bodies—naked, cauterized by the heat—the burning hanks of cloth and hair, the stunned survivors wandering about dazed, the medics overwhelmed. It was carnage. More than twenty dead, dozens injured.

And yet something wasn't quite right with this account. In Afghanistan, there are ways you know things. Outsiders call it rumor mongering or conspiracy theorizing, and when they ask you for some evidence, for something concrete to substantiate this gut feeling of yours, you shrug a little sheepishly because you have to admit they're right—you're only speculating. But still, you know. There is a tuning fork vibrating inside you to the true pitch. A tuning fork forged through years spent here, absorbing the underlying pattern. Because there is a pattern, despite the surface chaos. It just takes some time to grasp its contours.

An Arab suicide bomber does not fit the pattern. We just know it. But now is not the time to prove it. Now we have to go through the motions.

The streets of Kandahar, the dirt roads weaving through baked mud villages, are lined with people, standing silently, watching our cortege pass by. At the left turn leaving Arghandab, about a half hour outside of town, Mullah Naqib and his men, dressed in flowing tunics, turbans or lengths of cloth tied about their heads, have grouped themselves beside the road, symbolically ushering us through their territory. I'm sitting in the middle, and I catch a glimpse of them through the window and my daze. Mullah Naqib, the old warhorse who drove the Soviets out of the Afghan south, looks bowed, his sheep's fleece of a beard shot with gray, his shoulders a little stooped despite the urgency exuding from him as he waves each truck past. Akrem was his armor commander during the decade-long anti-Soviet resistance.

We leave them behind; they will board their trucks and join us shortly, guarding our backs. With them, we leave behind the last vestiges of human habitation. The road mounts the wall of a ravine on a diagonal, then clambers among jagged rocks and hoists itself up over the lip of the plateau. There the peeled, windswept expanse spreads out, uninterrupted to the next set of mountains on the horizon.

The mud-brick village blends in with the landscape. Our trucks pull up and park in rows. Child-sized table-and-bench sets have been dragged out of another schoolhouse and piled up against its walls. The packed-earth yard inside is spread with carpets and seating mattresses. Tents are strung overhead for shade. Akrem's brother waves me to a far corner. Obediently, I step out of my shoes and pick my way across the carpets. But I can't stay a full minute. I can't stay there all by myself, apart from everyone. I skirt the mattresses on my way to the first row, right by the compound door that everyone is entering through, and sit back down. I hear Akrem's brother mutter something about "completely in the way." I know it. I'm in the way. I'm an eyesore.

I shouldn't be here at all, in fact. Women do not attend funerals in Afghanistan. I am the only one. And the only foreigner. I had thrown on charcoal-gray hiking pants that morning, military-looking, a blue-and-white striped man's shirt, and a white embroidered shawl to cover my hair. I watch the graybeards do their double take as they notice me and, distracted, stare. This isn't even Kandahar, this is Khakrez, back in the hills, one of the most conservative villages in this conservative country. And by some miracle I have been allowed to come here, to share this moment. I say a silent word of thanks to Akrem's brother.

The schoolyard is filling now, as people find places on the mattresses; I get up and return to my corner. Friends of Akrem's sit on each side of me: a businessman, the security chief of Spin Boldak district. We start talking. A little later, Akrem's brother summons the bodyguard who was at the wheel of Akrem's car that morning, easing it up to the gate of the mosque, when the bomb exploded.

The young man in his police uniform kneels in the hollow of our circle, eyes cast down, and describes what he saw. Someone left the mosque, crossed the street, and turned around to watch. "And when the *Dram!* came, the man did not appear surprised." I exchange looks with the boy, and with Akrem's brother.

I know we ate something. It is mandatory. Afghan hosts feed their guests and ply them with cups of fragrant tea, should their own children have to go hungry. Akrem would apologize for having only "soldiers' fare" to give me. But I don't remember it. I remember someone berating himself for not thinking to bring a generator. I remember gas-fired lights arriving, hissing and burning white. I remember leaving the schoolyard at last, under a canopy of stars, four or five of us trailing behind Akrem's brother, who lit our way with a flashlight, escorting us in person to one of the family's mud-walled compounds.

Inside, great loads of spindly twigs are piled everywhere—in chest-high stacks filling half the courtyard, in drifts against the compound walls, spread across the low flat roof of the front room, which is sunk partly underground in the local fashion for insulation against the murderous heat. I know almost at once, even before snapping off a stem and seeing the precious grains clasped at the extremities of its fine, jointed ends. Cumin. Black cumin. It perfumes the night.

Several people offered me their homes and their womenfolk so I would not have to sleep with men. But like a waif, I clung to the people I knew:

the bodyguards, bless them, with whom I had hardly exchanged words before, when they would respectfully enter the room where I was meeting Akrem, bearing tea or a dish of grapes. I ask if we can sleep outside, in the clean air, next to the cumin and the stars. My companions humor me. The businessman is with us, Akrem's fast friend and benefactor, as well as a criminal investigations officer from the Kabul police department, who keeps aiming barbs at me.

He is an adept of the suicide bombing theory, and has been describing things to suit it. I had goaded him into going to look at the mosque that afternoon. "The concrete underfoot was unbroken," he proclaimed when we returned, and he repeated the assertion to the assembled company in Khakrez. "It was perfectly flat," he said, sweeping his hand out in a gesture meant to brook no opposition. "No way a bomb could have been planted."

The kneeling bodyguard contradicted him. "The ground was not unbroken," he said, glancing at me for corroboration. I gave it. And so we shamed the investigations officer. In a rage at his disloyalty and his swaggering incompetence, I stared broiling embers at him all evening.

The bodyguards start hauling bedding from the mud-brick house. They arrange pallets for themselves in a square in front of the door. Off to the side, a few yards away, they spread a straw mat for me and place on it a cotton-filled mattress and an overstuffed pillow. Two of them, remembering their training, stake out a position by the opposite wall.

No one slept much that night. The welcome unconsciousness would not last. In the morning, things would be just as bad.

I marvel at the sharp stars, at the Milky Way, stretched across the sky like a thick, illuminated cloud. Before too long, I notice I can make out the lines of the outhouse hugging the compound wall a dozen yards away. I get up and make my way there, then come back and pin my thick blanket underneath me against the desert chill. It will be hot soon. This is luxury.

But I was right. Things are no better this morning, they are worse. The huge anvil that plunged down onto my heart the instant I awoke won't be budged. It's cutting off my breathing. We're going to lose him today, forever.

Shortly, the others stir, call out to me. Someone comes with a thermos of tea, a metal box of sugar, a spoon, a stack of glasses, four or five sheets of flat bread; we gather at the bodyguards' square of pallets and spread a plastic mat on the ground for a tablecloth. I feel the hot, sweet tea spreading through me. Maybe I didn't eat last night after all.

And then it's time to go. Some people take their vehicles; some walk along the dirt road; most of us set out across the denuded hills. We look like some silent exodus. Loyal Karim, who works for me, is by my side. I reach down to snag a sprig from a wild shrub; they're gripped in clumps to the face of the bald clay. I crush it lightly between my fingers. The smell is pungently fragrant, like sage, or absinthe. *"Terkhe,"* someone pronounces for me.

We reach what must be the graveyard and stretch out in long lines, cotton shawls unslung and laid on the ground in front of each man for prayer. There is no wall enclosing this place, just the windy hills, and the sky and the mountains on the horizon. No gravestones, just scattered mounds, some marked with tall poles at head and foot, scraps of cloth fluttering like flags in the light breeze. Before us are three bodies: Akrem's and two more casualties from yesterday; I don't know exactly who they are. They lie on ample beds made of dark wood, carved with an ancient pattern. Akrem's blanket has been exchanged for a velvet cloth, richly embroidered with holy verses in silver thread. Men stand like human tent poles at the corners of great lengths of cloth, shielding the biers from the sun; they are hoisting the cloth up and down to fan the air. It has grown hot. The bodies are decomposing. We can smell them.

We are told that we must wait a little longer. Some important people are coming. No one from Kabul—not President Karzai, nor the interior minister, nor any of the American officials whom Akrem consulted with so often and so generously, nor the journalists who used to interview him. But his tribesman and successor as police chief of Mazar-i-Sherif in the far north is on his way. People from Mazar have been arriving all morning: Uzbeks with their bushy hair and angled eyes, Persian-speaking Tajiks, northern Pashtuns, grateful for the peace that Akrem achieved for them in that bitterly divided town. Mazar was supposed to do him in. But it didn't. He won it over, with all its disparate people; he pacified it.

The governor of Kandahar, Gul Agha Shirzai, is coming too. I am aghast. Shirzai is gloating over this death. I know it. My tuning fork hums with it. In Kandahar, Akrem stood up to Shirzai. Shirzai loathed him, wanted him out of the way. How can we tolerate Governor Shirzai here? What is this culture that makes the Afghans, the famously bloodthirsty

Afghans, welcome their mortal enemies into their midst, and show them courtesy?

Someone shouts something at me. Angrily. Pointing. He won't be quiet. I retort, temper flaring. Someone else turns and makes a gesture to calm us down. It is a gesture of prayer. I am ashamed. I have overstepped myself. I am a woman, and my presence in line will render the collective prayer unclean, unacceptable to God. That's what the man was shouting at me. Nastily, insultingly. I drop it and stand aside—coming apart. I go to the black van, empty now, slide back the door, and sit inside. There is a small puddle of blood on the floor.

After the prayer I can return. The men hand the body into the grave. Two of them climb down and start bricking him in. It is an oddly physical labor. They work like master masons, slapping on mud to caulk the joints. I help pass the big flat bricks down to them. Then, when they are done and have climbed out, younger men take turns with shovels. When the earth is filled in and piled up, we begin choosing stones to stud the mound from a heap behind us. Two cut saplings are anchored at head and foot. Someone loops the thin strip of cloth that had bound the body around the saplings, and ties it off. And it is done. He is really, truly gone.

I pick up a stone from the mound and put it in my pocket.

General Muhammad Akrem Khakrezawal, chief of the Kabul police, was forty-six years old. Barely two months in office in the Afghan capital, he was already loved by the population, gruff Pashtun from Kandahar though he was. Akrem was, bar none, the most able public official I encountered in Afghanistan.

And he was my friend.

I don't know if I will ever be able to find out who killed him. But I will try. By God, I will try. And the obvious way to start is to determine who did not.

CHAPTER 2

COVERING CRISIS

1990S-2001

WHEN AKREM WAS KILLED, on June 1, 2005, I had been living in Kandahar, with a few interruptions, for almost four years. The place had drawn me into its entrails, snapping me out of a disturbing malaise.

I had arrived there in late 2001 as a reporter for National Public Radio. The identity was one I had come to by accident, but it seemed to fit, for a while. Years before, I used to inflict NPR on my evening customers when I was working at a cheese shop to put myself through grad school. NPR was this crazy experiment in public radio financed by you or people like you who actually wrote out checks and sent them to their local stations. It was a main source of news for the community I grew up in— more intellectual, a little quirkier than most others. But I never dreamed, when I was cutting Stilton or offering customers a taste of torte mascarpone with one ear cocked to the radio, that my voice would be coming out of that box one day. And then, in a violent allergic reaction, I abandoned grad school and groped my way to journalism.

I reported for NPR from Paris through the late 1990s, gradually being folded into the lineup of "smoke jumpers": foreign correspondents flung at crises wherever they arose. I had a long and rich stint in the Balkans, watching as the splintered peoples there tried to get out from under the wreckage of their savage post-Communist downfall. I covered the evolving international consciousness that grew out of that trauma, including the proceedings of the War Crimes Tribunal at The Hague. When this run came to an end in 2000, I found myself back in Paris, reporting on food. Perfect, no?

Not for me. I had never felt entirely at ease in Paris. I was always struggling over the sense in what I was doing.

For some years, I went for the lowest common denominator. I convinced myself—in the desert of international coverage that the U.S. media had become—that just *being* a foreign correspondent was a kind of salutary subversion. I followed issues in France that had resonance in the United States: labor conflicts at a time when globalization was displacing industrial jobs, struggles over society's investment in public services like railroads and the post office, day care for working women, a big protest by undocumented immigrants in 1996. I wanted to show how the solutions that Europeans reached to these familiar problems differed from America's. I told myself that just convincing some Americans that the United States was not the only country in the world would be a service.

But once I was plunged into the center of the Kosovo conflict in 1999, reporting day and night from NATO headquarters and later from the ground among the devastated refugees, questions about the value of my work were suspended for a time.

I stayed in the Balkans, crossing and recrossing the Serbia/Kosovo divide, later adding Bosnia to the territories I explored in my rented Yugo. At length, I returned to Paris and spent a year covering ethnic conflicts that I could not take seriously, like Basque separatists or Corsican politico-mafia insurgents, and filing a seemingly endless series of food stories. I chronicled how bakeries were turning into fast-food joints, serving sandwiches to lines of Parisians who no longer took two-hour lunches—a story that was at least ten years old. I did a piece on a three-star restaurant that had switched to an all-vegetarian menu, a sacrilege in carnivorous Paris. And then the mad cow crisis. I went to a slaughterhouse for that one.

But all the while I had a sense of foreboding. I felt I was marking time as the world was heading toward a perilous turbulence. It seemed the precepts I believed in, the principles I thought my society was founded on, were fading. Instead of the struggle for justice, knowledge, good neighborliness at home and abroad, we seemed to be taken up with entertaining ourselves and amassing fortunes, no matter what the cost to the planet or human dignity. America and Europe seemed to be missing something basic. Something was wrong, and nothing I was doing was helping to right it.

Then September 11 crashed into the world. It snapped everything into a shocking light. This was it, I thought. Like so many others, I was instantly sure the moment was a watershed. As I joined millions of people watching those Manhattan buildings sink down in a horrendous, helpless, inexorable curtsy, it was clear we had come to a turning point. This was one of those moments that define their century. It was as though the plate tectonics of history were shifting.

September 11 shattered me, in ways that took me by surprise. Reporting on the ceremony at the centuries-old headquarters of the French National Police, with the great, booming bells of Notre Dame Cathedral throbbing in the background, I found myself weeping, out in the open, unable to wipe my eyes because I had to hold my microphone. I was so grateful to the French for just dropping all the contentiousness that has characterized our peoples' long and intimate partnership. For days, they waited in line outside the U.S. embassy to pay their respects. Conversations struck up during those days between Frenchmen and -women and Americans were profound. I began to feel—but the thought took days to surface—that the horror that had befallen us might just hide a miracle. It might shock the United States awake, get us to adjust our course. It might goad us to go to work again, to *be* what we kept saying we were: the champions of human dignity, the exemplars of public participation in government, of government acting in good faith, the mentors of peoples struggling to be free.

Or it might not.

For there was something about the reaction to 9/11 that disturbed me. Along with the new openness, the self-questioning in America—the e-mail messages people were sending around and reading aloud to their friends, the searching conversations between strangers—another tendency was emerging, and it was gaining emphasis. It was a reflex to divide the world in our hearts into two opposing blocs: We the West versus Them, now embodied by Islam, which had suddenly appeared on the world stage to fill the role left vacant by the vanquished Soviet Union. The shorthand term for this notion, taken from the title of a book, entered our vocabulary: the clash of civilizations.[1]

It was clear to me that the Al-Qaeda terrorists who flew their planes into those enormously symbolic American buildings were trying to force people everywhere into splitting apart along these lines. Quite aside from the terrorists' use of mass murder, it was this intent that made them abhorrent to me.

But some of us seemed to want the selfsame thing. And some of our leaders seemed to be showing the way, deliberately blurring all the myriad distinctions that gave our world its depth and richness. Suddenly the world was being described in binary terms, and instinctively I knew that was wrong. An us-versus-them reaction may be normal in humans who are attacked, but is it accurate? Is it productive? Is it the reaction that those to whom we look for guidance should be bringing out in us? Is this the best we can do?

I don't think so. I don't believe in the clash of civilizations. I believe that most human beings share some basic aspirations and some basic values: the right to participate in fashioning the rules that govern them, accountability, access to learning, and the reasonably equitable distribution of wealth, for example. The extent to which different peoples have been able to achieve these things depends a lot on what has befallen them over the course of time—not on some irrevocable cultural difference.

And so it seemed urgent to me at that assumption-shattering moment—that moment full of potential and peril—to counteract the tendency to caricature, to help bring out the human complexity of this new exchange. My background and abilities equipped me. I could talk to people on both sides of the alleged divide. I could help them hear each other. This was a way for me to serve.

I called my NPR editor: "If you need me," I told him, "I'm yours. I'd like to make a contribution."

So he sent me to Quetta, Pakistan, exactly where I wanted to go. Considered the most conservative and anti-American town in all of Pakistan, it had been the cradle of the Taliban movement. It was from Quetta that the Taliban, a reactionary group that used a radical reading of Islam as the basis for the world's latest experiment in totalitarianism, had set off in 1994 to capture nearby Kandahar—to widespread indifference internationally. A few years later, Usama bin Laden joined the Taliban leadership there, as their welcome guest. In return for financial and military assistance in their effort to conquer Afghanistan, the Taliban offered Bin Laden a haven where he could nurture and develop his Al-Qaeda network. Kandahar became the base from which the Taliban and Al-Qaeda forces took over ever-larger amounts of Afghanistan, until an opposing militia called the Northern Alliance was left clinging to only a tiny sliver of the country in the far north.

Because of this foothold, it was in the north that most of the U.S. bombing had been concentrated after 9/11; and it was to the north that flocks of journalists had been dispatched. For the story most Americans seemed anxious to hear—of relieved Afghans welcoming American liberators—could be most plausibly reported from the north.

The south was different. Well after the start of the war, U.S. planners were still struggling for a similar scenario there. They were looking for local insurgents, like the Northern Alliance, that U.S. bombing could be said merely to support. But it was harder to find them in the south. Seen as hostile and dangerous, shrouded in a darkness to match the Taliban's black robes, home to the core of the elusive Al-Qaeda network, the Afghan south seemed impenetrable.

But it could not be ignored. Kandahar had been the first capital of Afghanistan, and it was still the marrow of the nation's bones. And now, after 9/11, it was the antipode, the very place where the attacks had been planned. Quetta, Pakistan, with its promise of Kandahar once the Taliban fell, proposed just the challenge I hungered for. I arrived in the last days of October 2001.

As expected, it proved a difficult time and place to be an American journalist. But not for the reasons I had foreseen. The difficulty lay not in local hostility, but in reporting back to a traumatized nation.

"The worst period in my entire career," a friend and revered colleague confided to me as we compared notes afterward. He sent me a list of story ideas that his editors had rejected. "Our people simply didn't want us to do any reporting," my friend, a Pulitzer Prize winner, complained. "They already knew the story they wanted, and they told us what it was. We were just supposed to dig up some stuff to substantiate their foregone conclusions."

A CNN correspondent told me that she had received written instructions not to film civilian casualties. And I remember a confab in the marbled hall of the Quetta Serena Hotel with BBC reporter Adam Brookes in mid-November 2001, the weekend Kabul fell, listening to how he'd had to browbeat his desk editor to convince him that Kandahar was still standing.

It was as though, because the 9/11 attacks had taken place in New York and Washington, the American nerve centers, they had blown out the critical-thinking apparatus in the people we have always trusted to have one: the editors, the experienced journalists.

National Public Radio was not immune, though my one civilian casualty piece did enjoy the full support of my editors, to their credit. It was a story that simply had to be reported, for the Afghan refugees I interviewed every day could think and talk of nothing else. Their hearts shattered by decades of gunfire and explosions, these refugees had seen nothing like the bombs that were ploughing up their country now. With no experience of precision ordnance, they were almost mad with fear, as their imaginations overloaded their fragile mental circuitry with remembered images of carnage. That U.S. bombing *was* accurate was an important point. But that the bombing was traumatizing the Afghan civilians whom it was supposed to be liberating was just as true. The anguish I heard every day—the pleas to tell President Bush, for the love of God, to stop the bombing—was not an act; it was real. And it seemed important to expose Americans to the psychological impact that this war was having, not the least because it might have future repercussions. Ideological movements like Usama bin Laden's are rooted in collective psychology just as much as in matters more concrete.

So I did the story, visiting a hospital ward in Quetta, where most of the patients were children. I chose one small boy to open my report—at random really, because doctors were just coming in to examine him, and their activity would give me some ambient sound to record, the kind that radio reporters are always looking for to set their scenes. The boy was terribly injured; I wondered how he had ever survived the drive from Kandahar. It was so bad that I decided to censor myself. I took out the reference to the gash across his back—he had just had an operation for something torn up in there. On top of his other wounds, it would just seem too much. Even so, my story drew vituperative reactions from listeners. One said he was so angry that he almost had to pull his car off the road to vomit.[2]

My editors never even questioned me about it. But as time went on, I began to sense a certain impatience in Washington with my reporting. That same period between the fall of Kabul and of Kandahar, when the BBC's Brookes had trouble with his desk, a senior NPR staff member whom I deeply admired wrote me an e-mail message saying, in effect, that he no longer trusted my work. He accused me of disseminating Taliban propaganda: I, like Brookes, was reporting that Kandahar was still in Taliban hands. He called my sources "pro-bin Laden," for why else would they be leaving Afghanistan at the very moment that the Taliban were losing control and anti-Taliban Afghans were celebrating?

For that report, I had interviewed truck drivers who were transporting loads of Kandahar's trademark pomegranates across the border to merchants in Pakistan. Were those workingmen "pro-bin Laden?" A withering U.S. bombing campaign was under way. In that context, could not villagers be simply fleeing their homes under the rain of fire, without guilt by association with the Taliban? And—a most difficult question for Americans to untangle—was pro-Taliban necessarily the same as pro-Bin Laden?

These were the sorts of distinctions, I was learning, that it was imperative to make. Otherwise, we were going to get this wrong, with devastating consequences.

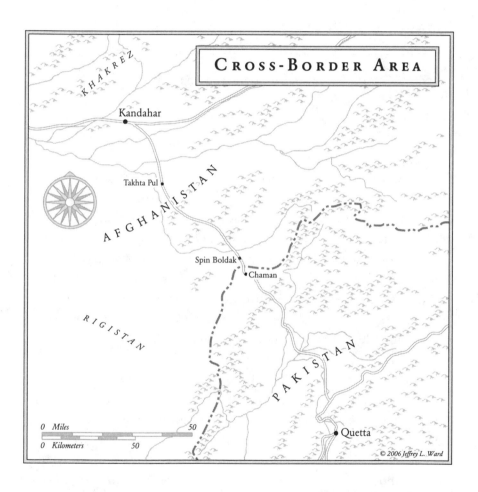

CROSS-BORDER AREA

KHAKREZ

Kandahar

Takhta Pul

AFGHANISTAN

Spin Boldak

Chaman

RIGISTAN

PAKISTAN

Quetta

0 Miles   50
0 Kilometers   50

© 2006 Jeffrey L. Ward

CHAPTER 3

MOVING IN ON KANDAHAR

ZABIT AKREM (as he was called then, for the lieutenant's rank he had earned in military academy) was in Quetta the same time I was—sometimes a few streets or a building away, no doubt. Those days, it seemed like the whole world was in Quetta, Pakistan.

The polluted, crowded metropolis, crawling with disaffected Afghan refugees, had been Akrem's home for several years. Penniless, he had survived on handouts from more fortunate countrymen, among them, future Afghan President Hamid Karzai. He had not even had the means to send for his family; his wife and a little boy and girl remained inside Afghanistan, tucked away on that windswept plateau in Khakrez.

Akrem had been thrust into this humiliating position by a principle: his early and implacable opposition to the Taliban. In 1994, when the black-robed militiamen were rattling the gates of Kandahar, Akrem had quarreled with his own tribal elder about it, through heated nights of palavers. That elder was Mullah Naqib, the same thick-bearded Mullah Naqib who, the day of Akrem's death, had stood at the left turn in Arghandab; the same Mullah Naqib by whose side Akrem had weathered the decade-long war of resistance against the Soviets. That late summer of 1994, Mullah Naqib was going to allow the Taliban into Kandahar. And Akrem refused to be a part of it. The council meetings among the leaders of their powerful Alokozai tribe were tempestuous. In the end, Akrem and his friends were dissuaded from open mutiny. Instead, they held out for weeks in nearby Helmand, then, defeated, left their native Afghan south.

Akrem made his way northwards, spent time fighting against the Taliban alongside the legendary leader of what came to be called the Northern Alliance, Ahmad Shah Massoud. He went to Iran to try to rally Afghan refugees from his own Pashtun ethnic group to the anti-Taliban cause. And at last he landed, impotent, in Quetta. For Akrem too, 9/11—with all its horror—was like the crack of a starting gun. This was it. He knew it. This was the end of the hated Taliban regime.

Akrem was right: the U.S. government moved fast. CIA agents were dropped almost immediately into northern Afghanistan, with briefcases of money, to set about buying allies. Other officials sent out feelers to their contacts in the south, primarily in Quetta, Pakistan.

Alongside the thousands of day laborers, bakers, trinket sellers, hustlers, and Taliban recruiting agents who clogged the streets of Quetta's Pashtunabad neighborhood—the flotsam of Afghanistan's various wars—a community of Afghan elites had also taken up quarters in the Pakistani town: engineers, many of them, the heads of humanitarian organizations or demining agencies, former officials of political factions, former resistance commanders like Akrem. It was to this community that the U.S. government turned after 9/11 in its search for anti-Taliban proxies to work with.

Two sharply contrasting candidates quickly emerged: dapper, bald-headed Hamid Karzai, whose father had been speaker of the Afghan National Assembly in the golden age, before a 1970s Communist coup, and Gul Agha Shirzai, an uncouth former Kandahar provincial governor who had presided over unspeakable chaos there in the early 1990s—the same Shirzai who showed up at Akrem's burial.

American planners decided to enroll them both. The notion was to mount a pincer operation against the Taliban stronghold of Kandahar. Karzai would sneak inside Afghanistan, pass Kandahar, then work his way back down toward it from the north, gathering followers. Gul Agha Shirzai would collect some fighters of his own, and push up toward the city from the south.

It was Hamid Karzai who first called Akrem and asked him to stop by his house, in a leafy Quetta neighborhood. This was a day or two after U.S. jets had started bombing, in early October.

"We're going in," Karzai told Akrem, as they sat together privately in an upstairs room. "I need you to organize some fighters." Armies, in Afghanistan, are personal affairs. Each commander brings his own liege men.

Karzai gave Akrem 300,000 Pakistani rupees, the standard commander's share. "We'll talk later," Karzai assured him breezily. Akrem contained his explosion of energy, focused it down to a burning point, like sunlight through a magnifying glass.

But suddenly Karzai was gone, vanished inside Afghanistan without warning. Akrem was left behind, frustrated, humiliated again.

Then Gul Agha Shirzai came to him for help with the other arm of the pincer, the thrust toward Kandahar from the south. Akrem mistrusted the man. They had had some run-ins back when Shirzai was governor; Akrem had reason to doubt his seriousness. "You're not putting me on?" Akrem challenged, his face like a gathering storm.

"Not a bit," the former governor swaggered. "The Americans have promised more than a million dollars for this job. They told me that when we get to the border, every vehicle but ours will be bombed. Only we will be able to move."

A "good-looking young American" was sitting in on this meeting, Akrem told me. He was wearing Kandahari clothes, the front of his tunic glistening with intricate local embroidery. The American didn't interject into the conversation, and Shirzai introduced him with an improbable title, a journalist, or the neighbor of a friend. "From this," said Akrem, "I knew he was CIA."

Despite his misgivings, Akrem was not about to miss this chance to help finish off the Taliban. With Hamid Karzai already deployed, Shirzai's was the only game in town. Akrem signed on with Gul Agha Shirzai.

A professional soldier, graduate of the national military academy, a veteran of fighting against both the Soviets and the Taliban, Akrem immediately flipped to combat mode. "We asked Gul Agha Shirzai for details: Who would give us food, who would take our wounded back to Pakistan to the hospital, what was the budget, who was providing the money, what kind of weapons we would have. But he wouldn't give us anything solid." Akrem remembered the former governor making two trips to Pakistan's capital, Islamabad, during those weeks. A State Department official told me years later that Pakistani intelligence officers introduced Gul Agha Shirzai at the U.S. embassy there, launching his career as an anti-Taliban proxy.

On October 23, 2001, just before I arrived in Quetta, Shirzai was boasting to the *Los Angeles Times* that he could raise 5,000 fighters. "We are ready to move to Kandahar and get rid of the evil there," he told reporter Tyler Marshall. "Our men are inside and ready." But Shirzai swore he wanted no role in a post-Taliban government. "I don't have any desire for this," he insisted. "I want to work for a more national, more liberal, more developed Afghanistan."[1]

Not a week after that article came out, I was checking in at the Serena Hotel to begin covering the drive to oust the Taliban. A reporter's first imperative upon landing in a beat is to develop "sources." That means striking up acquaintanceships with people who are part of the story, and who, for whatever reason, wish to talk about it. It took awhile, after I fused into the mass of my colleagues grappling to report the same story, but eventually I found one.

It was not Akrem. I would not meet him till later. Those early days, my source was a fighter I discovered in a public call office[2] in Chaman, the Pakistani border town that rubs up against Afghanistan with the greedy voluptuousness of a spoiled cat. His name is Mahmad Anwar. He was a small-time commander also with Shirzai's operation, and I relied on him for my account of it. He became a friend.

He proved to be a very good friend, and I never think of him with anything but gratitude and warmth—even though I discovered later that he had pulled my leg with a charming shamelessness back then, recounting the events not as they had actually transpired, but as Shirzai and his American advisers wished people to think they had. He took a boyish delight in the bright and convincing colors he threaded through the tapestry he wove for me.

When I asked Mahmad Anwar, months later, to tell me the *real* story of the move on Kandahar, he agreed with relish. He recalled the excited preparations for the strike against the Taliban capital. "We met secretly at Gul Agha Shirzai's house," he recounted. It would have been about October 12, 2001.

It was a solemn session, as the fighter recalled it. Just three men were there. Taking turns in a tiled bathroom, they accomplished the ablutions Muslims perform before prayer, rinsing their mouths and nostrils and their faces, splashing water with a practiced ritual grace on their arms to the elbows, their hair, their ears, their feet. Next, they took a copy of the Qur'an down from its niche in a wall. Every Afghan house has one, placed aloft, above any other book.

Shirzai unfolded the cloth that was wrapped around the holy book to protect it from the ever-present dust, touched the volume to his lips, and the three men placed their hands upon it.

"By God Almighty, we will fight the Taliban to our deaths, if we must. And if, when we defeat them and they are gone, we are still alive, we will turn over the government to educated people. This by God we vow."

Mahmad Anwar darted me a look to be sure I grasped the significance: "It was a sacred oath. We swore to surrender our weapons and go home once the Taliban were done for."

Such was the mood of self-sacrifice, and the feeling of optimism about the implications of the coming Pax Americana, as many Afghans remember it. In that pregnant moment, they abruptly shed their bitterly earned cynicism. They were electrified by the belief that, with American help, the nightmare was going to end, and they would at last be able to lay the foundations of the kind of Afghan state they dreamed of: one united under a qualified, responsible government.

Grasping a wad of bills in his left hand, Gul Agha Shirzai licked a finger and paged through them with his right, counting out about $5,000 in Pakistani rupees for Mahmad Anwar, to pay for his men and their supplies. As the meeting wound up, Mahmad Anwar warned Shirzai: "Do not tell Pakistan what we are doing."

The role of Pakistan in Afghan affairs is one of the most contentious issues in Kandahar, and indeed throughout much of Afghanistan. After more than two decades in which the Pakistani government has meddled industriously in the destiny of their country, almost all Afghans—even those who might once have benefited—mistrust the motives of their southern neighbor.

The Soviet Union invaded Afghanistan in 1979. During the savage decade-long war that followed, Pakistan gave aid and shelter to Afghanistan's anti–Soviet resistance, not to mention to millions of Afghan civilians who fled the carnage. Still, most Afghans think that Pakistani officials tried to determine the political results of that war, tried to replace the Soviet puppet at the head of the Afghan state with a puppet of their own. And Afghans resent it. They resent what feels like Pakistan's effort to run their country's economy. They breathe on the embers of a boundary dispute, "temporarily" settled more than a century ago, but in their view still legally open. And they resent the swarms of intelligence agents that Pakistan dispatches to Afghanistan in the guise of students, manual laborers, diplomats, and even Afghan officials, won over or bought during years of exile.

If the Pakistani authorities got mixed up in the anti-Taliban offensive, my border-dwelling friend Mahmad Anwar feared, it would mean danger for him and the rest of the force. For Pakistan had supported the Taliban regime from its very inception. From his vantage point in Chaman, Mahmad Anwar had observed the kind of assistance the Pakistani army and intelligence agency had provided the Taliban over the years. And now, in the wake of 9/11, the Pakistani state apparatus was suddenly turning on its black-turbaned protégés? Converting to the antiterror cause? The switch was suspect in most Afghans' view. Mahmad Anwar was sure that he and his men would be ambushed and shot to pieces if Pakistani spies found out about their plans. Or even if the fighters did survive, a Pakistani connection with their activities must hide some ulterior motive, Mahmad Anwar believed.

Shirzai nodded absently at his warning, and the men filed downstairs, where they bumped into a tall Westerner—probably Akrem's "good-looking young American." Shirzai introduced him as "an envoy from the forces in the Gulf." The presence of this man, at such an early stage, indicates how much it was at U.S. bidding that Shirzai rounded up his force at all. On his own, Kandaharis assure me, Shirzai had no followers. Only U.S. dollars, transformed into the grubby bills he had just counted out for Mahmad Anwar, allowed him to buy some.

About a month after that meeting, on November 12, 2001, a messenger arrived at Mahmad Anwar's house: one of Gul Agha's men. The rendezvous is tonight, he told Mahmad Anwar, at the crossroads where the Gulistan road branches off from the blacktop, halfway to the Afghan border. Be there by eleven. And the messenger was gone, off to inform other commanders.

The dozens of assorted fighters left Quetta a little before 10:00 P.M.—under the noses of more than a hundred foreign journalists, not one of whom got the story. Pulling up at the turnoff, Mahmad Anwar gasped. At the head of a line of vehicles, two Pakistani army trucks were idling.

"Yeah, sure, we tried to hide from the Pakistanis," he remarked to his men. "But here they are."

It is hard to believe that Mahmad Anwar or anyone else involved really thought it possible to keep this venture secret, given the legendary omniscience of the Pakistani intelligence agency, the ISI, and given the close U.S.–Pakistan cooperation on the anti-Taliban effort. Still, the overt collaboration was a sore point with the numerous Afghans who knew about it at the time.

Soon, headlights probing, another several dozen trucks drove up—Gul Agha Shirzai's personal contingent—and the militiamen gunned it for the border, Pakistanis before and behind. The herd of trucks thundered through a half dozen police checkpoints along the rough dirt road, Pakistani escorts signing to their colleagues to lower the ropes. When they reached the border, the Pakistanis stopped and pulled aside.

The Afghans' trucks leaped forward, shouldering one another aside on the inky road, passing and being passed in a testosterone-fueled competition. Mahmad Anwar boasts that only he was able to keep up with Shirzai. It was wintertime in the desert night—opposite as negative is to photograph of the withering summer days. "We could hardly move our fingers." After a while, the former governor stopped and had his men collect some twigs and light a fire. "We didn't even have any weapons yet," Mahmad Anwar recalled, still dumbfounded at the memory. What kind of an invasion was this, anyway? "And now the Pakistanis knew all about us. I was terrified. I was sure we'd all be killed." Furious, he strode over to join Gul Agha.

"We agreed not to tell Pakistan about our plans. What happened?"

"We couldn't cross the border without Pakistan's permission," replied Shirzai.

"We have the Americans with us," Mahmad Anwar retorted. "What do we need with Pakistan?"

Looking back, Mahmad Anwar thinks Gul Agha Shirzai was putting his fealty on display. He assumes the Pakistani government must have realized by then that its protégés the Taliban were doomed. And, with characteristic versatility, it was already switching its bets. It was maneuvering to get some trusty of its own placed in charge of strategic Kandahar under the new Afghan regime. Gul Agha Shirzai, it seemed, was the man.

A few hours later, the ragtag invasion force reached its staging point just inside Afghanistan. "I couldn't make out what was going on," Mahmad Anwar remembered. "How could we fight without guns? So I asked Shirzai: 'Where are we going to get weapons for this fighting?' Shirzai answered, 'Maybe the Americans will give us some.'"

As if on signal, the fighters sighted a ball of dust spinning toward them across the barren landscape in the pale, rising light. It was a truck. When it pulled up and a press of excited men rolled its tarps back, Mahmad Anwar eyeballed some six hundred brand-new Kalashnikovs and machine guns and grenade launchers—straight from Pakistan. He watched his comrades crowd around the truck like starving men at a food distribution. So this was why Shirzai had been so blasé, he thought.

Throughout the morning, meanwhile, new fighters were drifting in to join the force. Among them was Zabit Akrem.

A year and a half later, when I was fitting the pieces of this story together, realizing how much of it I had gotten wrong in my reporting at the time, I asked Akrem for his version. "Could I have an interview?" I said, with teasing deference—in other words, not one of our usual comparisons of notes between co-conspirators. He invited me to come by his house around four in the afternoon, when he had some quiet time. It was July, hot beyond imagination. Most of Kandahar was still asleep, the afternoon's leaden torpor not yet broken. I joined Akrem at his silent house, and, as he spread himself comfortably on his side, leaning one arm on a carpet-covered cushion, I flipped back the cover of a new notebook, bought especially for the purpose.

Akrem recalled the truckload of weapons that had arrived the same morning he did, confirming Mahmad Anwar's estimate of six hundred automatic rifles, plus sixty to a hundred rocket launchers. "I asked Gul Agha where he got them; they were not the kind you find in the bazaar. He said the Americans had given them to him."

A second weapons delivery came about a week after Akrem joined the force. "They told us to build fires to guide the plane," he said, grimacing at the strenuous nighttime hike. The airdrop included heavy machine guns, ammunition, and food—cases of standard-issue MREs (meals ready to eat) sealed in heavy, dun-colored plastic. You have to open up the outside envelope, pour about two fingers of water in, and lean it up against a rock to let the chemical heat warm the food. Whether the Afghans figured that out is anyone's guess.

In any case, they got a tutorial the next day. Two U.S. helicopters angled noisily at them and, touching down in a blizzard of dust and stones, deposited a half dozen Special Forces soldiers near the Afghan encampment. The Americans set up their sophisticated communications devices on the hoods of some trucks Gul Agha provided, all stems and antennas like a daddy longlegs.

The next day, this patchwork anti-Taliban force struck out toward the main road to Kandahar. The plan was to cut the Taliban's supply lines.

Circling overhead—droning away, then tipping to circle back, in maddening figure eights like flies—two U.S. jets followed the force. The sound reassured the Afghans, with its promise of overpowering backup. But it also emphasized the danger of their position as their convoy picked its way along a stony track.

"We were really scared." An unadulterated admission. "We thought the Taliban would kill us any second."

But apart from the noise of the planes—mosquito whines in a lower register—silence. At sundown, a moment of chest-constricting peace in that desert, when the slanting light paints the hills in burnished gold, the militiamen stopped at a stream to wash and pray.

And then the moment shattered like exploding glass. The stuttering bark of automatic weapons ripped the air, the sound ricocheting against the rocks, amplified a thousand times. The men scattered from the stream. They dove for cover. Stony splinters shot past them; the whine of deflected bullets lanced their ears. And this irreligious attack was not all they had to deal with: another group of Taliban fighters was closing in behind.

"The American soldiers told us they had heard some phone calls on the Taliban's satellite, and they were after us," recalled Akrem. "The Americans said their friends in the planes would try to bomb them."

The Special Forces soldiers struggled to bring some order to their proxies' pell-mell retreat.

The droning bombers did manage to get a bead; they let loose, blowing up some seven trucks, Akrem estimated. And that settled the fight. The anti-Taliban militia captured a heavy gun and twenty prisoners. But the next day, Shirzai let the Taliban captives go, even giving them some money to speed them on their way. Hamid Karzai did the same thing, say men who were with him on the far side of Kandahar, in the mountains to the north. Asked why, the fighters shrug their shoulders, disapproval manifest, if unspoken.

Perhaps the leniency was aimed at postwar reconciliation, making a distinction between the Taliban rank and file—conscripted boy soldiers, mostly—and the leaders of the movement. Maybe it indicated that the lines separating the opposing camps were not traced as sharply as they were in the mind's eye of Western observers.

The next day, the fighters reached the main road, at a strategic pass. They were alone, unopposed. Celebrating their fortune, they began deploying in the hills above, when a car approached, a single Arab at the wheel. "He thought we were Taliban, and when he realized his mistake, he started shooting," Akrem recounted. "But we caught him and tied his hands." Half an hour later, a second vehicle drew up, guns blazing. Its occupants were shot to pieces inside the death trap they were driving.

After that, for fully three weeks, Akrem said, "not a single Talib, by God, did we see."

Mahmad Anwar remembers the same thing. "There was no fighting at all," he confesses. "The Americans did everything." After the one skirmish by the brook, the Americans laid down the rule: " 'From now on, don't you move without our order.' We didn't kill a single person with a gun," Mahmad Anwar swears, innocently. Indeed, he remembers a rather embarrassing exchange with some of the U.S. Special Forces soldiers after they all had reached Kandahar. "So," he remembers boasting to the American troops. "We brought you to Kandahar at last."

"What are you talking about," the U.S. soldiers retorted. "We brought *you* to Kandahar."

I must say I blushed to hear these revelations after the fact.

Being a journalist, even one of good faith, is always an exercise in approximation. There is just not enough time, at least in radio, to be sure you got it right. *Morning Edition* has a four-and-a-half-minute hole in tomorrow's show. You have to come up with something by the end of the day, almost anything. So you charge around talking to as many people as you can lay hands on in the closing window of time. You sort through the suspected manipulations. You work to put a story together that adds something, and feels plausible—given what you've been told and what you think of the people who did the telling. And, when in doubt, you stick close by your colleagues. It is the safest course, and it is the course your editors feel comfortable with. That stuff about scoops was never my experience. NPR, at best, strives to add a new angle or some needed depth to a story someone else has broken. My editors never really wanted me to do the breaking. They never liked having me out on a limb.

But Afghanistan is a place of too many layers to give itself up to the tactics of a rushed conformity. Afghanistan only uncovers itself with intimacy. And intimacy takes time. It takes a long time to learn to read the signs, to learn how to discover behind people's words a piece of the truth they dissemble—to begin to grasp the underlying pattern.

Like other journalists that November of 2001, I reported frequent fighting between the Taliban and Gul Agha Shirzai's militia, the two sides, for example, "battling for control of the main road to Kandahar."[3] I told of the strategic pass changing hands;[4] I told how, by contrast, the forces under Hamid Karzai "negotiated—not fought—their way toward the Kandahar from the north."[5] The military pressure that Shirzai's group was exerting from the other side, to help accelerate Karzai's negotiations, seemed at least partially to warrant the friendship that developed between the warlord and his American patrons.

But the whole picture was false. This din of battle was an illusion that both elements of the anti-Taliban alliance south of Kandahar wanted conveyed—the Americans to demonstrate the strength of the local resist-

ance to the fundamentalist militia and Gul Agha Shirzai, displaying a brilliant flair for the value of PR, to "gain prestige," as Akrem put it. "Gul Agha
kept saying there were battles," he told me. But *"Hitz jang nawa."* (There
was zero fighting.) The ruse would repay Shirzai handsomely in the months
to come.

And I, like so many other reporters, fell for it.

CHAPTER 4

REPORTING THE LAST DAYS

NOVEMBER 2001

DURING ALL THIS TIME, my colleagues and I, at least a hundred strong, were stuck in Quetta. While Akrem was picking his way with Shirzai's force toward Kandahar from the south or was dug in among the rocks overlooking the main road, while Karzai's people were approaching the city from the north, "reasoning" with tribal elders along the way, we foreign journalists lived in the marble-clad luxury of the Quetta Serena Hotel, under the close and many-eyed scrutiny of the Pakistani intelligence agency.

From that remove, by way of the unverifiable and sometimes disjointed accounts of Afghans fleeing the bombing, and pronouncements by members of the exiled Afghan elite, we struggled for purchase. We fought to glean some sense of what was going on in Kandahar. How did it look, how did it feel, to be living the last days of the outlandish and now doomed Taliban regime?

Missing from the harlequin Quetta scene were any visible representatives of the country that was making all this happen: the United States. When once I tried to get some input from the Pentagon for a story, I received a curt editorial knuckle rapping. NPR had plenty of correspondents in the Pentagon, I was informed. I was to do the Quetta story. And so I operated in a strange kind of bubble: isolated from the gripping events unwinding across the border in Kandahar, and just as cut off from the prevailing American understanding of those events. I had no idea what kind of spin they were being given back home. And so I had no idea whether, and to what extent, my reporting clashed.

Yet it clearly came as an unpleasant surprise when the November 13 capture of Kabul by the U.S.-backed Northern Alliance did not automatically equate to the fall of the Taliban regime. Washington, like Moscow before it, had apparently mistaken the trappings of the Afghan state for Afghanistan itself. But the two are separate.

In the excitement of the day that saw jubilant Northern Alliance fighters pouring into Kabul, I, too, parroted the received prognostications that Kandahar would go down "within twenty-four hours." I quickly had to revise that prediction.

Abandoning token Kabul, the Taliban fell back on what had always been their true capital, Kandahar. And they stopped there for a moment, suspended, as the BBC's Adam Brookes and I began reporting almost immediately—and as I was to fully understand the minute I made the trip from Quetta up to Chaman on the Afghan border.

It was an ordeal to get there. The Pakistani government imposed police-state conditions on journalists. Before leaving our opulent digs at the Serena, we were required to make room in our vehicles for a police "guard" whose job was not so much to protect us as to report to his superiors on where we had been. The hotel crawled with Pakistani intelligence agents, many of whom landed jobs as our interpreters.

Each time we wanted to make the two-and-a-half-hour trip up the switchbacking road to Chaman, we were required to submit an application to the Home Office, the equivalent of the provincial interior ministry, for an "NOC": a no-opposition certificate, I think it meant. Each such application—even if we had just submitted one the previous day—had to be accompanied by a formal request on letterhead, photocopies of our passport picture and visa pages, and sign-offs by at least two different administrative offices.

Once all these formalities were accomplished and authorization was duly received, we and our assorted drivers and guides and interpreters were only permitted to travel to Chaman in a convoy, escorted by several vehicles of ISI intelligence officers, who, radios in hand, would herd us to the border crossing and hover over us as we worked. The convoy lumbered out the hotel gates sometime between 10:00 and 11:00 A.M. I knew from local taxi drivers that the busy time for border crossing was around eight in the morning.

My aversion to pack journalism was such that I avoided these guided tours, doing most of my work in Quetta among the Afghan refugees there. Still, after the fall of Kabul, a trip to Chaman was mandatory. Indeed, I ended up spending much of my time there in the three weeks or so that remained until Kandahar finally succumbed on December 6, 2001. I even managed to evade the ISI and spend a few nights up there.

True to the lawlessness of the two countries that meet at its gates, Chaman, Pakistan, is the archetype of a frontier town. It is like a seashore under a menacing cloud, its life defined by the incessant tide of travelers, traders, laborers, refugees, soldiers, scavengers, scholars, spies, trucks piled with crates or sacks of wheat, scrap metal, smuggled electronic goods, contraband, dust, rumors, and news that sweeps back and forth across the border each day. The time I spent there in late November 2001, real clouds gathered for the first time in months, and a warm wind filled the air with blinding dust. Everyone had his shawl pulled tight across his face, crossed over his mouth in a perfect V.

It was Ramadan, the Muslim month of fasting. Hungry believers obsess about food, and the roads were an indescribable crush of carts bearing mounds of oranges, dates, big lumps of caramelized sugar, raisins, long, mild white radishes, pomegranates, but also socks, shirts, and other sundries, and men walking in their gorgeously embroidered shawls or crowding around the fry stalls cooking up Ramadan delicacies. It could take fifteen minutes to drive three hundred yards. Once, a hobbled donkey was planted in the middle of the road, making an even more inextricable tangle of the traffic. No one seemed overly troubled. Amid my young interpreter's stricken cries ("No, Sarah, get back in the car!"), I hopped out and began to drag the creature bodily to the curb, to the hilarity of onlookers. They came and "helped" by delivering thudding blows to its rear end. We circled past ten minutes later and they were still kicking the poor donkey.

The way to talk to travelers, unfortunately, was to stand by the border gate—a bar across the road—and try to snag them on their way past, walking beside them as they hustled along, exchanging greetings and begging them to stop for a moment and give some news about the situation in Kandahar. This under the eyes of the border police, who invariably hovered and tried to listen. But seeing me often there alone after I had begun overnighting in Chaman, the officers warmed to me a little and helped by swatting away the clouds of barefoot young adolescents who made the job a trial. On one occasion, a rather older adolescent made a specialty of slipping behind me in the crowd and touching my ass, looking innocently away when I whipped around. The third time he did it I warned him, wagging a finger; the fourth time, I hauled off and slugged him.

It was in Chaman that I made a decision that people have asked me about ever since. I began to dress in the traditional clothing worn by Afghan men: vast trousers gathered at the waist with a woven belt, a flowing calf-length tunic of the same fabric, and a large shawl, embroidered at both ends, wrapped around the upper body, draping to a point between the heels. The decision was based on a rudimentary notion of optics, nothing more sinister.

Before leaving Islamabad for Quetta in October, I had some Pakistani women's clothes made up in the bazaar. The outfit is similar, but more closely tailored and done in bright colors. This is what I wore while reporting in Quetta. But Chaman, a mere two-hour drive away, on the border with Afghanistan, was in reality very distant indeed. There was not a single woman to be seen on the streets, let alone one without a burka, that ghostlike, powder-blue garment the Taliban made famous.[1] My—to Chamani eyes—garishly bright Quetta clothes were the textile equivalent of flashing neon lights. People would rush to flock round me from a hundred yards away when they spied me stepping out of my car. It made for difficult reporting, not to mention psychological discomfort. So I considered: What were my choices? I could wear a *burqa.* Fat chance. I could give up the effort altogether and don Western garb. That would not solve the problem, since there were no more Westerners in Chaman than there were women. Cargo pants and a parka would draw gawkers to me just the same.

I remembered the principle of optics: that the human eye does not actually see everything the brain registers; it only picks up most of the visual data, and the brain, trained, connects the dots. I decided to go for the optical illusion. If I wore men's clothes, I figured, then idle observers, from a distance anyway, would "see" me as the man they expected and leave me alone. It worked, more or less, and I could get on with my job.

Every kind of person was crossing that border those November days—

from children trudging to and from jobs on the "auto mile" across the Afghan border in Spin Boldak, or other children, their faces painted with a foundation of desert dust and their eyes lined with kohl to protect against it, who guided donkey carts of scrap metal along desert tracks well away from the main road; or wood gatherers driving tractors loaded with towers of brush from in the faraway Rigistan Desert, which stretches from Kandahar to the Iranian border; to neatly tricked out Taliban, who did not bother to disguise their affiliations to the Pakistani Frontier Guards, who never asked them questions; to the latest representatives of the region's ever-present transit traders: truck drivers, sitting on the bumpers of their riotously decorated vehicles, waiting to be checked in by customs officers. I wanted to evoke a picture of these trucks in one story, so I squatted down to jingle the ornaments that hung about the skirts of one of them, with microphone cocked to catch the sound. The drivers found this behavior exceedingly peculiar, even in a foreigner—that infinitely peculiar breed.

Kandahar, as the various cross-border travelers described it in late November 2001, was still firmly in the Taliban's grip. But tension was rising. It seemed the "Arab Taliban," as Kandaharis dubbed Al-Qaeda members, were growing nervous and tightening their direct control over the town. There was a strict curfew, and by sundown each day they would take over the main checkpoints themselves. The Arabs had begun to mistrust their Taliban hosts, some of whom were now negotiating Kandahar's surrender. The drivers told about probing searches, the Arabs literally turning people's pockets inside out. A man who was caught with a satellite phone was ostentatiously hung in the middle of town. The Al-Qaeda fighters swabbed dirt on their trademark Toyota four-wheel drive pickup trucks as camouflage for runs into the desert, where they would spend the nights for safety. But they were still arrogantly cruising around in those trucks.

In other words, though the end was inevitable, I could no longer report that it was imminent. I tried to depict the complexity of the situation, with alternating negotiations between Taliban leaders and Karzai's representatives for the bloodless surrender of Kandahar, and military posturing by the American proxy forces deployed on either side of the city—the whole punctuated by the deafening, implacable message of the U.S. bombing.

This was when I first encountered Mahmad Anwar, sitting with some of his men behind the darkened windows of a public call office. They were Achekzais—hard-swearing, ill-famed rogues who dominate the border area and its attendant opportunities for a thousand forms of smuggling. With an ancestral feeling for their territory predating any international boundary, members of the Achekzai tribe move easily between their fiefdoms of Chaman, Pakistan, and its sister town across the border, Spin Boldak, Afghanistan. They are known as people with no loyalty, except maybe to themselves.

Tribal epithets like this were entering even my vocabulary by then. I kept hearing them, so it was hard to miss how key such labels were to the way most southern Afghans defined each other, even if they denied the fact. I would sit around in my Serena hotel room, trading jokes with my driver and cousins or friends of his in what developed into an evening tea ritual, and I discovered I could make the guys laugh—and warm up to me—with self-deprecating comments, playing on the tribal stereotypes. Then and there I decided to bone up on the tribes.

They were an intimidating lot, the Achekzai fighters lounging in the neighborhood public call office, sporting characteristic hooked noses and great mats of hair. And yet they welcomed me kindly—and were having difficulty removing the smiles from their faces. This, more than any other sign, foretold the end of the Taliban for my driver and interpreter. "These people were afraid to *breathe* around here three months ago," my young interpreter exclaimed. One of the fiercest looking of the lot, with wild black hair and beard, kept bringing a little bouquet of flowers up to his positively ferocious nose. A picture out of a Persian miniature.

I think I amused these Achekzai fighters with my unabashed persistence—once picking my way all the way to Mahmad Anwar's house on Chaman's frayed, baked-mud edges. They became my chief informants. They gave me the satellite numbers of their commanders in the field, whom I would call from Quetta, and who, it is true, often led me astray with tales of fierce fighting. After announcing ultimatums before a threatened battle to the death, they would inform me that their absolute final deadline for the surrender of nearby Spin Boldak had just been delayed for yet another twenty-four hours. "Some tribal elders reasoned with us, saying we should do things differently this time," Mahmad Anwar would explain. "For the past twenty-three years Afghanistan has been destroyed by war, and too many people were killed. We don't want to repeat this mistake. That's why we keep changing our minds and putting off our deadline."

Trying to make sense of these things—the bewildering oscillation between ferocity and patience—I emphasized in my stories the Pashtun penchant for negotiation. For I had a tutor. My other main source of information during that month of November was Hamid Karzai's sharp-eyed uncle, Aziz Khan.

We journalists would troop over to the Karzai family residence every day. Every day we were ushered to a receiving room by a turbaned servant, and served green tea in a china cup and a dish of almonds and raisins from Kandahar. It was Ramadan, but we were foreigners. I had joined the daytime fast, so I did not eat. But it was unthinkable for a Karzai to receive a person into his house without at least such scant marks of hospitality as these. Even if the visitor was there on business.

It was not Ahmad Wali, Hamid's younger brother and the target of our attentions, who most helped to explain the subtle ballet going on in Kandahar; it was the elders. I would linger in the yard after my interview and squat beside the old men while they clicked their prayer beads and listened to the radio. Or I would go next door to visit with Uncle Aziz, sitting in his own peaceful garden. These elders introduced me to the unwritten tribal code called *Pashtun Wali* and the tradition of mediation and negotiation it enshrines.

Pashtun society—lacking in the mechanisms of a strong state—tends to settle disputes among its members not by striving for some ideal of justice that would need enforcing, but by means of practical conflict-resolution techniques. The aim is to achieve a workable settlement that satisfies both parties sufficiently for it to stick, and not immediately spawn further conflict.

A typical dispute might go something like this: If someone commits a crime—steals an animal or kills someone—a meeting is called between respected relatives of the two parties. These elders talk the matter out. They get the animal back; they negotiate a fine; they pressure the victim's family to forgive; they obtain women from the killer's family for marriage into the victim's family. (This solution, which women abhor, has the double advantage from the male perspective of saving the victim's kin the prohibitive cost of brideprice, and healing the wound between the two families by joining them.) If all else fails, the elders deliver the murderer to the revenge of the victim's family.

During these parlays, however, the criminal is protected. The honor of both families depends on it.

This custom might explain a lot, I realized. Thinking of the Taliban as criminals in the eyes of other Pashtuns—criminals with ancestral rights to such protection while the elders deliberated—I began to understand the apparent lull we were experiencing, while much tea was drunk late into the Ramadan night.

Two main sticking points were obstructing the progress of the parlays. One was the fate of Taliban trapped in Qunduz, a city near Afghanistan's northern border with Tajikistan, which had fallen to the anti-Taliban Northern Alliance. The Taliban in Kandahar rightly feared their friends trapped there would be massacred, and wanted to hold out for their release and safe passage. The other issue was the intransigence of the Al-Qaeda Arabs. They had nothing to gain in a postwar settlement and were, more than any Afghan, motivated by a radical Islamist ideology with pretensions to universality. The Al-Qaeda Arabs and a small core of Taliban close to the head of their movement, Mullah Muhammad Omar, were gunning for a fight to the finish.

On November 20, 2001, these unconditionals made a last-ditch effort to impress the foreign press corps. They invited us all to a press conference in Spin Boldak, Afghanistan. It was, bar none, the most surreal experience of my reporting career.

We suffered through an exaggerated version of the usual ordeal to obtain our Pakistani authorization for travel to the border, and worse for the coveted Afghan visa. None of us found it worthy of mention that though Kabul had fallen a week before, the Taliban consulate in Quetta was still manned and functioning.

The rumor that this consulate was issuing visas was only vague—no one knew for what, for where, or how long. Yet we would turn up and wait aimlessly. I predicted we would get to go to Spin Boldak for a briefing on the hard-line Taliban position, period. This was not a popular forecast. The action-starved newshounds, whose colleagues assigned to the Northern Alliance had been whooping it up during the fall of Kabul, were salivating to reach Kandahar for a scoop of their own. I confess I let the *Los Angeles Times*'s endlessly patient Alissa Rubin do much of my waiting for me. It is thanks to her that I was along on the venture at all.

I was feeling some foreboding. Soon rumor had it that the visa would be an open one after all, good for the whole country, and we would be able to travel to Taliban-held Kandahar. But, even in "liberated" territory around Kabul, conditions were hardly safe, let alone in this lair of die-hard fanatics. A few days earlier, four journalists traveling in a convoy to Kabul from the eastern city of Jalalabad had been pulled from their cars and shot. "If I were Al-Qaeda," I pontificated to my colleagues, "I would post some artillery on the hills overlooking the road to Kandahar, and take out a hundred foreign journalists. If you want to go out with a bang, what better way?"

I am not inordinately fearful, but I believe in calculating risks and reducing them where possible. In my view, a reporter's safety in such circumstances lies not in numbers, but in discretion. I kept remembering Albania during the 1999 Kosovo war, where the TV folks in the four-by-fours they rented for $250 a day would get stripped to the bone by highway robbers. For $7 I would take the minivan the locals ride up to the Kosovo border, to the delight of the (all male) passengers, who would teach me Albanian and make me drive the tortuous mountain road when they discovered that I—a woman!—had a license.

But it was impossible to address these safety concerns my way. NPR had already informed me that if I crossed the border illegally, or alone, I was fired. It was the convoy or nothing.

So I teamed up with the *Los Angeles Times*. Afghan and Pakistani formalities finally complete, the whole herd of journalists and their retainers charged for the border on the morning of November 21. My team of three—my interpreter, my driver, and me—suffered a single bad moment just as we crossed into Afghanistan. A crowd of yelling, kicking, stone-throwing men arrayed themselves in a gauntlet that we had to gun through, ducking our heads uselessly. A well-aimed blow shattered the back window of our yellow taxicab, and I felt sorry for my funny, streetwise, dignified—but sticky-fingered—driver. "My poor car," he lamented, with a pantomime-mournful face. I more than made it up to him.

The convoy turned in at a former UN High Commission for Refugees (UNHCR) compound, where the BBC, CNN, and others had already staked out their ground: tents pitched, cases of bottled water stacked like earthworks, satellite dishes in parallel rows pointing south, and flies buzzing absolutely everywhere. There was no electricity, not really any water, no shelter for sleeping. The first priority was to stake out some space to spread our bedding—such as it was—and send our staff to the bazaar to buy extra blankets. The *Los Angeles Times*'s Tyler Marshall was at first authorized to go out with a guard, but fifty yards outside the gate the Taliban turned him back for "security reasons."

In itself I found this a telling sign. The Taliban, fabled authoritarians, could no longer cow the people? Crowds of locals would jump up on the compound walls and squat there like great carrion crows, staring and mocking us. Our hosts sent fighters around with sticks or lengths of thick rope to chase them off, but they kept coming back.

Word coming from locals we sent our staff out to interview was equally telling. One prominent doctor said he was feeling so insecure he slept in different places every night, just as he had during the chaotic time after the Soviet withdrawal from Afghanistan a decade before. But this sense of danger made him happy, he claimed, because it was a portent of changes to come.

The promised press conference finally took place the second day. Much of what was said was false, much of it disingenuous. For example: "Forget about September 11. That doesn't have anything to do with this." But the spokesman—a poised twenty-five-year-old who spoke in English, in unswervingly measured tones despite the often hostile nature of our questions—laid out some of the recent history of the region. He explained the bloody chaos ushered in by the 1989 Soviet withdrawal, when for several years, the former resistance factions turned their unspent rage on one another. And he argued that the Taliban had taken power only because people outside the south wanted their lands pacified too.

Despite the self-serving aspect of his version of events, I was not unimpressed with the performance. I wondered how many Americans his age would have been able to handle an equivalent situation with such aplomb.

As I persisted in asking questions, I got looks of frank, but smiling, astonishment from the Taliban, who had probably never seen a woman participate in a public event.

The most stunning part of the trip, for me, was what happened when
word got out that I was fasting for Ramadan. I had kept the month-long
dawn-to-dusk fast when I lived in Morocco as a Peace Corps volunteer in
the 1980s, and it never occurred to me that I should not do so again, as a
gesture of respect for the culture I was working in. But I was the only journalist who did, and it made the Taliban, to my astonishment, adopt me. Najibullah, head of security for the event, invited me to break fast with him.
A scraggly bearded young Talib solemnly presented me with me his Parker
fountain pen. Another came to me during the night, as I was sitting under
the one electric light writing my story, bearing a precious apple.

The best were the cooks: two Tajiks from the cosmopolitan northern
town of Mazar-i-Sherif who were desperate to go home but couldn't, because a front line cut the road that leads that way from Kandahar. They took
me under their wing, made me sit in their warm kitchen, gave me their
bed—a stack of mattresses in an alcove in the wall—and served me endless cups of hot green tea all through the night. I slipped them dried apricots for the predawn meal, as the Taliban filed in to take away dishes of
rice amid a din of clanking pots and clattering plates I was too tired to get
up and record.

So there was I—an American female—the pampered pet of the Taliban during the death throes of their regime.

The final day of this bizarre jaunt was a textbook study in what is
wrong with journalists. The rumor that the Taliban might take us to Kandahar was dying hard, and my colleagues were determined to keep it alive.
At the press conference the previous day, the spokesman had said our hosts
would hold a meeting to decide. But now it was clear they wanted us to
leave. "Expelled," snarled some TV crews, furious that they wouldn't get a
shot at "the only story in town." They proceeded to put the heat on, demanding the Taliban take us to Kandahar, or at least let us stay in Spin
Boldak for a few days.

The *LA Times* and I started packing. We called in the two closest Taliban contacts we had made, the security chief and a former deputy foreign minister, for solemn thanks, expressing our gratitude for the time

they had taken with us, the hospitality they had shown under difficult circumstances—telling them it was a mark of their honor that they had done so much to protect us, that though our countries might be in conflict, as people we didn't have to be, and similar well-intentioned efforts at bridging a gap whose contours we would never fully discern.

Two more tenets of *Pashtun Wali*, hospitality and the protection of guests—be they mortal enemies—lie deep as bedrock among Pashtuns, as I came to understand fully in that improbable place. The deputy foreign minister was displaying unfeigned anguish at what he felt to be the poor welcome his Taliban had shown us, and at their inability to guarantee our safe passage to Kandahar amid the turmoil of a finishing war.

To me it seemed fairly clear—after four journalists had been executed on the Jalalabad road—that if your hosts, with whom your government is at war, ask you to leave their care for security reasons, then you do so. You do not insinuate that they are breaking their word, or being frivolous, or that they merely have something to hide. In my group, we had an ear close to the ground, and knew just how dicey the situation had become. I told other colleagues I thought they were out of their minds even to contemplate doing anything other than leaving for Quetta.

But the frenzy was on. I overheard journalists offering to pay drivers *anything*—a thousand dollars, five thousand dollars—to take them to Kandahar. Meanwhile, the crowd on the walls was getting hungrier and hungrier looking. We heard rumors they had been encouraged to loot. The previous night the Taliban had beefed up security to include a man with a rocket launcher posted near us. The *LA Times* and I loaded our cars.

Then transpired an interesting scene. A tall black man—Nubian looking, from southern Egypt or Sudan, maybe—appeared from nowhere, sporting a belt bag emblazoned with the flame-shaped emblem of the Qatari cable television station Al-Jazeera. Immediately the Taliban crowded around him. A few minutes later we heard the final order for all of us to return to Quetta. The *LA Times*'s well-connected translator murmured to me, as we sat for a moment on a stoop taking in the scene, "Don't look at the Al-Qaeda guy."

I jumped. "What Al-Qaeda guy? Where?"

The translator discreetly eyed the black man. I said he looked like a Jazeera crew member.

"Of course," said the translator. "They support Al-Qaeda a lot."

The role of the Qatari station in the events following 9/11 was a running debate among journalists and the public at large, as the U.S. government lashed out at Al-Jazeera and pressured American news organizations not to air its footage derived from Al-Qaeda sources. Over several years, the station had earned respect worldwide as one of the only Arab news outlets with any independence, and its exposure of something other than the official U.S. line about this war was, I thought, useful. At the same time, Al-Jazeera's degree of access to the Taliban regime and its status as the chosen recipient for Al-Qaeda videotapes did raise doubts about its affiliations.

I only wished the debate over Al-Jazeera would draw a clearer distinction between its journalism, which hardly seemed to violate the codes of the profession, at least no more than Fox News did, and actions its management or staff might take to provide concrete assistance to one party to the conflict—such as what I witnessed in Spin Boldak.

I later asked my driver: "Did you see that tall black guy working for Al-Jazeera?" He confirmed the Al-Qaeda connection. "He's doing *jihad*," he said. He had asked a Taliban counterpart about the man, and had been told that this "Al-Jazeera crew member" had called Taliban leader Mullah Muhammad Omar on a satellite phone from outside our compound, and received the order to make us leave.

We were given an hour and a half. I ambled over to the BBC, whose Adam Brookes was becoming a friend, to let him in on what I had learned. I was thunderstruck that he and his crew were even hesitating. When I explained about the Nubian man, they said: "Well that's that, then," and very efficiently set to breaking down their camp. At CNN, by contrast, the frustration boiled over like lye. The producer got on the satellite phone to Quetta to ask contacts among Pakistani Taliban to intercede with our minders to let us stay. What value any protection might have had if extracted under such duress apparently didn't enter into his calculations.

At length, more or less on schedule, we decamped. I gave my driver my French jackknife, and he tenderly took the compact disk bearing a traveler's prayer that hangs from his rearview mirror between thumb and first finger. "It's like you people cross yourself," explained my interpreter. I didn't need it spelled out. And we roared out of the gate, in a cacophony of beeping horns. Three truckloads of stick-wielding Taliban preceded us to scatter the crowd. Najibullah, the black-haired, bespectacled security chief we had gotten to know, kept driving up and down the length of the convoy like an anxious herd dog. And he posted himself, radio in hand, at the border crossing to see us through.

The exercise was an empty one, of course. No matter how stiff a front the hard-liners tried to put up, their regime was disintegrating. This was the third week in November, 2001.

KANDAHAR
PROVINCE

Helmand

Khakrez

ARGHANDAB

Maywand

Arghandab

Kandahar

AFGHANISTAN

Takhta Pul

Spin Boldak

PAKISTAN

Quetta

0   Miles   50
0   Kilometers   50

© 2006 Jeffrey L. Ward

CHAPTER 5

THE FALL OF THE TALIBAN

BY EARLY DECEMBER, the two anti-Taliban proxy forces stood poised on each side of Kandahar. Future President Karzai had set up a base camp in a village about an hour's drive to the north of town, and Shirzai and his patchwork troops were dug in at that strategic pass on the road to the south, ready for the American command to move in on the airport. The Al-Qaeda Arabs had retreated to hardened shelters there, where they were being subjected to an earth-gutting pounding by U.S. bombers.

Under pressure of this persuasive variety, the drawn-out negotiations inside the city of Kandahar were finally bearing fruit.

The man Karzai had chosen to lead these talks was Akrem's tribal elder, Mullah Naqib. That's the Mullah Naqib who posted himself at the left turn in Arghandab waving our funeral cortege on. The same Mullah Naqib who had permitted the Taliban to seize Kandahar in the first place in 1994—over Akrem's furious opposition. How these bewildering reconfigurations came about is part of the underlying pattern of events in Kandahar. Not for months did I begin to perceive it.

Without contest the most celebrated resistance commander locally, credited with driving the Soviets out of the region all the way north to Urozgan Province, the leader of one of the most populous and warlike local tribes, Mullah Naqib is an important power broker in Kandahar. And yet he is a curious rendition of a fearsome Afghan gun lord. He greets you enthusiastically, an irrepressible grin splitting his oval, bushy-bearded face. In a country where shrewd lying is the accepted mode of communication, Mullah Naqib is guileless, if prone to exaggeration. I gave him a small pocketknife once, on my return from a U.S. trip. He treated it like the Hope Diamond, turning it over and over in his hand, showing it off to his son, and proclaiming that if he had been to the United States himself and looked in all the stores, this was the very knife he would have chosen. Even in the thick of bitter factional fighting in 1992, when a rival group rocketed one of his trucks and killed all thirteen fighters inside, Mullah Naqib refused to seek retribution. He was just back from a pilgrimage to Mecca. "I can't be killing Muslims now," he told his angry men.

To put together my puzzle of those late November days of 2001, the final spasms of the Taliban regime, I needed Mullah Naqib's account too. And he, a year and a half later, was happy to oblige.

"Three days after President Karzai went inside," he told me, "he sent me a satellite phone." By then Mullah Naqib had withdrawn from Kandahar proper to his tribe's heartland just to the north. Leafy Arghandab is blessed with a river. Tangled orchards, like unkempt forests inside their earthen walls, could hardly offer more of a contrast with dun-colored Kandahar. When the farmers flood their land to let the trees drink, you have to pick your way through the groves on small raised paths, or sink ankle deep into the muck. Mullah Naqib was living in the fort he built to direct the anti-Soviet resistance.

"The Karzais' man brought a satellite phone to me in Arghandab," he remembers. "He said Mr. Karzai wanted to talk to me. So we called the president, and he asked me: 'What do you need? Money? Guns?' I told him, 'Both!' "

From then on, the two friends talked every day. "I was giving Karzai advice on tactics," Mullah Naqib grins. "I'd say, 'Do this, now do that' because he doesn't know anything about fighting. And he told me to try to separate the Taliban from Mullah Omar."

And so began the delicate task of prying the Taliban subcommanders—never quite subordinate, always semi-independent—away from their failing leadership. It is the time-honored ritual, another form of customary dispute resolution. It is the process of talking people out of conflict before it ever erupts.

Once, the Taliban defense minister sent a car for Mullah Naqib. The men met secretly in downtown Kandahar. "Don't fight against Hamid," Mullah Naqib told the minister. "He won't do anything bad to you if you surrender." Not two months after the 9/11 disaster, indeed, there was talk about a "broad-based coalition government for Afghanistan," which might include top Taliban leadership.[1]

By late November, Mullah Naqib's Alokozai tribesmen were itching to attack the spasmodically kicking, but clearly drowning, Taliban. Mullah Naqib sent an envoy to Taliban leader Mullah Omar with a letter: "Surrender by the day after tomorrow, or all Arghandab will take up arms against you." This was a potent threat, since Mullah Naqib's Alokozais had never been beaten in a fight. It is accepted truth in Kandahar that the only reason the Taliban were ever able to capture the city in 1994 is because, after those heated arguments with Akrem and like-minded commanders, Mullah Naqib ordered his Alokozais to let them do it.

Mullah Naqib's ultimatum prompted another meeting in Kandahar, on December 5, 2001. The Taliban officials threatened to go ahead and fight if Mullah Naqib did not agree to their terms for the surrender. "You want to make war on us?" the tribal chief says he challenged. "You want to destroy our homes? Why didn't you fight in Mazar-i-Sherif, or in Kabul, or in Qunduz?" The Taliban had precipitously abandoned those faraway cities to the Americans' proxies from the Northern Alliance weeks before. In reply, the Taliban negotiators demanded to speak directly to Hamid Karzai.

"I'm like this with Hamid Karzai!" Mullah Naqib held up his two twined fingers. "My words are his, his words are mine."

Karzai, just named interim president of the country, was spading his way through a blizzard of tasks: planning the tactics of the final move on Kandahar with his U.S. advisers, receiving local elders, considering the names of potential cabinet ministers, conducting key discussions with the Taliban leadership, sometimes talking on the phone to Mullah Muhammad Omar himself. The group in Mullah Naqib's house was insisting on a face-to-face meeting at Karzai's village headquarters a half hour north of town. Mullah Naqib remembers their asking for his satellite phone to try to raise the interim president. But the line kept breaking off and they could not get through.

With good reason. Just hours before, an errant U.S. bomb had almost killed the new president. Three U.S. Special Forces officers were dead in the accident, and twenty Afghans. These were Karzai's faithful tribesmen who, with that unique blend of unshakable devotion leavened by an irreverent egalitarianism, would have served him down to the bones of their bodies, and did, many of them. One, named Qasim, took days expiring. Both of his arms were torn off, and he begged his friends to finish him off. Finally, he died in the care of U.S. doctors at the desert marine base where they had medevaced him. Needless to say, Karzai's camp was in an uproar when the Taliban leadership was dialing the number.

Still, the delegation, led by Mullah Naqib, made the trip there across the bald, rock-strewn landscape. At the time, from conversations in Quetta, I was under the impression that the bombing raid was aimed at this very group of ranking Taliban. I was infuriated that U.S. trigger-happiness could have shattered the prospect for a negotiated settlement.

Mullah Naqib may be overstating his role in these eleventh-hour parlays, but he maintains that Karzai, face bandaged where shrapnel had nicked him, did not want to speak with the emissaries, that he, Mullah Naqib, was the one who talked the interim Afghan president into it. "You have to reason with them," Mullah Naqib admonished. "Because if we fight, there will be blood in the streets of Kandahar, and we will look bad." Karzai sat down with the Taliban officials, and instructed them to turn over the city to Mullah Naqib.

"But when they got back to Kandahar," Mullah Naqib pursues, "they changed their minds. They said they wanted to see the president again the next day."

Again the delegation traveled to the camp. Again the Taliban officials met with Karzai. Again they agreed to surrender Kandahar. They set the deadline for two days later. But once more, their word did not withstand the trip back to town—with significant repercussions for an orderly transfer of power.

"When we reached Kandahar," recounts Mullah Naqib, "the Taliban declared they were not going to wait two days to pull out, they were going to leave tomorrow. Then, that very same night, they called me on the satellite phone and announced: 'Our people are going.' I wasn't ready. I didn't have enough men. I spread the forty or fifty fighters I had around town."

It wasn't enough. As the Taliban fled that nearly moonless night, Kandahar slid into precisely the kind of pandemonium that Afghan refugees in Pakistan had been nervously predicting to me for days. This was the one thing they feared, they kept saying, when they contemplated an end to the Taliban regime: a return to chaos.

A doctor at the main city hospital lived through a Dantean scene that night. Several hundred wounded Arabs and some Taliban had flooded the leprous hospital grounds—survivors, no doubt, of U.S. bombing at the airport. They were outside, lying scattered about on the ground. "When they brought them here, we were doing triage," the doctor told me a week later. "It was the last night, when the situation was very bad—the night the Taliban were leaving and they were surrendering power to Mullah Naqib." The doctors worked furiously to sort and stabilize the patients in the cold and the encroaching dark.

As abruptly as they had first come to drop off the wounded, a fleet of Al-Qaeda pickup trucks roared back to the hospital, and Arabs, shouting at the doctors to stand clear, began pulling the patients from their hands and loading them, with their half-applied bandages and IV tubes, back into the trucks for the headlong flight from Kandahar. "Immediately cars came and took them all, with the Taliban. The cars belonged to the Arabs," said the doctor.

Just fourteen badly wounded men, including one Australian, were left behind in the hospital, where they were the target of at least two U.S.-led raids, which degenerated into gun battles right on the hospital grounds.

Niyamatullah is the son of a Kandahari almond merchant. He was working with his father at the wholesale almond and dry fruit market those days. Great mounds of almonds of different classes and qualities lie on tarps in the courtyard, men wading in them shin deep, or else weighing them out in sacks on brass balances. Surrounding the courtyard on three sides is a columned arcade, just a shade darker than the almond shells, housing shops and storage cellars for the different merchants.

"Right next to our market is a big mechanics' yard," says Niyamatullah. Such auto repair yards are grease-smudged obstacle courses, hidden from the street by the buildings that enclose them, with different mechanics working out of the back of cargo containers, bits and pieces of cars studding the trampled, oil-soaked ground. "There were lots of Taliban vehicles that had been left there for repairing. Suddenly gunmen appeared and snatched all the cars, then another group came and took them away, then the first ones came back. And they fought over the cars. I thought we were back to the civil war before the Taliban time." Like Wall Street after 9/11, the almond bazaar closed its doors and battened down its hatches for three full days.

The free-for-all that engulfed Kandahar was a repeat of the scene in Kabul three weeks earlier. America's proxies from the Northern Alliance had ridden rambunctiously into the Afghan capital, after U.S. bombing had emptied it of Taliban. Chaos reigned for days. The same thing would happen a year later, when U.S. soldiers conquered Baghdad in Iraq, and then proved utterly unequipped to deal with the human hurricane that shrieked into the vacuum they had created. It seems that planners underestimate the centrifugal forces that can be unleashed when a regime—no matter how unpopular—is toppled.

Even so, the transfer of power in Kandahar might have gone differently. Had Zabit Akrem been there, with his instinct for order and his ability to command, he might have been able to rein in the boisterous fighters and save the city two days of looting. But Akrem was still outside town, with Gul Agha Shirzai at the airport. In fact, Akrem was standing next to the former governor when a call came in over the satellite phone.

"President Karzai called Gul Agha. I was there. Mr. Karzai said, 'You will be the commander of the airbase, and Mullah Naqib will be governor.' "

Botched though the transition in Kandahar may have been, Akrem was saying, the intended division of power was clear. All the eyewitnesses concur with him: President Karzai designated Mullah Naqib to accept the Taliban surrender and take command of the city.

A young fighter from Chaman told me so a day or two after the fact. "The Taliban handed over power to Mullah Naqib," he said. Niyamatullah the almond seller remembers that "all the Taliban were going to see

Mullah Naqib and giving him their weapons." My Achekzai friend Mah-mad Anwar confirms: "It was the Alokozais who cleaned the Taliban out of Kandahar. Mr. Karzai gave Kandahar to Mullah Naqib." Mullah Naqib himself refers to outside authority for proof: "The BBC broadcast that I was to accept the Taliban surrender and take over the province."

That is how it was supposed to be. But that is not what happened.

CHAPTER 6

THE ROAD TO KANDAHAR

DECEMBER 11, 2001

"WE ENTERED THE CITY BY FORCE!"

I wonder how many times that has been said about Kandahar.

It is four days later, and I am on my way there. I am riding in our yellow Pakistani taxi, its back window repaired, on my way to Kandahar, at last.

I've managed to talk my frightened driver and interpreter into coming with me. This time I did not bother with a visa; I hitched a ride on an Achekzai motorcycle that headed out a desert trail. At the isolated shack that passed for a border post, my escort lifted an arm in greeting; the border guard did the same, and we were across. I rejoined my staff and our taxi on the main road. First stop was a barracks belonging to Mahmad Anwar's Achekzais. They detailed me a young fighter named Fayda, supposedly as a bodyguard, but in fact to afford the most potent protection of all in these parts: a visible mark of tribal affiliation.

Now we're on the road. Fayda is sitting in front. Kalashnikov cradled between his knees, he is casting loving glances at his reflection in the side-view mirror, adjusting a lock of hair that lies languidly upon his forehead. Perched on the edge of the backseat, straining forward to hear, I have my microphone out; I'm trying to prop my arm against the driver's jolting headrest, tilting the mike casually toward Fayda so I can catch his words without its presence distracting him. I know the effort is futile. For broadcast purposes, a microphone has to be within about two inches of the speaker's mouth—no hope of discretion. Anyway, above the noise of the car engine and the sickening lurches, my recording will be unusable no matter how I hold the mike. Still, I have to try.

I lean forward. "We entered the city by force," Fayda is exclaiming as we jounce along. He gestures out the window at a stony rise, not far from the Kandahar airport. "We left from here!" Eyes alight, he describes how the motley anti-Taliban fighters in the train of former governor Gul Agha Shirzai stormed the city three days before. Not to rid it of remnants of the Taliban who remained behind after the surrender, or holed-up Al-Qaeda fighters with hand grenades taped to their vitals. The Taliban and all but a handful of Arabs were gone, vanished the night they grabbed their wounded from the hospital four days back. The war was over.

The attack Fayda is describing was part of the quarrel afterward, among the victors for the spoils. Gul Agha Shirzai decided to disobey President Karzai's order. He decided to wrest control of Kandahar for himself.

This is crucial. I know it. My tuning fork is partly forged, and it is ringing. This incident, I am sure, will be decisive in shaping the character of the "new" Afghanistan. It indicates the kind of Afghan nation that will be built under U.S. aegis—this experiment upon which the world's eyes are trained.

But I cannot work out the precise meaning of the prophecy. The picture in my mind, from stories I have been hearing for several days, is too blurry, drawn thirdhand. Fayda was there. I pump him for absolutely everything, all the details.

"*Speed, speed,* we went," he reaches for one of the English words he knows to stress the excitement of the moment. "Mr. Karzai ordered Gul Agha to stay outside Kandahar, at the airport. But we didn't accept."

I am trying to think visually, for the story I will write. I try to picture this impromptu invasion of Kandahar: dozens of battered Toyota pickup trucks, their open backs packed with fighters rank from weeks in the field, signature embroidered shawls crossed tightly over their heads and shoulders against the chill December wind as they streamed across that sullen plain, their mismatched arsenals of Kalashnikovs, Chinese-made machine guns, and the occasional stub-nosed artillery piece bristling like hackles on a mangy dog. And for banners, grenade launchers tied up in bunches to the vertical struts of their trucks.

"No one invited us," Fayda exclaims defiantly, "so we didn't fly Afghan flags out the windows of our trucks. We stuck our guns out."

"What about the Americans," I ask, working to quell a rising disbelief. "Where were they?"

That U.S. "advice" to this proxy militia included a group of American Special Forces soldiers planted in its midst is hardly a secret by now. I reported their presence days back. Several Afghans saw them and mentioned them to me. Mahmad Anwar boasted about them, with an oblique glance and pantomimed solemnity at conveying the secret news.

"The Americans?" Fayda answers. "They *told* us to move on Kandahar! All our instructions were given by the Americans."

I actually gasp. How could that be? When Kandahar was in the hands of the other anti-Taliban militia, advised by its own special forces group, and led by President Karzai?

Karzai's people held the town by then; even I know that. They moved in quickly to reinforce Mullah Naqib's Alokozais. Shirzai and his contingent, with Akrem and Mahmad Anwar and this Fayda, were still out by the airport when Karzai's call came in on the satellite phone, ordering them to stay there. Why, I wonder, aghast, would one set of U.S. advisers tell its protégés to attack Kandahar when the enemy—the Taliban and Al-Qaeda—was beaten and the city was already held by another group of U.S. protégés? Why would U.S. soldiers tell Shirzai to disobey the president? It beggars belief. And yet the bare-faced innocence with which Fayda let this sentence escape, his genuine surprise at my question, are too spontaneous to be feigned. I admonish myself to verify this later on, but, with a stone in my gut, I register that it is probably right.

Foreboding rises in me: The Taliban have scarcely fallen, and already U.S. policy seems at cross-purposes with itself.

Well, what a story, anyway. I can't wait to reach town and begin writing it up.

We crawl along. The road is in appalling repair. Just inside Afghanistan, the paving disintegrated. First, pieces broke apart like chunks of ice on a melting river, lethal to tires and shock absorbers. Then the asphalt gave way altogether, leaving only the underlying river of iron-hard clay, pitted and rutted and studded with rocks. Drivers are negotiating it like rapids, careening from one side to the other in search of a channel through the hardened chop.

At last, by the airport access on our left, asphalt returns and knits into a decent surface so we can drive properly again. We ascend a rise. It is a saddle, really, with rocky hills stalking away from us on right and left. And suddenly, Kandahar appears, spread out wide in the distance, across our line of sight.

Mountains, glowering masses of cragged rock, tower over it from behind, coloring to a purplish blue as the sun tips toward evening. Dwarfed at their feet, the town is sketched in tawny lines, barely distinguishable from the land around. Between us and it, nothing. Not a tree, not a river or a road sign, not a patch of grass.

At this juncture, when we catch our first glimpse of it, Kandahar's reputation could not be worse. It is the Other Ground Zero, the epicenter of the explosive forces the world is suddenly confronting, the place Usama bin Laden made his home as he ratcheted up his campaign against the United States and what he thought it stood for, notch after notch. It is foreboding, glowering, mysterious, defiant. In other words, irresistible.

We cross the plain. The fabled city is finally going to come to life.

But no. As we pass under the arched gateway that marks the entrance, it is as though we are entering a ghost town. There are no cars on the avenue we drive upon, except the occasional pickup truck packed with fighters, speeding past with an urgent pride of place. Rows of mud-brick shops are barred and shuttered. There are no people out walking; there is no sign of joy or emancipation or anticipation, no sign of anything. It is as though we are driving through the corpse of a city, or through a city that has retreated deep behind its walls, to a small dark corner of itself, where it can watch and wait, unseen.

Built out of the living clay of its harsh plateau, of bricks fashioned by hand in wooden molds and hardened in the sun, Kandahar is like some austere sand-fort city. Soviet-era destruction has torn off great chunks of buildings. With time the scars have softened, and the jumbled rubble has been carried off for reuse, or else has melted back into the contours of the earth, as if the sand fort were partially washed away by the sea. Only a few pastel-painted villas stick out. Al-Qaeda Arabs rented them, and several were bombed. The American bomb damage blends in; just the edges of the debris are sharper.

We are looking for a building called the Maymuria. This is where, I was told at the Achekzai barracks on the border, I will find my friend Mahmad Anwar. He'll fill me in on what is going on.

Following someone's directions, we reach quite a stately building, set off from the main road by a broad dirt midden, planted with trees. It has a round tower marking one corner, with a dome on top. In front of the narrow door stands a line of cars idling, like the others that seem to have the streets to themselves this day: two newly minted Toyota SUVs, plastic still covering their immaculate interiors, and behind them, three pickup trucks packed with rowdy fighters. The men in the second truck wear the distinctive, loopy black turbans the Taliban made famous. Before I have a chance to wonder what I have blundered into, Mahmad Anwar bursts out of the front SUV: "Sarah!" The first syllable is long, *SAH,* the *r* the slightest kiss of the tongue behind the front teeth. Mahmad Anwar grips my hand, claps my shoulder, and bundles me into his SUV, right next to him. I do not have a chance to decide. My staff finds room in one of the pickups.

Mahmad Anwar was the follower of a particularly brutal and treacherous 1980s gun lord, whose wild-eyed marijuana-smoking devotees are to this day known for their lack of restraint. Yet he, too, strikes an unlikely figure as a cutthroat. Apart from a great scar that plows a furrow down the length of one forearm, much about him exudes a wide-eyed sweetness. He boasts shamelessly, in pure Achekzai style, elaborating on his enemies' fear of him. But there is something boyish about these tall tales. His voice cracks, especially when he laughs, as though he has laryngitis. And he is endlessly tender with his friends, no matter who they are or what their station.

We have hardly made it a half mile down one of Kandahar's dirt streets when he slams to a stop, leaps out of the Land Cruiser, and rushes to enfold a stick of a man in his arms. It is a tattered, impoverished Hindu, selling fried food from a cart. The two were friends long ago and lost sight of each other. The friendship is dearer to Mahmad Anwar than any lapse in dignity the gesture may carry. That is Mahmad Anwar.

Our convoy's trucks bristle with Kalashnikovs, a machine gun or two pointed out the back of each, and rocket launchers taped, according to the local fashion, upright to the backs of the cabs like menacing flag poles. Our fighters—fierce looking in their Taliban-style turbans, ammo belts criss-crossed under their shawls—are piled in every which way.

We may not look like it, but we are the police. In fact, we're working for Zabit Akrem. But I did not know that; I did not know who Akrem was yet. Our mission, I learn, is to start establishing some order. In the chaotic few days since the Taliban collapse, aid offices were ransacked and taken over by militia toughs. We are going to clear them out of their newly acquired aeries. First stop, the Kandahar Red Crescent office. The riffraff there refuses to budge. It takes Mahmad Anwar long minutes of discussion, Pashtun style, to "reason" their leader into leaving.

Next, we make for a former den of Al-Qaeda fighters to pick up gear they left behind. I swarm with the men up narrow steps, crowd into one cell-like room, then a second, then watch as the fighters divvy up the Al-Qaeda stuff. Within five minutes, half a dozen have exchanged their tra-ditional Kandahari garb of loose trousers and a long blousy tunic for dappled United Arab Emirates desert fatigues, struggling into the tight pants. I watch blankets and other useful accoutrements disappear, while ammo boxes and a couple each of Kalashnikovs, rocket launchers, and old-fashioned pie-plate machine guns are hauled downstairs and turned over to Mahmad Anwar. I even confess to taking a trophy, the wooden stock of an Al-Qaeda gun, for my brother Lincoln in Los Angeles. It never got to him.

The sun is closing in on the horizon now. We have to hurry. This is Ramadan; we've all been fasting since dawn. We have to rush to be in our places, ready to attack our food the instant we hear the first notes of the hungrily awaited call to sunset prayer.

We make for the house of one of Mahmad Anwar's relatives. I re-member a narrow passageway, and going down some steps to the guest room, where visiting males are received. The floor is covered in rich rugs from Herat and Mazar-i-Sherif. The furnishings are familiar to me from years I spent in the Peace Corps in Morocco: carpets on the floor, mat-tresses around the edges of the room for seating, and not much else. You settle down cross-legged, in a rough circle. On a plastic mat spread over the rugs, communal dishes are placed within reach of everyone, along with great sheets of homemade bread, two feet long. There is chicken in a kind of caramelized onion sauce, and lamb in something else delicious. Salad consists of slices of long, mild radishes, bunches of mint and coriander, and some scallions. I remember a white-headed uncle of Mahmad Anwar talking endlessly, God knows about what. No one else could slip a word in. The uncle is an elder; he has to be respected.

After dinner, Mahmad Anwar gives me my own room upstairs in a neighbor's house, with a guard whose job seems to be to serve me tea and make the occasional round outside on the roof. I look at my watch, one of those double-dial jobs I bought from the duty-free shop on British Airways. It is just about 7:00 P.M. Kandahar time—10:30 in the morning in Washington, the lower dial informs me. I have less than five hours to do it: to turn the kaleidoscopic hours I have just lived through into a four-and-a-half-minute radio report for *All Things Considered*. And somehow I have to convey the biggest piece of news: that the chaos I experienced that afternoon in Kandahar was due to U.S. policy. American soldiers escorted the gunslingers into town.

I set up my minidisc player and start listening back over the tape I've recorded, banging out notes on my laptop as I go along.

Four hours later it's done. My tea-pouring guard has gone to sleep. I have set up my folding satellite dish on the roof outside. And I have managed it. I have written up the tale young Fayda told me on the road—awkwardly, I grant. But I have at least sketched the unbelievable story of American soldiers egging on a warlord to snatch Kandahar away from President Karzai, who is also guided by American soldiers. I e-mail the script to Washington over the satellite.

And it flops.

I am reporting to a new editor now that I have crossed into Afghanistan—thus is the world carved up in newsrooms. And the new editor doesn't like the bit about the warlord. I dig my heels in. He sends the script up the chain of command to the international editor, a hard-drinking ogre we have all feared and respected and detested at one point or another. The ogre explodes. We have a shouting argument over the satellite phone. "There isn't shit in your story," he yells. The misunderstanding is this: he was looking for Mullah Omar sightseeing, the kind that filled the pages of the *Washington Post* he had opened that morning: descriptions of the tacky compound Mullah Omar had built with Usama bin Laden's money, descriptions of the horrors he had committed, landmarks made famous by his Al-Qaeda guests. "There will be plenty of time later to get into squabbling among the Afghans," my editor snaps.

I feel that everybody knows by now how noxious the Taliban were, and further expansion on that theme is superfluous. It is just gratifying Americans' sensibilities. The time for writing the Taliban story was five years back, I think. This is the story that matters now, I am sure of it. Because we are across the watershed. It is terribly important for America to get this right—important not just for Afghanistan and the United States, but for the planet. The world is watching us in Afghanistan. How we perform here after defeating the Taliban will determine where a lot of people come down on the clash of civilizations.

My editor wins, of course, half an hour to airtime. Fayda's testimony and its implications are cut from my report. So I never get to tell the story I already guess is key to what kind of Afghanistan will emerge from U.S. intervention.

I'm doing that now.

CHAPTER 7

TAKING THE CITY BY FORCE

DECEMBER 2001

It took me a long time to flesh the story out. I had to get to know the cast of characters—get to know them well enough to go to them, one by one, and ask them how it really happened. I did not plan it that way. But eventually, by stunning happenstance, I did come to know them all. Mahmad Anwar remained a friend even after he left his post in the Kandahar police. I took another Achekzai ride across the border more than a year after the fall of the Taliban to visit him at his home in Chaman. I got to know Akrem and Mullah Naqib. My acquaintance with President Karzai and even Governor Shirzai grew personal enough that I could call and set up appointments to talk about these things.

The only main character I was not able to track down was an American: Colonel David Fox of the U.S. Special Forces. All of my Afghan sources assigned him an important role in the events that would ensue.

My first priority on this quest was to confirm that American soldiers really did encourage Shirzai to "take Kandahar by force." That was easy.

The airport, where President Karzai had ordered Shirzai to hole up, is a crucial piece of real estate. Set among sparsely growing pine trees about a half hour's drive east of town, it is endowed with an abnormally long runway, tribute to its strategic location. The Soviets expanded the U.S.-built facility in the early 1980s so they could land their bombers to punish the countryside or potentially strike into Pakistan. After Taliban leader Mullah Muhammad Omar invited Usama bin Laden to join him in Kandahar in 1996, the hunted Al-Qaeda chief hardened some compounds at the airport for himself and his key followers. Die-hard Al-Qaeda fighters withdrew there in the last days of the Taliban regime, to play out their last stand in Afghanistan.

In early December 2001, U.S. jets started bombing the airport. A withering barrage of ordnance thundered down, cracking runways, plowing up acres of the brick-hard earth, and sending neighboring villagers fleeing to the homes of friends and relatives, or across the border to Pakistan. My sources inside Shirzai's militia—Mahmad Anwar and his Achekzais— regaled me with stories of bitter fighting for control of this airport between Shirzai's men and Al-Qaeda Arabs. But I never could get truck drivers to confirm a ground battle at the time, when I interviewed them on the Pakistani border.

With their dogged Afghan way of going on living no matter what kind of hell was breaking loose around them, these drivers ran their painted vehicles, loaded with leaning towers of pomegranate crates or magenta-stamped sacks of Afghan wheat, past the airport and up the main road to Chaman, Pakistan. I asked them about the airport, and they described new gun emplacements and a large herd of pickups pressing their noses against the gates. But no fighting.

This is the type of counterintuitive evidence it is wise to give credence to. The vaunted ground battle at the airport never took place. It was part of the fiction Gul Agha was concocting—with tacit U.S. approval, I came to understand—to secure his future reputation.

Not till the bombing had sufficiently "softened" this final target did U.S. handlers allow their Afghan protégés anywhere near the airport. Akrem remembered it this way: "On the eve of our assault, the Americans told us, 'Tomorrow we will go as far as the first tower of the airport.' Some of our friends went farther, and three of them were killed. So we retreated again, to the bridge. The Americans bombed some more, and then they said, 'You can advance now.' "

When Akrem reached the outskirts of the airport, a vista of carnage opened before him. "Wherever there were Arabs, they were dead. They were sitting with their weapons, dead. Curled up in corners, dead." Akrem counted just six or seven of the wounded that Gul Agha's fighters finished off. For a couple days, witnesses reported to me at the time, bodies lay by the roadside stiffening, before militiamen and townsfolk gathered them and buried them in what was immediately dubbed the Arab Cemetery, on the north side of Kandahar.

Then came Karzai's satellite call to Shirzai. Akrem, standing right beside the former governor, overheard it. He heard Shirzai shout insults. "I don't take orders from Hamid Karzai. I don't know Hamid Karzai, and I don't know Mullah Naqib. Kandahar is mine."

Gul Agha Shirzai does not deny his disobedience. I was at last able to confirm it with him during the appointment I made for the purpose, in 2004. "Yes, I spoke with President Karzai on the phone," he boasted. "I told him, 'Don't put Mullah Naqib's Alokozais in charge of Kandahar. Don't make that mistake.' "

And so the gloves came off.

"Then Gul Agha started his propaganda," says Mullah Naqib. "He said I was allied with the Taliban, that I had hidden Arabs and passed them across the Pakistani border, that all Alokozais do this."

Gul Agha Shirzai, advised by an Americanized Afghan factotum named Khalid Pashtoon, was making strategic use of the media, as I saw him do for years afterward, impressed at the deftness that lurked beneath his loutish exterior. He was adroitly staking out his position on the airwaves of the widely respected British Broadcasting Company.

The terms of Gul Agha's diatribe on the BBC were, according to my friends, "Mullah Naqib is a member of the Taliban; there's no difference between them." Mahmad Anwar said Shirzai told the Americans the same thing: "He won't help you hunt Taliban; he'll help them against you."

I did not catch Shirzai's stormy interview verbatim, when as a guest in an Achekzai compound across the border in Chaman, I was pawing the ground to get inside Afghanistan. But I certainly heard about it. It was the talk of all the refugees: how Gul Agha Shirzai had announced he was going be governor of Kandahar, no two ways about it. The reports I was filing to NPR were filled with accounts of a chaotic—tense though not openly violent—struggle for control of the city. President Karzai even threatened to resign if his supporters could not sort things out among themselves.[1]

At this dramatic juncture, the president gave Akrem permission to leave the airport and head for downtown Kandahar, to join up with Mullah Naqib. The groups were reconfiguring along more natural lines.

"Things aren't clear," Mullah Naqib told Akrem. "Let's wait a few days to see what develops."

"The next day," says Mullah Naqib simply, "Gul Agha Shirzai came to the governor's house."

That is, he "entered the city by force." This was the race up the jouncing road, guns sticking out every window, that young Fayda described to me as we retraced the route. Mahmad Anwar was the first of my friends to confirm the key detail: the U.S. role in Shirzai's move on Kandahar. "The Americans escorted Shirzai to the governor's palace," he remembered. "There were six planes circling in the air."

I suddenly heard an echo resonating: the voice of a refugee. At the time, he had described the Americans handing out new rifles to Shirzai after he reached the city. The man had been present; he had claimed an armful of MREs. He had described the guns with precision. "New ones," he had said. "The stocks were plastic, not wood."

When I put the question to Akrem sometime later, he nodded with a curt finality. "When Shirzai entered Kandahar, he entered with the Americans. And no one was fighting the Americans. Mullah Naqib told me, 'This is not the time for more war. If they push forward, you pull back.' Everyone felt the Americans were backing Gul Agha."

Mullah Naqib confirms: "I told my men not to fight. And the president ordered: 'Don't fight against Gul Agha.' I drove out to his camp to ask him."

And so, outgunned, Mullah Naqib surrendered Kandahar to the invaders from the south, as he had to the Taliban seven years before.

Gul Agha made straight for the governor's palace in the heart of the city. Built by the founding father of Afghanistan itself, Ahmad Shah Durrani, it stands opposite two shrines to the twin emblems of the nation's legitimacy: the mausoleum over the grave of the same founding father and the graceful mosque that houses a holy relic of the Prophet Muhammad. The Palace, as it is known, was a very symbolic place for Gul Agha to be.

Casting about for a headquarters of his own, Mullah Naqib lit on Mullah Omar's former compound—big, gaudy, partially bombed out, nestled in a pinewood on the edge of town.

And thus began a tense face-off between the two men. For some forty-eight hours, the situation remained deadlocked. No one could be said to control Kandahar.

On December 8, Defense Secretary Rumsfeld ruefully told the *Washington Post,* "The Kandahar situation is a bit like a wild west show. It's very untidy."[2] What he neglected to add is how his own troops had helped orchestrate this show by ushering Gul Agha Shirzai onstage.

CHAPTER 8

A CHOICE OF ALLIES

1980—2001

THERE WAS AN ESSENTIAL DIFFERENCE between the two sides confronting each other inside Kandahar—that's how I saw it, anyway. Gul Agha Shirzai, according to the picture I was getting from every Kandahari I talked to, was a predator—uneducated, irresponsible—who had no legitimacy except force and money. Hamid Karzai, by contrast, represented inspired political leadership for the new Afghanistan. And not just for Afghanistan, I felt. He seemed to be offering his vision to a cynical world—an example for us all: popular participation in a nation's destiny, individual freedoms, and steps toward healthy economic development. Perhaps he was the answer to the malaise I was feeling. Perhaps he was the spark that could jolt our stalled-out democracies back to life.

Hamid Karzai had played a rather discreet role in the preceding bloody decades of Afghan history. When, in 1979, the Soviet Union sent its army to prop up a puppet Communist government in Kabul, Karzai joined the Afghan resistance. He threw in his lot with one of the factions least known for religious extremism. The scion of a noble clan, Karzai took his place not in the field, but in the back office, handling contacts with rival factions and international supporters, and marshaling aid to fighters. He was among the early direct contacts Americans established among Afghan resistants.[1]

The choice to turn to him again in 2001 was well advised. Karzai's humble but elegant manner, his ringing exposition of the reasons for overthrowing the Taliban, set forth in daily radio interviews from his redoubt in the mountains north of Kandahar, had in large part swayed the stubborn Pashtuns to embrace the coming change. The vision Karzai expounded of an Afghanistan ruled by its people through traditional participatory structures, reclaiming its position among the commonwealth of nations, inspired his compatriots and made of him the obvious—and only—candidate for the role of a God-sent visionary who might finally end Afghanistan's twenty-five-year nightmare.

"He's the only one without blood on his hands," Afghan refugees in Pakistan told me when I asked them about Karzai the day he was designated interim Afghan president. These refugees were still profoundly shaken by the violence they had experienced during the Soviet occupation of the 1980s, and also—perhaps more devastatingly—during the civil war that followed it. The memory of those years haunted them. It pervaded their thoughts and words.

The Soviets finally abandoned Afghanistan and, in the winter of 1989, pulled the last of their troops out in a long and limping line across the great Amu Darya River, Afghanistan's northern border with the crumbling Soviet Union. In the wake of the breathtaking Afghan victory, it was the former resistance commanders' claws-bared struggle for power, their barbaric internecine fighting, that bled Afghanistan white and made it ripe for picking by the Taliban.

"They called themselves religious leaders," refugees told me. "They would swear on the Qur'an. But they weren't Muslims. Dogs wouldn't do what they did."

In the scramble to fill the vacuum left by the retreating Soviets, the former resistance commanders did not just kill their countrymen and fellow Muslims. They cooked them alive in cargo containers; they hanged them till their limbs started twitching, then let them down to catch their breath and hoisted them into the air again, and cheered when they finally died.

This behavior was not prompted merely by some innate evil lodged in those who perpetrated it. The cause also lies in the wounds to the spirit many of these fighters suffered during the prolonged anti-Soviet war—a war that shattered every notion their traditions had bequeathed to them about how honorable war should be fought. It was a war whose primary victims were civilians, women and revered elders and toddlers whom the humiliated fighters were powerless to protect. Now we have put a name to the psychological anguish these fighters suffered afterwards: we call it post-traumatic stress disorder, or PTSD.

Combat veterans afflicted by this psychological aftereffect of the hell they have been through typically remain in "combat mode," often turning to criminal activity. It is a kind of self-medication. The skills they acquired during wartime find a purpose that way, and the unaccountable rage they experience finds an outlet. Former soldiers caught in this particular trap of PTSD are incapable of achieving what they so desperately desire: a homecoming to peace.[2]

But only sophisticated psychological analysis can reveal these underlying explanations of the 1990s *mujahideen* behavior. For ordinary Afghans who had suffered ten years of Soviet violence, to suffer likewise at the hands of their own Afghan champions was a betrayal beyond words. Even a decade later, in 2001, Afghanistan remained profoundly traumatized. And most Afghans did not want these former resistance commanders rehabilitated; they wanted them tried and executed for war crimes.

But gentle, conflict-averse Hamid Karzai was different. Not only was he remarkably cultivated, he seemed uniquely devoid of brutality and arrogance. One shrewd former Communist government minister praised his style to me this way: "When he came, he was in our local dress, with a turban. He would introduce himself to the people, saying: 'I grew up in your land. I am the son of Abd al-Ahad Khan; I am the son of you.' Because of his dress and his speaking our language, and because he was speaking simply, the people found a place in their hearts for him."

In another conversation, an ordinary Kandahari—a small-time opium dealer, in fact—described how Karzai's radio broadcasts during the U.S. anti-Taliban bombing campaign had helped him process information he had been taking in for years, but had never fully understood. It was as though, during that earsplitting, terrifying month of November 2001, Karzai provided the Kandaharis with a new and wider context in which to place their recent Taliban experience.

"We saw the Arabs," the dealer told me, referring to followers of Usama bin Laden. "We saw them even more than the Taliban. Our government

was not in the hand of the Taliban as much as it was in the hand of the
Arabs. And we were not allowed to be with them in their council meetings. But still we didn't understand."

They did not understand, this dealer was trying to tell me, that their
country had been hijacked, wrenched from the grasp of ordinary Afghans
and put to ideological purposes beyond their ken. Lapsing into the sort of
poetic exaggeration Middle Eastern languages delight in to convey emphasis, he tried to spell it out: "We didn't know that twelve hundred countries and fifteen hundred countries were interfering in ours. Only now we
came to know it. Now we came to know that there were foreigners and
terrorists going around. Now we came to know that our country had dark
nights."

Surely the dealer could not have been so naive. After watching neighboring Pakistan expend itself without counting for two decades to achieve
control over Afghanistan, after watching Usama bin Laden cruise the town
in a heavily guarded motorcade behind darkened windows, surely this
streetwise dealer could not have thought the Taliban were wholly home-
grown. His explanation was a self-serving whitewash, more than likely.

Still, Karzai offered his touchily proud countrymen that: He offered
them a face-saving way out.

Most important, for nearly all the Afghans I interviewed at the time,
was Karzai's emphasis on negotiation. "He was telling the Taliban leader,
Mullah Muhammad Omar, to hand over power peacefully and not to destroy the country," the dealer told me. "From that we came to know he is
a good person. By negotiations and by the help of the tribal elders and their
councils, he came into Kandahar. With the people's consent, that's how he
came. He did not enter Kandahar by force."

During the days of pandemonium that immediately followed the Taliban flight, with the shoot-out over the cars by the almond merchants'
warehouses, and the tug-of-war for the injured at the hospital, and looting all over town—humanitarian offices turned inside out, cars stolen, papers strewn, furniture carried off—Karzai's soldiers were praised for their
comportment. They acted like public servants, people said, assisting the
frightened population, refraining from pillage and theft. They seemed to
represent the new Afghanistan the population so fervently desired.

America's other group of proxies, by contrast, Gul Agha Shirzai and his gun-slinging acolytes, embodied precisely the kind of violent chaos Afghans dreaded.

Shirzai was also from a Kandahar family. His father had a reputation across the province as a champion dogfighter. He poured much of his energy into this passion, breeding the barrel-chested fighting dogs local nomads keep, organizing matches, tallying bets. In a country where a man is known by his lineage, by the deeds of his forebears, these were not auspicious roots for Gul Agha Shirzai.

When the Soviets invaded Afghanistan in 1979, Shirzai's dog-fighting father also joined the resistance, calling up tribal followers and marshaling them into a rebel force. But according to the word spread by many in Kandahar, the Soviets lured him secretly to their side, and he served as a spy for the occupiers while pretending to fight against them.

Such betrayals and counterbetrayals were a feature of that bitter war. Pakistan, which had the most to lose from a Soviet victory, according to the Cold War calculus of the day, and invested heavily in the Afghan resistance, wanted the elder Shirzai assassinated, the story goes. He died of sudden, violent stomach cramps.

Gul Agha Shirzai is a great hairy bear of a man, with legendary rough manners. Stories about his wiping his mouth on his turban, or squatting to pee in the street, abound. Yet these things matter not at all to his constituency. There is a populist charm to him, something refreshing, almost endearing, about his in-your-face directness. And—key attributes—his generosity, his loyalty and kindness to underlings win wistful praise even from the liege men of his opponents.

It was not until 1992, two and a half years after the Soviet withdrawal from Afghanistan, that the holdover Communist governor of Kandahar was finally driven out. He was a member of Gul Agha Shirzai's tribe, and to ease the transition, Shirzai was invited to take over the reins of the province in a power-sharing deal with Mullah Naqib and other key leaders. Most Kandaharis remember him as a weak figurehead, presiding over that awful civil war—the goriest, most rapacious, and chaotic period in living memory.

"He was governor in the governor's palace," says Hayatullah, a happy-go-lucky man with a lion's mane of curly hair, who was a bus driver at the time. "He was governor in the palace, but nowhere else. If you had five men, you were governor on your street corner, and someone else was governor on his street corner. That's how it was."

This early 1990s "*mujahideen* time" was the incarnation of Afghanistan
as *Yaghestan*, a word that has often been used to caricature it. For centuries, courtly Persian monarchs flung this epithet at the rock-strewn
land that lay at the far fringes of their empire. The early Muslim conquerors broke their teeth on the place for decades and never really reduced it. By "*Yaghestan*," the Persians meant a land of the rebellious, of
the incorrigibly ungovernable.

Reverting to *yaghestan* served again and again as a fallback position for
a people who, every once in a while, did grudgingly gather under one banner into something like a nation. But ties of kin and clan always remained
strong. A tribe's feeling for its ancestral territory ran deeper than its loyalties to the institutions of national government. So when that empire or national government came under attack, Afghans were quick to dissolve it,
and run like water between the fingers of their would-be conquerors.[3]

The Soviet Union was only the latest predatory empire to be confounded by this trick. "It took the USSR thirty-one years to seize the machinery of the Afghan state," writes Michael Barry, in a brilliant analysis
of Afghan history called *Le Royaume de l'Insolence* (*The Kingdom of Insolence*). "The Soviets' mistake was to assume that controlling the government and army of Afghanistan was enough to place the whole country
in their grasp. . . . Whereas, the real country slipped away from them by
resorting, in a desperate lurch, to the *yaghestan* reflex."[4]

The Soviets, like many predecessors, finally acknowledged the task of
controlling Afghanistan beyond them and pulled back across its mountains
to their windswept steppes. But what they left behind, after ten years of
mortal combat, after countless atrocities and reprisals, and repeated decimation of civilians and their livelihoods—with continued funding afterward from the United States, the USSR, Saudi Arabia, and others, and with
neighboring countries egging on the various rival factions—was a *yaghestan* in its most extreme form.

All the invisible bonds that weave a country together into a single
polity had been dissolved. All the renunciations of personal sovereignty
in exchange for the comforts and protections of a joint destiny had been

retracted. Anyone claiming the allegiance of a few armed men felt enti-
tled to strike out for himself. Scores of petty commanders fell to preying
on their countrymen. This version of *yaghestan* was a metastasized can-
cer; it had grown beyond the capacity of traditional tribal structures to
contain it.

In Kandahar, the bloodletting was less systematic than it was in Kabul.
With the 1992 defeat of the rump Communists, only one full-blown military campaign remained: for local resistants to rid the countryside of the
forces of one of their chief erstwhile allies, and an ominous one, Gulbuddin Hikmatyar. The most radical Islamic fundamentalist among the resistance leaders, Hikmatyar was a precursor of the Taliban.

In the obsessive Cold War context of the day, the likely consequences
of his radicalism were ignored by the foreign countries that supported
him: Pakistan and the United States. Indeed, the extremist religious ideology he professed was seen as a spur to resistants whom it might inspire to
take up arms against the atheistic Communists.

The United States had not overlooked the potential impact of the
Afghan war in its global contest with the Soviets, a contest that had preoccupied it for more than thirty years. Like Latin America, Afghanistan was
seen as a key battleground where the overextended Soviet empire could
be bled. From at least 1980, the U.S. Congress was allocating ever-
increasing funds to the Afghan rebels. Over the course of a decade, Washington had poured an average of more than a quarter of a billion dollars
a year into the Afghan resistance, in perhaps the biggest covert operation
in U.S. history. Obsessed by the threat of communism and blind to other
dangers, American officials waxed enthusiastic about the potency of religious fervor as an antidote to Communist ideology.[5]

But it was Afghanistan's neighbor, Pakistan, that really drove the policy. In those times, the implications of a direct confrontation between the
United States and the Soviet Union were beyond contemplation. So Washington could not be seen to support the Afghan resistance directly. Instead,
in a fiction all parties chose to wink at, the United States channeled its support for the Afghan rebels through Pakistan. Thus Pakistan, via its intelligence agency, the ISI, was able to decide how and to whom all that U.S.
money would be distributed.

Pakistani officials harnessed Islamist ideology to further their regional agenda. The U.S. funds were lavished on religious extremists. Hikmatyar alone got more than half the manna.[6]

Although Hikmatyar's faction was the richest, however, it did not enjoy the widest support among the Afghan population. Afghans were seduced neither by its ideology nor its money. Once alerted to Hikmatyar's designs on their city in 1992, Kandahari forces under the command of Mullah Naqib and Zabit Akrem quickly drove the fundamentalists out.

This campaign was the last organized fighting in the Kandahar region. But the place was infested with petty commanders and their men, action addicted and armed to the teeth. Conditioned by a decade of war, in which trauma and mutual betrayal had pulverized any sense of right and wrong, these shattered men rushed to fill the power vacuum left by the fighting factions in Kabul and the weak, dull-witted Gul Agha Shirzai in Kandahar. They went back to plying a time-honored local trade: highway robbery.

Kandahar's most valuable natural resource, after all, was its road, the obligatory route for trade, travel, and expansionist adventure between Iran or Central Asia and the Indian subcontinent. For centuries, Kandaharis had been farmers and herders, true enough, cultivating almonds and pomegranates, drying perfumed grapes into exquisite raisins, stacking stalks of cumin against their compound walls, sending their children out with flocks of sheep and goats. But arable land is scarce on the moonscape around their oasis. Kandaharis' noblest callings had always been connected with their road. They were raiders, swooping down on India more than half a dozen times in the reign of a single king, the one who is now revered as the father of the Afghan nation. They were traders, dominating the lucrative commerce in horses, for example, between Central Asia and British India. They were tollbooth operators and protection racketeers. And beating their own occasional attempts at a system, they were accomplished smugglers.

During much of the decade-long war against the Soviets, Kandaharis had been deprived of their road. The resistants had blown its bridges and sowed it with mines to keep the Soviets from possessing it. In turn, the Soviets had planted antipersonnel charges to thwart resupply of the rebels.

Once a river, channeling a constant tide of human traffic, this ancient road became a wasteland. The only way to get from Quetta to Kandahar was by tracing a wide loop part way around the city, crossing the Kabul highway to the north and east, then hugging the chain of hills that leads southwest toward Kandahar. Lumbering transport trucks painted with designs in a riot of colors and caparisoned with jingling ornaments struggled and swayed along this route, sometimes bogging down for days in the rainy spring. Tiny village crossroads became bustling bazaars as the traffic of five provinces jostled through.

As soon as the Communists were defeated in 1992, that road became the top priority of demining agencies. "The very first day the main road to Kandahar was reopened, I drove it," recalls one Abdullah, an engineer who was working under a UN Development Program contract in Quetta, Pakistan, at the time. It was early 1992. Deminers working furiously from both ends of the road had managed to pry open a narrow channel—three yards wide, marked off on each side by a wobbling line of stones painted red.

The river in Arghandab had flooded, and the UN wanted to dispatch a team to take stock. "It was late, after lunch," Abdullah remembers, "but my supervisors asked me if I could go straight away." By 8:30 P.M., the team had made the drive from Quetta up the switchbacking road to the border, stopping when they got there to pick up one of Mullah Naqib's fighters for protection inside Afghanistan.

Then they entered the gauntlet, easing their white truck inside the double row of red stones. "There were no cars, at all. Then, after maybe half an hour, we saw two headlights, coming toward us." Nose to nose, the two vehicles came to a stop. "We were like this!" Abdullah raises his hands and lets them tremble in a remembered palsy of fear. "I am too scared of mines." He told his driver to pull the truck carefully to one side, right up onto the red stones. "We stopped there; we didn't move." The other car inched past.

After that, the only vehicles the team saw were tractors, chugging toward Pakistan in blissful disregard for the mortal danger under their tires. "They were carrying planes. New ones! The jets they used for fighting." Head tilted and arms akimbo, Abdullah mimics the broken planes, lying like wounded birds on the tractor beds. "They broke them in parts," he says. The dismembered Communist government MiGs were being carted to Pakistan for sale as scrap metal.

Once open in that spring of 1992, Kandahar's road soon regained its status as a main artery linking Iran and Central Asia to Pakistan. And with the Soviets gone, it didn't take long for the underemployed, overarmed former resistance fighters to set to extracting profit from all the traffic. "There were a hundred hundred chains between Kandahar and the border," recalls Abdullah. These "chains" were in fact dirty ropes strung across the road, with a tent or mud-brick guardhouse on one side, manned by somebody's fighters. Ammunition belts slung across their torsos, waving Kalashnikovs they did not hesitate to use, the gunmen shook down every car, truck, or bus that passed by. "Every fifty yards, hundred yards, there was a chain. You had to give them money." If the fighters were displeased with the take, or if they were just bored or having a bad day, they might drag a passenger out of a vehicle and shoot him, or her. Or rape him first, then shoot him.[7]

Any Kandahari will tell you stories of the nerveracking trial that road became during the "*mujahideen* nights," as that era is styled. Bacha, a typical traveler, is a tall, weatherbeaten fruit grower from the walled gardens of Mullah Naqib's Arghandab. With a partner he used to run great truckloads of pomegranates and grapes to the Pakistani border. "At every chain we had to give them a crate," he says. "Except at that mountain with the smooth round rocks near Spin Boldak. Hikmatyar's fighters were there. They wanted twenty or thirty crates each time we passed. One time my partner got out of the truck. 'I can understand you need two crates, three, four crates for eating,' he told the soldiers. 'But twenty?' "

The gunmen went for him, slamming into him with their rifle butts, again and again. After that, Bacha and his partner would heft down the crates, silently.

Bus driver Hayatullah had his toe shot off by one such gang of gunmen. They absconded with his bus and all the money everyone aboard was carrying. Hayatullah thanks God his sunny disposition kept the gunmen calm and every one of his passengers alive.

The worst offenders were the two most populous tribes in the region, the Popalzais, nominally loyal to Hamid Karzai's father, and Mullah Naqib's Alokozais. Both elders were quick to admit that they had lost all control of their men. "The sons of dogs," the elder Karzai used to grumble. "What are they doing?" Mullah Naqib laments: "I couldn't discipline them. If I told them to stop, they'd just join another faction. Even now they're no good."

When Kandaharis count back over the chains that made a nightmare of the simplest trip in that period, they don't remember too many belonging to the governor, Gul Agha Shirzai. But he does not earn much credit for this absence on the roads. It was not from lack of wanting to be there, but because his small tribe did not have the clout. Shirzai's term as governor is cited with revulsion as the heyday of the thugs. And he, like the rest of them, was run out of Kandahar when the Taliban swept into town in 1994.

This is the one deed for which the black-turbaned militiamen are to this day remembered with gratitude in Kandahar. They rid the countryside of the vultures that were picking the very marrow from its shattered bones.

And when, against the backdrop of U.S. bombing in October 2001, Gul Agha Shirzai cobbled together an anti-Taliban proxy force, he called a lot of these very same vultures up out of retirement.

My friends the Achekzais, who had held countless chains on the road to Pakistan, are still infamous for their smuggling, irreligion, foul language, love of money, and expert thievery. "Among the Achekzais, it was considered an honor to be skillful enough to steal a neighbor's sheep," laughs tribal elder Mahmud Khan, who lives across the border in Pakistan. "If someone managed it, the owner would salute the deed with a reward."[8] Gul Agha Shirzai did not waste much love on these shysters, who had once kidnapped him for ransom, but since the Achekzais control the border, he was obliged to invite them along to guarantee his force safe passage into Afghanistan.

A commander from the Karzais' Popalzai tribe was with Shirzai, as Karzai's eyes and ears. During the "*mujahideen* nights," this man's comrades manned chains from the eastern gate to the city out to the airport fifteen miles away. Kandaharis remember how the fighters used to shake down former Communist soldiers at their headquarters near the gate. "You know how they would kill them?" one witness says. "One would take their hands and the other would take their feet, and they would throw them up against the ceiling, and let them fall down to the ground. 'Where are your weapons?' the gunmen would shout. 'Where is your money?' These weren't leaders, or Communist Party members who might deserve revenge. They were simple soldiers. The gunmen were working them over for money, nothing else."

With such people poised to take charge again when the Taliban were defeated, it is no wonder many Kandaharis viewed the coming change with some trepidation.

"Now will be the era of the robbers," a young auto mechanic told me in late November 2001, after tribesmen had looted a warehouse for refugees just inside Afghanistan, in the last days of the U.S. bombing. I asked if he didn't trust the tribal elders to maintain order after the Taliban departed.

"No, I don't." He was emphatic. "They held power before, and they plundered the people and did bad things to them."

Other shopkeepers and small businessmen told of reverting to the defensive measures they had learned during the mujahideen nights: sleeping in different places each night, bringing all their wares home at the end of the day, and shuttering their empty stalls.

One further emblem of the post-Taliban free-for-all that these refugees so accurately foretold has burned itself into my memory. The scene took place in mid-December 2001, a few days after the Taliban ouster, after I had arrived in Kandahar. I had gone to the hospital because those fourteen wounded Al-Qaeda fighters, left behind when the others fled, were barricaded in there, cradling grenades against their stomachs. Some were reciting holy verses to the others, hands spread before them to symbolize an open book, bobbing back and forth in their intensity. It was hard to get near the Arabs, and, waiting, I looked in on another ward. I found it full of children, limbs ripped off in accidents with mines and unexploded ordnance. While I stood in the doorway, a new little patient was wheeled in, blood gushing from his upper arm where a chunk of flesh was missing. I felt my head go light. Suffering children do it to me every time. Fighting nausea, I asked the father what had happened. He told me his boy had seen a couple of soldiers smoking. The month-long Ramadan fast was not yet over. Smoking, along with eating or drinking, was still prohibited from dawn till dusk. "Why are you breaking your fast?" the boy had asked. In reply, one of the gunmen had idly leveled his Kalashnikov and fired, almost blowing off the child's arm.

That soldier was a member of Gul Agha Shirzai's forces.

And yet, this very Shirzai—symbol of the arbitrary, bloody madness the populace feared—was the one U.S. advisers had urged on to attack Kandahar and snatch it from Hamid Karzai, the battle-shy mediator.

CHAPTER 9

DEALING FOR THE GOVERNORSHIP

ONCE IN POSSESSION of the governor's palace, Gul Agha Shirzai dug in. His thick-tongued voice blanketing the airwaves, he transformed the precious radios everyone crowded around into his personal mouthpiece. Kandahar was his, Shirzai declared; no one, by God, would budge him.

In a culture where polite formulations, even if hypocritical, are the strict norm, Shirzai's public and explicit defiance of both President Karzai and Mullah Naqib was a verbal slash on the cheek.

Yet no one took up the challenge.

The invincible but oddly lamblike Mullah Naqib was at a bit of a loss. He turned to Karzai, the man he had followed thus far. Allergic to bloodshed, Karzai commanded peace. "The president told me: 'Don't fight against Shirzai.' And I kept telling my men, 'Don't fight; the time for war is finished.' "

At checkpoints all over town, Shirzai's men moved in on the fighters Mullah Naqib had posted, flinging blows and curses. The shaggy-haired bus driver Hayatullah witnessed the scene at the crossroad marking the center of the old bazaar. "They fought them," Hayatullah says, smacking the place on his own back where neck meets shoulder, to illustrate the blow from a gunstock. "Shirzai's men said: 'We battled Al-Qaeda at the airport; where were you? Get out of here.' " I meet Hayatullah's eye, knowing now how little fighting Shirzai's men actually did. The Alokozais, Hayatullah confirms, did not respond. "Mullah Naqib told them not to."

The man to whom it fell to enforce this command—to restrain his Alokozai tribesmen—was Zabit Akrem. With his usual crisp analysis, unalloyed by emotion, he looked back on the moment: "I think Mullah Naqib's decision was a good one," he judged.

The fundamental problem, in Akrem's view, was the credulity of the U.S. officers on the scene. "The Americans were such amateurs," he said. "They were honest to the point of simplemindedness. Anyone Shirzai or his interpreter told them was a Talib, they would take it on faith—and act on the accusation."

By this time, Shirzai's propaganda campaign was in full swing. It was quickly obvious to Akrem that his tribal elder Mullah Naqib was irrevocably tarred in the Americans' eyes as a Taliban sympathizer. Taking on Shirzai, under those circumstances, would have meant taking on the Americans. And the Americans, as the sheer sound and fury of their bombing campaign were meant to demonstrate, could not be taken on.

So Gul Agha Shirzai, unopposed, made himself at home in the governor's mansion, the palace built by the Afghan founding father, the symbol of Afghanistan's identity as a nation; and Mullah Naqib settled on the remaining emblem of power: the gaudy compound that reclusive, one-eyed Taliban leader Mullah Muhammad Omar had just abandoned.

The place looked like a circus tent after an earthquake. Its private mosque and living quarters were adorned with wedding-cake curlicues. A clumsily painted landscape scene covered a main wall. Behind it, U.S. bombing had reduced an entire segment of the building to ragged chunks of rubble. Mullah Naqib and Akrem arrayed their Alokozais around the jagged holes, and were shortly joined by President Karzai and his retinue.

Then began the congratulatory visits that are a feature of Pashtun culture. For three solid days during major holidays, Pashtuns go about to pay their respects: to their families and tribal elders, to their employers, to their colleagues. It is a kind of ritual renewal of bonds: of family, of fealty, of friendship. I have seen graybeards of the noble Popalzai tribe stoop to kiss the hand of President Karzai's younger brother Ahmad Wali, and the whole household follow suit—even the young servants who live in an intimate egalitarianism with him the rest of the year. Mullah Naqib's receiving room never empties, as Arghandab villagers descend on Kandahar to join the communal prayer at the cathedral mosque, making the obligatory trip to their elder's compound on their way home.

December 8 and 9, 2001, it was as if the whole of Kandahar filed through Mullah Muhammad Omar's house to pledge allegiance to the new *ra'is,* or "headman." With the elegance that is a family trait, lightened by a whimsical turn, Hamid Karzai accepted the devotion generously, touching the necks of the conscripted Taliban boy soldiers as they bent to kiss his hand, then paying them $5 worth of back wages and sending them home to the rocks of Ma'ruf District, or Arghestan, or Urozgan Province, where they would resume their efforts to scratch out a livelihood from the unforgiving land.

When the flood of well-wishers had subsided a little, Karzai told Mullah Naqib they would go to see Gul Agha Shirzai, and sort out the governorship. The way Akrem remembered it, Gul Agha sent an invitation, and the president accepted.

Culturally, this was a telling gesture for Karzai to make. In Afghanistan, it is the subordinate who makes the effort to travel to the seat of his superior. The superior plays the role of host, receiving guests and providing for them, or else summoning liege men into his presence. For the president-designate of the country to bestir himself to visit a boorish underling—an underling who had just disobeyed a direct command—was a reversal of protocol that could only have signaled to Gul Agha Shirzai the degree of de facto power he possessed.[1]

Just recalling this meeting made Mullah Naqib boil with indignation when I asked him about it. He said Shirzai was there, and his ever-present Afghan-American "interpreter," named Khalid Pashtoon, along with the U.S. Special Forces colonel David Fox, some CIA agents, Karzai, and himself.

I was sitting in a cool room of Mullah Naqib's home in Kandahar for this conversation, one of those vaulted cellar rooms sunk underground for protection against the heat. I was leaning against the wall opposite the old fighter, taking notes. Mullah Naqib had lifted off his turban; it was lying upside down next to him, for air.

"Khalid Pashtoon was barking like a mad dog," Mullah Naqib said. "He said I was hiding Al-Qaeda fighters. He said there were sixty of them in my own house. 'What?' I told him. 'What are they, ants?' You know, ants?" He held up thumb and finger a hair apart. "Where would I even put sixty of them? Then Pashtoon said other Alokozais were hiding Al-Qaeda fighters. I answered 'Oh yeah? Where? Show me some! By God, if you find a single Al-Qaeda in Arghandab, you can cut off my head.' It was lies, all of it lies."

Gul Agha Shirzai again conceded this version of events when I put it to him later. He was a minister by then. We were meeting in his office in Kabul, with at least half a dozen officials seated on ornate chairs around us. "I said that if Mullah Naqib had a government position in Kandahar, the old tribal warfare would break out again, just like during the *mujahideen* nights." I pressed him about the rest, about calling Mullah Naqib a Talib. Minister Shirzai smiled. "Yes, Khalid Pashtoon said that. He said Mullah Naqib *brought* the Taliban to Kandahar. He said he gave them three hundred thousand dollars and nine cars and thirteen hundred guns." The Americans, according to Shirzai, hardly intervened in the discussion.

They hardly had to. They were all sitting on his side of the table.

This is the sort of body language that speaks louder to Afghans than words. The American attitude was clear to Karzai. "They were supporting him," he told me, his tone final. That, for Karzai, was decisive.

I knew something like this had transpired when—on December 10, 2001, the day after this private meeting took place—my translator ran up to me, exclaiming he had heard on the radio that the standoff was over. Mullah Naqib had declined the governorship, pleading old age.

Old age. That's the cover story. I presumed a blackmail inked in Afghan blood. I assumed Shirzai had threatened to take up arms to keep the governorship, and that conflict-averse Karzai had given in.

In fact, as is so often the case in Afghanistan, the details of the threat were not even spelled out. They were implicit in Shirzai's "entering the city by force." That bit of U.S.-backed body language communicated the threat with perfect clarity. And mediation—*Pashtun Wali* style—played itself out the way it usually does. He who credibly threatened violence got what he wanted. The more reasonable parties, Karzai and Mullah Naqib, were induced to renounce their claim. For if they did not, conflict was likely to erupt. Thus can a certain style of dispute resolution contribute to the phenomenon of warlordism.

This scenario followed logically from the circumstances and the personalities of those involved. Still, I wondered how Hamid Karzai had actually reacted to the insolent power play. How had he behaved during that decisive meeting? Had he stood up for his ally, Mullah Naqib? Had he mediated?

The answer was neither.

"The president didn't say anything," Mullah Naqib told me. "He just translated for the Americans."[2]

According to Akrem, "Mullah Naqib was the only one who could have brought a peaceful end to the Taliban in Kandahar. He told the president, 'Gul Agha may say I'm a Talib, but you've been in touch with me all this time. Why don't you speak up in my favor?'

"The President answered: 'It seems the Americans aren't listening to me. They're listening to Gul Agha. Wait a while.'

"But Mullah Naqib was outraged. 'Gul Agha is a liar!' he cried out. 'He's spreading rumors!' And he made the president translate."

Such passivity on Karzai's part stunned me. And yet, by the time I heard it described, I knew the reason for it.

The story goes as follows.

"It was summertime," says Mullah Naqib. "A little later than this." He waves a hand at the garden he's just been tending: a riot of magenta nasturtiums, yellow and orange marigolds. He has laid down the small sickle he was using to break up clods and has come to sit beside me on a mat under an arbor. Soon the grapevines will put out their leaves and make the place a heaven of respite from Kandahar's murderous sun.

The year he is talking about is 1994, at the height of the chaos that engulfed Afghanistan following the withdrawal of Soviet troops. Kandahar was splayed on a rack operated by the warlords. Gul Agha Shirzai was governor; Mullah Naqib commanded the army; the Karzais' Popalzai tribe manned half a dozen chains on the east side of town; the Achekzais' chains started a little farther out, at the airport. On the road leading northwestward toward Herat, Popalzai chains alternated every five yards with those of yet another tribe. Mullah Naqib's Alokozai fighters, he is the first to admit, were doing their share of "bad, bad things." The sinews of tortured Kandahar were just about parting.

Mullah Naqib continues: "Hamid Karzai came from Quetta here to Kandahar. I was in my office at army headquarters. He came to see me there. Those days, the Taliban had already started working. Their leaders were coming into town, talking to people, telling them: 'We don't want power; we don't want government positions. We just want to clear the chains off the roads.' "

Mullah Naqib says he was impressed by the modesty of the demands put forward by these men, many of whom he knew. At the meeting, he says, Karzai echoed their arguments. "Mr. Karzai told me: 'These religious students only want to take the chains down. They won't get involved in the government. You should help them.' "

"Hamid Karzai said the country was torn to pieces, and the Taliban will bring some unity." This is Akrem's account. "He said 'They will bring the king back, and the Americans are supporting this.' "

Mullah Naqib was at a loss for a better solution. "I said to Mr. Karzai, 'Sure I'll help them!' "

President Karzai remembers the episode differently. When he and I talked about it in September 2004, Karzai said it was Mullah Naqib who called him, asking him to come visit him in Kandahar. Mullah Naqib's message, President Karzai told me, was that Kandahar was going to ruin because of infighting among the former mujahideen. It was impossible to rein them in, Karzai remembered Mullah Naqib's lament, because if you tried to discipline an unruly commander, he would just join another faction.

" 'You have buddies at the checkpoint by the airport,' " Karzai recalled Mullah Naqib's words. " 'Tell them to come see me. Let's do this. Let's help the Taliban.' "

I started. "*He* convinced *you*?"

"He called me," Karzai confirmed. "He proposed it."

It is possible. And yet, knowing the men involved, having gained a feel for their personalities, having spoken with their friends and family members, and having considered external evidence, I do not believe it. Mullah Naqib is a military tactician, not a political strategist. He is not a sophisticated political thinker. To me, it is just not plausible that he would have shown the type of initiative needed to forge these alliances. Karzai, by contrast, is a political dance master. Moreover, his version does not explain the strategy sessions with Taliban leaders that more than one witness has described him holding throughout that spring in his Quetta home. Nor does it account for a visit he made to the U.S. embassy in Pakistan in 1994 to discuss American support for the movement.[3] I believe, with full knowledge I may be wrong, that it was Karzai who persuaded Mullah Naqib to help the Taliban take Kandahar.[4]

The issue of what Karzai's motivation might have been is even more complex. It may be that he was genuinely duped, that Karzai took his Taliban friends at their word. More likely, perhaps, he overestimated his own power over the force he helped unleash. One family retainer describes Karzai thinking he could ride this Taliban tiger, while the Pakistani ISI, whose project the Taliban movement really was, looked on delighted at the help he was providing. Some part of personal ambition must have played a role—a patient kind of ambition that Karzai's lighthearted exterior belies.

I do not believe that Hamid Karzai ever actively subscribed to the Taliban's radical ideology. What seems clear to me is that his actions—even those he admits to—amounted to connivance. Such connivance may be morally ambiguous at best, but we should remember that the United States was doing nothing different all those years. *"The Americans are supporting this."* Negotiations between Taliban and U.S. officials about an oil pipeline were quietly continuing throughout the 1990s. Taliban leaders were visiting America. It was only the determined protests of American feminist groups that kept the U.S. government from officially recognizing the regime.

But after the 9/11 watershed, no one was remembering such things.

The meeting between Hamid Karzai and Mullah Naqib at army headquarters in Kandahar that summer of 1994 proved crucial to the revolution that would shortly take place. As a result of that discussion, the veteran anti-Soviet commander provided the Taliban with what amounted to a decisive piece of assistance: abnegation. Mullah Naqib did not stand in their way; and he prevented Akrem and his dissident group from standing in their way. And so, the way was clear. The Alokozais, led by this innocent man and unbeatable tactician, were the most powerful fighting force in the south.

I wondered, a decade after that fateful spring, how decisive Mullah Naqib's decision really was. "Do you think you could have stopped them?" I asked Akrem. His answer was swift and categorical: *"Bsyar bale."* It means, "Extremely yes."

A few commanders from other tribes did eventually throw up a last-ditch resistance to the Taliban; but without the Alokozais, they were doomed.

In that sense, what Shirzai's people told the Americans was true, and all Kandahar knows it. Mullah Naqib was the Taliban's friend; by refusing to defend Kandahar from them, he handed them the keys to the city. What escaped the official history, however, is that he most likely did so at the behest of Hamid Karzai. In front of Gul Agha Shirzai and the CIA, at that tense meeting in December 2001, President Karzai could hardly defend his ally without indicting himself.

Gul Agha Shirzai emerged from that meeting the governor of Kandahar.

CHAPTER 10

KANDAHAR, AFGHAN CAPITAL

DECEMBER 2001, 1500—1765

THE CITY GUL AGHA SHIRZAI laid hands on is arguably the most significant in Afghanistan.

Situated precisely on the fault line dividing two great civilizations—the Iranian and the Indian—Kandahar appears from the perspective of each to be on the extreme fringes of the known world. For Persians, wrapped in the comfort of their ancient and elaborate culture, Kandahar's very name has become a metaphor. *Safar-i-Qandahar* in Persian is the equivalent of "an odyssey"—a voyage so long and fraught with discomfort and danger as to be beyond telling.

And yet Kandahar is founded upon voyages. It lies on a rare route piercing a most strategic land. Like a wall, Afghanistan rises up between Iran and India, and also a third region, Central Asia, with its vast, fertile steppes and explosively mobile populations. Only two roads connect these worlds across forbidding Afghanistan, and Kandahar straddles one of them. Kandahar, on its plateau of packed earth, sheltered by bulwarks of jagged rock, constitutes a mandatory way station for traders, warriors, immigrants, and invaders moving from one of these zones to another.

Despite its impoverished aspect, despite the conditions in which most of its citizens survive—in the dust amid their chickens, forced to defecate in a corner of their unplumbed houses and shovel the dirt outside to a street without sewers—it is in some ways a wealthy town. I once saw a decent piece of real estate—a distinguished but dilapidated two-story yellow house on a piece of land fronting a main street—go for one and a quarter million dollars. This in a town with no banks, no commercial airport, little running water, precarious electricity, and hardly a paved road in sight. Only cash—in certain hands—is abundant.

Kandahar, like much of Afghanistan, has survived through the years on three main sources of revenue: pillage, tribute or tolls, and subsidy. This latter is dutifully handed out by the Great (foreign) Power of the day, in an effort to buy docility from the denizens of *Yaghestan*.

The last quarter of the twentieth century was no exception. Subsidy came in the form of lavish funding for the anti–Soviet resistance, dispensed by the CIA, the Saudi Arabian government, and the Pakistani ISI. Trunks of cash would be handed over to commanders and faction leaders, who took their cut while their soldiers sometimes did without blankets. Subsidy also took the form of humanitarian aid: money earmarked for reconstruction projects, not half of which were implemented. Mountains of wheat donated in the 1980s and 1990s by the UN World Food Program to pay for labor were measured off and sold in the bazaar, and not a workman hired. Monitors—who got a share of the take—signed off on fictional reports of the projects' progress.

Kandahar did count one local item among the sources of its wealth: opium. The Taliban made a show of banning poppy in the last year of their regime. But that was only in 2000, when there was such a glut on the world market that the price was falling. Officials made sure they had plenty of paste in stock before they started burning poppies. Before that, the Taliban would attach special security details to convoys running loads of opium from Farah Province down to Kandahar. Opium gorged the Taliban treasury.

And the time-honored transit trade continued to make Kandahar-area smugglers rich. The Taliban worked with them, too. In a deal that favored their interests over those of the Afghan state, Taliban authorities slashed customs dues. The local transit mafia had a field day.

But Kandaharis have a reputation for hiding their gold in rags and bones.

The city's bad name is not only a Western invention, tied up with Al-Qaeda and the Taliban. Even within Afghanistan Kandahar is reviled. Its people are known as the greediest, the rudest and most unruly, the most treacherous of all. More than one Afghan has assured me that the Taliban were the best thing that could have happened to Kandahar.

And yet there is obviously something about this place, something that goes right to the marrow of Afghanistan's bones. "Whenever change has come to Afghanistan," several locals have explained to me, "it has come from Kandahar."

Soon after the Taliban collapse, people began to arrive, as if on pilgrimage.

There is a building in the heart of town they flocked to visit—that mausoleum right across from the governor's palace. It has a graceful dome, something like a smaller, Afghan version of the U.S. Capitol. And, I gradually came to understand, the people were coming to see it just the way Americans go to visit the U.S. Capitol, or in family groups with paper cups of frozen yogurt and sweatshirts tied around their waists, walk the Freedom Trail in my native Boston.

It is the mausoleum of Afghanistan's George Washington, the country's founding father, Ahmad Shah Durrani. It is a symbol of the Afghans' nationhood. Unruly though Afghans may be, they cleave with fierce pride to this nationhood. It is their collective manhood. So, especially since the events took place on the very ground I was treading, it seemed incumbent on me to find out how this nation came to be. Without understanding what binds the disparate and chauvinistic Afghans together, I would never understand them very well.

But it took awhile to begin learning about their creation myth. I was not able to read into the history until some months later—after I finished my NPR rotation, left Afghanistan, visited the United States, and then left reporting and moved back to Kandahar to live.

That happened in the spring of 2002. I moved back under the aegis of the Karzai family: the president's older brother hired me. I'll explain all about that later. For now, the relevant point is that the only English books at my disposal are—incredibly—President Hamid Karzai's college textbooks. My de facto deputy at the nonprofit I'm running, a Karzai family retainer, has kept them squirreled away under his bed all these years, along with boxes of papers from the anti-Soviet *Jihad*, and now we've dusted them off and lined them up on a shelf built into a niche in our office wall.

I smile at Karzai's signature, inked neatly on the flyleaves with a fountain pen. Most of the books are Cold War–era treatises on international relations from a third world perspective. But there are also some quaint volumes on Afghanistan. These have titles like *The Pathans* or *The Kingdom of Afghanistan*. They are written by members of the class of Englishmen that seems not to provide its children with first names, but just pairs of initials. Several authors served as officers in British India. Their tone is shamelessly judgmental, soaked in superiority. I have my doubts as to the accuracy of their accounts, but nothing I've found in the bookstalls clustered near that mausoleum in the bazaar seems a lot more reliable.

So I plunge in, the way I used to do it in grad school. I fan four or five old tomes around me. There is one on an arm of the wood-framed easy chair where I've ensconced myself; I've got another two, one inside the other, on the coffee table by my knees; and there's one more lying open on the floor. I pick up one book and then another. Then I reach for the first one again, trying to piece together a coherent narrative.

Here is what I come up with.

We're in the middle of the eighteenth century. Appropriately, this Ahmad Shah Durrani seems to have birthed his country on a highway robbery. I keep toggling between the different books because they disagree on the details. One version describes the haul as booty: the treasure looted from conquered India—including the fabled Koh-i-Nur diamond—passing through Kandahar on its way to the shah of Persia, who had done the conquering.[1] Iran's sway, at that time, reached rather farther east than it does today. A different account, written by a successor of Ahmad Shah's, describes the load as tribute duly paid to the Persian overlords: 13 million rupees worth, or several years' tax from the subject provinces of Kabul and Peshawar.[2]

Either way, the young Ahmad Shah laid hands on a fabulous trove. That much is par for the course. What is more interesting is that instead of going on some gigantic spending spree, he used the money to bind to him the chiefs of the same tribes I have come to know: his own Popalzais (the Karzais' tribe), the rival Barakzais (now headed by Governor Gul Agha Shirzai), Akrem and Mullah Naqib's Alokozais, and one or two others.

Frustratingly, the books are short on images of Ahmad Shah's raid, perhaps out of discretion about the nature of this founding escapade. No one bothers to describe what must have been an impressive train of camels, piled high and decked out in dyed woolen tassels, swaying up the road to Kandahar. Protected by outriders and maybe a cannon or two rumbling on wood-wheeled carts, probably including some heavy-footed elephants, the caravan would have kicked up a storm of dust. Just the polished metal of a saber or the sun glinting off a piece of glass would have thrown off a flash.

Did Ahmad Shah ambush this cortege where the old road leading north from India mounts the edge of a hill just shy of Kandahar? Or did he dash out eastward and surround it in the plain crossed by travelers coming down from Kabul?

He was privy to breaking news: there was no more shah of Persia to accept the treasure this caravan was bearing. The shah had just been decapitated by his own men. So why not keep the money? Maybe Ahmad Shah encountered the caravan before he even reached Kandahar, galloping with his Pashtun and Uzbek horsemen away from the scene of the assassination.[3]

This Ahmad Shah was the youngest son of a proud family. His forebears had enjoyed the favor of their Persian overlords. They were settled in the city of Herat, located on modern Afghanistan's border with Iran. Their whole tribal confederation had moved there in the late 1600s, in a confusing and perhaps forced exodus from Kandahar.[4] Their new home, Herat, was a former imperial capital whose heyday had come some two centuries before. Great mosque complexes and minarets from that time, redolent of arabesques in turquoise mosaic, dominated the cityscape. They still do.

In the first quarter of the eighteenth century, Ahmad Shah's headstrong kinsmen were growing turbulent—that much I can make out. I've been going over and over the story for several days now, but I can't get the versions to add up. In sum, it seems they broke off Herat, this fabled seat of Persian culture, from the shahs' dominions, making it a kind of independent city-state.

What is clear is that the shah of Persia's court was in full decadence. Ministers and eunuchs, engaged in a murderous ballet around the debauched person of the monarch, were too busy stabbing each other in the back to see to the shredding at the borders of their lands.[5] All of this was taking place during the final decades that consummated the demise of two of the greatest empires the world has seen: the Iranian Safavis and the Indian Moghuls.

These empires met along a fault line that has persisted down the millennia, as though the raw geography of the region has forever determined its political configuration. They split much of the Asian landmass between them, with the Safavis ruling the Iranian plateau and the Moghuls the Indian subcontinent. Kandahar's lot—as it was before and would be ever afterward—was to mark the cusp between the two. It changed hands a dozen times.

Of course I've heard of the Moghuls: they built the Taj Mahal. I've heard of the Safavis too, but I can't dredge up much beyond the name. I decide I just have to delve back a little further in time, to try to picture the context at the eve of Afghanistan's emergence as an independent country. Without some sense of the situation that allowed a whole new country to be born, the details of the labor pains aren't going to mean very much. There must have been a crack somewhere, it seems to me. Some kind of geopolitical fissure that the budding Afghanistan was able to force open, the way the sprouting root of an apricot kernel splits apart the hard shell. The opportunity Ahmad Shah cleverly seized to capitalize on Kandahar's location and its road must have been more profound than the passage of a single caravan.

I don't see any way to avoid plunging into some more research. I note down a few titles and authors' names from footnotes in Hamid Karzai's schoolbooks.

I find the books on a U.S. trip, in my university library. I photocopy them cover to cover for reading at my leisure. That happens later. The fat copies, held together with black binder clips, stick out over the edge of the wooden bookshelf I had a carpenter make up in Kandahar. I've adopted a baby goat as a pet and cannot bring myself to bar him from my room, since he cries so plaintively when I do. He loves munching on one of these volumes in particular, a book by Laurence Lockhart called *The Fall of the Safavi Dynasty*.

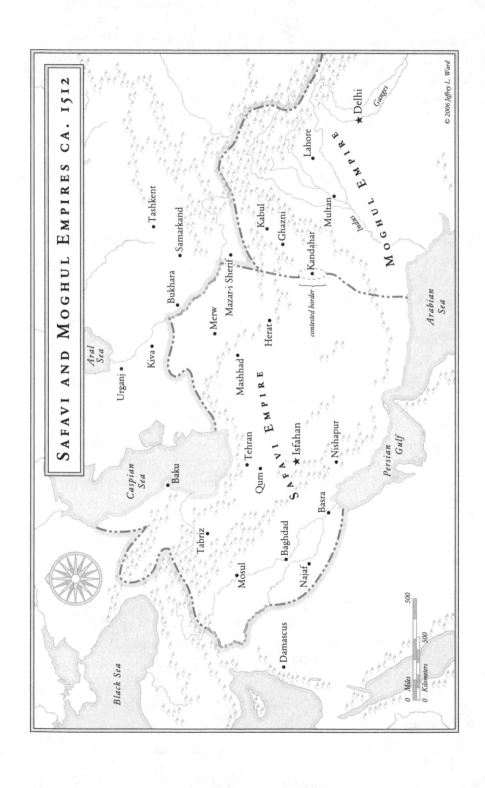

SAFAVI AND MOGHUL EMPIRES CA. 1512

© 2006 Jeffry L. Ward

Delhi

Ganges

MOGHUL EMPIRE

Lahore

Tashkent

Samarkand

Kabul

Multan

Ghazni

Indus

Bukhara

Mazar-i Sherif

Kandahar

contested border

Merw

Arabian
Sea

Aral
Sea

Herat

Kiva

Urganj

Mashhad

SAFAVI EMPIRE

Caspian
Sea

Tehran

Isfahan

Nishapur

Baku

Qum

Persian Gulf

S

Basra

Tabriz

Baghdad

Najaf

Mosul

Black
Sea

Damascus

0   Miles   500
0   Kilometers   500

Once smoothed out and taped back together, its pages inform me that the Safavis, from around 1500, revived and recentralized the old heartlands of the Persian Empire. They had been laid utterly to waste during massive invasions by the Mongols, among others, in the thirteenth and fourteenth centuries.

Originally followers of a tolerant and mystical religious order, the Safavi family and its acolytes grew into militant devotees of the Shi'i branch of Islam. Isma'il, enthroned as the first Safavi shah in 1501, embarked on the wholesale conversion of Iran to Shi'ism. The two words seem synonymous now, but it was not a self-evident thing to do, and was often furthered by way of violent persecution. In effect, the Safavi government became a theocracy, with a monarch who ruled by divine right at least—if not by the assertion that he actually embodied a spark of divinity in his person. Thus was Persia to witness, under cover of Islam, a recrudescence of some of the traditions of its ancient empires.

The religious underpinning of the shah's legitimacy was often belied, toward the end of the dynasty, by the gruesome behavior of the shahs themselves, who would spend whole days in a drunken stupor, issuing orders whose capriciousness and cruelty could not excuse terrified courtiers from executing them.

Still, the Safavis reorganized the vast and disparate lands of Persia into a functioning whole. It was an exercise in state formation, in stark contrast to the *yaghestan* that lay just to the east in what was not yet Afghanistan. They erected a capital that would symbolize their pretensions to a grand and opulent permanence. It was called Isfahan, *Nesf-i-Jehan:* "Half the World."

Isfahan was (and is) a fairyland of brick tracery and celestial blue faience. Shah Abbas built a many-arched bridge, gardens, and public buildings that personified decorum. He expanded its bazaars, building an entire new quarter south of the river for thousands of Christian Armenians he brought in from northwest Persia. The presence of these industrious folk was conscious policy.[6]

For the Safavis relied not just on land taxes and tribute from subject peoples for their wealth. They also deliberately emphasized commerce and industry. They tried to establish a royal monopoly over silk and oblige foreign merchants to buy it at fixed prices. They erected workshops to produce carpets and illuminated manuscripts for export. And they invested heavily in the infrastructure, comfort, and safety of their nation's roads. A chain of caravansaries blossomed along the major overland routes, where watchmen were posted and villages subjected to collective punishment if merchants were robbed. The idea was to promote the flourishing trade in luxury goods with India—which passed predominantly by way of Kandahar.[7]

For on the other side of the city, to the east and south, lay that second great empire. In India, a certain Babur, descended from the Central Asian conqueror Tamerlane, fathered the Moghul dynasty. Babur was a brilliant military tactician who mastered the use of muskets and light artillery in the dawning gunpowder age. He was a cultivated man of letters who wrote an unparalleled personal memoir. He was an epicurean who never ceased longing for the delights of the fragrant orchards and snow-fed rivulets of Kabul and his native Ferghana beyond it.

Driven from Central Asia by the latest warlike Turkic tribe, the Uzbeks, Babur abandoned the richer prizes of Samarqand and Herat for Kabul, then captured Kandahar from a rival in 1507 on his way to Delhi.[8]

Babur's grandson Akbar structured and centralized the Moghul empire. In some ways it resembled Safavi Persia. The Indian Moghuls made Islam—if of a syncretic variety—the state religion of India. They were of Central Asian Turkic blood and, like their counterparts in Isfahan, expressed themselves in a dialect of Turkish. And yet, like the Safavis, they were beguiled by Persian culture and adopted it, patronizing it richly.

And so the two great empires—sprung from a twined rootstock, communicating in the same religious and cultural idiom—faced off across an age-old continental divide. They were bound together by their shared history and their continual artistic, intellectual, and economic exchanges. And yet the rivalry between the two houses, often violent, ran just as deep as their similarities.

Kandahar, on its road, was caught in the middle. While the rest of what would become Afghanistan enjoyed peace for almost two hundred years under the Persians or the Indians, Kandahar was the place where one empire kept encroaching on the other. The city changed hands no less than nine times in a single century. Twice at least during the lifetime of a normal resident, Kandahar was "entered by force."

One reduction of the city, by Emperor Babur in 1507, is immortalized in the monarch's remarkably forthright autobiography, translated by my own college Arabic teacher. Babur's troops had made the march from Qalat (now a two-hour drive up the Kabul road) and, famished, were foraging for food. The defenders charged out from behind the city walls, and Babur was forced to fight at half strength, he reckons. His left wing ends up splashing around in a great irrigation canal, like the one that runs by Akrem's house, "exchanging sword-blows right in the water."[9] Babur's men eventually rout the enemy and, after a parlay, the city gates are opened. It was Kandahar after all, and from a glance at its dull walls, Babur could not have dreamed of what he would find inside.

Lucky Babur.

"Never had so much silver coin been seen in those countries," he writes. "In fact, nobody had heard of anyone who had seen so much."[10] After the battle, the future emperor went off to do some sightseeing, and returned to find his camp transformed. "What had happened to the place I knew? There were beautiful fine horses, strings and strings of camels and mules with fine textile trappings, brocade and velvet tents and canopies."[11]

Babur's conquest of Kandahar was the first of many that century. Even the most authoritative historians throw up their hands at the effort to get the battles straight.

Why such an obsession, I wonder. Why this city? Nowhere else along the lengthy frontier separating the two empires was there such contention. It is as though Kandahar became a symbolic spot where the two giants acted out a virile display of reciprocal challenge. As though neither could quite bear to let the other kingdom simply be, inside recognized boundaries, but had to make a show of encroaching on its rival's land. Was the choice of Kandahar as the stage for these theatrics haphazard? Or was there something about the city that warranted such a heavy military investment?

The answer seems to lie, naturally, with Kandahar's road. "In the 17th century," writes Rudiger Klein, in his study of the caravan trade under the Safavis, "the way via Qandahar and Tabas to Isfahan had become the main overland axis between India and Iran."[12] Contemporary accounts describe a city bursting beyond its walls, as suburbs sprang up to cater to the booming traffic, with merchants renting out donkeys and camels, selling food stuffs, cordage, and burlap, mending gear, renting lodgings, helping organize traders into caravans. So active was this route that the European maritime companies that were aggressively moving into the Indian Ocean trade—the Portuguese, then the Dutch and British East India Companies—were hard pressed to compete. In the first half of the century, extrapolating from Klein's figures, some forty thousand camels passed through Kandahar each year,[13] carrying choice indigo, silks and broadcloths, pepper, spices, and sugar by the ton. No wonder the empires on either side coveted the city. It was the strategic valve on the pipeline linking them.

Ironically, the frequent battles for Kandahar undermined the very source of the city's allure: trade. An invasion of Kandahar meant the whole imperial court at Delhi or Isfahan would take to the field, dislocating the end markets for luxury goods. When war was on, demand for finery tended to be off. Then there were the commercial blockades, the requisitioning of goods and services in the countryside around Kandahar that were otherwise available to merchants, not to mention the sheer uncertainty and danger of passage anywhere nearby.

From the middle of the 1600s, when the Indian Moghuls finally gave up on capturing Kandahar, the city lived for a time in relative peace under the Safavis. Then it brought the dynasty down.

Now we're getting warm. History is pregnant now with the coming Afghanistan.

By the end of the seventeenth century, demographic forces were pushing on both India and Iran. Turkic peoples were riding in from Central Asia, as they had done with devastating regularity since prehistory. And for the first time, a people called the Afghans was expanding outwards—and downwards—from the wall they were perched on, the great barrier of mountains that rose up between the empires. In earlier histories, in Babur's memoirs, for example, these Afghans are mentioned as a small tribe inhabiting just the highlands of what is now Afghanistan. Now, not a century later, they are everywhere, spreading south and east into India, to Kandahar and the fertile Helmand valley.[14]

These Afghans were divided into two rival branches, the Abdalis and the Ghiljais. This is still the major split within the Pashtun ethnic group.

Toward the end of the seventeenth century, the Abdalis (with Ahmad Shah's forebears) left Kandahar, moving northwestward to Herat. Their rivals the Ghiljais occupied the city they left behind. This population exchange may even have been a Persian attempt to use ethnic cleansing to weaken the Afghans. In any case, disgruntlement at the displacement went deep.

The Afghans were not held in check for long. While the Abdali branch was busy making Herat an independent principality, a Ghiljai chief murdered the Persian governor in Kandahar, throwing off Persian rule there too. That chief's mausoleum just outside town is almost as popular as Ahmad Shah's. In 1722, the mad son of this Ghiljai chief brought down the whole Safavi Empire. Afghan fighters bent on loot poured into beautiful Isfahan.

What followed was a dance of vultures on the Safavi corpse. The Ghiljais were outclassed, and a certain Nadir Shah emerged the victor.

Nadir Shah immediately turned to reconquering Persian lands from the upstart Afghans. The Abdalis in Herat were especially hard to reduce because they kept retracting their surrender and making him renew his siege.[15] In a move uncharacteristic of the age, Nadir Shah did not slaughter the Abdalis once he had finally vanquished them. He rehabilitated them, incorporating many into his army.[16]

These Abdali Pashtuns were accomplished fighters, and they served Nadir Shah well. As his victories piled up, with their attendant distributions of booty, more and more came to join the adventure. Legend says that the chief of Akrem's Alokozai tribe was especially favored, and earned the promise that if the rival Ghiljai branch was driven out of Kandahar, the Abdalis could move back to their ancestral home. That promise must have served as a powerful incentive.[17] In 1738, Kandahar, the Ghiljai redoubt, fell to Nadir Shah and his Abdali mercenaries.[18]

Nadir Shah kept his word and gave the city to the Abdalis, divvying up the lands around among the tribes.[19] The chief of the Alokozais was made governor, and his tribesmen were assigned a choice prize: well-watered Arghandab, where Mullah Naqib's mud-walled fort stands today.

Young Ahmad the Abdali joined his tribesmen in the fighting force of this successful new shah. It befitted his heritage as scion of the rulers of

Herat, as well as his station as younger son. For nine years, he helped command the troops that Nadir Shah took south, on a tear through Moghul India. The pillage and massacres don't bear retelling.[20] Through them, Ahmad Shah could not have missed two salient points: the land was rich, and it was easy to harvest.

Most accounts tell of Nadir Shah growing erratic, suspicious, and despotic as he gorged on war and its fruits. One chronicle describes in nauseating detail the kind of punishment he meted out: cutting off people's noses and ears in his paranoia, putting out their eyes, making a tower of their severed heads.[21] Nadir Shah had his own son blinded, and feared that the chief nobles of his clan were plotting to assassinate him. They probably were.[22] He was about to arrest them, according to some stories, when they moved faster and struck off his head as he lay in bed.[23] Another version has those nobles growing jealous because of the favors Nadir Shah was bestowing on the Abdalis, including young Ahmad.[24]

So. At last I have circled back to the very moment of Afghanistan's founding, the legend that has the same resonance here that the battle of Concord Bridge has at home, or the storming of the Bastille in France. But suddenly, there are no more footnotes in Hamid Karzai's schoolbooks. It is infuriating. I have no idea where the authors are getting their tales. My journalist's training—my historian's training, for that matter—is enjoining me to find some corroboration. I have to dig up a primary source.

So on a trip to Kabul, I decide to visit the public library. I wasn't even sure Kabul had such a thing, given what the city has been through. But there it stands, set back across a weedy vacant lot not far from the U.S. embassy. The history section is on the top floor, where a librarian courteously leads me. He is a short, gray-haired man, surprised and pleased by my interest. He cannot suggest a specific book, but points me at the relevant region of the rarely visited shelves.

I am impressed with the collection. All six volumes of the *Cambridge History of Iran* are there, and several of the authorities cited in Karzai's books. I trail my fingers along the spines, turning my head sideways every now and then to read a title.

Then I find it: *Tarikh-i Ahmad Shahi* (*The History of Ahmad Shah*). The volume I excitedly pull down and start leafing through is a glossy-paged facsimile of an eighteenth-century manuscript, written, I find in the brief English introduction, by Ahmad Shah Abdali's own court historian. The book was published in Moscow. That makes sense, after a second. The Soviets were always rather utilitarian about their scholarship, and Afghanistan was clearly on their strategic radar. I check the date. 1974. How interesting. Almost six years before their invasion, the Soviets were already investing in this kind of research.

It takes some begging to get the librarian to let me carry this book out of the building. It is against the rules. But I have to make a copy. I leave him my U.S. passport as collateral. An insane risk.

The book is written in Persian, naturally, which I don't speak. And the Russian critical apparatus is just as unintelligible to me. I inform one of my employees that he is going to be helping me on this. And every single day for the next two weeks, I drag him through the translation. It is interesting to watch. An educated man with loudly opinionated views about his country's history, very conversant with the 1970s and 1980s period, he is at sea with this story, key though it is to the Afghan national identity. And he keeps whining about the difficult eighteenth-century Persian.

The book is everything I was hoping for. Ahmad Shah's historian, who may have heard a firsthand account, describes the assassination of the Persian ruler Nadir Shah in riveting detail.

It happened, he writes, when "the velvet of darkness" had settled on the shah's camp. One of the conspirators penetrates the sanctum of the royal sleeping tent. A guard, an African, rears up before him. The white globes of his eyes, piercing his inky face, pierce the night. "Who are you!" he snarls. "Where did you find the courage to place the edge of your *foot* inside the Shah's tent at this time of night? I think you are sick of life!"

The assassin laughs and strikes a heavy blow on the chamberlain's shoulder, and strides past. Nadir Shah has heard the noise; he's awake, he's grasping a torch to see by. "Ungrateful!" he shouts at the conspirator, his erstwhile friend, "What do you want?"

"I am the Angel of Death," the assassin answers. "I have come for your soul. Speak no more; your appointed time is done. Put out your neck for cutting." And he brings his sword crashing down on the shah's helmet, cutting into his skull bone. Nadir Shah falls to the ground, stunned but not dead. The killer plops down on his chest and hacks his head off.[25]

At dawn on June 20, 1747, the shah's bloody torso is discovered. All the accounts speak of stark pandemonium in Nadir Shah's camp after the murder. Then the scene in Karzai's books skips to Ahmad the Abdali and several thousand horsemen breaking from the camp at a gallop and heading for Kandahar.

It is perfectly possible—though no historian suggests it—that the young Afghan cavalry captain knew about the caravan of treasure making its way at that very moment toward Nadir Shah.[26] Its load of coin and goods would have made a cogent argument for the Abdalis to abandon the royal camp and its strongboxes to the squabbling nobles. Otherwise, given the Abdalis' description as the cream of Nadir Shah's forces, it does not make sense that they would just give up their share of the loot.[27]

But leave they did. The account of their trip to Kandahar in the facsimile manuscript indicates the kind of chaos that was reigning in those days of the dissolution of empires. That route that had made Kandahar's fame, once studded with caravansaries and dependable wells for the benefit of long-distance traders, innocent of robbers or freelance tollbooth operators, had been the pride of the Safavi nation builders. But Ahmad Shah's troop keeps encountering bands of thugs perched in forts above the road, poised to rob travelers.[28] Just like the twentieth-century gunmen who mercilessly harried truck drivers during the "*mujahideen* nights."

The scene of Afghanistan's founding myth unfolds at a shrine just outside Kandahar.[29] I heard this famous tale when I first arrived in the city: the story of the *jirga,* or council meeting among the elders of all the Afghan tribes, called to settle the matter of their leadership. You can practically smell young Ahmad taking his seat, the sweat of the road barely scraped off his skin, his horsemen spread out in the surrounding fields.

Now those fields are a haunted landscape of ruined *kishmish khanahs.* Fortlike buildings of mud brick, their walls are scored with rows of window slits, like the ones for protecting medieval castles. Here they pierce the thick baked mud to allow air inside to dry grapes into raisins. Most of the arched roofs are blown off, and the low-slung domes that capped end rooms are shattered. Anti-Soviet mujahideen used to camp out in these structures, and the Communists shelled them. The fields around are dried out; just the earthen walls where the grapevines once spread their tendrils testify to a forgotten abundance.

According to the story, the *jirga* at the holy precinct lasted for days, for none of the chiefs would give up his own claim to lead. Young Ahmad the cavalry captain is depicted as a proper Afghan youth, sitting silent in the presence of his elders.[30] A holy man was there, a *darwish,* a kind of half-coherent itinerant hermit who decks himself with amulets and utters prayers as he begs his way from here to there. Nowadays, one of these men stakes out a spot on the seamed concrete road by the turn-off to Khakrez. He is so hilarious as he calls down God's munificence on my head that I never fail to stop and give him money. The eighteenth-century *darwish* is said to have ended the argument at that founding *jirga*. Drifting off from the fringes of the group, the story goes, he broke a sprig of wheat from an adjacent field, then pushed through the circle of elders to young Ahmad Shah and slid the green blade among the folds of his turban, "crowning" him.[31]

Thus was the Afghan nation born.

Ahmad Shah was a member of the Popalzai tribe, like President Hamid Karzai. Reading the accounts of this story, I notice that his prime competitor for power was Hajji Jamal Khan, the chief of Governor Gul Agha Shirzai's Barakzais.

Well, that explains a lot.

Here then lay the roots of the rivalry played out at that tense meeting at the governor's palace 250 years later—a rivalry in which I will soon be caught up.

Ahmad Shah Durrani, as he called himself after that day, was a consummate politician. His first recorded deed after gaining leadership of the Abdalis, or Durranis as they are now known, was to parcel out positions in a Persian-style bureaucratic government to the chiefs of the various tribes, finding something for everyone.[32] His reign lasted twenty-five years. He expanded his new kingdom of Afghanistan northwest as far as Mashad in Iran, and southeast beyond the Indus River. He raided the Moghul lands nine times. Throughout, he consulted regularly with his *jirga* of tribal elders.

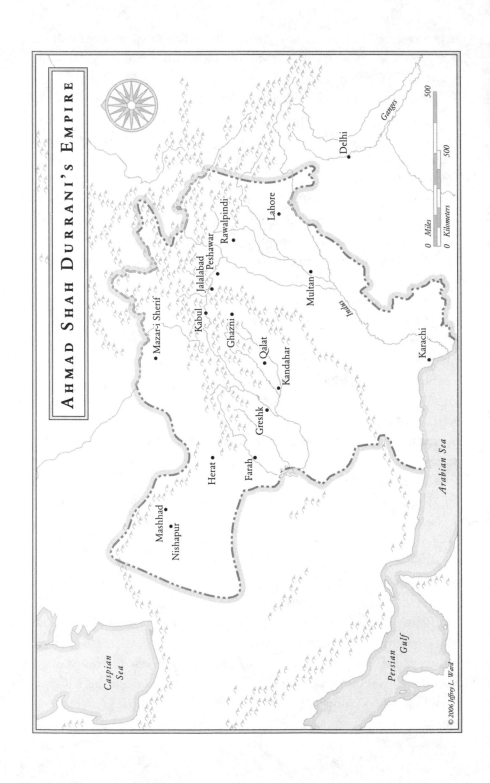

AHMAD SHAH DURRANI'S EMPIRE

Ganges

Delhi

Rawalpindi

Lahore

Peshawar

Jalalabad

Multan

Kabul

Mazar-i Sherif

Ghazni

Indus

Qalat

Kandahar

Greshk

Karachi

Farah

Herat

Arabian Sea

Mashhad

Nishapur

Caspian Sea

Persian Gulf

0 Miles   500

0 Kilometers   500

© 2006 Jeffrey L. Ward

Thus does Ahmad Shah Durrani appear to combine the contradictory Afghan tendencies toward *qanun,* government under some kind of national law, and *yaghestan,* dissolution into tribal units whose vertical ties are reinforced by the distribution of booty.

As Michael Barry analyzes it, leadership among Pashtuns is acquired by a pretender's ability to extract wealth from a lowland power in one of those three familiar forms—plunder or tribute or subsidy—and distribute it among his men.[33] Ahmad Shah's ability in this regard was undeniable. That was the significance, the coded meaning, of capturing the caravan.[34] By the same token, in early-twenty-first-century Kandahar, Governor Gul Agha Shirzai's visible proximity to America—the lowland power of the day—and his ability to spend American money on his followers, is what allowed him to solidify his power at the expense of Hamid Karzai's central government.

Ahmad Shah Durrani's other key move was to establish Kandahar as his capital. He broke with the timeworn tradition of tribal marauders who, like cuckoo birds, loved to nest in the capitals of the great empires they brought down. Ahmad Shah did not covet either Isfahan, the blue-domed Safavi capital, or Moghul Delhi. Instead, in what is now described as the first stirring of an Afghan national consciousness, he founded a new capital in his tribal stronghold, Kandahar.

Ahmad Shah's city is the Kandahar I have come to know. And, by laboriously tracing and absorbing this long story, I begin to sense just how this Kandahar is coequal with the genesis of Afghanistan as a modern state.

It is a state founded not on a set of thoughts held in common and articulated through texts and institutions, but rather a state founded on the strategic nature of its territory—the crux between empires. It is a state founded on a fluid and tenuous interaction between collective structures, structures of nation, of tribe, of family, and a highly developed sense of freedom, a violent aversion to submission.

Ahmad Shah Durrani laid out his new city just east of the ancient fortress his master Nadir Shah had razed nine years earlier. British Envoy Mountstuart Elphinstone, writing in 1810 (about a city he asked travelers in Kabul to describe for him), lists four main bazaars, meeting at a covered point called to this day Chahar Sou, "four ways."[35] My favorite mosque in town is one of Ahmad Shah's, on the street lined with sellers of used goods that leads southward from this same Chahar Sou. The low, sand-colored dome of this mosque is framed by four minarets, the whole softened by coats of mud plaster smoothed over the bricks, as though the artist who drew it had, with a thumb, rubbed away the sharpness of his penciled line.

It was in this mosque that Zabit Akrem was murdered.

CHAPTER 11

REPORTING KANDAHAR

DECEMBER 2001-JANUARY 2002

FOR SEVERAL DAYS after I arrived in early December, Kandahar remained as it was: drawn tight into its shell, playing dead. On the lumpy streets that make up the city's bazaar, almost all the shops were shut. Corrugated metal barriers were pulled down and padlocked to the ground, wooden shutters closed and barred. Just a few hardy exceptions proved the rule: some wooden vegetable carts, a few fabric shops with multicolored bolts of cloth stacked against the walls, and stalls that stock the sparkly local caps set with chips of glass that young Kandahari men adore. The month-long Ramadan fast was almost over, and Afghans celebrate its end with new clothes. These few merchants were catering to preholiday customers.

The opium bazaar was also busy. In a small, dead-end warren, narrow stalls with heavy wooden doors stand a few inches up from the curb. Customers step out of their shoes and sit cross-legged on a carpet. The only furnishing is a small locked counter with a brass scale on it and a telephone. The walls are daubed with brown smudges, where people have tested the quality of the opium paste then wiped their fingers off.

Except for the pickup trucks packed with fighters cruising around as if they owned the place, the streets were empty. At night there was a curfew. To get past the ropes slung across the road and manned by flashlight-toting adolescents, you had to know the password. We would pick it up from Mahmad Anwar. I still have the folded-up paper he wrote it on one night: "rocket," with the reply: "radar."

Slowly, like some great beast shaking itself awake after hibernation, Kandahar came to life. It was the music shops that marked the change, tiny stalls that drew crowds of men straining over one another to lay their hands on a cassette. A few great buses and trucks began making their appearance in the streets, piled high with bales and bundles and crammed with refugees returning home.

For me the most moving symbol was the kites: bright-colored squares of tissue paper stretched on curved bamboo ribs, which blossomed on the folded-back doors of market stalls or hung in rows from their awnings. The Taliban had banned kite flying in their drive to stamp out not just idle pleasure, but also gambling. Kandaharis pit their kites against one another and bet on them, sometimes gluing ground glass to the strings for sawing another's asunder during airborne battles. Now, like sparks and flecks of ash above a fire, the kites danced back into the air, darting and bobbing like swallows. As a silent tribute to freedom and newfound joy, I couldn't imagine a better emblem.

On the holiday marking the end of Ramadan, Kandahar erupted in earnest. All the new clothes came out, and clutches of little girls, decked out in matching magentas or peacock greens, fluttered like confetti through the streets. There was even an amusement park of sorts. Ferris wheels made of wood and pushed by hand hoisted squealing children a few feet into the air. After the communal prayer at a sky-blue mosque on the edge of town, there were horse trials, for the first time in six years. Chargers with high saddles and tassels hanging from their bridles flung their legs out across the plain.

The other high point of adult entertainment was the hard-boiled egg matches. Two contestants would buy ten eggs, judiciously testing each one against their front teeth for shell density before choosing it. Then one man would clasp his egg in a fist, with the domed end peeking above his curled thumb and forefinger. The other man would tap his egg against it, and the one whose egg cracked first lost it to his opponent. This riveting sport drew crowds of forty and fifty spectators in amusement-starved Kandahar during those early post-Taliban days.

But this was anticlimax. For we journalists—all of us—had missed the story. After our strident, petulant, ground-pawing rush to get to Kandahar, Kandahar had abruptly ceased to be a story. We hid from this truth, busying ourselves anyway. We chased around importantly, finding features to write. But the key moments in the drama had taken place well out of our line of sight. The visit by Taliban leaders to President Karzai in his shattered encampment and the surrender deal struck there—that was the story. Or, the same night at the hospital, the Al-Qaeda trucks swooping down to gather up the wounded; the congratulatory visits to the new president; the ceremony with the Taliban boy soldiers—those things were the story. The story was the meeting at the governor's palace, and the Americans enthroning Gul Agha Shirzai as governor. The story had gone unwitnessed.

I spent the month left in my rotation obediently—ignoring, as I had been ordered, what seemed to me to be the only other story: the palpable return of warlordism to the city's packed earth streets. My reporting fell into clichés that appealed inexhaustibly to my ogre of an editor: human rights abuses committed by the Taliban, resistants to the Taliban regime inside Kandahar, a merry chase behind a convoy of U.S. and British Special Forces who were scouring caves for terrorists, the inevitable Christmas with the marines.

On that one I got into another argument.

At the U.S. military base now established at the airport, I stopped to chat with a group of marines draped over the sandbagged rim of their foxhole, which was dug into the hard dirt near the airport terminal building. They shared their MREs, ripping open the heavy plastic envelopes and leaning the main course up against the sandbags to let the chemical heat do its work. It was pretty chilly out there.

One of the marines, a thoughtful twenty-two- or three-year-old from Ohio, turned the tables on me.

"You live right in town?" he started questioning. I allowed as how I did.

"Tell me something. How dangerous do you really think things are out there?"

The answer was, they were not.

Kandahar, in those days, shimmered with a breathless hope. Afghans, even there in the Taliban's former den, were overcome by the possibilities opened up by this latest "revolution," as they referred to it. They were in a rush to get their children educated, to have competent people in charge of them—officials who wouldn't pocket all the public funds that were supposed to be devoted to reconstruction, and who could hold their own with foreign governments. They couldn't wait to see the ruins of their city fixed up, to have some roads laid down under the tortured tires of their trucks. They were hungry to participate again in the shaping of their national destiny, the way they had back in the golden age before the Communist coup and the Soviet invasion.

I remember a discussion with a dozen petty opium dealers who had invited me to break the Ramadan fast with them. I asked to see some of their wares, and they obliged, fetching four and a half kilos of pure opium paste in a plastic bag. It smelled a little sweet, like new-mown hay. Microphone cocked, I had them put it on a brass balance and comment on its quality, so I could use the sound for my story.

Once I had wrapped up my formal interviews and we were sipping our after-dinner tea, we began talking about the future. The dealers said they would love to have a school right there in their neighborhood. They wanted "the foreigners" to build them one. I cut the fantasy short, lecturing: "You know what? The Americans are not going to drop a fully formed education system out of some helicopter like they dropped their bombs. It's just not going to happen that way. If you want foreigners to help you, you are going to have to take some initiative. If you start something, then they'll help you finish it. Why don't you get to work on that school yourselves?"

To illustrate this apparently alien notion of pitching in, I found myself describing Work and Play Day, a tradition at my own elementary school back in Boston. On the last day of the year, we kids would be assigned to different classrooms and spend the morning doing heavy cleaning for the summer. The afternoon was a schoolwide game of capture the flag. We looked forward to it all year long.

It took some talking to get my point across, but eventually the Afghan opium dealers warmed up. One thought that maybe there was room for that school on the roof of his own house.

Such conversations were infectious; I found myself having them again and again.

The point is that this was Kandahar, yet there was no hostility to the American presence. On the contrary, Kandaharis were looking to the

Americans for help. They expected the Americans to help them gain their country back, help them rein in their own leaders' well-remembered corruption, help them come up with a new version of *qanun,* of law and order, which would be a little less oppressive than the Taliban's rendition. Help them start making something of themselves.

I told this to the young marine. I told him U.S. soldiers were in zero danger. They were seen as Kandahar's ticket out of backwardness.

"That's really interesting," the marine replied. "I had a feeling that's how things were. See, they keep giving us these briefings about the situation here, and I've been wondering if they're bullshitting us. They keep saying this is a combat mission. 'Combat?' I'm saying. 'What combat?' There's nothing happening out here. I'm feeling pretty dumb in this hole in the ground. And I'm getting a little ticked off too. I think they're taking advantage of us. I feel like we're just a symbol—like a great big American flag stuck in the dirt out here. What's the use of that? I'd like to do something real. I'd like to get out there and start building that road."

I wanted to throw my arms around the kid. "And you know what?" I said. "If you built the road, it would do more for your security than another thousand guys out here in foxholes. The Afghans would protect you. If they saw you helping them, they would take care of you."

I had this entire conversation down on tape. It was going in my story. Because, like the tale young Fayda had told me on the way to Kandahar a couple of weeks before, it seemed to hold the crux of what was already going wrong.

But my editor nixed it. She said there was nothing new or interesting in this conversation. Soldiers are always disgruntled. This marine was just the same as every other grunt.

Looking back, I wonder what I had left to put in my marines at Christmas piece after she chopped that conversation.

I made a second lifestyle choice after a week or so in town, next to which my decision to wear men's clothes seemed positively mainstream. I decided to take up quarters not with the rest of the journalists at the one hotel, but in a private home, with a family of Achekzais.

I was guided in this choice partly by my sense of security—a hotel full of Western journalists felt like a target to me—and partly by my irrepressible reflex to get down on my hands and knees and roll around in stories I was covering. The company of fellow journalists always seemed to be too distorting a lens through which to observe a foreign culture.

I asked Mahmad Anwar if he could possibly find me a place to live. The same afternoon, he signed my driver to insert our yellow taxi into his convoy, and he led us up a stony road to the dodgy north side of town. Across a small bridge and to the right between a baker and a vegetable stall, and then abruptly left, our cortege emptied out into a graveyard.

It had to be the loneliest place I had ever laid eyes on. It was not set up like Western cemeteries, with headstones in rows, or funerary sculptures, or lovely landscaping, or marble mausoleums. It was bare ground. The graves were body-length mounds of stones, sometimes marked with a pole at head and foot, and decorated with scraps of cloth. To signal the resting places of heroes or saintly men, these slender poles were hung with flags, usually green or black.

About a hundred yards ahead, across this eerie landscape, stood my new home. Its impassive walls hid a mud-brick compound, the typical Kandahar construction, half underground, with a room for receiving visitors, the *maelmastun,* and separate family quarters where women could walk unseen.

There were twenty-two of us in there, counting a dozen kids, not counting the cow and her calf and two oversized brown Turkmen sheep. We had no running water, but we did have our own well and good reliable electricity, pirated off the city mains. I spent the nights with my driver and my youngest host-brother, in the public part of the compound, the *maelmastun.* We slept on the cotton-filled mattresses that hugged the four walls, doubling as seating during the day and bedding at night. A window niche was my desk; I kept my computer there, and an English-Pashtu dictionary that would lead me on tortuous quests, and the digital decoder that sent my stories out in crystal quality across a satellite link to Washington. The livestock and the well and latrine, and the small room we used for washing with a bucket of water heated over a fire, and a vegetable patch, were all back in the private quarters where the women lived, separated from the *maelmastun* by a narrow, low-roofed corridor.

Deprived of the services of my male translator when I was back there, I never really got to know the three young wives of the married brothers. I did not even learn their names. The only females who could cross back and forth to the *maelmastun* or stray outside like men were the little girls, and occasionally *Mur,* the family matriarch. For one fattish girl who was reaching puberty, it was already becoming a problem. At about thirteen, she was no longer allowed outside.

In the evenings, the brothers and their gleefully foul-mouthed father would gather for card games, slapping a winning card down with a triumphant *thwak,* and keeping up a running commentary. (A scant two weeks before, even such an innocent vice as this was punishable by beating.) My driver would join in, or some male friends or relatives who had stopped by. I would play too sometimes, or butt into the conversation with one of my laboriously acquired Pashtu words.

Meals were eaten communally, but segregated by sex, the women in the house, the rest of us in the *maelmastun.* The youngest brother, whose lifelong task it is in Afghan families to serve the others, would shake out a long plastic tablecloth on the floor. He and the children would carry dishes of food along the corridor: a chicken stew, rice, and a few raw vegetables, including my favorite—long, mild white radishes. There would be a dish for every two or three people. And within reach of everyone, a big metal bowl filled with a Kandahar delicacy: *shlumbi.* It is watered down yogurt, sometimes embellished with chopped cucumbers or mint. I don't like sour. I made everyone laugh by pointing at my stomach and saying that if I drank *shlumbi,* there would war down there. *War* was one of the first Pashtu words I learned.

After a while, I almost stopped noticing the stony mounds outside the door. You had to pick your way among them to get to your car, or if you wanted to go outside to pee at night. One day I saw one of our little boys playing knucklebones, with real knucklebones. *I wonder whose they are,* I caught myself thinking with macabre humor.

In another corner of our graveyard was the Arab Cemetery, where many of the Al-Qaeda fighters killed in the final assault on the airport were buried. It was starting to gather crowds. In a typical example of Afghan self-contradiction, Kandaharis who had resented the Arabs' arrogance when they were alive began visiting their graves now that they were dead, in hopes of intercession on high. I remember relatives of my staunchly anti-Taliban host family arriving all the way from Quetta in Pakistan, with their sick daughter. They had come to the burial place of the Arab "martyrs" to pray for a cure. An embarrassed Governor Shirzai tried to close the area to prevent gatherings of fervent pilgrims.

In keeping with Achekzai tradition, the family's five adult sons worked in the transport trade. Nazir Ahmad was a machinist, honing auto engine parts on his spinning lathe. The others worked in the shop of the eldest, Nissar Ahmad, in one of the city's oil-splotched car yards, tricking out huge cargo trucks with fanciful decorations: panels painted with elaborate scenes and framed by metal curlicues, meeting in a towering point high above the truck's cab like the prow of a ship. And around the skirts, a fringe of jingling metal ornaments that would lend a truck's struggle over bumpy roads the sound of a glad-hearted festival. In one of the most impoverished countries on earth, truck owners will lay down thousands to tart up their prize possessions. My Achekzai brothers made sure they got their money's worth. The shop was famous for Nissar Ahmad's embossing on chrome plates. I would visit him sometimes and watch him work, sitting cross-legged on the ground, holding the plate down with one bare foot. He still owes me a fish, complete with scales and an eye, like the ones he uses to finish off the bottom panels of the truck broadsides, sometimes five or six feet long.

The brothers were short and a little stocky. When they left the house in the morning, piling into their white station wagon with their shawls slung around them against the cold, I could not shut out the picture of myself as Snow White, with the brothers playing my five dwarves. "Hi ho, hi ho, it's off to work we go . . ."

Each of the four older ones had four or five kids. I never did get completely straight who was whose. Willowy, black-haired Gulali used to follow me everywhere, getting into my stuff, pouring water for me to wash my hands, and fetching a thermos of tea or my notebooks for me. Unable to speak more than a few words in her language, I must have seemed like a toddler to her, and she would mother me importantly, as though I were her doll. Sadia was the mischievous one, always scrapping with the other kids. Four-year-old Guldani flirted inveterately, sidling up to my imposing driver. One of the baby boys, Tawwab, took an unaccountable shine to me. He would sit in my lap as I lay on a mat spread outside in the evenings, lean back against my raised knees, and place his feet, with careful deliberation, in my face.

Mahmad Anwar would come over with some fighters every once in a while to check on me. Sometimes he would spend the night with us in the *maelmastun*. And I often stopped by his headquarters to hear the latest. Despite its dignified exterior and its location on the main thoroughfare, it was an utterly unsalubrious place: walls discolored and flaking, no running water, leftover food drying in the corners.

Mahmad Anwar welcomed me unquestioningly. With a warm salutation, the nappy fighters on the door would usher me upstairs, accepting me as one of their own. I learned how to greet the people gathered in Mahmad Anwar's office with the ritual that Afghans perform when they enter a room. Everyone stands up, and you shake hands all around, greeting each person in turn. If you know someone well, there is a kind of dance step you do: left hand to your friend's right shoulder, right hand to his waist. Then you take a half step back and let your right hand slide across to his, and clasp it. One of Mahmad Anwar's friends did this with me once, and put his right hand smack on top of my bosom. He almost died. The optical illusion had worked too well; he had actually thought I was a man. Handshakes done, everyone sits back down, and the greetings go around again, the newcomer meeting the eyes of each person in turn, wishing him peace, asking after his health and family.

It seemed oddly contradictory to me: the dignity and ceremony of this salutation, performed by the otherwise wild Achekzais.

Mahmad Anwar never tried to hide anything from me. When I showed up, day or night, I was ushered into his cramped and misshapen situation room: dirty carpet on the floor, dirtier mattresses as a bedding/seating combo, a leaning stack of ammunition boxes in a corner, a few Kalashnikovs and rocket launchers. Whatever he was discussing, I was welcome to follow along. Often it had to do with disarming leftover bands of Taliban in Helmand Province to the west. In private, I would give him advice, similar to what I had told those opium dealers. He really had to clean up his headquarters, I said. And he should not be allowing his men to smoke pot. It was giving them a bad reputation.

Mahmad Anwar loved to swagger around in the olive green U.S. Army parka the Americans had issued him, with its fur-trimmed hood. His men were wearing the traditional Afghan outfit of baggy trousers, long tunic, turban or sparkly cap, shawl slung over one shoulder. But a rough sort of uniform was starting to shake out in Kandahar. Western-style clothing was coming to be a badge of the new regime. Security officers like Mahmad Anwar wore fatigues, provincial officials wore shirts and ties, even teachers wore Western clothes in school. But they would not be caught dead in them on the street; tight trousers, exposing the shape of a man's legs all the way up to his crotch, were just too unseemly by local standards. Teachers brought their school clothes to work and changed in the cramped communal space of what passed for a teachers' lounge.

And so I spent my time trying to describe life in post-Taliban Kandahar to my unseen audience a world away.

One afternoon, I was working on a piece for *Morning Edition*. My deadline was coming at me like a cavalry charge, and I was transfixed with concentration. Suddenly—I could have killed him—one of my host-brothers shattered it. He rushed into my sanctum with some flustered noise about the chief of police. On his heels scampered the little girls to straighten up the room. It was like the flight of wild creatures ahead of a forest fire.

A moment later a mighty man entered, one of the largest I have ever seen. He was surrounded by four or five bodyguards. Their presence seemed to use up all the space in the room. It was Zabit Akrem. *So this is the big man I've been hearing about.* Mahmad Anwar's boss.

For, when Shirzai seized the governorship, President Karzai gave the provincial security apparatus to Mullah Naqib's Alokozais, to preserve some balance of power. Zabit Akrem reaped the police department.

Akrem and his soldiers sat themselves down and began making small talk. After a curt salutation, I turned and went back to smacking my keyboard.

"Sarah," my host-brother interrupted after a minute. "Mr. Commander wants to speak to you."

"I'm busy. He'll have to wait till I'm done." Unbelievable affrontery.

"Sarah." My host brother's tense voice broke a silence. "Zabit Akrem is a big person. He doesn't have much time. He wants to talk to you for a minute."

I sighed and flounced around to face him.

Foreigners, Akrem informed me, were forbidden to live in private houses. I would have to move out of the compound for my "safety," and take up quarters at the hotel.

I was indignant. Suddenly there were laws in Afghanistan, and staying in a private home was against them? That filthy excuse for a hotel was infested with fellow journalists, not to mention seedy-looking Afghans haunting the halls. There were only one or two women reporters, and I didn't fancy walking around with my hair drying in front of a lot of unknown Afghan men. I knew my safety and ability to work in hidebound Kandahar depended on my reputation. Living as part of a family put me in a category that made sense, culturally. And it fit in with the protection precept I was going by. I was here under the protection of the Achekzai tribe. Staying with an Achekzai family offered a lot more security than living with a bunch of other foreigners guarded by a few paid gunmen. And another thing. Those gunmen, I understood, were Akrem's tribesmen. Their other job was to keep tabs on where reporters went. Just freed from police-state conditions in Quetta, where we had to dream up ruses to shake the intelligence agents assigned to us for our "protection," I had no intention of submitting to that nonsense again.

"Sorry, I'm not going," I informed Akrem. "I have a father here, and five strong brothers. I'm much safer here in 'my' house than in any hotel. Besides, I'm leaving in a few days."

We haggled for a while, the brothers backing me up. Finally I won out, Akrem agreeing that I could finish out my rotation in the house.

I met him again a little later, the first week in January 2002, in his office at the police department. A crack journalist from *Time* magazine, Michael Ware, and I had come up with a harebrained scheme to strike off across the vast deserted wasteland of Helmand Province to the west of Kandahar, in search of fighting with Al-Qaeda. Mick wanted to take along some police fighters for protection. And when Akrem found out and wanted to talk, Mick conveniently had an urgent deadline and asked if I would go.

It was more than a little intimidating to face him in his office, stars on his shoulders, surrounded by uniformed fighters, scarcely glancing up from behind his massive wooden desk.

"I thought you were leaving," he said. Yeah, well . . . Heart pounding, I told him a fairy tale about having some friends I wanted to visit in the Helmand Province capital. I said I would only go that far. "So, you've got a lot of buddies with black turbans," Akrem retorted, meaning Taliban. I let it go and retired, just about backing out of the room the way courtiers did in ancient Persia before the king of kings. I heard him say in a stage whisper aside: "These foreigners tell a lot of lies."

"It's true," I told him later, when we became friends. "I was lying. But you lied to me, too!" He threw back his head and laughed.

With the exception of one other hostile meeting the next spring, Akrem and I did not exchange another word for almost a year.

One day in early January, school was ready to open. It would be the first time in about a decade. I simply could not resist taking my three littlest girls up the road to register, with hundreds of other yelling, zooming, laughing, excited neighborhood children, after they had all but somersaulted into the *maelmastun,* where I was at work, squealing and mimicking the act of writing with fingers on their miniature palms: "We're-going-to-school, we're-going-to-school, we're-going-to-school!" It seemed a historic errand, a more important task than finishing my piece for *All Things Considered.* My grip on precisely what my mission was here in Kandahar was loosening.

From rueful experience, I could recognize signs of approaching burnout: a frenetic tinge to my energy when it rose, and, like a background monotone, a fatigue, a growing lassitude that had been creeping up on me and was now upon me, blinding me to stories. Even so, I eyed the approaching end of my NPR tour, in early January 2002, with a sense of dislocation and some loss.

I ended up overstaying my scheduled departure date. And only with some difficulty did I resolve to turn my back at last on this uncouth city that had wormed its way into my heart. I stopped off for a series of raucous or formal good-byes: with my adoptive family—they sprinkled water behind my departing yellow car in a Pashtun tradition—and with Ahmad Wali Karzai, the younger brother President Hamid had left behind to hold down the fort in Kandahar, and, when I set off on that bone-crushing road to Spin Boldak and Pakistan, with my various Achekzai comrades at the border.

At the barracks where I had first been assigned the young bodyguard Fayda, one of the scruffy fighters asked me, "Are you a journalist?"

"She's *our* journalist," his comrades chorused.

And so the love affair began.

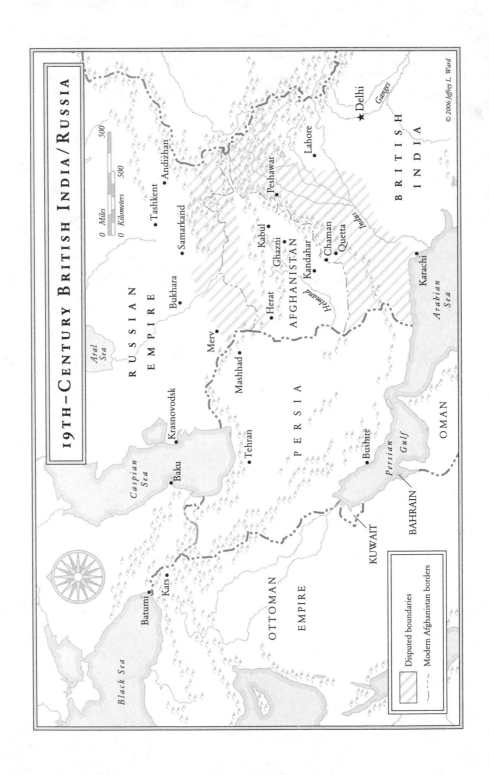

19TH-CENTURY BRITISH INDIA/RUSSIA

© 2006 Jeffry L. Ward

RUSSIAN EMPIRE

Aral Sea

• Tashkent
• Andizhan
• Samarkand
• Bukhara

Caspian Sea

• Krasnovodsk
• Baku
• Tehran
• Mashhad
• Merv

PERSIA

• Herat
Helmand
AFGHANISTAN
• Kabul
Ghazni •
• Kandahar

• Peshawar
• Lahore

★ Delhi
Ganges

BRITISH INDIA

Indus

• Chaman
• Quetta
• Karachi

Arabian Sea

• Bushire

Persian Gulf

OMAN

KUWAIT

BAHRAIN

OTTOMAN EMPIRE

Black Sea

• Batumi
• Kars

0 Miles 500
0 Kilometers 500

Disputed boundaries

Modern Afghanistan borders

CHAPTER 12

THE BORDER

1838-1898

I STOOD WEDGED against a table that took up three quarters of a room at the cramped Pakistani border post. A stumpy, round-headed bureaucrat refused to glance up in my direction. Before him was a vast ledger, its pages rising in symmetrical hills from the center binding and extending at least two feet across on either side. He would glance at it, then page through my passport, rubbing each leaf voluptuously against its neighbor, then run his finger down the hand-printed names and dates in the book. Because of that Achekzai motorcycle ride a month back, which skirted this very border post, my passport lacked the stamp he was looking for. Having not legally exited Pakistan, I was going to have a hard time legally entering it again. I wished there was a way to get to France without setting foot across the border.

That border is a sore subject, and has been for a century. Where precisely the line separating Afghanistan and Pakistan even lies is a subject of violent contention, a lightning rod for seething resentment, animosity, and mistrust between the two deeply entangled neighbors. The porosity I enjoyed in the company of my Achekzai friends; the thoroughfares that insurgents could take across the frontier—unpaved tracks across crags and sandpits, or gates opened by acquiescent Pakistani border guards—the repeated Pakistani encroachments, as troops strayed across the line to tumble into firefights with U.S. soldiers, or as officials edged the line forward, moving Pakistani border posts into Afghanistan; all these manifestations of the unsolved conflict would enormously complicate the U.S. mission in southern Afghanistan in the months ahead.

The manifestations are the symptoms of an underlying attitude. During my stay in Quetta, I came to sense that much of Pakistani officialdom thought of Afghanistan as something like the vacant lot behind their house. A place they effectively owned, could unload their junk in, or put to more serious use should occasion require. I started hearing about a notion called strategic depth. In the calculus of their ongoing confrontation with India, it seemed that successive governments in Islamabad postulated Afghanistan as an extension of their territory, land to fade back or retreat to, or base their missiles on, if it ever came to war. And it seemed that much of Pakistani policy in recent decades had been aimed at securing unrestricted access to that territory.

This attitude has hardly been kept secret. Kandahar's telephone exchange under the Taliban, for example, was the same as Quetta's—with a Pakistani country code. In 2003, Zabit Akrem received a most unsettling warning, delivered in person by the messenger of a well-known colonel of the Pakistani ISI named Faisan. "Where you are now," the messenger said, "will soon be part of Pakistan."

Akrem sent back the reply that Afghanistan has a rather longer history than Pakistan's, and will likely outlast it.

Afghans, meanwhile, nurture a reciprocal proprietary attitude toward much of northern Pakistan. Just about all the refugees I met in Quetta considered the ground under our feet to be part of their native country. I had a hard time taking them seriously, but they were quite worked up about it. Even the scarcely literate would go on at me about something called the Durand Line. Everybody had something to say about it, none of it complimentary. This line, which constitutes Afghanistan's border with Pakistan, was no longer valid, the Afghans kept insisting.

Local lore holds that the treaty establishing the border expired after a hundred years, meaning the line was now defunct. Clearly, the root of the trouble went back to that treaty, to the original drawing of the line. If I was to begin to sort out in my mind the legitimacy of the competing assertions, I was going to have to examine the circumstances that gave rise to it.

A hundred years, I mused, listening to the Afghan refugees. That puts

us in the middle of the Great Game. The term conjured up Rudyard
Kipling for me, and not a whole lot else. All I really knew was that it was
another face-off between two empires across the Asian landmass, with
Kandahar marking the centerline, as usual. I hate the nineteenth century,
but I could see I was going to have to get into it. Otherwise, the persis-
tent Pakistani interference in Afghan affairs, and Afghans' burning resentment of a neighbor that shared their religion and their recent opposition
to the Soviet colossus, were not going to make much sense.

The two seminal works about the Great Game available in bookstores,
when I finally made it home, proved mind numbing.[1] But by shutting out
a lot of the details, I could begin to discern the main lines of the story.
This border, it emerged, had been a running argument for decades among
the amirs of the young Afghan state—the successors of Ahmad Shah
Durrani—and the heirs to the Moghul dynasty in India, the imperial
British.

Throughout the nineteenth century, as Britain extended and tightened
her grasp on lands in India, her policy toward Afghanistan, India's northern neighbor, was, in the understated words of the most important
Afghan ruler of the day, "subject to occasional fits and changes."[2] In fact,
British policy tacked quite radically back and forth, like a sailboat in a
contrary wind.

Britain, at that time, was caught up in a huge worldwide contest between superpowers—the Cold War of the day. Its rival was Russia. And
Russia, during that century, was relentlessly expanding across Central Asia
at the expense of Muslim amirs who ruled oasis city-states in such ancient
capitals as Tashkent, Bukhara, and Merv.

This Russian expansion, in the view of most British policymakers, was
not aimed merely eastward, to push the borders of the czars' land toward
the edge of its continent—much as the United States was expanding westward across her own continent during those years. The British were sure
that Russia had designs on English lands in India too.

The two books I was reading disagreed strongly about the nature of
this Russian threat to the English Indian dominions. So did the British
at the time.

The conservative Tory Party's assessment of the Russian threat was
alarmist, and its reaction to it, hawkish. An imminent Russian danger was

the postulate in all the Tory leaders' equations. Their consensus on how best to counter it was that the best defense was a good offense. That is, most Tories judged that the best way to keep the Russians out of India was to move forward *toward* Russia and take over Afghanistan in whole or in part. As it happened, this "forward policy" led the British Empire to one of its most scorching military defeats since the American Revolution.

The Liberal Party, by contrast, was sometimes inclined to make light of the Russian threat. And the favored liberal solution to the Russian problem was rather dovish: to stay put in India, befriending a locally acceptable Afghan leader and allowing him and his fanatically independent people to serve as the subcontinent's gatekeeper. This course effectively halted Russia's military advance on Afghanistan until 1979.

The abrupt tacking back and forth between these two policies—the "occasional fits and changes" that occurred every time one party lost an election and the other gained power—made the British rather difficult for their Afghan interlocutors to read. This I gathered from my first good primary source for the period: more memoirs, dictated by the late nineteenth-century Afghan amir quoted above: Abd ar-Rahman Khan. He was to play a decisive role in the events, and in the tracing of the famous Durand Line.

Regarding the reliability of British promises, this Amir Abd ar-Rahman once remarked acidly to a British viceroy of India: "I am sorry that I am not a prophet, neither am I inspired to know whether at some future time, if I am in trouble, a Liberal or Conservative Government will be in power." Abd ar-Rahman found it a brilliant feature of the British constitution that it always provided for "one party or another to put the blame upon when mistakes are made."[3]

The first really appalling mistake the British made in Afghanistan was to interfere directly in the old rivalry between the Popalzai and Barakzai tribes—the same two tribes that vied for power at the founding *jirga,* the same tribes whose rivalry I would bear witness to so many years later.

When Dost Muhammad, the first Barakzai to displace the founding Popalzai dynasty on the Afghan throne, agreed to meet a Russian envoy in Kabul in 1838, Britain decided to remove and replace him. Though Afghanistan was nominally independent, the overwhelming firepower of neighboring British India made such a decision seem feasible to politicians and bureaucrats in London and the Indian capital of Calcutta. To take Dost Muhammad's place, the British chose an aging and repudiated member of the Popalzai house, an exiled grandson of Afghan founding father Ahmad Shah. The British decided to put him back on the throne he had occupied some three decades earlier. But doing so, and maintaining him there, required the deployment of a garrison in Kabul. This debauched amir emphatically did not qualify as a locally acceptable ruler. He was seen by Afghans as despicably beholden to the English, and their move to install him as a poorly disguised effort to take over the country.

Underestimating Afghan hostility, the British underestimated the type of investment that would be required to control Afghanistan through their puppet amir. This mistake has been repeated by powerful foreign meddlers in small countries, right down to the United States in the twenty-first century—before my eyes in Iraq, for example.

The British army that escorted the new amir into Afghanistan reached Kabul fantastically encumbered: more servants rode with it than soldiers; the camel train stretched for miles. One account describes a pack of foxhounds among the baggage, and saddlebags straining with angular bulges from crates and crates of cigars.[4] This supporting force was stationed on the outskirts of Kabul, billeted in absurdly exposed barracks: a mile from town, dominated by hills and separated from its own food storehouse.

It did not take long for the disgruntled Afghans, bitterly resentful of the puppet amir and his vast foreign army, to begin exploiting the British position. By late fall 1841, two British envoys lay hacked to pieces in the Kabul bazaar and the hills about the garrison bristled with Afghan fighters and their long rifles, picking off Redcoats who risked a sortie. Without reinforcements from a British contingent based in Kandahar, the Kabul garrison had no hope. A surrender was negotiated with Dost Muhammad's son, who was leading the revolt. It stipulated the total withdrawal of foreign troops from Kabul. The Army of the Indus, the fighting force of the richest and most powerful empire on earth, picked its freezing and starving way up through the hills toward the breathtaking passes on the road that led eastward to Jalalabad and India beyond. There, in those passes, the troop was cut to pieces, despite the treaty. Only a single British fighting man survived, and a few hundred camp followers who were taken prisoner. The force of mighty Britain had been annihilated by a bunch of Afghan villagers.

This exchange was dubbed the first Anglo-Afghan war. It was to burn a sizzling scar into the flesh of British history. Like the story of the founding *jirga,* the tale of it has become a legend for Afghans, to whom it serves as a kind of second founding myth. For the British, it became a painful object lesson in how, in global politics as well as the Bible, pride goeth before a fall. Coming a decade before a bitter and savagely bloody mutiny and uprising in India, the slaughter in the Afghan highlands marked the beginning of Britain's inexorable retreat from empire, which culminated a century later in independence movements across the globe.

The first Anglo-Afghan war has also sent a chilling warning to all other Western powers that have considered following Britain's footsteps into Afghanistan. It is from this story more than any other that the legend of Afghan invincibility was born.

The Barakzai amir whom the British had tried to remove in the first place, Dost Muhammad, returned to Afghanistan. And the British—displaying as much facility for shifting alliances as the Afghans themselves—entered into an agreement with him. Under its terms, he would let the British viceroy in India run his foreign policy in return for a yearly subsidy.

A rough peace was thus achieved for some decades. During this time, the frontiers of Afghanistan were never clearly defined. To the south and east, they faded into a kind of tribal belt—which even Afghanistan's rulers called a *yaghestan*—separating their kingdom from the principalities to its south, which were tributaries of British-held India. To the north and west, Afghan lands were subject to repeated attacks from expanding Russia, which had swallowed vast tracts of steppe country, snapped up ancient silk road capitals, and was nipping at the fringes of Afghanistan.

The peace with India was broken, inevitably, by a second Anglo-Afghan war. It erupted in 1878, again because the reigning amir had had the temerity to receive a Russian delegation. Britain had failed in its promise to defend Afghanistan from its giant northern neighbor, and the amir felt he had to open talks with the Russians. A three-pronged British invasion to punish him achieved an easy initial military victory, and the masters of India, for a second time, installed a puppet on the Afghan throne.

Even more openly than before, the British action aimed to move the border of India upward to the line running between Kandahar and Kabul. The Tory hawks were in power, and they wanted to advance *toward* advancing Russia.

And so the British forced upon their new pet amir the Treaty of Gandomak. This was the first legal document to officially sign away swathes of land the Afghans had considered theirs for time out of mind. Quetta and Peshawar, those key outposts on the two roads piercing Afghanistan, went to the British—along with tens of thousands of Pashtun tribesmen who, ethnically anyway, belonged with their brethren in Afghanistan.

"Though England does not want any piece of Afghanistan," Amir Abd ar-Rahman noted wryly in his autobiography, "still she never loses a chance of getting one!"[5]

Having signed this humiliating treaty, and after widespread Afghan mutinies against its terms and vicious retaliation by the British, the puppet amir resigned. Suddenly, Afghanistan had transformed itself back into *Yaghestan*. There was no interlocutor, no ruler, no one for the British to treat with. Tribesmen withdrew their recognition of the Treaty of Gandomak and their nominal submission to the British Crown, bestowing their loyalty on one or another scion of the ruling Barakzai house. "You broke it; you own it," the Afghan tribes might as well have been chanting to the muscle-bound British. There was no way for Britain to control the country in this condition except by moving in en masse and colonizing it. And this they were not going to do.[6] Afghanistan defeated the British, as it would the Soviets a hundred years later, by dissolving.[7]

Enter, at this juncture, Abd ar-Rahman Khan, the amir quoted above, who, apart from graciously leaving behind his astute autobiographies, one in Persian and another in English, was perhaps the most brilliant statesman ever to rule Afghanistan. He had spent the previous decade in exile as the guest of the Russians. At this propitious moment, they propelled him back across the border to his homeland. But Abd Ar-Rahman Khan would disappoint any in Moscow who may have hoped they had bought his allegiance by financing his exile. More than any other ruler, he would come to personify Afghanistan's fierce and cleverly preserved independence from both of her powerful neighbors.

British policy at this point called for a partition of the country, with one amir in Kabul and another in Kandahar. In fact, some British experts thought Kabul was a military irrelevance anyway, and Kandahar was the key defensive position.[8] Many Tories urged the course of annexing Kandahar outright, adding it to the Indian dominions, and leaving Kabul to a "friendly" amir. But at that moment, though there were many fractious rivals, there was no obvious candidate for the position.

This is why Abd Ar-Rahman's sudden appearance was so well timed. Though somewhat uneasy about his links to Russia, the stymied British were relieved to offer him Kabul. Kandahar they planned to hold apart.

In his autobiography, Abd ar-Rahman has this to say about the shattered land he was poised to take in hand: "The weakness of the kingdom of Afghanistan was so great that whenever the King went a few miles out of his capital, he used to find some one else King on his return."[9] The shrewd amir responded to the British offer of Kabul by playing hard to get. His aim was to consolidate some local support before accepting anointment from the foreigners, and at the same time to make himself desirable to them so as to improve—however slightly—his bargaining position. Though too weak in guns, treasure, and political legitimacy to reject the partition of Afghanistan at that point, he hoped to be able to reverse it one day. For, he wrote, "The kingdom of Kabul, without Kandahar, was like a head without a nose."[10]

The art of patience. This was what Abd ar-Rahman Khan mastered with such genius: the ability to assess lucidly his own frailties and flex with them, while waiting till the course of events helped overcome them. "A great ruler and a great man," concluded Sir H. Mortimer Durand, the envoy who finally did negotiate the Indo-Afghan border with him a decade later.[11] Durand's superior, the viceroy of India, called Abd ar-Rahman "a strange, strong creature."[12]

Looking thoughtfully at the camera, he sat for a photograph in the 1870s, his feet in tall leather riding boots resting on a curved footstool, a walking stick in his hands, his face displaying "more roundness of contour than is customary," as another British officer put it, "while a certain heaviness of limb gave little indication of his well-known active habits."[13]

Amir Abd ar-Rahman deeply impressed Sir Mortimer Durand, who sat opposite him for the historic boundary parlays. Though "not altogether easy to deal with," he had a head for business, Durand said; he spoke with a directness unusual to the region, and conducted negotiations in all their details himself, dispensing with interpreters—even making Durand address Afghan tribal elders in his imperfect Persian, rather than through an intermediary. He was dignified but not ostentatious, resolute, true to his word, and forward thinking. Durand's description of his boisterous sense of humor brings the amir right to life: "He had a way of making a joke and looking at you with eyes and mouth open, to see if you had caught it, and then going into a roar of laughter, which was very infectious."[14]

To the British peer, "there was something which went to one's heart about the man, standing there between England and Russia, playing his lone hand."[15]

One of the best examples of Abd ar-Rahman's flair for turning weaknesses to advantage in this nerve-racking game came immediately after his inauguration as amir of Kabul, in 1880. He allowed the British to administer a thrashing to the scion of another noble house, his main rival for control of Afghanistan. The rival, Ayyub Khan, was popular, and it would not have been good policy, imagewise, for Abd ar-Rahman to take him on himself. Doing it for him, the British put Abd ar-Rahman on the road to reuniting Afghanistan—including coveted Kandahar—under his own rule.

For Kandahar is where the action took place.

Afghanistan was still *Yaghestan* at this point. Britain's puppet amir had resigned after signing the hated Treaty of Gandomak, the provinces were in open revolt; the British had only just selected Abd ar-Rahman from among a handful of potential claimants to the throne in Kabul. A few weeks before his inauguration, in July 1880, Ayyub Khan, based in Herat, marched toward Kandahar to attack a small British garrison that was holding the city for the crown. By rejecting British interference and ejecting Abd ar-Rahman as its apparent instrument, this amir determined to take the political as well as the military offensive.

Browsing in the stacks on the fifth floor of my university library, in the section marked "Ind" for India, I fell upon an old collection of letters—binding cracked, chips of pages sifting to the floor—written by British officers who were part of the Kandahar garrison. The letters provide a priceless picture of the events that the correspondents' well-trained powers of observation, together with their epistolary habits, enliven so vividly that reading their letters feels like watching a film.

The Kandahar these British officers depict, a little before the turn of the twentieth century, is rather different from the one I came to know. For starters, the place is positively lush. The officers describe mango and coconut groves, no less, where today trees of any kind stick up wan and lonely like spindly aberrations. "On three sides of our city we have smiling villages, clustering orchards, gardens, vineyards, cornfields, and groves of palm."[16] Apparently, the savage drought that accompanied Taliban rule in the 1990s was only a sort of meteorological exclamation point, punctuating a long, gradual drying out of Kandahar's oasis.

The city itself resembled Ahmad Shah Durrani's eighteenth-century capital more closely than it does today. Great battlements, thirty feet high and studded with sixty-two towers, surrounded it. The British officers, with an eye toward defense, found this wall "poor and weak," since it was made only of leprous dry brick and rubble with no stone revetments, and the gates were of "rotten timber," which would have been vulnerable to a medieval battering ram.[17] Swilling down double rations of beer in the heat, the British toiled during that spring of 1880 to reinforce the defenses.

These walls are all gone now, and as the city has grown up around it, the area they once bounded has shrunk in relative size to a mere neighborhood of Kandahar. It is now the teeming and lively bazaar where my red pickup truck can scarcely squeeze by the vegetable carts and rickshaws and loaded donkeys. Still, the traces of the old walls linger in the names of certain street corners: Herat Gate, where no sign of a gate remains, just the mouth of a narrow street lined with cloth merchants' stalls; Kabul Gate, on the other side of the bazaar; or Shkarpur Gate, facing the old road south toward India, where caravans bearing precious goods for Safavi Persia used to pull to a halt, camels roaring throaty indignation.

Like the U.S. military base today, out at the airport, the British cantonment was well outside the nineteenth-century town, to the west, right about where the younger Karzai brother's house now stands. Kandaharis call the neighborhood *Shahr-i Naw,* New Town.

As the dates on the officers' letters enter the month of June 1880, foreboding starts seeping in. The writers know Ayyub Khan, in Herat, is gathering a force to march against them, and they feel undermanned and vulnerable. "We are beyond all question too small a garrison for the size

of the defenses," one comments.[18] Meanwhile, rumors about the impend-
ing clash fan skittishness among the Kandaharis. The officers describe the
"consternation" of friendly Afghan merchants, and families packing their
things and fleeing the city. The Kandaharis' fear is contagious. It darkens
the mood of the bluff British officers.

On July 2, a foot and horse contingent is sent out to try to block
Ayyub's force before it reaches Kandahar from Herat. The British plan to
meet up with a friendly Afghan commander a little way outside Kandahar
and, together with his men, take on the hostile Ayyub.

In those days, the British imperial army was not even half British; the
small force included such units as the Third Bombay Light Cavalry and the
Sind Horse. For little more than 700 Englishmen, there were close to
2,000 Indian troops.[19] One of their commanders admires them for almost
two pages: "splendid-looking specimens of the race from which they came;
long-limbed, lean and sinewy . . . and a muscle well developed by constant
lance and sword exercise."[20] The officer appraises their mounts and horse-
manship with a practiced eye, and points out some of the advantages of
their equipment over that designed in London:

[The] cumbersome sabers, that won't cut and cannot point, with their
heavy steel scabbards, are not to be compared with the native *tulwar*, whose
keen, razor-like edge enables its owner to lop off a head or a limb as easily as cutting a cabbage. Our English regulation scabbards . . . are heavy,
difficult to clean, glisten in the sun and moonlight . . . while they make
such a rattle that a secret reconnaissance with them is impossible.[21]

Reading these comments, I thought of the complaints of British soldiers in Kosovo in 1999, about their shoddy standard-issue rifle. Or the
American troops in Iraq, driving Humvees with cloth doors. I wondered
why such enormously rich nations, which pour money into their defense
budgets, can never seem to fit out their soldiers in the field properly.

Along with the cavalry and foot soldiers, the retinue included bullocks
and pack mules, camels howling over the high-pitched curses of their Indian drivers, wood-wheeled artillery pieces lurching over the uneven
ground, a field hospital, a quartermaster, and cooking gear. This crowd ad-

vanced at about two miles an hour, never fully taming its own chaos, while the cavalry units grew daily more restive. One officer vowed he would take three days' fighting over twenty-four hours' marching any time.[22]

The first clash took place on the Helmand River, a mighty waterway that is to this day the throbbing artery of southern Afghanistan.

It was a battle that was not supposed to have happened. As the British approached the encampment of the "friendly" Afghan unit with which they were supposed to be joining forces, the putative allies abruptly deserted. The *yaghestan* principle was operating again. Rather than be seen fighting with the foreigners against their countrymen, the Afghans switched sides. They corralled the artillery pieces the British had armed them with and swept down the Helmand River to put them at the service of Ayyub.

The British set out after the mutineers, one of the Indian cavalry units giving chase at a "swinging gallop."[23] The stolen artillery pieces were retrieved, and some of the Afghans killed and wounded, but close to 4,000 dashed to safety and the open arms of the force approaching from Herat.

British morale suffered another blow when orders came down to withdraw halfway back to Kandahar. All of the letters deplore the move. One officer calls the new position at the village of Maywand—exposed and surrounded by high ground—"simply a military rat-trap."[24]

Adding to the unease was the fact that decent intelligence was not to be had. It was as though the Afghan force were operating inside a dust storm, which blinded the British to its makeup and intentions. This same handicap consistently dogged the American forces I observed in Kandahar.

The Battle of Maywand finally took place on July 27, when the Afghan cavalry burst upon the British troops after outflanking them in the night under cover of some hills. Today, Kandahari legend depicts this battle as a desperate stand by a handful of Afghans against the mighty British, complete with a local heroine firing up her countrymen in epic style, and for rations, flour and dried mulberries. In fact, it was a formal pitched battle, in which the Afghans outnumbered the British by something like four to one and brilliantly outfought them.

> It is impossible to deny the bitter fact that from first to last we were outmaneuvered by Ayyub, who not only chose a position we should have occupied, but lured us from the one we had taken into an ambush, where

his [artillery] had the best of ours, where his cavalry had the advantage, and where his infantry were better handled than our own. These are sad and humiliating truths, but it would be idle and useless to try to extenuate their existence.[25]

Close to half the British force perished in the engagement, and the panicked flight back to Kandahar sounds frankly hellish. "In one confused mass European and native, officer and private, old and young, brave and coward, fled along the road."[26] Mounts were bleeding from shrapnel and slashing sword wounds; donkeys and ponies and camels were held back in a jostling mass to pick up the wounded; Afghans were mixed in with the British at such close quarters that fighting could only continue by means of knives and bayonets, and "the road was soon slippery with blood." To add to the uproar, thirst set in; the frenzied British almost began killing each other to get at the water when they finally reached a stream.

Writing from his hospital bed afterwards, one of the embittered officers lashed out at the boardroom generals whom he was sure had commanded this operation from the comfort of faraway India: "Playing chess by telegraph may succeed, but making war and planning a campaign on the Helmand from the cool shades of breezy Simla is an experiment which will not, I hope, be repeated."[27]

But it is repeated, again and again.

The British disaster worked to the advantage of the newly inaugurated amir in Kabul, Abd ar-Rahman Khan, and his hopes to unite Afghanistan. It fortified the Liberal view in London that Britain should not seek to hold either Kabul or Kandahar. A decision was made to withdraw all troops from Afghanistan.

But the smarting British did have to avenge the mortifying defeat at Maywand, and rescue their garrison now besieged in Kandahar. And so, under an able and ruthless general, the Redcoats left Kabul for India, taking not the most direct route via Jalalabad, but the longer southern road that passed through Kandahar.

Amir Abd ar-Rahman contentedly paved their way. "I will merely say that our march up to the present time has been a veritable picnic," writes one pleased officer, "not unaccompanied by a rubber of whist in the afternoon, or a little duck and quail slaughter."[28] Abd ar-Rahman did everything he could to make the journey agreeable. For it would be to his political advantage if Ayyub Khan, his arch rival and the hero of Maywand, was defeated, and even more so if it was the British, not Abd Ar-Rahman himself, who did the defeating. So when, at the end of their pleasant journey, the British did indeed thrash the Herati amir, they put Abd Ar-Rahman well on his way to uniting Afghanistan.[29]

Still, it took him about a decade of intense and sometimes savage fighting, as well as several forced relocations of population—ethinic cleansings, in effect—to complete the job, to force his unruly countrymen to submit to him. Once he did, once he was solidly possessed of the whole country, it was, in his view, "of the first and greatest importance to mark out a boundary line all around Afghanistan."[30]

This project, which both Britain and Russia had come to desire as strongly as Afghanistan did, was almost ruined by a fresh British election that replaced the Liberal doves with the hawkish Conservatives.[31] The viceroy in India sent letters to the amir "in a tone that I was not accustomed to," sniffs Abd ar-Rahman, "for he wrote in a dictatorial manner, advising me upon matters of internal policy in the administration of my kingdom, and telling me how I ought to treat my subjects."[32]

Still, the amir exercised his patience and eventually received a British delegation led by Sir H. Mortimer Durand, whose task was to reach an agreement on a permanent boundary between the two kingdoms. This mission traced the line that till today has marked out Afghanistan's southern and eastern frontier.

Durand, who later served as ambassador to the United States, remembered the boundary talks as being a bit knotty. The issues to be settled, he told an audience at the Central Asian Society in London in 1907, were "rather complicated, and it took us a long time to thresh them all out."[33] Durand claimed that the amir did not have a very good sense of geography, and was forever challenging the British maps. " 'Whenever you are dealing with one of my alleged encroachments, it is made very big on the map,' Durand remembers Abd ar-Rahman complaining. " 'When you are dealing with one of your own, I notice, it is quite a tiny little thing.' "[34]

That sounds just like the amir. And he was probably right. Then, as now, no one had much good to say about the border that was eventually agreed upon, as the medley of even Anglo scholarly opinion in the upcoming footnote indicates.[35]

Probably no one hated the Durand Line more than Amir Abd ar-Rahman, who was appalled when he saw an advance copy of the map Britain intended to use as the basis for the Durand Commission's work. "It is necessary to mention here that in the map sent to me by the Viceroy all the countries of the Waziri, Chaman and the railway station there . . . Chitral, and other countries lying in between, were marked as belonging to India."[36] You can almost hear Abd ar-Rahman gulp.

These were regions that had been cut out of Afghanistan under the Treaty of Gandomak. Abd ar-Rahman had been quietly courting them for years, seeking to bring them back inside his newly united Afghanistan.[37]

The amir made his reservations known in a letter to the viceroy in India, correctly predicting endless tribulation on the frontier if the British went through with their plan. But his arguments were rebuffed. The overwhelming power of the British Empire made further argument impossible. This appears to be another moment at which the amir decided the better part of valor was patience. In return for a 50 percent increase in the subsidy Britain was paying him, and some valuable weapons, Abd ar-Rahman gave up his claim to territories amounting to something like half of modern-day Pakistan.

Between the lines of the diplomatic language in his autobiography, the amir makes it clear that he felt forced into this agreement by the threat of war. And his hostility toward British advances into what he considers his territories never wanes. A new railhead in Chaman he felt most painfully: "They were pushing the railway line into my country just like pushing a knife into my vitals,"[38] he groans. It seems clear that Amir Abd ar-Rahman hoped some later course of events would allow him or his heirs to reverse his concession, just as he had been able to reverse his early concession of a separate, British-held Kandahar.

But so far, that course of events has never materialized. Afghan lore holds that the Durand Agreement expired after one hundred years—that would have been in 1993 or 1998, depending on whether you count from the sealing of the agreement during ceremonies in Kabul or from the final demarcation of the line. But nothing in writing actually stipulates a hundred-year deadline.

In 1947, India became independent of British rule, and in a violent and painful split, majority Muslim areas in its north were partitioned off into the new state of Pakistan. Thus, Pakistan has inherited the decades-old tension over a boundary that is unpopular with Afghans and its own Pashtuns alike. Even without an explicit hundred-year expiration date, the treaty's ongoing validity is cast in some doubt since one of its signatories—British India—no longer exists. Recent governments in Kabul, including the Taliban, have never been willing to revalidate it by explicitly reratifying it with Britain's successor, Pakistan.

To this uncertainty, the Pakistani government seems to react with a version of the British Tories' forward policy, assuming that the best defense is a good offense.

After the fall of the Taliban, for example, Pakistan quickly moved the Chaman border crossing up about a mile inside Afghanistan. What used to be a teeming Afghan bazaar was bulldozed, homes wrecked, shopkeepers ordered to clear their wares or lose them. For, as one of them later told me, they were informed that the "dust beneath their shops was Pakistani dust." At a ceremony in early 2002, Governor Gul Agha Shirzai laid the cornerstone of a towering new Friendship Gate straddling the place like an arch of triumph. This gate marks the new Pakisian-Afghan border. The U.S. overseas development agency, USAID, has invested in a new state-of-the-art customs and immigration complex on the Afghan side of this new line.

Thus has Pakistan, assisted by the Kandahar provincial government and the United States, and unhindered by President Karzai, nibbled away yet another morsel of Afghanistan.

CHAPTER 13

CIVIL SOCIETY

I CAN'T REMEMBER HOW, but I did manage to browbeat the Pakistani bureaucrats into allowing me back in their country. Rushing now to get home to Quetta, my big driver tried to skip the stop I insisted on in the Chaman bazaar to drink one last round of tea with my Achekzais. It was a delicious moment, suspended in time, infused with a loving kind of fellowship.

And then I couldn't delay it any longer. We climbed back into the long-suffering yellow taxi, and headed down the switchback road to Quetta. It was January 11, 2002. I was tasked to meet my NPR replacement at the airport and do a pass-off, before finally pulling out of the region.

What I was really looking forward to was dinner with Uncle Aziz Khan Karzai—King Uncle, as he is known. He was the sparkling and sharp-eyed gentleman who, during the drawn-out negotiations for the surrender of Kandahar two months back, had helped me understand the Pashtun propensity for consensus building.

We had a lovely evening. I remember Uncle Aziz aligning and re-aligning the fine, olive-green stones of his prayer beads on the sofa cushion beside him as he voiced his fears about what would come next for Afghanistan. By this time, his nephew Hamid had left Kandahar for his capital, Kabul, accompanied by a vast crowd of well-wishers and job seekers. He had settled in the sprawling, tattered royal palace, where, bereft of the most elementary infrastructure, he had set about creating a nation-state out of whole cloth.

Aziz was troubled by the humanitarian free-for-all he knew would be unleashed as opportunists poured into the Afghan vacuum, riding the projected tide of aid. "They are sharpening their teeth and sharpening their knives," he said of the old barons of local nongovernmental organizations (NCOs). War profiteers, they have lived for years off the humanitarian bonanza, the latest incarnation of the foreign subsidy that has long sustained the Afghan tribes. "The word NGO should be struck from the English language!" Uncle Aziz cried. He knew something about it. He had placed several of these barons in charge of local branches of big international nonprofits, back in the pre-Taliban heyday of the aid biz.

At last I rose to leave. I turned in the doorway to thank Aziz one last time, and abruptly he asked me:

"Wouldn't you come back and help us?"

The question hit like a bolt from a crossbow. My ears registered with surprise what my mouth replied.

"Yes."

And then our thoughts started tumbling out, in an excited jostle. "You find someone to send you here," he said, "someone to pay your salary, and we will give you all the authority."

Almost without faltering, as though hypnotized, I set out upon the course so abruptly opened by that brief exchange.

For this was what, unwittingly, I was waiting for. Well before 9/11, a part of me had been casting about for such a sense of potential as I was feeling now. I could no longer bear to watch our Atlantic democracies go through the motions, in a business of democracy, while half our people didn't even vote. That couldn't be right. Through my reporting, I had gained the conviction that somewhere out there, from one of these postconflict disaster areas, a phoenix was going to rise. Someone from some other place—not America or Western Europe—was going to winch us up out of this rut.

Though I searched, I did not find it in the Balkans. The very worst tendencies of that region's peoples had been stoked white hot by cynics and by disillusionment. Everyone in the Balkans was out for himself.

This was different. The context was much bigger. The context was the alleged confrontation between the two great cultural and ideological rivals of the day: Islam and the West. Both of them were part of me. Hamid Karzai was different, too. He was the most inspiring political leader I had come close to in my adult life.

And this man's uncle wanted me to help?

I went to the United States, instead of home to Paris, and spent two months casting around for a way to do it.

The time was punctuated by calls to Uncle Aziz in Kabul to reaffirm the reality of it all. He had joined the team in Kabul and would describe life in the leprous presidential palace, the Afghan equivalent of the White House—an empty, echoing place, without steady electricity to stave off the midwinter cold, or telephones, or a single computer, let alone the Internet, or a satellite dish to catch coverage of nephew Hamid's first, acclaimed visit to the United States.

Karzai's elegant style and ringing eloquence took Washington by storm. Newspaper reports were comparing him to South Africa's Nelson Mandela, and commenting on his dazzling sense of fashion, as, grafting together typical clothes of different Afghan regions, Karzai invented a new national dress. The acclaim was only reaching Kabul in tiny fragments.

Stunned by Aziz's description of the home front, I wondered: how anyone could possibly start building a country in such conditions. Everyone knew how backward and shattered Afghanistan was even before the latest conflict, after centuries of isolation and three straight decades of war. Given the notoriety of the place and the symbolism of the moment in the wake of 9/11, I was astounded that someone like Microsoft's Bill Gates had not thought to pack off a half dozen computers and the $5,000 satellite dish it would take to establish an Internet connection. All of the postconflict zones of the past decade had been in similarly desperate shape when the shooting stopped. I thought that if the United Nations wanted to do something really useful, it could organize a rapid-reaction force for public utilities: a team of engineers on call to dash to countries emerging from war and restore communications, electricity, running water.

In the end, at Aziz Khan's suggestion, I fell in with another one of his nephews, Qayum, President Karzai's senior by a decade. Qayum Karzai and his wife, Patricia, had founded a nonprofit organization four years earlier in Baltimore: Afghans for Civil Society (ACS). After a brief telephone conversation, I suddenly found myself field director for ACS's as yet un-born operations in Afghanistan.

In a similarly noninstitutional way, I roped my older sister Eve Lyman into the venture. Radiating a dazzling gold, like a human sun—not just from the color of her mane of curls and the golden clothes she wears to set them off, but from the intensity of her passion and drive for life—Eve was at a turning point too. She jumped in with all her being, and side by side we set about inventing an NGO.

It was like being poised at the lip of a bright, churning, intoxicating tract of white water. The twinned feelings of urgency and opportunity were overpowering. With inspiring Karzai at the helm and Americans of good faith in the field, it actually seemed Afghanistan might be the place where some of the damage could be repaired—the damage caused by years of ignorance and neglect, arrogance and withdrawal; the damage caused by the surrender of the force of ideas, in much of the United States and the Muslim community, to those who would split the world into op-posing civilizations, irrevocably hostile. Afghanistan might just prove them wrong.

And how fitting: Afghanistan, which for seven years had symbolized the twisting of Islam into a glowering fascism—bent on social control, isola-tion, extirpation of difference—could regain its ancient role as a connec-tor of empires, facilitating the exchange of riches, people, and ideas between them.

This vision for post-Taliban Afghanistan was always, and openly, the in-spiration at Afghans for Civil Society. We never espoused the traditional hu-manitarian credo of rigid political neutrality. It was not our aim simply to ease physical suffering indiscriminately. Rather, we wished to focus our necessarily limited activities to influence, in whatever tiny way, the direc-tion the new Afghanistan would take. And unashamedly, we wished to promote awareness, understanding, and mutual appreciation between Afghans and Americans.

The window of opportunity seemed unparalleled. Here was a Muslim country that had twice in two decades rid itself of tyranny thanks to U.S. assistance. I thought of the Kosovo Albanians' indelible gratitude follow-ing the 1999 expulsion of the Serbs by NATO, the United States in the lead. On September 12, 2001, the light of a thousand candles lit the Kosovar capital as Albanian Muslims thronged the streets in condolence for America's loss. A Kosovar friend called me in Paris to say that a group of his peers wanted to enlist in the U.S. army to fight against Al Qaeda, and what should he tell them?

I hardly entertained any delusions of the same kind of outpouring from the prickly Afghans. And yet this historical juncture was pregnant with a unique potential. In contrast to the Balkans, Afghanistan was blessed with visionary leadership in Hamid Karzai. But the Afghans had suffered from too many leaps of faith in their recent turbulent past to sustain another if it did not pay off fast. Eve and I judged there were about six months to make a palpable difference before the moment would be lost. I went back to Afghanistan to meet Qayum in person and search for likely projects.

Qayum and I hit it off instantly, connecting, fanning the embers of each other's enthusiasms.

One decision I urged upon him during that exploratory trip was to base Afghans for Civil Society in Kandahar, not Kabul. I knew how it went with postconflict capitals. They always draw the bulk of the international resources, as humanitarian organizations devise projects within driving distance of their spacious headquarters, and new restaurants open up to cater to the foreign crowds. I felt that it was important to reach beyond the capital and the artificial world that develops there. Only by that extra effort can money be distributed with any fairness through the country being assisted. And only by that effort can any sense be gained of the country's real conditions. In the capital, solutions are viewed as abstract models, while the details—the local anecdotes that illustrate the projects' true impact and meaning—never come to light.

A new culture takes root in postconflict capitals like Kabul. I am not sure—to adopt the terms of a debate among some humanitarians and some of their beneficiaries—whether humanitarian action as currently practiced constitutes a form of colonialism. I do find, however, reading those accounts of the nineteenth-century British in Afghanistan—with their servants, foxhounds, and cigars—a certain parallel with at least the lifestyle of Western aid workers in Kabul.

They live apart from Afghans in guarded compounds. They do not walk about, but are driven by chauffeurs. They eat special food, imitation Western, bought in special stores—instead of popping down to the corner for fresh-baked local bread. They indulge in riotous drinking parties, with almost no thought for how this may offend their Afghan staff, almost no realization that such behavior in itself constitutes a security risk: in a strictly dry culture, many Afghans take exception to the injection of such taboo behavior into their country, seeing it as exactly the kind of corruption that Westerners bring with them—another reason to keep Westerners out.

My bias in favor of local action immersed in local knowledge was to be confirmed and reconfirmed during my time in Afghanistan.

Such a bias would have argued in favor of any provincial town over Kabul. Even more so Kandahar, with its special symbolism as Afghanistan's former capital and the native region of all its rulers. Kandahar, I knew, also had a special symbolism as the native region of the Taliban. In the new Afghanistan, it was a pariah. But I was sure that if Kandahar was left behind, the rest of Afghanistan would not be going anywhere.

Besides, I loved the place.

That spring of 2002, residents of the city dizzied by this latest revolution—their fourth in a quarter century—wore out a path to the house of the younger Karzai brother, Ahmad Wali. As the de facto representative of the new president in his home base, the de facto elder of the Popalzai tribe now that President Hamid was off in Kabul, and as a man known for getting things done, Ahmad Wali Karzai was one of the few fixed landmarks in sight.

Like most houses in Kandahar, his consists of two separate buildings, one for the family, one for receiving guests. The private residence is set back from the public one across a few feet of dry rose garden, where birds in wicker cages sing. Small bedrooms, a kitchen, and a Western-style living room for private talks or honored friends open onto a carpeted hallway with cushions on the floor, which serves as the general gathering place. Tea and glass dishes of raisins and pistachios, and meals laid out on a plastic cloth, are served here in shifts: first family and friends, then the platoon of young men who keep the place running. They are "Karzai's people," utterly devoted, utterly respectful, but reveling in a certain irreverent intimacy. Inside this sanctum the Karzai magic reigns, a kind of gracious calm, in the face of the hot, dusty whirlwind—human and meteorological—buffeting the house.

The front building is dedicated to the tribal elders and petitioners who fetch up at all hours, and must be welcomed and heard out without exception. Five separate receiving rooms are arrayed about its two floors. The indefatigable, beturbaned Lajwar guides each delegation to its appointed place, according to its rank, and whether—because of some feud or private confidence—it might be inopportune for its members to see or be seen by some other party present. Lajwar executes the steps of this complicated minuet with a surefootedness born of a detailed but unspoken familiarity with the private histories of all comers.

That spring of 2002 the building hardly emptied. You could tell with a glance if Ahmad Wali was home by the crowd of shoes waiting outside the door.

The tale of one group particularly moved him. The delegation, led by an elder with a running sore on one hand, explained that their village, Akokolacha, was in ruins. Abutting the perimeter of the Kandahar airport, it had been caught in that last withering barrage of U.S. bombing that delivered the deathblow to Al-Qaeda in Afghanistan. Of some thirty mudbrick houses, ten and the village mosque had been reduced to misshapen mounds of earth. Families had scattered to Pakistan or were doubled up with friends in nearby hamlets.

Ahmad Wali Karzai made the trip to Akokolacha, a half hour out the airport road, to survey the damage. He came back genuinely distressed, and mentioned the villagers' predicament to me.

There it was: a perfect project. Again I was reminded of Kosovo, where the rebuilding of houses the Serbs had trashed and burned in their final, furious bout of ethnic cleansing became the symbol of a new era. Within weeks of the Serbs' retreat, the defiant skeletons of dozens of new homes aimed their limbs at the sky, with, snapping from their roof beams, the black eagle of the long-banned Albanian flag splayed wide against a red ground.

I was surprised at the contrasting lack of attention in Afghanistan to "shelter," as it is termed in the aid biz, especially given the staggering number of refugees who had been camped out in neighboring countries not for days or weeks, but for years. Rebuilding the village of Akokolacha would be an important symbol, I thought, and even more so if American soldiers, in uniform, were to do the work.

I thought about the marine I had interviewed in his foxhole on Christ-

mas day. How eloquent a message, if Americans were to be seen repairing
what Americans had destroyed. What better way of demonstrating that
President George W. Bush's proclamation at the beginning of the bombing campaign was sincere: that the war was not against Afghans or
Afghanistan, but against the criminal regime that had taken power there.
Akokolacha's impoverished farmers, long-distance taxi drivers, or small-
time mechanics, who had fled the deafening violence of the U.S. bombing, could surely not be held accountable for Usama bin Laden. If they
could regain what they had lost in this latest Afghan regime change, maybe
they would understand that this one was different from the others, promising a better future for all Afghans, not just those whom chance had tossed
to the top of the pile.

That I had even conceived of such an idea, complete with U.S. soldiers
armed with picks and shovels, indicates how removed I was from contemporary humanitarian theory.

In the ongoing international debate about "humanitarian intervention," one of the arguments made by responsible aid organizations is that
troops participating in an armed intervention—even if the military action
is said to be motivated by humanitarian or human rights concerns—should
not be involved in postconflict relief and reconstruction. As parties to the
conflict, humanitarian theorists argue, soldiers have no business mixing
with civilian humanitarians in the field. The lines inevitably become
blurred, and the neutrality that is a credo of humanitarian action is cast into
doubt. Soldiers should keep to soldiers' work: maintaining the security
and freedom of access necessary for aid agencies to do their job, ministering to the people.

To me, I confess, these distinctions seemed a bit theoretical. I suppose
my thinking was stuck in the past, tangled up in the legend of the Marshall Plan in post–World War II Europe. Moreover, I could not efface yet
another memory from the Kosovo conflict. When, with explicit prior
warning, the Serbs deported tens of thousands of Kosovo Albanians to
Macedonia as the first NATO bombs fell, the United Nations refugee
agency was caught hopelessly by surprise. I stood in the NATO briefing
room in Brussels gaping up in horror at a television set on a wall bracket,
watching masses of wretched Kosovo Albanians corralled in the mud of a

no-man's land just inside the Macedonian border, at the mercy of the Macedonian army.

Thousands of NATO troops were billeted right nearby. If they boasted no other skill, they certainly knew how to pitch a camp. "Why aren't the soldiers building tents for those refugees?" I would practically shout to my fellow reporters, gathered in a knot below the TV. I later learned that it was the humanitarians' refusal of assistance marred by military uniforms that had kept the troops away for several agonizing days.

In this matter as in others, Afghans for Civil Society was iconoclastic. We went right to the U.S. soldiers for help. We argued that rebuilding Akokolacha would enhance their image, and thus their security, just as I had told that young marine.

We could have saved our breath. U.S. Army Civil Affairs, the branch of the army charged with interactions with local civilians, and in this case, with any relief activity the army sponsors, does not actually perform any reconstruction itself. It pays local contractors, then monitors the work. And in Afghanistan, U.S. Army Civil Affairs was not contracting out the reconstruction of private property.

As general policy, this made sense. Otherwise, there were bound to be inequities. The army might find itself obliged to drill a private well or build a house for every village chief as the price of permission to assist his people.

In our own view, Akokolacha hamlet seemed worthy of an exception, since its inhabitants had been rendered homeless as a direct result of U.S. action. And yet that fact seemed to make it even more taboo. Above all, a precedent must not be set, we were told. It must not appear that Washington was taking any legal responsibility for war damage, lest it be induced to pay compensation or reparations. We talked to USAID, the State Department's overseas development agency, which was spearheading the overall U.S. reconstruction effort in Afghanistan. We got the same answer. No precedents.

So we fell back on the goodness of ordinary American people. September 11 had unleashed such pent-up generosity and hunger to help, much of it frustrated; we hoped to tap into the receding tide.

In April, I returned to the United States from that quick Afghan trip for a period of intense, creative NGO conception side by side with my sister Eve. Some friends from the town of Concord, Massachusetts, Mary and David Clarke, had invited me to give a talk at the First Parish Church. In their farmhouse kitchen, familiar and comfortable to me as a pair of old jeans, Eve and I brought up the idea of rebuilding Akokolacha.

True to its central role in America's own founding mythology, Concord preserves the spirit of direct democracy and community involvement in public affairs that animated the Thirteen Colonies during the years surrounding the American Revolution. It is one of those places still governed by town meeting, a yearly gathering of all interested citizens to thrash out and vote on issues of municipal importance. In between, committees and forums marshal Concord residents' interest, energy, and money toward various worthy causes.

The Clarkes were enchanted by the Akokolacha idea, and went at it in their unparalleled way, mobilizing a whole network of Concord-and-beyond folks. A cabal of local activists (primarily women) dubbed themselves the Concord Friends of Afghans for Civil Society, and invited a select forty people to a fund-raising tea. The public middle schools joined in, holding a vote among the students on the slogan for T-shirts to send to kids in Akokolacha. "Concord and Akokolacha," they chose. "We are the Bridge to Peace." The declaration, traced in my laborious Pashtu, hung above an outline of the Concord Bridge where our own famous battle against the Redcoats was fought in 1775.

Struck by the similarities between the Pashtun tradition of the *shura,* or council of elders, and the selectmen who govern New England towns, the Concord Friends decided they wanted to send gifts and a letter from their selectmen to the Akokolacha elders. I called Ahmad Wali Karzai in Kandahar. He was thrilled and suggested sending radios. He said that when I came back we would go together to Akokolacha and convene a *shura* to explain the whole project and describe the special significance of Concord, and we would build a council room and name it the Concord Room.

I gave three talks in Concord in one day, the last one at the First Parish Church, which crowns the Puritan dignity of Concord's village square. As assorted Clarkes and Eve and I and a few other friends stood around the church basement wolfing turkey sandwiches, with Mr. Clarke enjoining me to "just relax," I realized this felt like nothing so much as the frenetic, exhausting energy of a political campaign.

Something like two hundred people showed up that night. It was an exercise totally unfamiliar to me. As wide a public as I might have reached during my reporting days, I never had to *watch* the people listening to me. I filed my stories from the privacy of my Paris apartment, often from under my winter parka, which I tented over my head to dampen the echo.

But I could feel the people with me. In a way, they knew me personally, since most of them listened to National Public Radio. Some had probably endured my company while they brushed their teeth in the morning. That night had the sparkle and intimacy of addressing a family reunion. For a grand finale, one lady asked me to do my NPR sign-off: "Sarah Chayes, NPR News, Paris." For some mysterious reason it captivated people more than my reporting ever had. Something to do with the final *s* being pronounced like a *z,* and the long *a* in the middle—the name rhymes with *haze.* I had never done this SOC-out, as it is called, for an audience, and it normally comes at the end of a story, not just hanging out there by itself. So to trick myself into it, I turned my back, solemnly read the last paragraph of one of our project proposals, and signed off, "Sarah Chayes, NPR News, Concord." To roars.

"It just about killed us," Eve told her daughter on the phone a few days later, "but we got the money."

And it went on like that. The people of Lincoln, Massachusetts, stepped up, in a neighborly competition with next-door Concord. Lincolnites turned out, another couple hundred of them, on a snowy Friday night at seven-thirty. I looked around the room, in wonder. *What are all these people doing here?* Like Concord's, Lincoln's commitment proved to be in persisting earnest. After a magic potion of a dinner Eve concocted one night, a brilliant, intuitive philanthropist named Greg Carr wondered if we could use an office in the middle of Harvard Square. He eventually funded the radio station we launched in Kandahar to the tune of $100,000.

We were stunned by the response we generated with our simple plea to do something concrete and direct and our promise that we would communicate our friends and donors about the fortunes of their project, in detail. We were not CARE or the American Red Cross, we promised.

Contributors would not be receiving glossy self-congratulatory pamphlets in the mail. They would hear exactly what became of their money, personally, in the flesh. Suicidally, we promised that every single penny would go to project activities. We would find our overhead elsewhere. It began to dawn on me that I was offering myself up to donors as a kind of human sacrifice. Was there enough flesh and blood in me to satisfy them? As we registered people's hunger for this approach, we grew almost frightened. What were we unleashing? What kind of sacred trust were we taking on by inspiring people this way? It got so that we almost avoided telling the latest new acquaintance what we were doing, lest the person offer to help.

And so we glimpsed the precious well of civil society lying frustrated and untapped just below the surface of apparent U.S. indifference.

CHAPTER 14

PLUNDER AND SUBSIDY

THE RULE FOR CASH IS $10,000. If you're taking more than $10,000 out of the United States, you have to declare it to customs. But having worked in various places lacking banks in my day, I was yet to be convinced of the value—for me—of that particular formality. So with $18,000 of Concord's money secreted in various private places about my person, I returned to Afghanistan in May, just in time for the first offensive of summer heat.

Nothing came easily. I moved back in with my Achekzai family in the graveyard, which felt familiar, though the promiscuity and lack of a toilet were hard to contemplate as part of a permanent arrangement. With the windfall they had reaped from me and the NPR reporter who had replaced me, they had bought a television set and a dented satellite dish that they had anchored precariously to their mud roof. Now, of an evening, my *maelmastun* was filled will male neighbors glued, agog, to raunchy Bollywood images. Our card games were over.

It did not take long for Zabit Akrem to catch wind of my presence back in the house. He sent over a flunky this time, bearing a letter on provincial government stationery. I was still not allowed to live with a private family. My oldest host-brother and I went to see the big police chief in his office.

The meeting developed into an argument between the two men, which I did not entirely follow. It seemed that Akrem was telling my host brother that if he insisted on having me in the house, he would be responsible for my security. In Afghanistan, that is a heavy obligation. My host-brother retorted that security is the job of the police, and if Akrem was putting the family in charge of me, he should issue them some weapons. Not that he didn't already have weapons, as he hastened to show me when we returned home. But it was a matter of principle, and both sides dug in. Akrem dismissed us by turning and looking fixedly at the next petitioner. We had ceased to exist.

I was determined to fight this ultimatum, though I could feel my host-family cooling off.

Then one day I crossed paths with my new boss, Qayum Karzai, when he and his brother Ahmad Wali were on their way to a funeral. They wondered what on earth I was doing in that insalubrious place. "She lives here," one of their men informed them. And that was the end of it.

"We're responsible for you," they remonstrated, aghast. "You can't possibly live out there." It was in fact they who were responsible for my security. By entering Qayum's employ, I had entered the Karzais' retinue, and overlordship in Kandahar bears certain responsibilities. For the Karzais' sake, I realized, for the sake of their reputation, I could not leave myself at such risk.

So I moved into a house on the other side of town with a big yard and three cows, which used to be Ahmad Wali's office back when he ran a local NGO. The chaotic months of U.S. bombing and its aftermath had scattered contents and occupants, leaving the place prey to friends and neighbors turned temporary looters. Abdullah, the Karzais' family engineer, lived there. But, as Ahmad Wali had often said, his habits were such as to render his own bedroom worthy of a UNDP-sponsored cleanup project. The place was a trash heap.

I spent the summer renovating, relegating myself to the roof in the process and spreading out my bedding and my nighttime effects each evening. We fixed the bathroom, laid tiles of local white stone in the hall, built, discarded, carpeted, and furnished. We hauled out all those books and papers of President Karzai's, which Abdullah had squirreled away, put the books on a shelf and sorted and filed the papers in a painted trunk. And then at last, we cleaned out a former storeroom to serve as my bedroom, and I could come down off my roof.

It felt as though I were—figuratively as well as literally—constructing the floor I was standing on, hopping on one foot while I laid down a few boards to put the other down on. Kandahar's telephone lines had been shot to hell, and the Internet was several centuries away. I had to go to a public call office or rely on the expensive fold-out satellite phone I had used as a reporter to stay in touch with Eve. She heroically held fast to the other end of the tenuous rope I clung to, grounding me, protecting me ferociously, and constantly reinspiring me.

For comic relief, there was Wooly and Big Dog.[1] Big Dog, a mournful German Shepherd, was manifestly suffering from post-traumatic stress disorder. When I first moved to the house, he would slink off with his tail tucked in and his head hung below his sloping shoulders if you ever penetrated his consciousness. I decided he needed some pet therapy. So I bought a lamb, named Wooly. I won't go through the complicated trilingual pun, via Albanian, which led me to *that* original name. The two became inseparable, Wooly first trying to nurse from Big Dog and later trying to mount him. Harried Big Dog cheered up.

An early trip to our project site, the bombed out village of Akokolacha, was obligatory. It lies just off the main road to the airport, about the only stretch of asphalt in the province at the time, and cars still had to swerve to avoid old shrapnel scars and the twisted carcass of a tanker-truck. All around lies the stark, dun-colored wasteland of rock and clay, hardened by the punishing sun. Only a fleet of nappy-haired camels, nomads' patchwork tents, some sheep spread out in a row to comb the stubble of a parched field, break the monotony. Scattered villages, camouflaged against the dirt they are built from, appear and disappear into its unremitting surface. At Akokolacha, the clods of the former huts were already blending back into the stony-hard earth.

My idea was to rebuild the houses just as they had stood before the bombing, never imagining there would be any trouble recreating the layout. A half hour clambering over the piles of clay shattered that happy presumption. The village men knotted themselves around us, famished half smiles playing on their faces. One so exactly resembled the Big Bad Wolf that the nickname stuck.

"I had nine rooms," the owner of one mound told us as we climbed atop, eyeballing it at about eight yards by four. "And there was a bathroom with every room."

Incredulous, I turned to the other villagers for a backup chorus of ridicule.

"It's true," they nodded gravely. "And I had seven rooms," someone else said.

I realized we would never know what the village had looked like. We were facing a conspiracy of exaggeration. No villager would expose another's lie for fear of losing his own chance at an American-financed mansion.

I was crushed, and immediately faced with a moral dilemma. What to tell Concord? If I described the scene accurately, all those wonderful people would regret their contributions and good wishes, I was sure. But could I possibly lie, or gloss it over: tread on the slippery slope that led to such cynicisms as—in one example I had heard of—an aid agency photographing gifts unloaded in Somalia, for the donors' benefit, then carting them off to the beach for burning?

I grappled for an explanation for the villagers' bald, ungrateful, unapologetic greediness. My own heart needed it as much as the Concord donors did.

What I came up with had to do with Big Dog's ailment: posttraumatic stress disorder. After twenty-three years of nonstop civil war, the whole of Afghan society was suffering from collective PTSD, I was coming to understand. I cataloged its symptoms: inability to bond emotionally, inability to plan for the future, inability to think beyond one's own needs toward a collective good, excessive guile.[2] People like the Akokolacha villagers had so often seen their destinies—appalling or miraculous—visited upon them from the outside, with no apparent reason or consistency, who could blame them for grasping at whatever they could obtain right now, and damn the future? What ever lasted into the future anyway? And then there was the matter of power. It is not especially empowering to be helped. And so, perhaps to try to redress the imbalance, proud beneficiaries make strident demands.

It seemed the very conception behind our Akokolacha project was out of sync with the Afghanistan of this particular juncture. Never mind, I thought. At least we'll get the houses built.

All of these deductions were valid. But what I did not thoroughly understand at that point was how my actions and those of ACS fit into the age-old Afghan pattern of extracting and distributing subsidy. This pattern went back at least to the days of the Great Game and the early Afghan amirs like Abd ar-Rahman Khan.

Back then Britain was the wealthy empire paying out the subsidy. But when Indian independence ended the Great Game, London turned off the faucet. A few years later, during the Cold War, the United States took up Britain's contest with Russia—by then the Soviet Union. Then, its cold war over, Washington, too, cut the Afghan subsidy. Now, in the post-Taliban era, the United States was paying out again.

In other words, the Afghan tribes have grown accustomed to receiving subsidy. It is a mark of their geostrategic importance. As such, it is not an embarrassing handout, but a badge of honor, a perfectly dignified way of making a living. Obtaining subsidy can even be seen as a mark of superiority vis-à-vis the lowland empire that has to cough it up.[3] The leader who distributes it commands his tribesmen's loyalty.

In this traditional dynamic, I was playing the role of the representative of the foreign power, coughing up the subsidy. All of our lofty words to the Akokolacha *shura* about Concord, and democracy, and citizen participation, and cultural exchange were, in this context, meaningless. What we were doing fit too closely with the familiar pattern for the villagers to see anything distinctive in it.

In the perception of these Popalzai villagers, Ahmad Wali Karzai was the tribal elder who had secured the subsidy and distributed it to them. He had visited them, eaten their food, and then produced a foreigner to rebuild their village. They took it for granted that I was bound by his pledges. Ahmad Wali had told them the village would get a council room, a promise construed by the village chief to mean a *maelmastun* attached to his house. To this head elder, it was an obligation. Never mind that the project was about replacing bomb-damaged houses only. My protestations that Ahmad Wali had no operational involvement in the project were simply unintelligible to the villagers. This was a misunderstanding that was to dog the work for its duration.

While we were deliberating over dimensions and floor plans for the new houses, another problem cropped up. Akokolacha's water supply went dry. The hamlet is built on the banks of a canal, part of a 1970s irrigation system that diverts water from the Arghandab River. A drought, so severe it had killed off most of the fruit trees not already splintered by Soviet shelling, had the region in its grip for the sixth straight year. The gates to the reservoir on the Arghandab River that fed the canal were closed. Akokolacha residents had to go to a neighboring village to collect water in plastic jerricans and lug it home.

A village well, we thought, is not private property. Here was something the American troops could do.

The U.S. Army Civil Affairs team, led by a tall redheaded hydrologist named Ben Houston, was refreshingly enterprising and practical. In those early days, when we humanitarians were still getting our feet under us, the Civil Affairs team was out there doing stuff: overseeing the building of schools and, yes, the drilling of wells.

But not one for Akokolacha, they regretted. They had had some bad experiences with villagers sabotaging expensive new wells, so they had called a temporary moratorium. Why didn't we try USAID?

The United States Agency for International Development is the arm of the U.S. State Department charged with distributing America's public foreign assistance around the world. As such, it was supposed to spearhead the effort to reconstruct Afghanistan. Behemoth USAID wields a budget of some $10 billion per year, and is staffed by two thousand men and women, half of them posted in the field, and fully half housed in the Reagan Building, a giant airless glass cube in Washington.

We had had interactions with a variety of USAID officials in Washington, at the newly reopened U.S. embassy in Kabul, and with an assessment team that had come to Kandahar for a week. I brought two of its members over to my house in the graveyard for dinner with my Achekzais. I introduced them to a group of prominent local women to discuss priorities. Our USAID contacts were friendly and enthusiastic, full of encouragement and promises: "Don't worry. I'm setting aside $70,000 for your radio station, whenever you're ready"; "A vocational school is a great idea—I'm sure we'll fund it"; and so on. The Akokolacha well request, backed as it was by support from private U.S. donors who had promised an ongoing commitment to the village, reaped a similar response. I wrote up a formal proposal for a $10,000 drinking water and irrigation well, complete with submersible pump. "A shoo-in," we were assured.

So we waited. And waited. I was reluctant to pester the USAID people, knowing how harassed they must be. When I finally did inquire about the status of our proposal, or of any of the other proposals we had submitted, I found that the person we had been working with was back in Washington; his or her replacement had just arrived and would be on it right away. Often his or her replacement would be unable to locate the file and would ask us to drop off another copy of our proposal at the U.S. embassy up in Kabul.

Such was the merry-go-round at USAID—and the U.S. embassy as a whole—those crucial first months after the fall of the Taliban. In the entire U.S. delegation, only one diplomat spoke an Afghan language, learned when he was a Peace Corps volunteer in Iran thirty years before. Called up out of retirement, he stayed at the embassy a record six weeks. Everyone else was on a two- to three-week "hardship" rotation.

The significance of such a rapid changeover was that the United States had, in effect, no policy in Afghanistan. During that crucial window of time that could make or break the future of the country, America's sails were luffing. There was no strategy for targeting reconstruction dollars so as to produce the greatest positive domino effect. Worse, there was not even a clear notion of what the desired "end state" in Afghanistan was. The embassy lacked seasoned political officers with regional experience or a coherent vision. And no guidance was coming from Washington. It was as though it had never occurred to anyone to think about what would happen once the Taliban were defeated. As a result, U.S. action was slipshod and haphazard, just when Afghanistan needed legibility, direction, and consistency.

In this void, decisions that most affected ordinary Afghans were made by U.S. infantry or Special Forces units conducting mop-up combat operations around the countryside. It was the military who decided not only which villages would be searched or which suspects captured or killed but, more significant, which local strongmen—like Gul Agha Shirzai— would reap the extraordinary benefits of an alliance with U.S. forces. These decisions were made in the heat of battle, based on the immediate usefulness in tactical military terms of the gun-lord in question. The longer-term impact of empowering him did not enter the calculus of the combat officer making the choice; politics wasn't his job.

And in the void—in the absence of a policy to guide the allocation of reconstruction funds—the big public donors like USAID resorted to an acronym: the QUIP, or quick impact project. QUIPs were school buildings or clinics, culverts by the side of a road, village wells. The notion was that it was important to get money out on the ground, quickly and visibly. To be funded, a project had to be a physical object and cost less than $30,000. Those were the operative criteria, across the board. The idea seemed to me to be to spread the money around, like whitewash slapped on a broken fence.

I believe that this was the big donors' way of hedging their bets on post-Taliban Afghanistan. Fear of failure, ironically, meant that money was not concentrated in ways that might have helped avert it. The alternative—a major project that could make a real difference, both symbolically and practically—snaked its way past Kandahar as it had for millennia. The road.

I had thought the route from Quetta, Pakistan, across the Afghan border and into Kandahar was the worst experience on four wheels I would ever inflict on myself. That was until I drove to Kabul. On my maiden voyage there, the Toyota station wagon I was riding in with my Achekzai host-brothers simply went to pieces. First we got a flat tire. Then the muffler fell off. Though I was accompanied by two auto mechanics, I ended up wedged under the car tying the thing back on with scavenged bits of wire and a strip of tire rubber. Finally, we suffered a compound fracture of the left front wheel. That forced us to overnight in one of the derelict roadside "hotels" that cater to the truck traffic. The ceiling of our mud-brick room was about six feet off the dirt floor, held up by a massive wooden pillar of unknown age. The furnishings consisted of a metal barrel with a cockeyed pipe for a wood stove and a plastic mat.

I came to know that four-hundred-mile, fifteen-hour nightmare quite well. My favorite part was where the deeply grooved dirt track resolved itself into a series of sine waves. If you got your timing right, gunning your motor just as you reached the crest of each rise, you could turn it into a rhythmic roller-coaster ride. I confess a certain joy, too, in the frequent games of chicken with oncoming trucks, tilting rakishly under their loads. A tacit rule prevailed, of course, encouraging drivers to stay to their right. But each encounter was in fact governed by the conditions of the road at that juncture, by which vehicle was bigger (size usually determining who got to choose the path he wanted), by which driver hit his brights first, claiming right of way, by which would dare to ignore the claim and face the other down, and, finally, by an ineffable intuition that instructed you where to go to avoid collision. Much of the time, in fact, was spent *off* the so-called road, driving on the smoother desert floor on either side. No matter how tightly windows and air vents were sealed, the pervasive talcum-powder dust was staple sustenance the whole way, its dried-clay smell sharp in your nostrils, its grit between your teeth. The wind would raise it in boiling pillars, spinning and writhing toward the sky, like Lot's wife after her fatal glance at Gomorra. Sometimes, engulfed, cars would have to halt, visibility zero. When the ocher cloud had passed them by, they could start up again.

It invariably took me two days to recover from the drive to Kabul. For me, it was a bruising inconvenience. For Kandahar merchants, it was crippling.

I attended a meeting on the topic between tribal elders and a U.S. embassy official more than a year after the fall of the Taliban. "We sell grapes," the graybeards opened. By late July, the crates start appearing beside the walled lanes in Arghandab, and bales of straw for lining them. The clusters of tiny oblong grapes, a translucent greenish gold and indescribably fragrant, are bedded in the straw like jewels.

"Before," the elders patiently explained to the U.S. official, "the run to Kabul took six hours. Our trucks could make a delivery to Kandahar shops in the evening, then leave for Kabul and get there before the bazaar opened at 4:00 A.M. Kabul was our main market, and we couldn't fill demand. Now cargo trucks spend seventy-two hours on the road. Who can send grapes? Our only outlet now is Pakistan, and we have to beg for buyers there."

No program would have had a more positive impact on the Afghan south, and indeed on the country as a whole, than rebuilding that road. Back in the sixteenth century, the Safavi shahs in Persia understood the critical importance of road maintenance to their nation-building project. Safe, well-kept roads, equipped with amenities for travelers, bound their disparate empire together, enhanced its wealth by stimulating trade, and served as a constant, visible demonstration of the government's power and ability to care for its people. The fortunes of the Safavi dynasty were gauged by conditions on the road through Kandahar.

But five centuries later, that lesson was lost on the international proponents of nation building in Afghanistan. Once I asked a USAID official what was holding up the project. She said, "If we financed that road, it would use up all our money. We could hardly be doing any other work in Afghanistan."

It would have been a better investment, I believe. That road was worth a thousand QUIPs.

If it had been tackled in a timely fashion, the road would have energized the new Afghanistan. It would have helped ignite the economy of a whole region, as canny entrepreneurs like those tribal elders with their grapes spontaneously renewed their activity, reviving old patterns of trade and inventing new ones. It would have tapped into the immediate post-Taliban enthusiasm for the new order, vivid but fragile, and converted its potential before it soured into disappointment. A fast road would have eased the isolation of the Afghan south—an isolation bound up with reactionary Taliban ideology. Encouraging travel and communication among estranged provinces, the road would have helped cauterize the wounds left by two decades of war and mutual grudges. It would have enhanced security by increasing traffic and speed of access. It could have served as part of a program to disarm the gunmen who had reinfested Afghanistan. Platoons of young men, organized into a kind of Afghan Civilian Conservation Corps, could have taken pride in their new role reconstructing their homeland. Such an undertaking would have redounded to the credit of the fledgling Afghan government. And it would have redounded to the credit of the United States. Only a project of this magnitude, in Afghan eyes, was worthy of such a superpower. Village schools, while needed, seemed beneath American dignity.

Work on the road finally did begin in the summer of 2003, a year and a half after the Taliban demise. Though welcome, it was very late. By then, enthusiasm for the new regime had died down; the people were disillusioned by yet another exercise in rhetoric. Resurgent Taliban had already regrouped. They turned the long, lonely construction site into a duck shoot, killing and kidnapping workers. Rather than serving as a means of demilitarizing gunmen, the construction work necessitated the arming of new ones. A private security firm, staffed by Afghan fighters, was set up to patrol the road.

I was at a loss to understand what it was that had kept this manifestly vital project in abeyance for so long.

Years later, a State Department official suggested an explanation. "Craig Buck," he emphatically replied to my still-unanswered question. Dour Buck was head of USAID Afghanistan in 2002 and 2003. "Craig said, 'We don't do roads, the World Bank does roads,' "recalled the State Department official. This sounded just like Buck, as I had experienced him at a meeting that verged on the insulting at the U.S. embassy.

According to normal decision-making procedures, the main lines of U.S. policy in a context like postwar Afghanistan should be defined on a political level, at the State Department, for example. Subordinate agencies like USAID would be expected to carry out their activities in support and furtherance of the policy goals set above their level. But in the case of the road, according to this State Department official and others I asked, the policy vacuum allowed the local USAID representative to make the effective policy decision himself—with dramatic consequences. It took the direct intervention of President George W. Bush, a year on, to reverse it.

There was another reason, as we discovered later, why the great machine that was supposed to deploy on all fronts churning out reconstruction for Afghanistan failed to gear up. The war in Iraq.

Many people asked me what impact the opening of hostilities in the spring of 2003 had on the reconstruction effort in Afghanistan. Was there a visible difference? Did the money gushing into Afghanistan suddenly dry up? The truth, as usual, proved to be unsimple. In terms of manpower, the Iraq effect was dramatic. Overnight, in early 2003, every one of our interlocutors at USAID was abruptly reassigned to Iraq. And yet that phenomenon does not fully explain the conditions we encountered. Off the cuff, my answer to the questions was different, challenging the assumption that underlay them: "What gush of money?" I wondered aloud, bemused. We never saw it on the ground in Afghanistan. It simply never materialized. Throughout that summer of 2002, we kept wondering what all the big players were waiting for. We would come up with different postulates. Later, information from officials on the ground as well as reporting in the United States indicated that resources were sucked away from Afghanistan before they even made it there. "As early as February 2002," the same

State Department official recalled to me, "assets were being pulled off of Afghanistan in preparation for the war in Iraq."[4]

Eventually, USAID did get back to us about our well. The project we were proposing seemed to fit all the QUIP criteria. And given Akokolacha's specific plight, we believed, it would send a strong signal as to U.S. intentions in Afghanistan; it enjoyed unique backing from a local community in the United States. It was exactly the kind of hearts-and-minds project that USAID should fall all over itself to support. We were sure of it.

The answer was no. The big public donors had jointly decided not to finance any more wells. An overall water strategy was needed first for drought-stricken Afghanistan.

That smacked of planning, and we approved, in theory. We had seen how wells drilled at random—without reference to the water table, local water-use patterns, or the needs of neighbors—could upset the economies of entire villages. The future of the Afghan south would clearly depend on how it allocated its water.

There were just two difficulties with USAID's argument. One was that the urgently needed strategy was not on anyone's drawing board. We had just approached the same Craig Buck at USAID with a plan to conduct a thorough interdisciplinary study of the Kandahar-area aquifer. We offered to develop a detailed map of the region's water inputs and outputs, geological projections as to where untapped resources might lie, and recommendations on how to enhance existing sources of water, as well as draft regulations governing water prospecting and use, and materials for a public information campaign on water conservation. "I'm not funding any studies," Buck had snapped at us. "I want to feed hungry children." Where was the water strategy USAID was waiting for to come from?

The second difficulty with the major donors' well moratorium was that it was undifferentiated. No one thought about examining the specific circumstances of different villages and giving exemptions to those that might fail without water and expel their residents into the tide of returning refugees and other displaced people already surging into Afghanistan's towns.

At a get-together with resourceful U.S. Army hydrologist Ben Houston and his Civil Affairs team, we poured out our woes. Houston repeated the stories of their experience with irrigation wells: generators breaking down, rich families who paid for the fuel monopolizing the water, children throwing stones down them for laughs and breaking the submersible pumps. He suggested we drill a hand-pump well. It wouldn't water crops, but it would keep people alive. He thought it would cost about a thousand dollars.

A thousand dollars, we thought; that's cheap. We could get a thousand out of our Concord money. We wouldn't have to ask for outside help.

We drove to Akokolacha to look for a site. Several village men generously volunteered their own land. Avoiding that trap, we chose a place near the dry canal where villagers were used to going to collect water anyway. In an impromptu ceremony, one of the elders balanced a forked stick in his hands as a divining rod and, following its indications, pointed out the spot for digging.

We hired a two-man crew, equipped not with a drill—no such thing was available in Kandahar—but a great length of steel pipe five inches across, some cables, and a rusty generator-powered engine. The men erected a tall metal tripod and suspended the pipe vertically from its center, like a pendulum. Then, with the aid of the engine and a simple gear contraption, they would hoist that pipe up and let it drop down with a re-sounding clang, like a pile driver. Thus was the well "drilled," or rather, punched into the earth. When water was struck, it manifested as rich mud oozing up around the pipe as it was heaved out of the ground.

We would go out almost every day to inspect the work, and encourage and cajole the two-man team tending the machine under the blazing sun. The job was almost complete when we noticed a pair of awfully familiar-looking tripods in the central part of the hamlet, right outside the chief elder's house, and hardly a hundred yards apart. *What on earth?* We ambled over to the driver of a white car marked with a local contractor's logo, and wondered who was financing these other two wells.

"The Americans," said the driver, Kandahar's term for the U.S. troops.

Surely not. Hadn't Ben Houston explained to us that Civil Affairs wasn't paying for wells? Wasn't he the one who told us to drill our own? Didn't he know that we had diverted some of our precious building funds for the purpose?

On our next visit to the U.S. base to see the Civil Affairs team, we put it to them: "Why did you guys finance two wells in Akokolacha when you

told us you couldn't do wells?" The CA officers swore they weren't working in Akokolacha. We shrugged, bemused.

It took Ben Houston's return from leave some weeks later to clear up
the mystery. The well moratorium had been lifted. The village where the
two wells were dug was indeed Akokolacha. But it had been identified to
the CA team by a different name, to induce confusion. With a skill honed
over centuries, our villagers had successfully played the foreigners for an
increase in their subsidy.

Never mind. Akokolacha hamlet now has three wells.

CHAPTER 15

SHOWDOWN WITH SHIRZAI

OCTOBER 2002

I took a running leap up the mound of one of Akokolacha's former houses, with a clap of my hands. Scrabbling for balance, I dug an undamaged mud brick out of the dirt. *"Kushnian-o!"* I called to the children. *"Rassi!* Come here!" A little boy with a smile that hovered between timid and entranced trotted up to the base of the mound and stretched out his arms. *"Rmm . . . Rmm . . . ,"* I mimicked a bulldozer. I loaded up the little boy with two mud bricks and sent him off.

Work had at last begun at our building site, and we were sorting, for nothing is wasted in Afghanistan. We were going through the debris, piling up usable mud bricks and leaving the hopelessly broken ones impacted in the mounds of clay that would later be removed. The children quickly got into the game. Even Hajji Baba, the crotchety old man the village chose to receive the first house, would urge me to pile yet another brick onto his spindly limbs. Though the kids, unused to this sort of attention, got a frenetic, shrieking kick out of it, and though the pace of work definitely picked up when we arrived, the village men kept their distance, squatting on the broken walls, smirking.

Progress was steady. Soon the new houses were laid out with string and wooden pegs; then lines were scratched into the ground and foundation trenches dug. Then one day the Karzais' family engineer Abdullah, now my de facto deputy, came into my office: "There's a problem with the stone for Akokolacha."[1]

Abdullah was a case. He was one of the pieces of broken wreckage thrown on shore by Afghanistan's twenty-five-year storm. His excessive generosity and attentiveness were beguiling. He was protective, funny, and indispensable. But his heart was corroded by anger and contempt for his fellow Afghans. "An atom bomb," he swore, was the only solution for Kandahar. And for the Hazaras, a minority ethnic group. And for residents of Wardak or Farah provinces. "If I were in charge," I later found out he had told the residents of Akokolacha, "you would *never* get new houses."

With unerring precision, Abdullah embodied exactly those caricature Kandahari traits he held up to me as objects of revulsion. He stole from Afghans for Civil Society, inflating receipts or skimming bills out of petty cash. But daily—hourly, often—he accused some local contractor or shopkeeper of theft. He tyrannized the staff, calling them names, withholding their money, and firing them if they dared speak up. But with the powerful, he hung his head and followed orders on the bound. This, he told me many times, was what was wrong with Kandaharis: they cowered at force and terrorized the weak. He ventured confessions about his sex with adolescent boys—"a lot," he beamed once, shyly, "five or six times a day"—while loudly condemning Kandahar society for enshrining this ancient habit. His was an elaborate double life, his deeds an almost perfect negative image of his words.

To my discredit, it took me fully two years to figure all this out. My judgment impaired by isolation, by my aching need for someone to talk to—someone to trust—I made excuses for his behavior, and I empowered him. Precisely the same way, I realized later with a gasp, that the U.S. military persisted in empowering the warlords.

This delayed epiphany gave me some insight, anyway, into the Americans' weakness for local allies who provided them with whatever they needed—trucks, gravel, "intelligence"—and who convinced them that everyone else was a lethal and cunning foe.

It was one September day, well before these things came clear, that Abdullah announced: "There's a problem with the stone for Akokolacha."

"What problem?"

"Gul Agha's soldiers stopped our tractors. They need the stone for themselves."

I ceased what I was doing: "What do you mean, they need the stone for themselves?"

Abdullah shrugged.

In this measure does relief work in Afghanistan resemble reporting: no truth is discernible at a distance; no one's word conveys the circumstances with meaningful accuracy.

"*Zu*," I said, pushing back my chair. "Let's go."

We swung aboard the ponderous black Toyota Land Cruiser that Ahmad Wali Karzai had donated to Afghans for Civil Society—a piece of Taliban booty, like Mullah Omar's cow, black and lyre horned, who lived behind the house. We left our compound and entered the fray that is Kandahar traffic.

Impatient white station wagons push past former Taliban pickup trucks; two-wheeled taxi wagons drawn by tasseled horses stop for passengers; minivans with children clinging to the roof racks among the bales and bundles, overloaded donkey barrows, similar barrows bearing similar burdens heaved along by men instead of donkeys, wheeled fruit stands, wheeled popcorn and ice-cream stands, bicycles bearing turbaned elders—all of these jostle for room on the lumpy roads. And like shiny dung-beetles, the brightly painted three-wheeled rickshaws tootle over, around, under, and through all the various obstacles. There is something joyous about this riot, and given Kandahar's small size, something inevitably sociable. Lights are flicked in greeting to friends in oncoming cars; hands are raised and conversations pursued regardless of honking tie-ups on either side; and, in my case, frequent traffic jams are caused by friendly cops at intersections loping over to shake my hand. I must be the first female they have ever seen behind a wheel.

Past the double gates that mark the edge of the city, where the jingling transport trucks line up to pay their tolls, it abruptly thins out. The confusion of the town is replaced by a silent, brown expanse.

Only one line of hills troubles the becalmed topography along the road that leads out to Akokolacha, and the airport and Pakistan beyond. The rock teeth of these hills, jutting up from gums of scree, close in on the road from the right, lifting it over a small saddle, then ebb away to its left. These are the hills that feed the stone quarry.

We turned up a sandy track to a rough cavity and called to the quarryman's son. In the amphitheater created by the gouging out of the stone from the hills, the workers gathered around us. "A totally bad person," their spokesman told us, had come the previous day with a Kalashnikov-toting tough, twisted a fistful of collar up under the young man's chin—he mimed the gesture—and warned that no one, but no one, was to take stone from the quarry.

The "bad person" in question was Razziq Shirzai, the brother of Kandahar governor Gul Agha.

Tires ground gravel as I wheeled the truck around to go see the quarryman, seated in a straw-thatched lean-to at the gas station he owns by the road. He is a smiling, portly man who leans back slightly, as though to accommodate the thick beard fanned out upon his chest.

The Shirzais were opening their own gravel and cement plant right next to his operation. They had imported Punjabi labor from Pakistan. Workers who did not even speak the local language were building the installation. In the meantime, the Shirzais had arrogated the quarryman's contract with the U.S. military base for the tons of gravel and stone it required. When they were not able to keep up with demand, they would buy gravel from this man at market rates, about $8 a tractor load, and then resell to the Americans for more than $100.

Now the Shirzais were forbidding him to sell any uncrushed stone at all. Nor could anyone else drive a tractor up to the exposed bone of a hill and break off rocks for personal use. At a time when reconstruction was Afghanistan's top priority, it was illegal, by government fiat, to obtain the raw material to lay the foundations. The symbolism of it almost felled me.

The quarryman's twangy voice startled me out of my swirl of righteous anger. "In Islam," he was saying, "the mountains belong to everyone. No one can call them his private property. But they showed me papers they brought from the ministry in Kabul."

It was the old practice of looting turned inward, I mused: Governor Shirzai, unable in this day and age to sally forth to India in search of plunder, was plundering the resources of his own province and constituents.

The only way around the ban, the quarryman was telling us, was to bring a written order from the governor himself.

"*Zu,*" I said to Abdullah. "Let's go see the governor."

The ancient governor's palace, the one built by Ahmad Shah Durrani, was being renovated according to Shirzai's taste. His temporary residence was in New Town, a quarter mile outside the invisible gates to the old bazaar. It is set behind high concrete walls in the middle of a park.

The governor was having his afternoon nap when we arrived.

We returned the next day. Given my mascot status with Shirzai's nappy fighters, who remembered me from the days of the capture of Kandahar, we were greeted jovially and offered plastic chairs under the crushing sun. But we had to keep the entrance clear: absolutely no one could see the governor till the next day.

"Just ask," I cajoled, and someone disappeared inside the walls.

We used the wait to drink in the scene: open-backed trucks sporting bunches of rocket launchers in the latest fashion, ranks of soldiers shoving back the flock of petitioners. Despite the mistreatment, that midday crowd never drifted far, swinging as if at anchor and incessantly attracting the wrath of the soldiers. Curses and the butts of Kalashnikovs would keep the people back.

Such soldiers and their ostentatious guns are the unspoken threat that cows Afghans. More than any turban or title, these are the operative marks of power still. And in Afghanistan, the exercise of power remains personal. There are no institutions; there are only powerful men. This is why the aggrieved or the needy—the women in filthy *burqas,* the befuddled graybeards, the touchy young men—suffered the abuse outside the governor's residence that day. There is no alternative. There is no institution they can turn to for redress. Village and tribal structures have been neglected or overpowered, and the central government has not stepped in to fill the gap. The people are bound, like subjects rather than citizens, to the person and the caprice of the governor.

Eventually we privileged "guests"—read Americans—were let inside. We stopped at the office of the chief of staff, who had his own press of petitioners. One sinewy old man, trying to lean into his line of sight, was positively begging—kissing his fingertips and touching them to his own eyes in entreaty—saying he had come three days in a row, please give him his opium back. The official snapped, without a glance up from the sheaf of paper he was busying himself with, that opium is illegal.

"Why is it illegal for me and not for Hajji Abdullah?"

Hajji Abdullah was a wealthy businessman reputed at the time to be the biggest opium dealer in the province. He also owned a large money-changing/money-transfer business, and was buying up property in fantastically expensive Kandahar, building houses and selling them.

Hajji Abdullah was at that very moment in a meeting with Governor Shirzai, and would shortly be having lunch with him. Plates and trays of food—rice pilaf adorned with raisins and strips of candied carrots, tomato and okra stew, scallions laid in a row with sliced tomatoes and cucumbers and sprigs of fresh mint and cilantro—began arriving in the air-conditioned private quarters where we were ushered to await Shirzai. Servants silently arrayed them on a table, garishly ornate in a country where most people eat sitting cross-legged on the floor.

We declined an invitation to join the party and waited through lunch outside in the park. It was a cool oasis of green in dust-swept Kandahar. Rows of squat eucalyptus trees shaded the grass. To accent the medieval pageantry of the scene, a small antelope with horns that arched back from its brow in a graceful curve ambled near. Then a soldier struggled up with another in his arms, a young female. The governor of Urozgan Province had brought the pair down as a gift from his mountains to the north.

Sitting there, watching the antelopes explore the park, I felt as though I were merging into a timeless cultural continuum. It was as though I had just stepped into a manuscript commissioned by the Safavi shahs of Persia.

At length, Shirzai's luncheon guests emerged, led by Hajji Abdullah. He walked at a sedate pace and frowned at our stares. Shirzai welcomed us. He had exchanged his local clothes and turban for Western garb, his thick black locks sticking out from a white bandage wrapped around his head. He had been grazed by a bullet in a recent heart-stopping attempt on President Karzai's life. Karzai, in town for his brother Ahmad Wali's wedding, had been riding with Shirzai in a motorcade when one of the governor's private bodyguards had taken a shot at them. Investigation into the incident had broken down under mysterious circumstances, leaving us all aghast.

After a gush of friendly greetings, I brought up the question of the stone. I launched into an elaborate brief. "At the end of the war, the only thing the people of Kandahar cared about was reconstruction of bomb damage. Remember? Akokolacha is the perfect project to signal the dawn of a new era."

Shirzai nodded at me kindly, his answer ready:

"We are making a cement factory," he said. "You cannot have any stone." He smiled broadly. "Let me give you some advice. Make your foundations from brick, with cement for mortar. It's much cheaper."

"But I promised the villagers I would rebuild their houses exactly as they stood before," I improvised. "And they had stone foundations. I need stone."

Still the governor refused. Eventually I did wrest a promise from him to send a delegation from his office out with us the next day to find another source of stone. We set the meeting for 8:00 A.M.

Rising to leave—and having learned a little bit about how it's done by then—I piled on a further dollop of public bonhomie.

"Mr. Governor, it goes without saying how relieved I am that nothing serious happened to you last week . . ."

Flattered, Shirzai offered me a look at his scar. So suddenly I found myself digging around in Governor Gul Agha Shirzai's hair and exclaiming at the white line traced across his scalp.

The next morning the soldiers at the governor's gate were less jovial. Again they refused to admit us. I insisted that we had seen the governor yesterday—

"That was yesterday," one of them snapped.

—and that we had an appointment this morning, and they were making us late.

It took us fully half an hour to bully our way inside. The chief of staff who had been present at our meeting was sitting behind his formica desk, and he showed no sign of remembering our 8:00 A.M. appointment. He feigned to ignore me, turning his attention to a staff member or the telephone, then standing up and folding a briefcase shut in preparation for leaving.

I did it with a smile, making a joke of it. But, as he rounded his desk to exit the room, I actually stood in front of him, barring his route to the door. "I'm not letting you go till we settle this issue of the stone," I said. Again the official tried to look the other way, or say something important to someone else. But there was nothing for it. Short of a physical confrontation, there was no way out of the room. Sizing the situation up, he gave in and led us down the hall to another official, the chief administrative officer.

The door to this man's office, too, was choked with petitioners, Showing rather more courtesy than we had encountered so far, he picked up the phone and called the provincial director of Mines and Industry. After a brief conversation, the administrator penned a note, which we pocketed, then set off to visit Mines and Industry.

That directorate was located across town, up a narrow flight of stairs in the arcade of buildings that line the main road near Mahmad Anwar's headquarters, affording dignity to the approach into town. We climbed the steps to a small dark room and sat down on some chairs against the wall, across from half a dozen graybeards. I made our case yet again. Leaning forward. Pleading. We are trying to rebuild a village. Winter is coming and the people need their houses. Can you please tell us where we can get some stone? The director of Mines and Industry, dressed in the uniform of the new Afghanistan—Western clothes, his white beard neatly trimmed—told us he would have to see the site before making a decision.

"*Zu*," I said. "Let's go."

Astonishingly, he agreed. I led the little troop back down the narrow stairs. We climbed into our trucks and headed out the main road toward Akokolacha. Just short of the line of hills that breaks the road, we could see three or four tractors crawling across the desert to our right, small in the distance, but clearly hauling loads of stone. Mines and Industry signaled for us to stop.

"They are breaking the law," he said as we alighted. He flagged a tractor down when it drew near.

"Where is this stone from?"

The driver jutted his chin at the hills.

"How did you get it?"

Silence.

"Soldiers weren't on the road?"

"They wanted money."

Mines and Industry admonished the man not to bribe the soldiers anymore, then turned to me. "If we let one person take stone, soon everyone will. The law is the law. We need this stone for our stone crusher."

Our stone crusher?

The line of hills swept back for several miles. I flung my arm out. "All of this?" I asked, playing it up. "You need all of this stone for your stone crusher?"

The official shrugged and climbed back into his car.

Not above a little deception by this point, I had told him that we had in fact obtained Governor Shirzai's approval to get stone from our friend the quarryman. It was a lie, but I was learning. At the gas station lean-to, the official duly instructed the quarryman to give us the stone.

"But he's not the problem," I interrupted. "He *wants* to sell us stone. It's Razziq Shirzai and the workers at the quarry." So we drove back up the sandy track, official in tow, and distributed our ACS business card. "If a tractor driver shows you this card," the official instructed, "you can give him stone."

Razziq Shirzai did not give up entirely without a fight. "I don't know any director of Mines and Industry," he stormed when he caught our tractor loading up the next day. "I know Gul Agha Shirzai. If they don't have an order with the governor's signature on it, they can't have any stone."

But it was bluster. He backed down; we got our stone. And Hajji Baba, the infuriatingly hilariously crotchety old geezer at Akokolacha, who had complained about our work every step of the way, got his house. He even liked it. Before the arrival of the first rains in six years, all of the bombed houses at Akokolacha and the village mosque had been replaced. So the story wound its tortuous way to a happy ending.

On our side, that is.

The quarryman landed in jail for a couple of weeks. Governor Shirzai in person, on a trip to Pakistan, halted his convoy at the quarryman's gas station and ordered his soldiers to take him away. Fortunately, an Amnesty International delegation was passing through at the time, asking a lot of uncomfortable questions about the treatment of prisoners in private jails. We put the quarryman on their list. He was all but pampered, but it easily could have been worse.

The Amnesty team came by for supper at our compound. Over tea, as we relaxed against the cushions on the floor, I asked them to give it to me straight: objectively, just how bad was the situation in this heart of darkness?

"Actually," countered their willowy team leader, "conditions in Kandahar are surprisingly good." Her team was having a most productive visit. "In other towns," she explained, "we haven't been able to find out anything. It's like a wall of silence. But the police chief here has been really helpful. He's amazing. He threw open the doors of his department. He told us quite honestly, 'I've got a problem. My men are fighters, not police officers.' He knows he's got human rights abuses, and he asked us for help. I've never seen the like in Afghanistan." She was talking about Akrem.

I took this in, dubiously, not yet willing to put aside my mistrust of the man.

The Akokolacha saga had the effect of confirming for me the value of our maverick style at ACS: our determination to be involved in policy and practice both. It was always a difficult course to try to explain to people, when they asked, predictably, "What do you do?" That simple question never had a satisfactorily simple answer, and I always heaved a sigh before plunging in. And yet Akokolacha seemed to prove the virtue of our approach. As deep as my misgivings about warlord government had been from the moment I had arrived in Kandahar, I never would have understood what it felt like to be subjected to it, I never would have been able to describe it cogently had it not been *my* tractor that was held up at gunpoint. By the same token, it was impossible for me to live through such events and then shut up about them in the name of maintaining a "positive working relationship" with the provincial authorities in order to win their permission to help the people.

That was the style of most of the other nongovernmental organizations and international agencies: a see-no-evil stance.

A few international actors, like USAID, did take the Afghan political framework into account, though they usually made what was in my view a well-meaning, but crucial, mistake. They thought in institutional terms. Their mission, as some of them understood it, was to cultivate, encourage, and foster the fledgling Afghan government. And for most of them, that meant shoring up its "institutions": its ministries, its courts, its provincial administrations.

Western political culture prompts us to think this way. Over the past three or four centuries, we in the West have designed and laboriously erected institutions as our bulwark against tyranny. And we have come to revere them, for they have indeed protected us. Westerners, to a degree unique in history, invest their loyalty in institutions, regardless of the individuals who happen to be staffing them at a particular time. The willingness, in 2000, of Americans to obey the ruling of a split Supreme Court in the most closely contested presidential election in their history is a striking example.

Western officials on the ground in Afghanistan were acting instinctively within this conceptual framework. "We're here to support the government," I heard again and again. "And Gul Agha Shirzai is the governor. So we've got to support him."

But Afghanistan is not there yet. In Afghanistan, loyalties and allegiances are to individuals. That is the system within which Governor Shirzai was operating, and to which he translated this international support. He applied all of the well-meaning Western aid—lavished on him in his role as a representative of the Afghan government—to the purpose of building up a *personal* power base. And this was a project that could only conflict with truly nationwide governing institutions for Afghanistan. It was to advance this personal aim, which remained largely invisible to Western eyes, that Gul Agha Shirzai diverted much of the plunder he extracted from his own province, and much of the subsidy he extracted from international representatives. In other words, their contributions were working in opposition to their stated aim.

Whenever I raised these issues with U.S. officials, they countered with a valid objection: What was the alternative? It was not up to them to decide who should hold office in Afghanistan. President Karzai had appointed Shirzai.

There were a number of answers to this argument. One was that it was disingenuous. Washington had played a very active role in the choice of Afghan officials, not the least of whom President Karzai himself. In the case of Shirzai, President Karzai had not in fact appointed him, as I knew perfectly well by then. He had appointed Mullah Naqib. It was the United States that, backing Shirzai with a cohort of Special Forces officers and everything such a show of force implied in an Afghan context, had forced him upon the president.

Setting aside these questions of fact, there was another point I tried to make to U.S. and UN officials. There was a difference, I maintained, between "working with" Gul Agha Shirzai and writing him a blank check. Kandaharis—as they told me during innumerable conversations, both casually and in a study setting—longed for three benefits from the U.S. presence in their town: security, reconstruction, and perhaps most of all, government accountability.

They had had plenty of experience with the abusive, predatory nature of their local strongmen (and even of their technically educated compatriots: the "engineers" who had maneuvered themselves into management positions at all the so-called local NGOs, and were helping themselves to a disproportionate share of foreign subsidy). These people had been artificially strengthened by lavish payments during the Soviet and *mujahideen* times. They had grown, like cancerous tumors, out of control. And now, with the Taliban gone, they were back in power again. Vulnerable Kandaharis were looking to the foreigners for protection against them. They saw us, on the whole, as more scrupulous, fair-minded, and hardworking than their fellow-Afghans.

And we, I believe, could have afforded a measure of that protection. American officials could have held Gul Agha Shirzai up to some kind of standard. They could have made their ongoing financial and moral backing of him contingent on better governance. They could have noticed that he was funneling the vast bulk of their aid to his family and tribesmen. They could have taken steps to spread the wealth. They could have disarmed his private militias. They could have sought out other community leaders and listened to their views.

In other words, even if obliged to work with Gul Agha Shirzai, they could have used their considerable leverage to force him to improve.

Akokolacha, which had brought so much of this into focus for me, became an object lesson. I wrote about it.[2] I used it as an example in talks to U.S. audiences and in radio interviews. I told visiting journalists the story, and they wrote about it.[3] (On one such occasion, the poor old quarryman wound up in jail again.)

Thus did Akokolacha launch what began to look every bit like a personal feud between the governor of Kandahar Province and me. In fact, there was nothing personal about it. My table manners are hardly faultless either. It was Gul Agha's system I objected to, the kind of governance he represented—the kind of Afghanistan that would result if his way prevailed.

CHAPTER 16

ZABIT AKREM

NOVEMBER 2002

MY FEUD WITH the governor led to one utterly unexpected consequence: friendship with the man I had studiously kept clear of, Police Chief Zabit Akrem. He was feuding with the governor too, and for the same reasons.

One day in late 2002, our weekly women's meeting was drawing to its garrulous close, women gathering their bags and draping their *burqas* like capes from their foreheads—they would leave them open in front so they could keep talking while they made their way downstairs, then flip them down over their faces when they got outside. This was a gathering we hosted at ACS of about a dozen women, several rather prominent, several unknown. One or two were illiterate, in fact, part of our effort to make sure the vast majority of Kandahar women were somehow represented. Our conversations those days were a little unfocused: we would talk about priorities for women in Kandahar, or about setting up an office for the female delegates to the *Loya Jirga*, the grand tribal council that had met in Kabul the previous June.

That afternoon, as I was waiting to walk the women downstairs, Mami Jan came up to me. Loud, big-hearted, melodramatic Mami Jan, was one of the *Loya Jirga* delegates, and administered a medical clinic for women.

"*Comandan Saab* wants to see you," she said, casually.

"*Comandan Saab?*" It means "Mr. Commander." I thought I knew who she was talking about.

"Zabit Akrem," she confirmed.

Nothing had happened to change my opinion of the man since that second nasty meeting in his office eight months before about my living in the house in the graveyard. Still, other westerners, like the Amnesty International team, were unanimous in their praise of him, something I did point out when people asked me.

His roundabout approach was enough to intrigue me: he could have sent a soldier with a summons, and I would have been obliged to appear before him. That he did not—that he chose a mutual friend as a go-between instead, and a female one at that—was obviously meant to signal a reduction in hostilities. I had no hesitation about going to see what he wanted.

Police headquarters featured a press of people hardly second to the one on hand at the governor's palace. So we arranged for him to come by my house that evening after dinner.

I remember scurrying to prepare dishes of nuts and raisins to serve with tea. I even persuaded a neighbor to contribute two plates of shucked pomegranate seeds, mounded and glistening like rubies. On that occasion and the countless times Akrem and I got together afterward, I felt keenly self-conscious about my awkward hosting skills. The size of him, both physically and in his rank and local stature, always made the space I occupied seem inadequate. I did not have a retinue, or a late-model SUV with an armed driver, or any of the other marks of power that do, in the end, matter in Kandahar. He wielded these things with grace—not because he coveted them inordinately for their own sake, but because he knew the value of their symbolism.

At that first meeting, I could see him taking stock of our spare compound and wondering if he had made the right move. I was always more comfortable at his house, on a private street behind police headquarters. We would sit in his snug receiving room, on floor cushions covered with tasteful but unostentatious rugs. A curly-haired bodyguard would appear unbidden with a dish of grapes or cans of soda on glass saucers lined with paper napkins. A new little daughter called Asma would clamber all over him when he allowed her in, tweaking his beard with bright-eyed, fearless devotion, till at last he would shoo her out of the room. And still, I cringed more than once when my incorrigible informality, the directness that I can't keep from tipping into impertinence, grated against the decorum of his flawless manners.

I seated him in a corner of our receiving room, furnished Afghan style with a rug on the floor and velvet-covered mattresses around the walls with matching cushions for backrests. In a niche I had placed two beautiful old brass water pipes that I had picked up for the equivalent of a couple of dollars on that street by the ancient mud-plaster mosque, where rags-and-bones men set out used goods on squares of dirty cloth.

As we talked, it slowly dawned on me that Akrem was scared. Physically afraid.

He was telling me a story that was having the strangest effect on me. It was utterly incredible, and yet it was confirming a lot of things I had begun to suspect.

An informant of his, someone who worked on Governor Shirzai's staff, had been reporting back about weapons deliveries—guns and equipment coming from Pakistan and unloaded directly at the governor's residence. On one occasion, Akrem said, a car had arrived with pistols and sophisticated walkie-talkies and some sort of motion detectors. "Where's the good stuff?" Governor Shirzai had demand, as he looked over the hardware.

"The car with the radar is following right behind us," the driver had answered, according to Akrem's mole.

Some of these arms, it seemed, were being transshipped out of Kandahar to a nearby battleground. Six days ago, Akrem continued, his mole had observed several vehicles setting out from the governor's residence, Kalashnikovs hidden under a mess of plastic water bottles. The convoy, said Akrem, was headed for Shindand, a town halfway up that seamed cement road that leads out of Kandahar, past the turnoff to Khakrez, and on northwestward to Herat.

Shindand was a hot spot, for it marked the dividing line between the Pashtuns to the south and the Persian-speaking Tajiks to the north. Herat, that former center of Persian culture that had become the stronghold of the Abdali Pashtuns just before the birth of Afghanistan, was back in the Persian orbit. It was ruled by a powerful Persian-speaking Tajik warlord named Isma'il Khan. He had been huffing and puffing against the southern Pashtuns since the anti-Taliban war a year before. While the Kandahar elders were negotiating the Taliban surrender in November of 2001, Isma'il Khan was stamping his foot with impatience, vowing he would take Kandahar by force. That would have really sparked civil war. The whole Afghan south would have risen up against him. As it was, several nasty fire-fights had broken out recently between Isma'il Khan and a Pashtun commander at Shindand who was defying him.

This, Akrem was telling me, was precisely the kind of ethnic conflict the Pakistani government was trying to foment, using Governor Gul Agha Shirzai as a stalking horse. The Pakistanis wanted to set Gul Agha up as the champion of downtrodden Pashtuns in Herat, and get him to lead a military expedition there in order to keep Afghanistan volatile and unstable—America's *yaghestan.*

"Oh," I twigged. "So all those declarations of Gul Agha's on the radio recently, about human rights abuses against Pashtuns in Herat . . . ?"

"Exactly," Akrem answered.

Then just yesterday, Akrem's mole had come to him with another story. At 9:00 P.M. the night before, the man had been in the governor's office. Two Pakistani army officers were there, berating the governor. "You're too slow. What's the problem?" Shirzai was not working quickly enough to ignite the hostilities with Herat, the Pakistanis charged. According to the mole, the governor had put the blame on two big problems he was confronting. One was Kabul. President Karzai would not have any patience for ethnic strife in the new Afghanistan. The other was Zabit Akrem. "He's blocking things on this end," the governor complained. "Every time I call a security meeting and propose some action, he speaks up against me. He's keeping me from rallying commanders to the anti-Herat cause."

"Zabit Akrem is making problems for you?" the Pakistani officers retorted. "Then make problems for him. Kill him."

So *this* explained the occasional clashes on the streets of Kandahar between Akrem's police and Shirzai's private thugs, I thought. There had been that shoot-out right in front of the old mud-plaster mosque, in the middle of the bazaar. Was a rocket launcher fired? I tried to remember. In any case, someone had been killed, I was sure of that.

From the way Akrem was talking, it was clear that he took this threat from Pakistan very seriously indeed.

I leaned forward. Did he mind if I took some notes? I flipped open the orange cover of one of the pocket-sized pads I had used for reporting. Did he have the sense that Pakistani intelligence agents were planted here? Akrem reeled off half a dozen: Seyyid Karim Agha, who used to be at army headquarters; right now he was in Islamabad. Ayyub Palawan, on the border, and Hajji Niyamat Nurzai. The list went on. We talked about the militia commander's hosting a U.S. Special Forces group in Helmand Province to the west of us. He was a loyalist of the fundamentalist resistance leader who had preceded the Taliban as Pakistan's protégé. The fundamentalist faction was back in business these days, and by working with one of its members, the Special Forces troopers might as well have staked their tent right inside the lion's den. I asked Akrem about the private prison supposedly run by Governor Shirzai's hatchet man, Khalid Pashtoon. It was behind the old governor's palace, Akrem confirmed. He named the two men in charge. If I wanted, he could get me together with some people who had been held there. He told me about a Pakistani-infiltrated gang of fighters posted on the U.S. airbase; they were working as American proxies by day and shelling the American positions by night. We discussed the attempted assassination of President Karzai that summer. Akrem shook his head at the lack of a serious investigation. He told me how the key witness had died while in the custody of Gul Agha's men at the U.S. airfield.

The picture he painted for me of the streets of Kandahar left me agape. With U.S. dollars, Governor Shirzai had constituted his own private militia. And—better armed and better paid—that militia was competing with Akrem's police force. He started naming checkpoints around town that Shirzai's "Special Force" had taken over. And I realized that Akrem's men, the legitimate police of Kandahar province, had been pushed back into a little corner of the city. The police patrolled just a few streets, commanded two or three of the precinct houses. Everywhere else were Shirzai's thugs.

I looked up, reconsidering this embattled man.

We talked deep into the night, while Akrem's bodyguards waited hours for him, leaning on his shiny forest green Land Cruiser, fraternizing with my staff. Akrem's answers to my volley of questions were considered, astute, constructive. It was a tone that never wavered through two and a half years of conversations.

We fell into a loose routine. We would rarely let more than a week go by without an exchange of phone calls or a visit. Something would come up that I wanted his take on, or he would have a piece of information to pass along. Or I would simply notice I hadn't heard from *Comandan Saab* in a while, and I would call him up to see how he was doing.

Zabit Akrem proved to be the most sophisticated political thinker I encountered in Afghanistan. The fact seemed somehow incongruous, beside the rough-hewn nature of the man.

CHAPTER 17

MILITARY MATTERS

---

2 0 0 2 – 2 0 0 4

PART OF WHAT prompted Akrem to break the ice between us was that he possessed information vital to the American mission in Afghanistan, and he wanted to communicate it. But the Americans were swaddled in their alliance with Gul Agha Shirzai. With Shirzai's eyes and ears hemming them in, the U.S. troops were unapproachable. Akrem had pegged me for a back channel.

He got the reasons for it wrong—my contacts with American officials were due to fluke and longevity, not professional affiliation—but in substance, he was right. I did turn out to be a back channel to army officers, among others.

The entrance to the airport, where the U.S. military established its base, has been gussied up a bit since Al-Qaeda's last stand there. A Soviet MIG that miraculously escaped being sold for scrap, painted with new camouflage and a menacing grin, guards the turnoff. Behind it, great metal gates with a plaque inscribed in honor of Gul Agha Shirzai bar the road. Spherical marble guardhouses, like big golf balls, flank the gates, and a matching marble-clad barracks has reared up just inside. It is for Shirzai's fighters, who secure—and control—the outer perimeter.

It was no mean prize President Karzai offered Gul Agha Shirzai when he told him to hold the airport as the Taliban regime was collapsing. Shirzai defied the president and took the governorship, and he kept the airport too.

Despite the visible expense, there is something desultory about his efforts at embellishment. Beyond the gate and its gaudy new protuberances, the road stretches for half a mile across the sun-baked, dust-swept emptiness to another set of gates. Tall, lopsided pine trees that once studded the grounds were mostly cut down by the U.S. troops in order to deny potential enemies cover. The rest, untended, have developed sickly, brownish-yellow blemishes on their drooping needles. For a time the earth was pocked with foxholes where the U.S. Marines were hunkered down that first Christmas, but gradually the holes were filled in and the soldiers moved to tents; then the tents gained plywood floors set up off the ground. Now most of the buildings on base are made of wood.

I dreaded going out there, because of the time it always took. You would park your truck at the far side of a kind of traffic island—without the traffic—then walk a hundred yards to a rust-brown iron bar slung across the road with a hinge at one end and a piece of rope at the other for hoisting it up and down. This was Gate 2. When the military police officer spied you through the slit in a sandbagged bunker set back about thirty yards behind it, he would amble over, his pace designed to not jack up his body heat, as he sweltered inside full combat gear: helmet, long-sleeved desert camouflage, twenty pounds of bulletproof plate inside his vest, ankle-high boots, magazines at his belt, black M-16 slung over his shoulder. He would inspect your ID, then walk back to the bunker and call in your details and the name of the person you wanted to see.

Then you would wait anywhere from one to three hours, in the scorched, dust-filled wind, for an escort to arrive.

Various things struck me about this process. The extremely rudimentary nature of the communications systems in use, for one. There was no way to reach a person on base from outside if you wanted to make an appointment, for example, to cut down the wait. Internet, which the soldiers relied on, was nonexistent in Kandahar. A few U.S. officers obtained hand-held satellite telephones, like old-fashioned walkie-talkies with fat antennas that you have to struggle to get pointed in the right direction, whirling around while you're talking or leaning over to get the angle right. But they were of the U.S.-owned Iridium variety, incompatible with the Thurayas used in Kandahar.

The consequence was an impregnability—not just of the physical barriers made of sand bags and cement tank traps and loops of concertina wire, but the barriers to any form of communication between the Americans and people of the land in which they were operating.

Within the army, communications were just as bad. It took more than a year for the MPs manning the gate to get handheld walkie-talkies so they would not have to keep trudging back and forth, bunker to gate, gate to bunker. The walkie-talkies, I later learned, were not even issued by the U.S. government. The soldiers had bought them with their own money. Worse was the link back to the base proper, a few hundred yards inside the gate. To call in your details, the MP would unclamp the receiver from a heavy military telephone set and connect to something called the TOC, or Tactical Operations Center. The soldier who picked up there would then make a similar call over to Civil Affairs or whichever unit you needed to reach. And that is where things broke down. It never took less than half an hour for that connection to be made, let alone for Civil Affairs to send someone out to the gate.

The thought of relying on such haphazard links in an emergency did not fill me with confidence. Early on, I made a mental note that should disaster strike, ACS would forget about the U.S. Army and throw itself at the SAS, the highly capable British Special Air Service team right in town.

What also baffled me about getting on base were the constantly changing rules. Inefficiency might be par for the course, but I had always thought the army stuck to ironclad procedures. Not at Kandahar Airfield. Each visit brought new variations on the theme. Usually I was searched going in, but often I wasn't. One MP team might invite us to have a seat in their bunker while we waited, passing us cold bottles of Gatorade and allowing us to make conversation. Another group might stare at us stonily, ordering us back from the iron bar to await our escort at the traffic island. Most Civil Affairs teams were happy to see us any time. But one rotation told us we could only come on Fridays.

For a few months—on the Shirzais' say-so—I became persona non grata and could not get on base at all. Various excuses would be made when I pulled up after the half hour drive from town: there was a security alert, no one was allowed on, or no escort was available. I would watch people I knew were working for Pakistani intelligence get waved on base, while I, a born and bred American, was left with my ruffled feathers in the dust.

The BBC's Adam Brookes and me, guests of the
Taliban, applying moisturizer under the rather
unnerving stares of Spin Boldak folk, perched on the
walls of our compound in late November 2001.

My Achekzai friends from the barracks at the border, showing off the haul from a drug bust, March 2002.

OPPOSITE, CLOCKWISE FROM TOP LEFT: Flirtatious Guldani is peeping from behind the window curtain.

Nissar Ahmad embossing panels for embellishing the trucks.

The littlest kids bringing my books and magazines through the corridor joining the "mealmastun" to the private part of the house.

An in-law helping at the brother's body shop.

CITY OF CANDAHAR, AFG[...]

Money changers at Chahar Sou.

The dry-good street on the edge of the old bazaar in Kandahar.

A rickshaw.

LEFT: View of Kandahar from the saddle in the road where the stone quarry is located, 1897.

TOP ROW, LEFT TO RIGHT: Rebuilding Akokolacha, summer 2002: the doorway of one of the bombed-out houses.

The master mason working on a mud-brick wall.

Brian Knappenberger behind the camera, filming his documentary, *Life After War* (Sundance) / *A House for Hajji Baba (Frontline)*.

Me with kids. (EVE LYMAN)

BOTTOM ROW, LEFT TO RIGHT: Akokolacha children loaded up with bricks.

Our new pump.

The Kabul to Kandahar road. For fifteen hours.

CLOCKWISE FROM TOP: Men at work: bringing fodder home, Helmand Province.

Selling pomegranates, Tirin Kot, Urozgan Province.

Baking bread, downtown Kandahar.

Spinning silk, Herat.

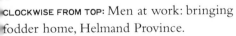

CLOCKWISE FROM TOP:

Spinning silk, Herat.

Threshing, Vrozgan.

Casting brass spoons,
Kandahar.

Feeding a wedding party at
the house in the graveyard.

CLOCKWISE FROM TOP:

A village council meeting, Arghandab.

Settling a dispute before the district council, Khakrez.

A nosegay, Tirin Kot, Urozgan Province.

A village elder in Helmand, explaining that water from the canal no longer reaches the village.

CLOCKWISE FROM TOP:

Bringing fodder home, Helmand.

A young shepherd, Arghandab.

Despite occasional intimidation, girls attend school.

A boy who just delivered milk to a collection point, Arghandab.

CLOCKWISE FROM TOP LEFT: Cleaning an air filter on the Kabul to Kandahar road.

A nomad boy on the move, Helmand Province.

Three girls at a gas station on the Kabul to Kandahar road.

A young shepherd across the street from the Arghand workshop in Kandahar.

POSITE, CLOCKWISE FROM TOP LEFT:
village woman, Akokolacha.

ree women who administer vaccines in Kandahar.
hen they saw me with a camera they came over,
ped up their *burqas*, and demanded that I take
eir picture. "Take it to America!" they cried. A
olutionary gesture.

omen from the nomadic Kuchi tribe (here, in
lmand Province) are far less confined than their
ban sisters.

diqa, one of the women who work with me at
e Arghand cooperative, shucking pomegranates.

President Hamid Karzai (right)
and Gul Agha Shirzai.

(AP IMAGES)

Muhammad Akrem Khakrezwai in July 2003.

I later learned Civil Affairs had been told that the army did not like ACS's views, and they were not to have anything to do with us. Then when the units rotated and the base came under new command, I was issued a pass and could drive on and off unchallenged. Such was the bewildering lack of system that seemed to characterize much of the army's activities in Kandahar. Apparently, each incoming captain liked to leave his mark by making a new set of rules. Sort of like a dog peeing on a post.

At the gate, the one constant was Shirzai's insolent young men with their dark glasses and newly minted pickup trucks roaring through.

When President Karzai gave command of the provincial security forces to Mullah Naqib and Akrem's Alokozais as a check on Shirzai's power, one obvious move remained to Shirzai on the Kandahar chessboard, and he made it. He formed his own personal security forces. Thanks to funding provided by the U.S. army, Shirzai—who before the war had had to scrounge for followers—was able to recruit and deploy two extralegal military units. *Nazmi Khass*, or the Special Force, was housed in palatial new barracks on the main road into town. This was the unit that competed with Akrem's police inside Kandahar proper, setting up its own checkpoints around town and coming to blows with the legitimate police. The second group of fighters was stationed out at the airport under the command of Gul Agha's brother Razziq. They continued to serve as U.S. proxies in the ongoing "war on terror."

Technically, their role was a military one. They were charged with providing outer rim security for the U.S. base and with joining U.S. troops on missions—both combat and assessment visits—around the countryside. In practice, just the way engineer Abdullah made himself indispensable to me, Razziq and his colleagues saw to the grateful Americans' every need. And before long, the U.S. forces were helplessly wrapped inside the Shirzais' friendly bear hug.

The troops needed pickup trucks? Shirzai provided them, on lease, at rates so high the army could have paid for the truck outright within five or six months. The base needed gravel? Shirzai crushed it at his new facility or bought it from our friend the quarryman at $8 a tractor load and charged the U.S. Army $100. The Americans wanted to make a contribution to the local economy by hiring local labor for menial work around the base? The Shirzais provided the workers, then extorted a quarter of their daily wage in kickbacks. A thousand laborers on base racked up $2,000 a day for the Shirzais. And the employees, grateful anyway, were almost all Shirzai's Barakzais. In assorted contracts with the two commanders of this militia, the United States paid out almost $100,000 to each per month. And that's without the perks: the free cases of soft drinks, the PX privileges—or the inestimable power and prestige this relationship with the Great Power of the day afforded these gunmen on the local scene.[1]

The outcome of most contests is determined by terrain, and the Americans had surrendered a choice position to Gul Agha Shirzai. "Outer rim security" meant manning Gate 1, the gate between the golf balls, behind the grinning MiG. By controlling the outer gate, Shirzai's men in effect controlled access to the base. No competitor could even approach the Americans to offer a better deal on goods or services. The consequences of this monopoly were not restricted to the waste of taxpayer money. The damage went to the core of the U.S. mission in Afghanistan.

When U.S. Army Civil Affairs bid out contracts for a reconstruction project—a village well or school, for example—the bidders' conferences were held at Razziq Shirzai's compound. Few who were not Razziq's friends got inside the gate. That meant the local contractors being subsidized in the interests of capacity and relationship building were all in Shirzai's orbit. Since the governor's suggestions for reconstruction projects were also largely followed, it seemed to most Kandaharis that the primary mission of U.S. troops in Kandahar was to service Gul Agha Shirzai and his Barakzai tribe.

During one of our chats in his cozy receiving room, Akrem put it to me this way: "The other tribes are frustrated, and they're starting to pull away." We were discussing some intensive political activity Shirzai had been engaging in, calling tribal elders to meet with him, giving them gifts of ceremonial turbans or rugs. Akrem could not understand why the U.S. forces seemed to be helping Shirzai so assiduously. "The Americans do everything for Gul Agha and Khalid Pashtoon," he remarked with wonderment. "The schools, the wells, all are for the Barakzais. But it's only a small tribe. Gul Agha doesn't even need this American money; he's got the customs revenues." Kandahar customs officials were all Shirzai's Barakzais, and so far, not a penny of the estimated $5 to $8 million dollars a month that was being collected at the gates of Kandahar was making it to central government coffers in Kabul.

The impression of American favoritism was exacerbated by Shirzai's fighters' wardrobe. Both *Nazmi Khass* and the militia at the base had been issued U.S. Army fatigues. U.S. soldiers wearing that uniform are subject to U.S. discipline and supervision. The Afghan fighters were not. And they interpreted the formidable shield afforded by their friendship with the U.S. troops as a blank check.

When idle conversations with Kandaharis veered to the subject of security, as they often did, I would keep count. Every time I heard of an ugly incident—a boy being shot in the leg by a soldier who wanted his bicycle, the driver of a wedding procession being shot because he refused to give a soldier some candy, a house being looted on the pretext that the soldiers were looking for opium—I asked what uniform the perpetrators were wearing. Almost every time, the witness would describe the particolor U.S. camouflage worn by Shirzai's gunmen.

What were Kandaharis to conclude except that Shirzai's men were operating under U.S. command, that they and their actions were part of U.S. policy?

In other words, much of the expenditure in effort and treasure that was aimed at building bridges and gaining friends in Kandahar did the reverse. It built a growing feeling of resentment against the U.S. troops.

Shirzai's gunmen gained a further benefit from their ownership of the airfield's outer perimeter: a chunk of territory that was free from scrutiny. The distance from Gate 1, the outside gate manned by the Afghans, to Gate 2, the inner gate guarded by U.S. troops, was about half a mile. That half mile, ringed all the way around the base, was a no-man's land, protected and peopled by Shirzai's henchmen. For a time, they were taking advantage of this privacy to load marijuana shipments for transport to Pakistan.

The racket, as I understood it, went like this: Among his other contracts, Razziq Shirzai had won the exclusive right to supply the U.S. base with diesel fuel. Tanker trucks would drive up from Pakistan or across from Iran and onto base, empty their contents into great rubber pouches like giant water beds partially sunk into the ground. Then, in at least one case, after an empty tanker had exited the base proper and entered the zone between the perimeters, Shirzai's men loaded it up with dope and sent it back toward Pakistan.

That particular truck was captured by Afghan frontier guards in March 2003. The chief of the border police at the time was one of my Achekzai friends—the commander who had detailed the young bodyguard to me on my first drive into Kandahar. That spring of 2003, I was on my way to Chaman to visit Mahmad Anwar, and I stopped at the border police headquarters for a motorcycle ride into Pakistan. Over the obligatory glass of tea, the commander told me how he had captured a tanker truck full of dope a few days back. He reached into his breast pocket for some papers that the driver had been carrying.

The border police chief unfolded one. What I saw first, inked in green across the top of the slip of paper, was the official letterhead of the Provincial Government of Kandahar. The note was signed Bacha Shirzai, the governor's other brother. It read: "The carrier of this letter is my man; he is doing my business. Please provide him with all necessary assistance." It amounted to safe conduct through every checkpoint from Kandahar to the Pakistani border and beyond.

The second piece of paper was a cryptic list: some names with numbers next to them, about forty in all: "Ata Jan 7," for example. "Najibullah 4." (I'm remembering the names. They may not be accurate.) It had to be a kind of cargo invoice, listing each drug trafficker and the weight of the shipment he had placed aboard the tanker truck. A *man,* the common unit of weight in Kandahar, equals appoximately four and a half kilos, or almost ten pounds. "Ata Jan" would have been shipping nearly seventy pounds of pot to Pakistan. A rough addition of the numbers on the list put the tanker's total cargo at around nine hundred kilos, or just short of two thousand pounds.

And the Shirzais, doubtless for a price, were apparently providing a safe place on the U.S. base to load this cargo, and then protection for it on the road to Pakistan.

There was another drug scam on base, involving U.S. soldiers this time. Shirzai's men would run marijuana *into* the base, for use by U.S. soldiers. The pot came with the tanker loads of fuel the Afghans were delivering. In payment, the soldiers would falsify the delivery records, signing in a full tanker of diesel when in fact the load was short.

These transactions were eventually discovered and the U.S. soldiers discreetly punished. But the Shirzais never suffered any consequences.

In both cases, the integrity of the U.S. mission was compromised because U.S. troops either appeared to be or actually were participating in the very drug trade they were theoretically supposed to interdict.

But to my mind, the very worst breach of U.S. security lay with the interpretation and translation services the troops relied upon for all their interactions with the Afghans around them. I can remember only one soldier who spoke Pashtu. Local interpreters were required for the army's every move. And those interpreters were provided, again, by Razziq Shirzai. They did not even receive their pay directly from U.S. personnel, though one Civil Affairs sergeant almost gave herself an ulcer trying to get the procedure changed. But she was ordered to keep giving the money to Razziq, and to let him pay the interpreters. They lived in his compound in the no-man's-land. In the Afghan context, this made the interpreters beholden not to the Americans, but to Razziq Shirzai. Whether by inclination or—as was often the case—by force, with physical abuse driving home the facts, the interpreters were Razziq's men, under his orders.

The result was a severely distorted picture of the situation in the Afghan south and nearly unintelligible interactions between Americans and Afghans. The information U.S. forces were receiving was frequently inaccurate or deliberately misrepresented. The messages U.S. officers were trying to communicate to locals were either not getting through at all, or were, time and again, twisted to suit the Shirzais' ends. Complaints and suggestions that some courageous Afghans—like Akrem—might step forward to offer U.S. forces were similarly bent and deformed.

It was on the basis of a picture this flawed that U.S. commanders were reaching their combat and reconstruction decisions in Kandahar. It made me want to weep with frustration.

CHAPTER 18

SECURITY

IN THE BEGINNING, given U.S. forces' stated mission in Afghanistan—fighting Al-Qaeda—their lack of communication with the Afghans around them arguably did not matter very much. For at first, there was not much Al-Qaeda to fight. Al-Qaeda and the Taliban were gone.

For about six months, there was a period of grace when those who were battling for the future of Afghanistan only had to battle the past's inert wreckage, not its resurrected ghosts. Even Kandahar, which separated from its Taliban affliction with care and some cynicism, was released for a moment. For a time, no alternative to the new U.S.-led experiment stalked. Kandaharis could give themselves up to the promise they perceived in it without a glance over their shoulders.

A trip to the bazaar drew a crowd, unsettling in its immobility, its insatiable, unsmiling stare, but nothing worse. A petulant clot of traffic blocking an unpaved street was just a frustration, not something that required the calculation of risk. I could drive across Kandahar without nervously eyeing the motorcycle that drew alongside me, or thinking to roll up my windows in case of grenades.

When the first signs came, we did not see them as portents, for they were silent—harmless, we thought—and they came not to Afghanistan but to neighboring Pakistan.

It was like some grotesque courtship ritual. Men, dressed in immaculate white or glowering black, their beards carefully frayed to untrimmed wisps at the edges, their heads wrapped in the loopy, outsized turban the Taliban had made their trademark, would appear on their doorsteps and stand for a while. Or they would collect in relaxed groups on street corners in the busy Pashtunabad bazaar, the Afghan neighborhood in Quetta. Like peacocks before a prospective mate, they were on display. Except it was hardly the rare *burka*-clad female whose attention they desired. The show was for their rival; they wished to gauge his reaction.

That rival, in the form of the new Afghan government and the Americans protecting it, did not react. And so the way was open for the next phase.

That was the "night letters" and the threats. A folded slip of paper tucked into a crack in the door of the mosque or passed around by a friend, declaring that the new Afghan government had rejected Islam and combating it was holy war.

This message began to lace the sermons delivered in the white-painted mosques of Quetta, with their quiet, arcaded courtyards, havens from the sooty chaos outside. Soon the imams added the obligation and the threat: anyone collaborating with the apostate government in Afghanistan could be—should be—killed.

A word about courage. Afghans are famous for it. They are legendary spillers of blood. Afghan songs and poetry are full of merciless exhortations to ferocity. Few Westerners recall the Afghans' successful resistance to the Arab invaders who tried to reduce their rocky land thirteen hundred years ago. But the Afghans do, and with pride, despite their fierce conversion later to the Islam those Arabs were carrying. The Afghans' rout of the British army in 1842—that massacre of the Army of the Indus down to one last man who was allowed to live so he could describe the horror of it—has haunted the imaginations of all foreigners who have even thought about spending time in Afghanistan ever since. It doesn't matter if they don't know the historical details of that butchery. The shadow of it haunts them.

Of course, a closer look at the historical details uncovers a good deal of shrewdness mixed in with Afghan courage. Afghan fighters know how to turn terrain, timing, and temporary alliances to advantage so as to reduce the actual spillage of their blood. Those Redcoats in 1842 were shot up in a canyon, with straight rock walls that rise almost to blot out the sky. The Afghans were ranged above, shooting down at the beefy English officers and their cold and homesick Indian troops, thinned out along the road like blood cells in a capillary. The slaughter of those men had more to do with the blind arrogance and incompetence of their generals than the Afghans' profligate courage. Sometimes the fighting of Afghans resembles a kind of stylized theater, a performance designed to bring the probable winner to light so that the terms of his acceptance can be negotiated.

The most egregious recent exception to this rule came during the 1980s Soviet invasion, when Afghans leading mules and carrying bolt-action rifles took on the Red Army. Even that was a guerrilla war, not one marked by pitched battles. The Afghan fighters allied themselves once more with their unfriendly landscape. They renewed their everlasting covenant with the treacherous rocks and the rough footpaths across them, and kept on shooting.

One man who fought the length of this war, Tor, a lanky man, inhabited by a miraculous innocence despite his haunted eyes, can even think back on his time in the mountains with some fondness. He remembers his horse—white, of all the nontactical colors—which would carry him all day, then munch down a handful of cookies dug out of a sack, and be eager to set off again. Tor's eyes glint like a boy's with a bicycle when he talks about that horse.

But it was a real war. And it took an appalling toll in the elements of civilization that were more painstaking for Afghanistan to acquire than other countries: the orchards, the irrigation systems hollowed out of stone and laboriously maintained for generations, and in blood, in innocent blood. The Soviets, shot at from a village, would come back with their invincible helicopter gunships and raze the village, bring down the mud-brick houses on their occupants, splinter the bones of the elders, eviscerate the women never once seen by a stranger's eyes, sow mines among the almonds and apricots so those who longed to tend the trees would be blown up trying. A million Afghans were killed in that decade of war, most of them civilians.

In time, the Afghans, with their rifles and their white horses, and finally with their U.S.-supplied Stinger missiles, won the war. But the victory, miraculous though it was given the odds, unimaginable though it was in its impact on the organization of the whole world, came too late to avert an irreparable loss. The Afghans lost their courage. For, before the Stingers arrived, courage could do nothing against a helicopter flying out of range, whose reinforced belly was immune to bullets anyway. The inequality in firepower between the Soviets and the Afghans was so great as to render courage irrelevant. The Afghans' courage was disempowered, as was their mythical hardiness. I saw the marks from entrance and exit wounds in my Achekzai host-father's lower gut. "But then what are you doing alive?" I exclaimed, eyeing a hand-breadth of scar tissue on his side where the slug blew its way out. "Oh, I just took my shawl and tied myself up in it," he answered, perhaps with a touch of bravado. Even the courage to do this, even this superhuman ability simply to survive, could not keep a million innocent people from dying. And so the Afghans' courage deserted them.

The meaning of this loss is that it is no longer necessary to kill Afghans to intimidate them. When I was reporting, I was astonished to find my big, strapping, dignified driver repeatedly malingering when I wanted to go someplace the least bit dangerous. I was astonished when my interpreter quit his fantastically well-paying job with me, citing the intolerable risk. The last straw came when I asked our driver to pull over, and I got out of the car to follow a dirt track toward the airport. "They'll shoot you," said my interpreter. I explained that U.S. Marines don't shoot on sight. "There are mines," he insisted. I pointed out the fresh tire tracks in the dirt, which showed me where to place my feet.

I was dumbstruck to discover myself more courageous than the fabled Afghans, and effortlessly. I gained a reputation in Kandahar, but it is false. I am not so very brave. Only, I have not been through their trauma. I am not violated and indelibly damaged by it, as Afghans are. Brutality and agonizing death have been visited on them in such unpredictable and unparriable ways that their ability to calculate risk is gone.

And so fear has grown to be a determining factor in Afghan society. Its power to paralyze can be invoked by the wisp of a threat. A "night letter," instructing families to remove their girls from the infidels' school lest something happen to them, produces results. A look, cast by a neighbor at the man who invites a foreigner to his home to take tea, can abort future invitations. All of the rituals and pantomime of courage remain, like fossils. But in today's Afghanistan the impact of an intimidation campaign cannot be underestimated.

In the autumn of 2002 the verbal intimidation got reinforcement. That was the time of the shelling, constant but apparently random. Not a night would go by without the sound of an explosion, a rocket-propelled grenade, fired from somewhere, at something, maybe. There was rarely much damage, rarely a death. We would talk about it, try to analyze the previous night's damage, wonder who the target might have been, who the perpetrators. Fruitlessly.

And we got used to it.

Then, with the new year, the aim improved. Something would blow up near the office of a humanitarian group, shattering windows. Or a stick of dynamite would be tossed over the walls of a compound when no one was there.

It was Akrem who pointed out these evolving stages to me, who helped me discern beneath the jumble of events the underlying pattern.

That winter, he managed to land a tribesman in one of the terrorist training camps that littered the Pakistani side of the border. The mole brought back the curriculum, a syllabus covering such subjects as demolitions and bomb making, especially with kitchen pressure cookers, or how to plan and execute the assassinations of public figures: how to track their routines, where to wait for them, how to aim. A Pakistani army colonel and two majors were the professors; Akrem gave me their names.

"The Pakistanis train people and give them money," he said, "and the people plant bombs. Then, if the Afghans and the Americans get angry, the Pakistanis catch a few 'Talibs,' and tell the real ones to stay quiet for a month or two. This is the Pakistani strategy: they advance by taking two steps forward and four steps back."

It was the first time Akrem told me this. He would say it again the night before he died.

By February 1, aid workers posted in Kandahar—the ill-omened city even Afghans were afraid to visit—were getting rattled. Several offices decided to suspend or curtail their missions. Security began to dominate the conversation at the weekly coordination meetings.

Of course, security had dominated conversation among Afghans for months.

But between the security concerns of the Afghans and the security concerns of the foreigners there was a gulf. The foreigners were worried about shadowy "former Taliban" and a putative anti-American insurgency. The Afghans were worried about the quite real depredations of the government those Americans had put in power.

For Afghans' fears about what would take place if the warlords returned had been realized. Perhaps not in their goriest excesses, but with enough precision to bring back memories of the "*mujahideen* nights," the early 1990s chaos that took the place of the retreating Soviets. There were chains on the roads again. Shirzai's militiamen who manned them were taking tolls from taxis. Mama Ubaydullah, in Spin Boldak on the border, according to my Achekzais, was kidnapping the beautiful sons of merchants for ransom and who knew what else. The younger brother of the carpenter who built the studio for our radio station was captured right in Kandahar. He was turned over to soldiers for a theft he did not commit. The soldiers made him cook for them and serve them, and they wanted to make him do other things for them, but could not quite go so far because we were on the case. Nazar Jan's men had a lean-to in my old backyard, the cemetery. Now women could no longer go to visit graves. The private prison was spawning tales, the one maintained by Shirzai's Afghan American factotum, Khalid Pashtoon, now provincial director for foreign affairs. Prisoners were tortured there, it was said, sometimes for money. Everyone had a story. Everyone knew someone who had been hurt. And the fear of it radiated through Kandahar.

Frustration was radiating, too. *This* was the new Afghanistan? people began to wonder.

That winter of 2002, I brought together some of the delegates to the previous June's *Loya Jirga,* or Grand Tribal Council, for a series of focus group discussions. The men and women, from rival tribes and hostile orientations, sitting in one room for the first time in six months, agreed resoundingly on one thing: they had had it with warlords. This is not a word that has been invented in the West. The concept, utterly familiar in Afghanistan, has a name: *topak salaran*, or "gun-rulers." The delegates agreed that the presence of these men had distorted the June *Loya Jirga*, and their presence in government since then was distorting the nascent Afghan democracy.

The former delegates were not at all impressed by the claims of some notorious warlords to be religious leaders—claims I had heard Westerners acknowledge. "They are using the name of Islam all the time; but their deeds are unholy. To speak out against them is not to speak against Islam," said one. Or "These people killed thousands of Muslims, and no one even mentioned it. We could have arrested them and put them in jail where they belong. But they were members of the *Loya Jirga,* so now we can't."[1]

This was the delegates' main complaint about the meeting that had affixed a seal on Hamid Karzai's interim presidency of Afghanistan. They felt it had proved, in part, counterproductive. Most of the delegates had been dispatched to Kabul with a clear mandate: bring an end to warlordism and establish law and order, or *qanun.* "We don't want schools or a hospital," one delegate quoted his constituents' instructions. "We want security." But instead of curbing the warlords, instead of expelling them once and for all from Afghan politics, the Karzai administration was augmenting their power. That was how the delegates felt. "Before, the *topak salaran* had hundreds of followers," said one, while the others in his group nodded. "Now they have thousands. Their position has been legitimized. Before, their hearts were shaking; now they are strong."

These men and women, like the vast majority of Kandaharis, blamed Karzai and the Americans.

"The foreigners must like *topak salaran,*" shrugged another delegate.

My friend Mahmad Anwar had put it even more starkly a few months earlier: "Why are we warlords still in power?"

I asked if he would please repeat what he had just said.

"We *topak salaran* should have been sent home by now. The Americans warned us that anyone who took power with their help when they came into Kandahar would have to leave after the *Loya Jirga.* They should have kicked us out. This was supposed to be a government of educated people."

Disgusted at how swiftly the solemn oaths sworn with Governor Shirzai had been forgotten, Mahmad Anwar resigned a few weeks after this exchange with me, and went home to Chaman.

I have often been asked whether we in the West have the right to "impose democracy" on people who "just might not want it," or might not be "ready for it." I think, concerning Afghanistan at least, this question is exactly backward. From my discussions with these elders and with countless others, I have found that Afghans know precisely what democracy is—even if they might not be able to define the term. And they are crying out for it. They want from their government what most Americans and Europeans want from theirs: roads they can drive on, schools for their kids, doctors with certified qualifications so their prescriptions don't poison people, a minimum of public accountability, and security: law and order. And they want to participate in some real way in the fashioning of their nation's destiny.

But Afghans were getting precious little of any of that, thanks to warlords like Gul Agha Shirzai, whom America was helping maintain in power. American policy in Afghanistan was not imposing or even encouraging democracy, as the U.S. government claimed it was. Instead, it was standing in the way of democracy. It was institutionalizing violence.

Unpredictability destabilizes the human spirit. It was clear, and Kandaharis said as much, that the Taliban oppression had weighed more heavily than the oppression they were experiencing now. And yet under the Taliban there was a system: there was law and order—there was some version of *qanun*. One knew the rules, for they were explicit. And if one only followed them, harsh and intransigent as they were, one could be relatively sure to be left in peace.

Now there was no law. Oppression was arbitrary. It struck without reason, and so it unsettled people. Perhaps the number of actual incidents in Kandahar was not so high. It was surely not so high as it had been during the *mujahideen* time, and Kandaharis did recognize that. They were grateful to the American presence for the comparative calm, swearing that if the U.S. soldiers left, blood would surge through the streets again like the Arghandab River in snow-melt flood. Still, the unpredictability of the incidents, their arbitrariness, gave them a disproportionate power to destabilize spirits.

And the people began remembering how it was under the Taliban. They told of driving to Herat at night, free from fear. They recalled that time they left a whole pile of money tied up in a shawl, right out in the street, while they walked away to buy some melons. They began harking back to the Taliban peace with some nostalgia.

In this way, the sketchy former Taliban began reconstituting themselves, in people's minds, as an alternative. Not an attractive one by any means, but one that was not exclusively hostile to the people's interests either. Nothing ideological entered this calculation. Ironically, Afghans are among the least ideological people on earth. Their thinking was practical, and they remembered that they had enjoyed some practical benefits under Taliban rule.

CHAPTER 19

THE COMING OF ISLAM

THE TALIBAN WERE infamous outside Afghanistan precisely for their ideology—their exaggerated and rigid interpretation of Islam. To the rest of the world at the end of the twentieth century, Afghanistan was a symbol for the Muslim faith, in its scariest manifestation. Yet Islam is not indigenous to Afghanistan. In fact, it took some time gaining a foothold in that rocky land.

Paradoxically, this makes Afghans proud. A man boasted to me once about some graves in Kabul believed to be the tombs of Companions of Prophet Muhammad. The holy men had died trying to conquer Afghanistan, he explained to me, manifestly proud that Kabul boasted such sacred resting places. But it was a source of equal pride to him that Afghans had killed the would-be conquerors. It was like the Arab cemetery near my first home in Kandahar, where people visited the Al-Qaeda graves for their intercession value, even though they had hated having Arabs rule their town.

Given the Afghans' fierce and obviously complex attachment to their religion—the one thing, many say, that binds them together despite the searing scars cutting across tribes and ethnic groups—it seemed critical to me to come to a documented understanding of how Islam really did reach Afghanistan.

The place to start this quest was C. E. Bosworth, another Brit with two initials. He is the don, the absolute authority on the region around southern Afghanistan in the early Islamic period. He had recently retired from his professorship at Manchester University, as I found when I sent him this chapter to see if it would fly.

I photocopied his seminal monograph, *Sistan Under the Arabs*.[1] To my surprise, I discovered among his sources for an early chapter several famous Persian poems. I hardly expected epic legends to be a foundation for a scholarly work of history. Nor did these particular poems seem to be all that relevant. They are the legends of Persia, as important to the national identity of Iran as Homer is to Greeks, even more visceral than Chaucer or Beowulf for England. But how, I wondered, did these Iranian folktales apply to the region that interested Bosworth—and me: southern Afghanistan at the time of the Muslim conquests?

I tracked down some volumes of this poetry to try to figure it out, and started reading in an old French translation:

"After terrible suffering and great travails, King Jamshid climbed up to Zabulistan," went one fairy-tale line.

Zabulistan? I put down the book and actually clapped my hands. I had my answer. Zabul is the province immediately to the northeast of Kandahar, on the main road to Kabul. This Jamshid fellow and the other Iranian folkheroes that I had always connected with the heart and soul of Persia were not from Iran at all, it seemed. They had lived in my neck of the woods, the region around Kandahar. That was a discovery in and of itself.

I picked up the copied page and went on.

> [Jamshid] caught sight of a city so beautiful it resembled paradise:
> its gates, its plain, its mountains were all gardens and cultivation.
> Its habitat was good, its fruits fresh, its prosperity recent, its earth
> joyful, its water light, its air soft. It was full of merchandise,
> crowds, and courageous men.[2]

The description didn't fit any of the dry baked-mud towns *I* had seen; but perhaps things had changed since those mythical days. For what I was reading was nothing less than a creation myth—every bit as gritty and anthropomorphic and pagan as the Gilgamesh story or the Greek tales of the Titans and the Olympians.

Just after the dawn of time, according to these epic poems, King Jamshid ruled Iran. His father had subjugated the demons and the birds and evil spirits, leaving Jamshid centuries of leisure to order the affairs of men. He invented armor and textiles; he divided his subjects into the classes of priests, warriors, and craftsmen; and he set the demons to work as masons and architects.

But Jamshid grew arrogant, and "a mighty discontent arose through-out Iran."[3] Disgruntled nobles replaced him with Zahhak the Evil-Doer, from whose shoulders two serpents sprouted; they had to be fed a daily ra-tion of fresh human flesh. Jamshid was in hiding, for Zahhak had pro-claimed that whoever caught him and delivered him bound hand and foot would receive a great reward.

And so Jamshid became a ghost of the byways, a sovereign reduced to beggary, in constant flight until he reached the land of Zabulistan—roughly the region of modern Kandahar. There he fathered the dynasty of Iran's national heroes.

It was during the eleventh century A.D., about five hundred years after the birth of Islam, that tales such as this began to be collected, translated from the archaic tongue that had conserved them, Pahlavi, and rendered into the exuberant poetry of a new language: Persian, or Farsi. This liter-ary blossoming was part of an extraordinary Iranian renaissance that was to transform the culture of Central and South Asia over the course of the next six hundred years. It, just as much as the religion of Islam, defines the character of modern Afghanistan.

I had some familiarity with this terrain, and found myself drawing on knowledge buried since my stint in grad school as I plunged into Bosworth's exposition.

In the early 600s, the great Persian Empire was sacked—morally and materially—by the conquests of the Muslim Arabs. They exploded on camels from the barren desert, armed with their novel religion, Islam. Iran, which included most of today's Iraq, was the land of the king of kings and elaborate courtly culture, of complex linguistic overlays and choreographed rituals in honor of absolutism. And it came crashing down under the lance thrusts of barbarians raised on a diet of dates and milk. Nothing like this had happened to Iran since Alexander the Great tore a swathe through it about nine hundred years earlier. Even compared to Alexander's uncouth Macedonians—rowdy drinkers and vocal egalitarians, violently suspicious of Persian hierarchy—the Arabs must have looked pretty rough. It took Iran centuries to recover.

But gradually, fertilized by the new sounds of the Arabic language and the elegant curves of its evolving script, by Islam's leveling piety, by the intellectual challenges of studying the new holy texts and seeking their meaning, of the quest for scientific knowledge and the struggle to hammer out new judicial principles in line with the new ethos, and by the eventual need for the administrative tools of empire, Iranian culture was reborn. Starting in the tenth and eleventh centuries, it spread eastward so powerfully and took such a hold that it was able to win over the hearts and minds of all the successive waves of later conquerors.[4]

The poetry that recounted the exploits of mythic heroes like Jamshid was at the forefront of this cultural reawakening. It was infused with a new Iranian consciousness. The Iranians are the good guys, beset on all sides by monstrous foes. And the language of the epics, an oral vernacular that had seldom been transcribed in the past, is defiantly Persian. While different from the old imperial Pahlavi or the Aramaic of the ancient scribes, it contains almost no Arabic neologisms, which were studding spoken Persian by then. The poets, reveling in the invention of their new literary language, took pains to avoid Arabic words.

Yet there is one striking aspect of these stories whose aim is to celebrate Iran—as I was only now discovering. Their heroes, the champions who time and again rescue Iran's honor and increase her lands or sail out to discover marvels for the shah, do not hail from the heart of the Iranian kingdom, but from its eastern marches. The heroes—Jamshid, Zal, Rustam, Garshasp—come from Kandahar.[5]

And so, though the actual details I was reading were fancifully ahistorical, I would surely discover some truths about the past of the Kandahar region buried in the epic poetry, like almonds studding a gossamer sweet.

By far the most renowned and influential of the books is the *Shahnama*, or the *Book of Kings*, written in the first quarter of the eleventh century by a poet named Abul-Qasim Firdowsi. Its chief hero is Rustam. In the story, his centuries-long life spans the reigns of several Iranian kings.

Born via cesarean-section, Rustam has already accomplished various exploits when the first event really defining his heroic identity takes place. He chooses a horse that will be his lifelong companion. "I need a horse of mountain height," he declares, "one that no man but myself can take with a lasoo."[6]

And so all of the horses in Zabulistan and Kabulistan are driven before him. Rustam places a hand on the back of each, and each one's spine gives under the pressure. They won't do. "At last there arrived a troop from Kabul, and a spate of horses of every color rushed before him." A colt catches his eye, whose "skin was bright and dappled as though flecked with the petals of red roses on saffron." But the herdsman warns Rustam away, for whenever anyone draws near this colt, his dam "comes forward and fights like a lion."[7]

Grasping the sense of the omen, Rustam lassos the mare, overcomes her, and gains his four-footed comrade in arms.

As a backdrop, this episode evokes the importance of the Kabul-to-Kandahar zone in the transcontinental horse trade that was crucial to war making for centuries. Neither Iran, nor especially India, was as suited to raising horses as were the highland plateaus of this region. The animals foaled there, or those driven overland from Central Asia of the grassy steppes, often spent a season near Kandahar to rest and fatten up. Chaman, the name of that Pakistani border-town where my Achekzai friends live, means "grass" or "field." The sight of those great herds of horses, pasturing in the city's environs as they awaited the spring and fall fairs, must have punctuated the rhythm of Kandaharis' lives. As late as the eighteenth and nineteenth centuries, Afghans from near Kandahar still dominated the horse trade that provisioned the British army in India.[8]

Examined more closely, the tale of Rustam and his horse Rakhsh echoes the historical encounter of Alexander the Great and his horse Bucephalas—which had momentous ramifications for Afghanistan.

The fiery steed Bucephalas, when presented at the royal court for inspection, was so aggressive that no one dared approach him, let alone throw a leg across his back. Disgusted, Alexander's father, Philip of Macedon, waved at the groom to take him away. But young Alexander instantly perceived the animal's worth. He made a bet with his father, and, understanding that Bucephalas was afraid, he mastered the creature with kindness and the complicit awareness of a shared destiny. And so was born one of the most profound friendships between a man and a beast in recorded history.[9]

It was Bucephalas who carried Alexander the Great on an earth-shattering campaign of conquest and discovery across Iran and Central Asia and through the border areas—where he founded a city near Kandahar on his way to India.[10] Alexander appears in many of the Persian epics, including the *Shahnama*. But he is a purely whimsical character who does little more than gallivant around discovering fabulous creatures and strangely garbed humans. It is not surprising that such a telling incident as the gaining of an unrivaled horse should be transposed to Iran's most emblematic hero, Rustam.

Another animal appears frequently on the field of battle in the Persian epics: the elephant. Rustam himself is often referred to as "elephant bodied," and his earliest feat was to kill the king's white elephant, which had gone on a rampage. The colossal elephant, with its utterly improbable nose and curving tusks, appears in the Persian poems not in the catalog of marvelous or mythical animals, as it did in Western medieval texts, but as an ordinary element of the royal household. For example, "The king's elephant advanced in the midst of the army, with golden bells and cymbals upon it."[11] It is a symbol of strength and courage in battle. The elephant's unremarkable presence in these stories attests to the cultural proximity, to their audience, of that other great basin of civilization: neighboring India.

In Kandahar, above the north side of town, a ragged chain of hills bars the way to leafy Arghandab and Khakrez beyond. The one on the end, a bit apart from the others, rests its trunk vertically along its front legs till it touches the ground. It is called Elephant Rock.

Kandahar has, age after age, marked the border between Iran and India. The struggle between the Safavis and the Moghuls was just a late chapter in a long tale. After Alexander's death on the road in 323 B.C.—and a murderous, double-crossing, eye-clawing struggle for his succession—his general Seleucus Nikator gained sway over the part of the far-flung new empire that included the lands of modern Afghanistan. But Seleucus abandoned the region to the first Mauryan emperor of India. In fact, he *sold* Kandahar to India for the sum of five hundred elephants.[12]

That delicious fact was lodged in another book I found on my visit to the Kabul library. It was an analysis of some inscriptions cut into a rock face, which archaeologists discovered in Kandahar in 1957.

The Indian ruler who ordered the inscriptions, Ashoka, was a grandson of the emperor who had bought Kandahar. Ashoka reigned from around 270 to 233 B.C.. Inspired by Buddhism, he published a series of edicts encouraging nonviolence and tolerance and giving advice on how to live a happy life. The westernmost of these edicts is carved into the face of a rock wall outside Kandahar. Constant warfare in recent decades has effaced the memory of its location. (In 2002, an official of the UN educational agency, UNESCO, asked me if I could locate it for him. I could not.)

The Ashoka Edict is written in two languages—not the emperor's native Sanskrit, the language of his Indian heartlands, but Aramaic, the official written language of the Persian people living from Kandahar westward into Iran, and Greek, spoken in the colonies left behind by Alexander.[13] Kandahar, then known as Harahuraka or Arachosia (later pronounced by the Muslim Arabs as the Rukhkhaj district of Zabulistan), still marked the very northwestern reaches of the Indian empire.

But in Firdowsi's much later epic poem, the hero Rustam is not primarily preoccupied with challenges to Iran coming from India. Though his native Zabulistan borders Hindustan, the bulk of his epic struggle is with an enemy from a different quarter: the kingdom of Turan, or Central Asia and China. Rustam is forever challenging the Turanians, or rescuing his king from defeat at their hands. The poem's obsessive focus on the lands to the north and east of Iran was to prove prescient. It was from those steppes that, two hundred years after the *Shahnama* was written, the next wave of devastating conquest would crash down upon Iran: Genghis Khan and his Mongols.

Throughout his long life, Rustam of Zabulistan behaves as a model vassal to the shahs of Iran. He marches all the way to China to rescue one, though agreeing privately with a friend that the shah "had not a brain in his head."[14] To his successor, Rustam proposes a great campaign against Turan with the aim of regaining a wayward territory.[15] The heroes always send back a generous portion of the gifts and plunder they win abroad to their liege lords, the rulers of Iran. And whenever Iran is in truly dire straits, it is to these heroes that the rulers dash off a letter of summons. And they always come.

Only once, toward the end of his long life, does Rustam disobey his king's command. The monarch of that age feared a challenge from one of his own sons, so he sent the disobedient prince on a risky mission to bring Rustam to court in chains.

For it appears that Rustam now "reckons himself no man's vassal." He will not raise a finger for the king. When a difficulty befalls his ruler, he is far from the scene. And he never visits anymore. "For such a time as he continues to exist," the king tells his son, "the lands of Zabulistan, Bost, Ghazni and Kabulistan belong to him." In other words, the bent tract of southern Afghanistan running from Helmand Province west of Kandahar, turning at the city, and heading northeastward up to Kabul.

The prince does not wish to fight the admired Rustam. So he suggests a ruse to conciliate his father. What if Rustam would just allow himself to be shackled in chains for form. Then, the prince says, "I will intercede with my father and change his heart. I will let no harm come to Rustam."

But though the hero offers to go humbly to the king, to kiss his head and foot and both his eyes and beg his forgiveness, this is one concession he cannot make. "Shame would overwhelm me . . . shame that would never be blotted out. No man will ever see me alive and in fetters." The two fight, and Rustam kills the prince.[16]

Thus, in the Persian epic poetry, Zabulistan—Kandahar—remains outside the royal power, an ungovernable *yaghestan*.

This theme—the incorrigible independence of Zabulistan—does indeed reflect reality. For, five hundred years before the epic authors penned their works, what is now southern and eastern Afghanistan did withstand the most important conquest of the age: the seventh-century onslaught of the Muslim Arabs, which swept one empire before it and rocked another, which within eighty years reached all the way across Africa to the shores of Spain. C. E. Bosworth's monograph confirmed the legend for me. For decades on end, the Muslims launched sterile border raids against that *yaghestan*, without being able to add it to their empire. When they hungered for India, they had to sidestep Kandahar, a few times even taking to their boats to attack the subcontinent by sea.

Thinking back over what I knew about the Bedouin Arabs, I realized

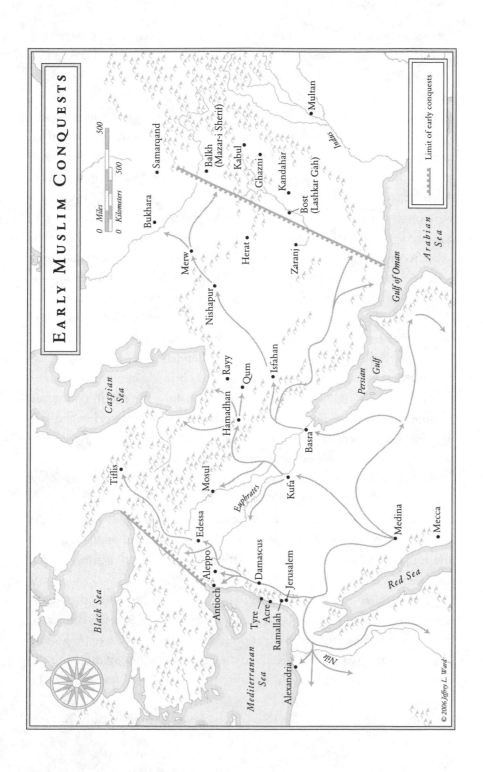

EARLY MUSLIM CONQUESTS

Limit of early conquests

0 Miles 500
0 Kilometers 500

Black Sea

Caspian Sea

Mediterranean Sea

Red Sea

Persian Gulf

Gulf of Oman

Arabian Sea

Tiflis
Edessa
Antioch
Aleppo
Tyre
Acre
Ramallah
Damascus
Jerusalem
Alexandria
Nile
Mosul
Kufa
Basra
Euphrates
Medina
Mecca
Hamadhan
Rayy
Qum
Isfahan
Nishapur
Merw
Bukhara
Samarqand
Balkh
(Mazar-i Sherif)
Kabul
Ghazni
Kandahar
Bost
(Lashkar Gah)
Multan
Indus
Herat
Zaranj

© 2006 Jeffrey L. Ward

that the original audience for the Prophet Muhammad's revelation resembled in many ways a bunch of Kandaharis. The Arabs' social structure was relentlessly tribal; they inhabited a trackless wilderness that supported little agriculture, so they lived off commerce arriving along the caravan routes, tolls collected on those same routes, and, of course, plunder and "protection" from plunder. For years, Arab tribes spent their leisure time raiding one another. Pre-Islamic Arabic poetry is full of the exploits of the *ghazis*, bold warriors who would lead sorties against neighboring tribes, driving away rustled camels and horses—much the way the Achekzais were forever stealing their neighbors' sheep for ransom.

The very first achievement of Islam was to federate these rival Arab tribes, to unite the Bedouin and offer them a focus of allegiance other than tribe. Battles following Muhammad's death in 632 were fought against groups that broke away from the nascent Muslim community. Called the Ridda wars, the wars of apostasy, they probably had little to do with apostasy in the sense of a rejection of faith or dogma—since the content of Muslim faith and dogma had yet to be fully defined, and since many members of these recalcitrant tribes had never even put aside their own religions. They had joined the Muslims in the traditional fashion of forging a temporary alliance. The Ridda wars were aimed at countering this traditional perfidy, at enforcing a new unity of the Arabs under the leadership of Muhammad's community in Medina.

But once this unity was achieved, once it was established that Muslims should not kill Muslims—that Muslim tribes should not indulge in raids against each other—what was to be done with the energies of the *ghazis*? And where were these desert dwellers, who produced only milk and meat and rough woolen cloth and some dates, to get the surplus they needed for a decent life?

It was largely to answer these questions, as well as to carry the teaching of Muhammad to other Bedouin living outside the Arabian Peninsula, that the great campaigns of Arab conquest were launched. As one leading scholar of early Islam, Hugh Kennedy, analyzes it, "Only by directing the energies of the tribesmen against an outside enemy could the unity of the Muslim state be preserved."[17]

These Bedouin Arabs, like Kandaharis, were famously unruly. To keep them under control, a tight discipline was enforced on the military campaigns. Tribesmen were sent out under a commander, and a garrison city was usually founded to house them as they subdued the land around, or to serve as a base for further expansion. Kufa and Basra in today's Iraq were the most famous. There the Bedouin lived apart from the local population, their unity and distinctiveness reinforced by the practice of their new religion, Islam.

It was Umar, the second caliph to lead the community after Muhammad's death, who instituted a code for religious practice in the garrisons. He promoted officials on the basis of seniority: those who had converted first to Islam. He sent out Qur'an readers, men who could recite the entire revelation of Muhammad from memory and instruct their listeners in its significance. He fixed the times of the five daily prayers and upheld the ascetic simplicity of the desert as a pious standard for men sorely tempted by the riches of the lands they conquered—was intransigent, for example, on drunkenness, that scourge of soldiers everywhere. Like U.S. army bases in the Balkans or Afghanistan, the Muslim garrison towns were strictly dry. This may be the origin of one of Islam's most distinguishing obligations.[18]

By the mid–650s, just twenty or so years after the death of Muhammad, the Muslim Arabs had established a foothold in the town of Zaranj, clear across the Iranian plateau from their Arabian heartland. It stands at the far eastern fringes of Iran, on modern Afghanistan's border, where it is now the capital of Nimruz Province. In another of the Persian epic poems, *The Book of Garshasp,* the hero discovers its oasis after traversing a windy desert "that lion and devil fled from; its soft earth was sand, its hard earth was salt."[19] Garshasp brings back famous engineers and astrologers from Byzantium and India and founds the town, erecting earthen ramparts around it, building the fort inside high as the moon, and diverting springs from the Helmand River to provide water.[20]

When the Arabs reached it, Zaranj was indeed a sturdy city, swept by the same wind that whips dust through Kandahar some four hundred miles to the east of it. Its battlements were probably designed to hold back the gale-driven encroachments of the desert as much as the attacks of enemies. Captured with difficulty, it rebelled several times against the Muslim garrison commanders appointed to rule over it.

As Zaranj was being subdued and turned into a Muslim garrison town, the first campaigns to push yet farther eastward clashed against the ruler of the land of legend: Zabulistan. That was the name of the region from Kandahar to Kabul in truth as well as in fable, and the title of its ruler apparently sounded something like "Zunbil."

Very little is known about this line of local princes, who spent their summers in Ghazni and their winters near Kandahar, or their subjects, except that they "inhibited the advance of Islam here for a long time to come."[21] Politically and ethnically, they seem to have been the flotsam of the Hephthalite kingdom, which took over the area in the mid-fifth century in one of the innumerable southward migrations of steppe peoples. By the end of the sixth century, the kingdom's glory days were over, but some of its provincial leaders clung to the rocks around Kandahar. As was the case in this region during the Soviet invasion, it appears that it was the dissolution of government into small units with tenacious local roots that allowed it to avert conquest by a foreign empire.

For the Muslim expansion ground to a halt here for some two hundred years.

As for the pre-Islamic religion of Zabulistan, it has aroused much unsatisfied curiosity. It does not seem to have been Buddhism, which had a rich history and a continuing presence in those parts. One story has a troop of Arabs entering the main shrine to the god Zun, in 654, where they broke off the votive statue's hand and put out its ruby eyes to prove its impotence.[22] Some scholars suggest a cult of sun worship. Another evokes a deity whose traces have come down to us in the Persian epic cycle: Rustam's father, Zal, a variant reading of whose name matches a variant reading of Zun.[23]

At times the Muslims enjoyed victories against the zunbils of Zabulistan, as in the late 660s. Commanders under orders from Basra fought in Zabulistan and finally secured the zunbil's surrender. The region was supposed to pay tribute to the Muslims ever after.

But whenever tribal factionalism or religious disputes broke out among the garrison Arabs, or during the ragged transitions from one Muslim governor to the next, the non-Muslim people of Zabulistan were quick to throw off their allegiance, sometimes even attacking westward into Muslim lands.

Thus did Bosworth, bless him, set the scene for me. But now I was getting hungry for a primary source. I wanted to know how this chronic confrontation on the Muslim frontier had actually gone down, since their protracted rebellion was such a key feature of Afghans' self-consciousness.

This time I didn't have to hunt in the back reaches of the Kabul library. Several early Muslim historians chronicled the Arab conquests year by year. I had read some of them in the text in Arabic class long before. Muhammad ibn Jarir at-Tabari was the greatest of these historians, who were often legal scholars as well. He died in 923. Tabari, like his colleagues, is careful to trace back the version of events he describes through a scrutinized chain of transmitters to an original eyewitness—roughly in the fashion of modern footnoting. Now an excellent translation of Tabari has been published in multiple volumes, each one edited by a different scholar, all working simultaneously, so the work did not take a lifetime to complete.

In the pages of this history I found yearly updates on the status of the Arabs' never-ending war against the zunbils of Zabulistan.

The following series of episodes, disastrous for the Arabs, took place at the very end of the seventh century. This was when the whole Muslim east was ruled by one of the most formidable characters in the history of Islam, al-Hajjaj ibn Yusuf. This viceroy to two caliphs—brilliant general, ruthless decision maker, and assiduous nation builder—almost single-handedly held the vast empire together for a quarter century.

"Zunbil had been under a truce, with the Arabs collecting land taxes from him," writes Tabari, in his *History of the Prophets and Kings*.[24] "But he had several times . . . refused to pay." (The *yaghestan* principle.) The terrible Hajjaj, from headquarters back in Iraq, dispatched orders to his Zaranj garrison commander to inflict an exemplary punishment on the zunbil. "Take the field against him . . . and do not return until you have plundered his land, pulled down his fortresses, killed his fighting men, and enslaved his women."

The commander set out from Zaranj and did rather well—at first. He "penetrated into the lands of Zunbil, seizing cattle, sheep, and other property as he wished, and razing strongholds and castles. He conquered a great deal of their territory, as Zunbil's forces fell back from one land after another."[25]

It is not hard to imagine what the Muslim camp must have looked like by this time, with flocks of sheep and goats trailing from its flanks, tents gaudily decorated with booty and frightened women, the Arab tribesmen heady with their easy victory.

And then things go wrong. Having lured the Arabs deep into hostile territory, the zunbil's forces deftly skirt them and take up positions along the highland "passes and defiles" behind them, cutting them off. This trick, which worked against the Soviets more than a millennium later, was a classic element of steppe warfare that the rump Hephthalites had apparently brought with them from their northern grasslands.

Like his predecessor who had fallen into the same trap, the beleaguered Muslim commander was ready to sue for peace. He even offered to pay the zunbil good money "in exchange for safe passage out of here." There followed a shouting match with his deputy, who argued that any ransom paid to the zunbil would be docked from all their wages, and that surrendering would weaken Islam on the frontier.

The mutinous deputy calls out to tribesmen wishing for martyrdom to join him. His commander snorts: "You are an old man and have gone senile." A few of the Arab *ghazis* do follow the deputy, and are cut to pieces by the zunbil's army.

And so the Muslims are forced to beat an ignominious retreat back across that rock-hard land to Zaranj. It was, like the British retreat over some of that ground in 1880, hell. The Arabs must have been starving, for some accounts have them eating their horses, and Tabari describes their friends riding out from the garrison to meet them with provisions, but "when one of them ate his fill of the food, he would perish."[26]

The commandant-governor of Zaranj dies of grief, no doubt fortunately for him. One can only imagine the temper of al-Hajjaj ibn Yusuf when he got wind of this latest disaster in Zabulistan. He fires off a letter to the caliph in Damascus. "I want to send out against them a massive force of men from the two garrisons," he writes. For otherwise, "I fear that Zunbil and his infidels will overrun the entire frontier."[27]

The caliph replies that Hajjaj is to follow his own judgment. The terrible viceroy appoints a new commandant-governor to Zaranj, 'Abd ar-Rahman ibn al-Ash'ath, whose abilities must have been hard to match, for Hajjaj is said to detest him. The bare sight of this man entering a room is enough to make Hajjaj whisper to a subordinate: "Look at the way he walks! By God, I would like to cut off his head!" Nevertheless, Hajjaj hires him.

Then the viceroy turns his prodigious energies to readying troops for the offensive, "devoting himself to this task with great zeal." The men get full pay up front and are ordered to muster with the very best in horses and accoutrements. Hajjaj reviews the troops with ibn al-Ash'ath, and pays out bonuses to fighters who have not stinted on their equipment. So dazzling is this huge force, the men decked out in gorgeous cloth, the sun glinting off stirrups and spear points, that it is dubbed the Peacock Army.

Ibn al-Ash'ath handles the campaign with rather more skill and foresight than his predecessors. When the zunbil of Zabulistan withdraws before him, as usual, ibn al-Ash'ath decides to occupy the vacated land, "sending out a tax official over it, accompanied by armed attendants. He also set up a postal service between the various areas, positioned lookouts in the passes and ravines, and stationed advance parties in every dangerous spot." In other words, ibn al-Ash'ath plans to annex Zabulistan, not just raid it for booty.

He understands that the effort to bring the denizens of this *yaghestan* into the fold of the Muslim empire will take time. Once his army has mastered a fair chunk of ground—probably extending to Kandahar—he halts, saying, "We will content ourselves with the territory we have conquered this year until we get to know it and we can collect the taxes, and Muslims can boldly travel its roads." And only then, he says, will the army push farther. He writes to al-Hajjaj ibn Yusuf, explaining this sensible course.[28]

This course, alone, has proven effective in modern instances of post-conflict nation building.

Hajjaj, however, hits the ceiling. He fires back no fewer than three letters, vilifying ibn al-Ash'ath, and his "weakness and confused judgment."[29] Heaping on further scorn in this vein, Hajjaj commands ibn al-Ash'ath to renew his attack on the zunbil, or see himself sent back to the ranks and forced to fight as a simple soldier.

And that, for a highborn Arab chieftain, is mortal insult. Ibn al-Ash'ath musters his Peacock Army and calls on his *ghazis* to join him in a revolt against the viceroy. He reminds them how he consulted with their delegates about halting the offensive, how he took account of their views. And Hajjaj, he thunders, "charged me with incompetence and weakness and ordered me to hasten the business of taking you far into the territory of the enemy—that being the territory in which your brethren perished but yesterday."

In rousing words, ibn al-Ash'ath tells his soldiers: "I am one of you. I go forth when you go forth, and I balk when you balk." Then he asks his men to "disavow Hajjaj, the enemy of God, and fight against him until God expels him from the land of Iraq." To a man, the fighters shout an oath of allegiance to ibn al-Ash'ath.

The ensuing Revolt of the Peacock Army almost brought down the Muslim Arab empire.

One of the reasons the troops were so willing to rise up is that Hajjaj was a relentless hard-ass and they had had it with his authoritarianism. Another reason is that the nature of the garrison cities was changing. Arab civilians had been migrating eastward to fill up the lands the Muslim armies had been capturing. Some soldiers began bringing their families to settle in the garrisons; others were arranging for local brides. Zaranj was turning into an ordinary Muslim town. And so the fighters were unhappy at the prospect of a prolonged campaign in murderous territory against the zunbil of Zabulistan. They had more to lose. They were less convinced of the point of the war.

The leaders of the revolt appealed directly to these sentiments. The tyrannical Hajjaj, one of them shouted, "does not care that he is taking chances with you." Another rebel predicted, "He will keep you out in the field in the manner of Pharaoh"—the pharaoh of ancient Egypt being the archetype, in the Qur'an, of the unjust ruler. "I think most of you will be dead before seeing your loved ones."

Before leaving Zabulistan, ibn al-Ash'ath sealed a pact with his erstwhile foe the zunbil. If the revolt succeeded, ibn al-Ash'ath promised, the zunbil's lands would be excused from tribute for the rest of his life. And if ibn al-Ash'ath was defeated and had to flee, the zunbil would give him refuge.

And that is what eventually happened. But it was a near thing. Ibn al-Ash'ath beat the great Hajjaj in a pitched battle in central Iran, then actually captured Basra and Kufa, the two tent poles of the Muslim empire. The caliph offered generous peace terms. Ibn al-Ash'ath would have accepted them, but his rebels, fired up, refused.

When they finally were overcome, it still took more than a year for the caliph's armies to force ibn al-Ash'ath back, in a fighting retreat, to the eastern frontier. There, the friend he had left in charge of Zaranj slammed the city gates in his face. Ibn al-Ash'ath pushed farther eastward to Bost on the road to Kandahar—now Lashkar Gah, the capital of Helmand Province. His deputy at Bost did worse: he welcomed ibn al-Ash'ath inside and then "pounced on him and put him in bonds," hoping thus to curry favor with Hajjaj.

It was the zunbil of Zabulistan who kept faith. He descended on Bost, besieged it, and demanded ibn al-Ash'ath's freedom. "By God," Tabari has the zunbil warn, "if you cause him so much harm as a speck of dust in his eye, or deprive his head of a single hair, I shall not leave the battlefield until I bring you down and kill all who are with you, take your offspring captive, and divide your property among my troops."[30] Ibn al-Ash'ath's treacherous deputy is sufficiently cowed, and releases the rebel.

The zunbil escorted ibn al-Ash'ath to Zabulistan, where he graciously "lodged him and did him honor"—him and the hundreds or perhaps thousands of defeated fighters clinging to his stirrup leathers.

It was not until 704, about five years after the revolt, that the zunbil finally gave ibn al-Ash'ath's head to al-Hajjaj ibn Yusuf. And the mighty viceroy paid a high price for it. Depending on the versions, Hajjaj agreed not to attack Zabulistan for a decade, or not to take tribute from it for some years. The Muslim empire was saved.

But so was the independence of Kandahar and surrounding Zabulistan. For the next 150 years, the best the Muslims could do was send the occasional load of plunder or string of slaves back from its border.[31]

It took a local boy to bring Islam to Zabulistan.

By the mid–850s, a century and a half later, the Muslim garrison town of Zaranj and its surrounding region had settled into the turbulent life of a perpetual frontier. This is C. E. Bosworth's domain, so I relied on him for a picture.

Far from the center of caliphal power in Damascus and later Baghdad, the eastern province of the Muslim empire never sent taxes back to the capital very graciously; it often did not send them at all. It became a proving ground for rowdy young sons bent on adventure, and a refuge for upstarts and insurgents driven out of the heart of the empire—much the way the American West harbored rebels-turned-bandit like Jesse James.

The most stubborn of these insurgents was a group of wooly-haired extremists called the Kharijis. The roots of their movement went all the way back to a struggle for leadership of the young Muslim community two hundred years before, between the Prophet Muhammad's brother-in-law Mu'awiya, and his cousin and son-in-law 'Ali. This is the same dispute that led to the greatest split within Islam, between the Sunnis and the Shi'is. The original Kharijis—many of them the pious Qur'an readers sent out to the garrisons to instruct the troops—had backed 'Ali. But they withdrew their support during the quarrel, feeling that he had violated their shared principles by negotiating a settlement and that all he was really after was power.

Most of these Kharijis were killed then and there, but a few escaped and collected in little bands and communities of fighters, set apart from the main body of Muslims. They developed an extreme, inflexible interpretation of their faith, rejecting urban influences and looking back to the Bedouin lifestyle. Living largely off plunder and booty, they insisted that only their reading of Islam was true: anyone who disagreed was an infidel.

The lines of transmission may not be direct, but their attitude resembles that of Usama bin Laden and his Afghan hosts, the Taliban. The Kharijis would cause trouble for the Muslim empire for hundreds of years.

By the ninth century they had been mostly cleared out of the heartlands and parts of the Persian Gulf where they had established colonies. They hung on along the eastern frontier of the empire, on the border with Zabulistan. There they were to be found in the countryside, preying on travelers and villages. Zaranj remained a garrison town manned by troops, so the Kharijis could not stray too near. Still, they did often raid, and sometimes concluded agreements with the commandant-governors of Zaranj or Bost to the east.[32]

Often they would join forces with their peasant neighbors and victims in revolt against the Zaranj tax gatherers, or with other displaced people who fetched up on the frontier. They also raided farther eastward, across the border of the empire into Zabulistan. Some evidence indicates they may have set down roots there, perhaps taking over the town of Gardez, to the east of Ghazni.[33] But by this time, it is unclear the degree to which the Kharijis were animated by questions of religious doctrine, or by the marauding lifestyle they had adopted.

Despite constant efforts, the commandant-governors of Zaranj were not able to eradicate them. The days when al-Hajjaj ibn Yusuf could extend his iron fist all the way to the border of the Muslim empire were long gone; the caliphate was beset by local risings everywhere, and could no longer supply the combination of supervision and support that a central government owes its provinces.

And so some townsmen of Zaranj and Bost began organizing ad hoc self-defense teams, taking upon themselves the task of battling the heretical Kharijis. But the name that has stuck to these posses—*ayyars*—translates roughly to "brigands." It appears that in choosing to live by the sword, these *ayyars* succumbed in turn to the lifestyle, and the fight against the Kharijis became an excuse for their own brand of marauding.

Into this swashbuckling atmosphere was born, somewhere around 835, to a coppersmith in a village off the Zaranj-to-Bost road, Ya'qub ibn Layth. It was he who would finally defeat the zunbil for the Muslims and bring Islam to Zabulistan.

True to local custom, stories pin the start of Ya'qub ibn Layth's career to a highway robbery. A great caravan, in one version, is approaching Zaranj from Iraq; its representatives send ahead to the governor for an escort through Khariji-infested country. Ya'qub and his band of *ayyars* find out; they hide in a tower and ambush the escort on its way to meet the caravan. Helping themselves to arms and horses, the brigands ride ahead to fall upon the caravan—whooping the Khariji war cry to confuse their victims.

Like Ahmad Shah Durrani nine hundred years later, if on a smaller scale, Ya'qub thus demonstrated to his companions that they had something to gain by riding with him.

Ya'qub and his followers joined another band of *ayyars*, and together they fought and faked their way to Zaranj, the provincial capital, which they captured and then quarreled over. In 861, Ya'qub ibn Layth had won out and was recognized by the people of Zaranj as their commander. But he still had to defeat his former *ayyar* chief, who had fallen back on Bost.

This he did in 864. The battle took place in Kandahar, where Ya'qub's *ayyar* opponent had joined forces with the zunbil of Zabulistan. The zunbil was killed in the fray, unhorsed, it is said, by Ya'qub himself.

The full annexation of the region and its conversion to Islam took many more years—Ya'qub waged another major campaign against Zabulistan in 870, and Kandahar proved especially hard for the Muslim invaders to reduce. But the determination of Ya'qub, a truly local Muslim ruler, who was schooled in the tricks of banditry and who enjoyed the support of the turbulent frontier folk from whom he sprang, would gradually break down the independence of Zabulistan.[34]

Like the poetic folk heroes Rustam and Garshasp, Ya'qub ibn Layth never forgot to send back a share of plunder to the liege lord of all Muslims, the commander of the faithful, the caliph of Baghdad. According to the chronicles, the capital was agog at the four-armed copper idol of a female deity, girt with two silver belts set with jewels, which arrived from near Kabul.[35]

But, again like Rustam and Garshasp, Ya'qub's submission to Baghdad was only token. At last he turned his armies westward, and pushed his conquests well into the lands of his nominal overlord. In 876, he was advancing on the capital, Baghdad.

For fifty years, Ya'qub's family, called the Saffarids,[36] ruled much of the Muslim empire. Their domain, bordered by Kandahar and Kabul in the east, reached westward across most of Iran. Then the tables were turned, and Ya'qub ibn Layth's successors were pushed back to their native Zaranj, where the Saffarids carried on as local rulers for almost a century.

The Saffarid conquests are seen as one of the first real breaches in the territorial integrity of the Muslim empire. After the turn of the tenth century, no one could ever again claim to unite the disparate Muslim communities under a single government. And so in a sense, the eastern *yaghestan*—including the Kandahar region—remained unfettered even after its conversion to Islam.

Ya'qub ibn Layth was a local boy, and he spoke Persian. One evening, after a victory at Herat, he is said to have cut short the poet who was singing his praises in Arabic. "Why must I listen to this stuff I can't understand," a local historian quotes him saying, more or less.[37] His chancellor hastily improvised some lines in Persian, borrowing an Arabic meter to distinguish them from the minstrels' ditties that were all that existed in Persian at the time.

This man became the court poet. He sang Ya'qub's exploits in his invented Persian meter, helping spark a literary revolution. It was his work that led the way to the *Shahnama* and the *Book of Garshasp*, which celebrated the exploits of those other east-frontier local boys, Jamshid and Garshasp and Rustam.

CHAPTER 20

HOW TO FIRE A WARLORD

THE SWASHBUCKLING, FRONTIER atmosphere of those ancient days never really left Kandahar. It is still present now. There is always a sense of unchecked power, a feeling that violence might strike, and with impunity. The feeling lurks beneath the surface; my usual tack was to vigorously ignore it, and get on with the day-to-day. Sometimes that was not entirely possible.

One chill morning we were bringing in a blackened metal barrel, belatedly blowing the dust off it and attaching a length of jointed pipe to make it into a woodstove. It would soon be truly cold on our plateau, after the insufferable heat. And not a radiator in sight. I would pile a wool blanket on top of a U.S. Army-issue sleeping bag—goodies handed out to anti-Taliban proxies during the war—and still I slept fully clothed.

As we were tugging on the pipe, trying to wedge it into the hole cut for the purpose high on one of the walls, and then sealing the joint with a strip of cloth dipped in gypsum, one of Ahmad Wali Karzai's men arrived with a message asking me to see him. This was rare.

We still ate Ahmad Wali's food at Afghans for Civil Society—a priceless donation. We would send someone around to the tiny outdoor kitchen where two or three cooks wielding washtub-sized pots prepared meals for a hundred over wood-fire embers. Our man would line up with the others and bring back the stewed lamb and potatoes and rice in steel bowls—and when we were lucky, some okra.

In this way we were included in Ahmad Wali's retinue. I would stop by a few times a week to eat at the house, sitting in the carpeted hall downstairs, or to join the audience upstairs watching Ahmad Wali play pool at night—one of his few releases from the incessant demands of his undefined job. If I had left it a little too long, he would crack one of his dry, deadpan jokes about my absence, hardly looking my way as I walked in. A further sign of belonging.

But he rarely called for me unless it was something urgent.

He met me upstairs, by the pool table. "Don't worry about this," he reassured me, pointing at one of the stuffed chairs. He sat down opposite. "It's not what it seems. I think I know what it is.

"The CIA wants to see you," Ahmad Wali said. They had, he told me, some information about a threat against my life.

I later found out the exact terms.

Someone in provincial government was keeping tabs on a terrorist cell through an informant. The group answered to that radical Soviet-era faction leader Gulbuddin Hikmatyar, Pakistan's protégé before the Taliban. This cell was preparing an attack, right now. Its target: "a CIA agent masquerading as a journalist" named Sarah. The terrorists disposed of details accurate down to the make and color of my car. Considerately, the informant's handler had passed this information on to the CIA.

Ahmad Wali hardly let me digest this before interrupting with his hypotheses. He did not think the threat was real. And the explanation he hastened to add sounded right. He suspected Governor Gul Agha Shirzai's unscrupulous factotum Khalid Pashtoon, the one with the private prison. Pashtoon had excellent relations with the CIA. Ahmad Wali guessed Pashtoon had provided the "tip" himself, in hopes of scaring me out of the province.

I agreed with Ahmad Wali. It was pretty transparent, in fact.

Still, I brought the matter up with Akrem in one of our early meetings. He dismissed the possibility with a toss of his head. The faction leader Gulbuddin Hikmatyar had no presence in Kandahar Province as far as he knew. A few people in Helmand maybe, but nothing active in Kandahar.

The next morning I drove out to see the CIA at Mullah Omar's former compound in the pinewoods. The irony apparently lost on them, the American spooks had set themselves up in the headquarters of the vanquished Taliban; so instead of creating a visible contrast with the previous regime, they invited comparison.

There had been some work to fix the place up after the U.S. bombing, but the wedding-cake mosque was still there, and that clumsy landscape mural on one of the walls. The intelligence agents had failed to inform the Afghans on the gate that I was coming, so it took a while to get in. I had not even been supplied with the name of the person who had summoned me, so it was a hard job persuading the careful Afghans.

Hostility was palpable as I entered the CIA quarters, weaving my way through a forest of exercise bikes to get there. A heavy-set agent in shorts, sweating on one of them, frowned down at me as I walked past. Two of his colleagues found a small room sufficiently barren of secrets to allow me inside, and alerted me to the threat, in fulfillment of what they informed me was their duty.

I suggested Ahmad Wali's analysis. They waved it away, then hastily rectified: "Of course, we can't rule anything out. But we don't have any reason to think the governor's people would do that. No."

The CIA agents were not even going to pursue the possibility, out of idle curiosity. Nor did they ever exchange words with me again.

To my embarrassment, this episode got blown out of proportion. The U.S. State Department representative at the Kandahar airport, a great guy if a bit eccentric with his head tilted back beneath a felt fedora, contacted U.S. troops all the way to Urozgan Province when he could not reach me on the phone—a common enough occurrence in infrastructure-starved Kandahar. Then he called Qayum Karzai's wife in Baltimore, who called my mother. The absolutely last thing I wanted to happen. It took a day or two to climb back out of that one.

But I was not frightened. I was closer to angry. I was sure that Ahmad Wali was right. It had to be the governor.

From the start, I had suspected warlordism was going to be the most serious problem facing the new Afghanistan. Our run-in with Governor Shirzai over the stone to rebuild Akokolacha hamlet had confirmed the premonition. Shirzai had proven to be just what Kandaharis had feared: arbitrary, predatory, brutal, if charismatic. The fact that Afghans for Civil Society had a mandate from Qayum to address matters of policy meant that we would be speaking out about warlordism as a policy issue, both in the United States and in Afghanistan.

But that sort of discussion was abstract at first, an intellectual debate. As time went on and to my intense surprise, nothing at all was done to curb Shirzai and other governors like him, and I had to witness the Kandaharis—people I knew—suffering yet again at their hands, the issue became a boiling frustration.

Now, suddenly, it had become personal.

Shared and rising disbelief at President Karzai's blindness to the threat these regional warlords represented became staple fare during my frequent chats with Akrem. We just could not understand Karzai's unwillingness to recognize and confront the problem.

One evening some weeks after the threat against me, I was sitting in his receiving room. Prayer beads of light-green Khakrez stone looped around his wrist, flipping them idly as he talked, Akrem was reclining against the carpet-laid cushions when he began to muse:

"President Karzai should be paying more attention down here."

I waited.

"I don't see why he isn't collecting the customs directly instead of leaving it to the governor's people. He should define his officials' responsibilities more clearly. That would solve a lot of the problems here—if he explained to the governor exactly what his powers and duties are and what my powers and duties are. And he should send a representative to supervise the work of the provincial administrative departments. The education department, for example. Teachers should be talking about the central government in school, not just 'Gul Agha, Gul Agha, Gul Agha.' Really, Mr. Karzai should have more *contact*. He should be meeting with groups of elders." Akrem used the slang word *whitebeards*. "He should be mobilizing them. He should send for them and sit with them in Kabul, listen to what they have to say. And then he should give them some little gift, a turban or something. They will be overjoyed. And they will support him."

I smiled. This was the kind of political strategizing that always seemed just a little incongruous juxtaposed with Akrem's police uniform and his bulky build. Once I asked him: "Do you talk to the president this way?"

"No," he shook his head. "With the president I talk like a soldier."

I don't know if this was true. If so, it was unfortunate.

In any case, and as usual, I agreed. It was over a year now since President Karzai had taken power, swept up to Kabul on an exuberant tide of hope, armed with an unequivocal mandate to fill his government with constructive, educated people, and to root out the predatory strongmen. The Afghan central government, personified by Karzai, was the population's only defense against the local warlords. It was supposed to contain these cancerous tumors, which the United States had injected back into the Afghan body politic. Kandaharis expected Karzai to act as their champion. They wanted him to provide *qanun*.

But instead of protecting the people from the warlords, curbing them, or removing them from office, Karzai seemed to be waltzing with them, an endless number up in Kabul. He was becoming a distant figurehead incapable or unwilling to weigh in on the level that counted for ordinary people.

Several times that year I had passed word to President Karzai in this vein by way of an odd channel his brothers opened up between us: letters I wrote at their urging, which they handed to the president. I emphasized how important it was for President Karzai to keep in touch with his people, especially his base in the south. He enjoyed a tremendous popular mandate, but few institutions of power. Mixing with the people, leading from their ranks, he could work miracles. But cut off from them, he was just another scrabbling jockey in the Kabul power struggle. In just about these terms, I told him as much.

After the assassination attempt against him in the summer of 2002, Karzai's U.S.-furnished security had become draconian. The bodyguards with their lethal accoutrements hardly let him out of the palace. So, if President Karzai could not go to the provinces, why not, as Akrem was suggesting, take the provinces to him?

Akrem, naturally, had something specific in mind. He had been meeting with some tribal elders himself.

They were Ghiljais—that branch of the Pashtun ethnic group that had been expelled from Kandahar in 1738 by Nadir Shah and his Abdali mercenaries. Now the Ghiljais were a minority in the province. And because many of them had joined the Taliban—Taliban leader Mullah Muhammad Omar was a Ghiljai—that had served as an excuse to exclude them altogether from the post-Taliban distribution of power.

I agreed to meet the Ghiljais. They had set up a tribal council with a president—a compact, intelligent man, silver-gray turban neatly tied, white beard trimmed to a tasteful point. He had a couple of deputies: a greasy-haired, ingratiating former Communist import-export merchant, and Mullah Omar's landlord at the roadside village where he used to lead prayers. Each one strove for exclusive and private access to me. God knows what I thought I was getting into.

We convened a meeting. At first the elders came off sounding like a disgruntled voting bloc after an electoral defeat. "The good people aren't getting government jobs," was their primary complaint.

Meaning you, right?

I listened further.

"The people in power took their positions by force, and by force they placed their friends everywhere."

That was sounding different.

"And reconstruction, it was supposed to be for everyone, but the money's being stolen."

I asked if the gentlemen thought these last two points were connected.

"Of course they are! That's the whole problem. The powerful people gave their friends all the seats, like the education department or urban development, and then those officials put the reconstruction money in their pockets. They share it among themselves. And no one else gets any."

I remembered the fate of my very first project, a campaign to link U.S. schools with newly opened schools in Kandahar, with American students collecting money and sending letters and pictures to their struggling Afghan counterparts. Some $1,200 dollars that students at my own elementary school had raised with great energy and excitement were pocketed by the principal of their Kandahar sister school, along with $600 of my own, which I unthinkingly left in my purse in his office. With a little investigation afterwards, we discovered that the principal split the money with one of his teachers and the two top education department officials, in a well-oiled routine. This larceny was minor compared to the wholesale theft of food supplies donated by the World Food Program and a Pakistani-based organization called Islamic Relief. None of the guilty education department officials, cronies of Governor Shirzai, was ever disciplined. These discoveries put me off working with Kandahar schools. Though ACS continued to do so, my heart was never again really in the program.

I broke off these recollections with a volley of queries to the Ghiljais. Their answers coming thick and fast, we reached the subject of warlordism: "The militiamen should be disarmed and put to work." The elders were emphatic.

This position, too, echoed what other Kandaharis had been telling me for some time. As a representative sample of views in Kandahar, I found the Ghiljais' concerns perfectly worthy of attention.

So I began organizing a trip to the capital for "my" elders—as I had started to call them. While I was at it, I thought, why not get them an appointment with the U.S. ambassador? I began meeting with their council, leading what could be termed advocacy-training sessions.

They gathered each week in a large rectangular room off a verandah brightened by a row of windows. I remember clouds of flies lighting on the neon-colored hard candies a boy served with tea. It must have been during the first warm days of March.

The first thing I pushed the elders to do was get to the point. "President Karzai is overwhelmed with petty requests," I told them. "People who want him to settle their boundary disputes or get their confiscated truck released." And it is true. To an amazing degree, Karzai's role as president of Afghanistan remained that of a tribal *khan* called upon to adjudicate the most trivial of matters.

"Don't make it look as though you are going to him for jobs," I said, though it was the Ghiljais' not-so-disguised objective. "You are bringing him questions of national policy, and you should phrase it that way."

It remained to help the Ghiljais distill what they wanted to say down to the essential. Pashtuns tend to circle their subject.

I took to leading the sessions I attended, shattering protocol by turning directly to the men around the circle and calling on them like students. In a pause, I looked around at the grizzled heads bent toward me, the elders raising their fingers to speak: Tukhi, with his broad beard and saucer-round eyes; wild-haired Gul Mahmad Kuchawal, hands on his gnarled cane, who claimed to represent the region's nomads; young Tukhala Khan, who had probably never spoken up in front of his seniors before.

There it was, another surreal scene: an American female presiding at an Afghan council of elders.

The points the Ghilzais made were precise, intelligent, and grew more and more daring as our sessions went on. For example, the elders thought it was impossible for the gun-lords to be brought to heel without concerted international intervention; they were too entrenched by now. The international community, read the United States, owed this service to Afghanistan.

"The foreigners are the ones who sold guns to these people, who gave them guns, who worked with the gun in Afghanistan. Now they call us warlords. They should help us get rid of these people."

I, too, was surprised at the lack of attention in Afghanistan to DDR, as it is called: disarmament, demobilization, and reintegration. Somehow, the theory seemed to be, the "free market"—in this poverty-stricken land—would absorb the gunmen if they could just be taught a skill. Like the elders, I thought disarming the warlords was going to take more work than that. I thought a more concerted program would be needed, perhaps converting the former gunmen into a kind of Afghan Civilian Conservation Corps, putting them to work on the roads and other major infrastructure projects. That way they would retain an esprit de corps, discipline, and the uniforms and badges that often give young men a sense of pride and identity. Later, arms long laid down and new skills learned, they could be reintroduced into civilian society.

The Ghiljais did not spare President Karzai in their assessment of wardlordism. "Karzai made the *topak salaran*," one grizzle-headed man ventured bravely, several sessions in. "Isma'il Khan, Gul Agha Shirzai—didn't Karzai bring them back?"

"You should tell him that. Don't be shy. Be tough on him."

I was sure that Karzai was just as impatient as we were to rid Afghanistan of these thugs. But for some reason, he was afraid to do it. Maybe he did not know he had the power. Maybe he just needed some clear evidence of local support. That's how I reasoned. It never dawned on me that President Karzai might be playing us all. That perhaps, despite his high talk, he no longer had the least intention of crossing the warlords.

I helped the elders distinguish which of their concerns to address to President Karzai and which to the U.S. ambassador. There is always a latent sense in Afghanistan, despite the country's fierce independence, that "the foreigners" control everything. So the Ghiljais drew up two petitions for my review, one addressed to Karzai, one to U.S. ambassador Robert Finn.

Next came the matter of logistics. And suddenly that Afghan fragility resurfaced. I had risked the drive to Kabul half a dozen times by then. But these men were old. Most had not set foot outside Kandahar in years. They were frightened.

We set about weaving safety nets. The council president got a hand-held satellite telephone; we arranged for him to call in along the way. I organized backup from the president's office for when the group arrived in Kabul.

They set off. Calls came in from the prearranged places at more or less the right times—I was not really keeping track, but to my elders it was important. They were proud of their achievement, and they needed encouragement. I cheered them on.

Then, at the Kabul gates, their fears were realized. Northern Alliance fighters looked askance at their dust-daubed cars unencumbered by license plates, at their Pashtun turbans and beards, and listened with revulsion to their soft, southern consonants. The Ghiljais were barred entrance to the city.

While the old men quietly pulled their cars to the side of the road to wait, I jumped on my cell phone, trying to break through to *anyone* at the president's office. Eventually an envoy was sent, and the Ghiljais were escorted into the capital.

It was a meaningful foul-up. What it signaled to the Ghiljais was that this central government of theirs, this central government that was supposed to be protecting them, was not even accessible without the intercession of a foreign woman. What it signaled to them was that Kabul, the capital of their country, did not belong to them. It did not belong to the Afghan people. It belonged to a clutch of warlords from the Northern Alliance.

The presidential guesthouse was the venue for the next crisis. It was not ready. There was no electricity or water. Food had not been prepared.

This lapse was simply unforgivable. I had been planning this visit for weeks. The aim was to improve mutual esteem between President Karzai and a tribal bloc that could anchor support for him in the south. Instead, the elders had been snubbed, in precisely the domain where an Afghan leader's power is traditionally put on display: his hospitality.

I could not believe the Palace had let this happen.

A high-ranking official was at last dispatched. Escorting the Ghiljais to a hotel where they were fed and settled, he saved the day. My elders called me and reported their satisfaction.

In the end, the visit was a great success. President Karzai's chief of staff e-mailed his thanks. The elders, he wrote, were of "much higher quality" than most of the president's callers. They spent nearly two hours at the U.S. embassy. And then, of course, they found their feet. They discovered some other Ghiljais, and they communed. Ministers sent for them. Their visits were covered on TV. My elders stayed in Kabul for two full weeks.

During that time I drove up to the capital myself, to engage in the most intense period of collaboration ever with my boss, Qayum Karzai.

Qayum had proved to be an extraordinary inspiration. He could make me literally catch my breath at his penetrating expositions of what was wrong with Afghanistan and why. Much of my thinking about the warlords was rooted in his analyses. Ever vulnerable to sheer brilliance, I was repeatedly swept away.

By now, though, I had painfully learned that Qayum's patience for the details of making anything happen lagged far behind his appetite for abstract analysis. He seemed blissfully unconscious of what it took. Some other characteristics had begun to unsettle me as well. There was a secretiveness about him, a cultivated ambiguity, and an excessive disorganization, which was belied by his laser-tuned powers of observation, and his allergy to saying anything of substance on the telephone. Something about him made me uncomfortable. But then that genius of his would sweep me off my feet again. It was very disconcerting.

Qayum lived in a modest house in the Wazir Akbar Khan neighborhood of Kabul. It was an NGO Row. Everyone's headquarters was in

Wazir Akbar Khan; you could walk from Oxfam to the Red Cross to Germany's GTZ to the U.S. embassy. Newly minted SUVs, emblazoned with logos or shielding their occupants behind smoked-glass windows, clogged the streets, dominating pedestrians from their tall wheels. The occasional fruit-and-sundries stall, the battered white-and-yellow local taxis, the limbless veterans begging from wheelchairs were dwarfed.

Qayum's house had a small patch of garden in front. A sitting room with heavy wooden furniture adjoined the dining room, with a curtain between. Upstairs were three bedrooms occupied by the president's chief of staff and that man's young nephew who also worked at the palace, and an older Karzai cousin of some sort, who would turn on his radio while the television was going, prayed for hours, and thought nothing of camping out indefinitely with Qayum and eating his food. In this way did the place remain Afghan, despite the Western-style furniture. My unannounced arrivals always entailed a shift in occupancy: someone ended up on the living room floor. But I was always greeted, no questions asked, with a tall thermos of tea and a dish of nuts and raisins set out on one of the black marble-topped coffee tables. Once, when Ahmad Wali was in town, his retinue of four stayed with us. They slept in their shawls under the stairs, next to the woodstove that had been installed for the winter. Somehow, there was always room. Qayum would pad around quietly like a long-limbed cat that noticed everything, his glasses perched on the polished dome of his forehead.

Those February days, I established my computer and printer on the end of the dining room table. Qayum's first priority was to produce a mission statement and an organization chart for a putative upcoming presidential campaign. Such a thing was called for in the blueprint for building Afghan political institutions that had been hammered out in Bonn, Germany, just before the fall of the Taliban. But as yet no date for the election had been set, nor had it even been decided whether other offices would be up for a vote at the same time. The assumption was that the presidency at least would be in play and that Karzai would run, though he had not announced any intention to do so and was certainly not busying himself launching a campaign.

Nevertheless, we had at an organization chart. The result of our labor

was structured and efficient looking—perfectly alien to the Afghan context, not to mention to Qayum's own impenetrably ambiguous style.
Qayum was fantasizing. If his brother did not want to campaign actively
for the presidency, as, for whatever reason, he apparently did not, there was
no way we were going to force him.

The next effort edged closer to what I thought was the urgent priority. We developed a long-term—and hopelessly elaborate—strategy for
eroding the power of the warlords. It would take years.

Then it was my turn. "Let's help the president out," I said over morning tea, flavored with cardamom. "Let's give him a plan for firing the
warlords."

I had raised the warlord issue repeatedly with expatriates over the past
six months—U.S. diplomats and army officers, journalists and humanitarian workers—when I met them at Qayum's house or the U.S. base or the
embassy, or when they came to visit me, which was happening more and
more frequently. Being one of the few U.S. civilians living in Kandahar
proper, and one with a surprising range of Afghan contacts, a person who
was willing to voice her opinions to boot, I was becoming something of
a tourist attraction. My interlocutors, spooked at the thought of an Afghan
conflagration or wanting to advertise their sympathy with President Karzai,
had been telling me: "But how can Karzai take on the warlords? He's got
no army."

I thought the question was disingenuous, a pretext for inaction. I didn't
think the president needed an army. Neither did the Karzai brothers. We
thought the governors were paper tigers, lacking popular support. Without the overt U.S. backing that kept them *rampant*, they would mew plaintively and crawl away. We were sure of it. Our tuning forks were
unequivocal.

But there was a chicken-and-egg problem. Americans and Afghans
each seemed to be waiting for the other to make the first move. American officials would repeat that as long as President Karzai gave these men
his confidence, there was nothing the United States could do.

*But we're the ones who brought the warlords back and rammed them down
his throat!*

Never mind. I let that piece of recent history go. Instead, I tried to explain how Afghans read body language, not words. "As long as we are visibly supporting these warlords with money, uniforms, and guns, that's the message President Karzai is going to read, not our verbal assurances of support against them."

Then I would shuttle back to the Afghans and explain that President Karzai really had to be decisive about this. He had to take clear and visible action. Then the Americans would follow his lead.

It felt like hauling on chains, trying to get two wild horses to nuzzle each other.

But as I told Qayum that morning over tea, we needed to get out of the realm of speculation. If we could just come up with a concrete proposal for how, practically, to eject the warlords, maybe we could break the deadlock. President Karzai, I said, needed a road map, something he could take to the Americans to demonstrate that he was serious.

"Let's do it!" Qayum put his teacup down on the marble table. I had piped up at just the right moment. The topic had been dinner fare at the Palace the night before.

And so we hammered out a document, in eight parts. Qayum, it emerged, could be quite practical when pushed. Here is what we wrote:

1. **Begin with Gul Agha Shirzai.**
2. **Choose a replacement:** Someone with strong administrative skills, integrity, and the stature required to mobilize allegiance.
3. **Call Gul Agha to Kabul,** without telling why. (Note: breach of this plan's security will allow him and those around him to prepare a riposte, so care should be taken to avoid leaks.) When he gets here, tell him your decision and explain that it is based on continuing governance problems in Kandahar.
4. Simultaneously, or slightly prior, you or your envoy should **contact the heads of the Kandahar security forces: Zabit Akrem, Khan Mahmad, Mahmad Shah, Amir Lalai . . . apprise them of your decision. Entrust them with maintaining the public order. Assign the one you most trust to pay special attention to Razziq Shirzai, Gul Agha's brother.** Explain that the integrity of the Afghan nation depends on them.

5. **Secure Spin Boldak on the border with Pakistan.** This is another place where disruptive activity might be launched.

6. At the same time as you are meeting with Shirzai, a trusted envoy whose dignity and stature are recognized in Kandahar should **gather the main elders of all the Kandahar tribes and explain your decision to them, enlisting their support.**

7. **Maintain all other provincial and municipal officials in their positions,** as an incentive not to resist the decision. The new appointee should begin the process of cleaning up his government after a month.

8. **Consult with key Americans—civil and military—on the elements of this plan.** Solicit their input, and **request specific support:** For example, assistance in securing Boldak and the border area. Or, since Razziq Shirzai's compound is on the airport grounds, the Americans could be asked to provide a minimal deterring presence, so as to maintain order there and keep him from mobilizing his men to mischief. Or, the State Department representative in Kandahar could be asked to contact Khalid Pashtoon and tell him the U.S. will hold him accountable for any breach of the peace.

I heaved a sigh of relief. There it was at last: how to fire a warlord, in eight easy steps. But I thought it needed a little something more.

During my days in the Balkans, I had absorbed some principles of military planning. NATO, I learned then, does not reason in classic best-case/worst-case terms. Its planning is a little more subtle. Officers are called upon to imagine what the *most likely* scenario will be and plan for that, and then think about what the *most dangerous* scenario might be and how to protect against it. We should adopt those technical terms, I thought. It might impress the Americans.

So we added a most likely/most dangerous section to our plan— adulterated, I felt, by Qayum's tendency to focus on the result he hoped to obtain, rather than the truth. I thought he downplayed the potential dangers a bit too vociferously, instead of simply assessing them.

Anyhow, I printed the thing out in several copies, Qayum looking on, almost boyishly jubilant. When he left for dinner at the palace that night, he put one in his briefcase.

For my part, I never went to Kabul anymore without stopping by the U.S. embassy. It had improved a lot since the days of the revolving door. The political affairs desk was in the hands of a savvy and thoughtful young man named Kurt Amend, who had spent time in Pakistan. The ambassador, a bit of an oddball, was a hero in Central Asia for his cultural sensitivity there in the 1990s. Flanking him was a dapper, upbeat, switched-on man named Bill Taylor, of ambassadorial rank, the most impressive diplomat I have ever met.

So I rushed off to give that chain another yank. I called on Bill Taylor, and I handed him a copy of our eight-point plan.

But I wasn't done meddling yet.

I returned to Kabul in early March for an International Women's Day conference, and I had to see President Karzai on another matter. Never once had Qayum bothered to invite me to the palace, though he went several times a day. I never did discover why he wouldn't take me along. That March, I decided to make the move myself.

After a bit of awkward circling, which finally left me seated in a cavernous waiting room upstairs at the palace, admiring the warm ochers of its two great rugs, I found myself alone with President Karzai, in his private office.

It was only the second time I had seen him face to face. The first time was at his brother Ahmad Wali's wedding, when he had narrowly missed being killed.

"So *you're* the one who writes me the letters," he had said then, stunningly cool and gracious after what had just almost happened to him.

This time, we sat at his elegant desk in the form of a T, with me along the upright and him at the crossbar. He was as direct, and charismatic, as I had hoped. At one point, he broke off a sentence, stood up, and ambled over to a low table to grab a fistful of raisins from a glass dish, then sat back down, sharing out my half.

Our other business finished, I ventured: "So, I hear you were looking for a plan for how to get rid of the warlords."

I suspected that Qayum had never given our document to his brother after all.

"I never asked for a plan," the president denied.

"Well, I have one."

"Let's see it." President Karzai smiled indulgently, stretching out a hand. I passed it over. He looked at it, folded it in two, and slipped it into his slim leather briefcase.

Well. That was that accomplished. I thought all I had to do now was wait a few days.

CHAPTER 21

MURDER

PRESIDENT KARZAI DID need to get a move on. During that spring of 2003, the atmosphere in Kandahar took a distinctly menacing cast.

One afternoon in late March, in his office at police headquarters, Akrem was taken up in conversation. Sitting not behind his imposing desk, but in a corner, on one of the overstuffed velvet chairs, he was bent toward a man who gave the impression of being out of breath, though he wasn't literally.

I could not understand what the man was saying. He and Akrem were conversing quickly and quietly, and I didn't know Pashtu yet anyway. Nor could I presume to interrupt for a translation. But as soon as the man left, Akrem turned to give me a synopsis.

The man was one of Akrem's informants, in from the field where he had been carrying out some surveillance. With a group of former Taliban, he had just crossed over from Pakistan into Afghanistan, on one of the innumerable dirt paths that traverse the vast, lonely frontier. The informant had accompanied the militants all the way to a trackless piece of country in northern Kandahar Province, where they were now arrayed, bunking in the villages or spread out in the hills around. "I never saw so many of them cross at once," the man said. "There were twenty-five of us, maybe thirty."

I took in this information, not immediately registering its significance. The militants, Akrem added, were being paid and trained in Pakistan. From this man and other informants, he had learned that the orders insurgents like these received were to cross into Afghanistan, to work first in outlying districts, and then move slowly in toward Kandahar, progressively tightening their ring around the city.

Three days after this conversation, a convoy from the International Committee of the Red Cross (ICRC) was ambushed, crossing the zone the informant had described. A foreign aid worker was murdered. That incident, more than any other single event, set in motion the gradual but steady withdrawal of international humanitarian and reconstruction agencies from the Afghan south.

His name was Ricardo Munguia, a hydraulics engineer. He was a man, I am told, who distributed the warmth of his native Latin American sun wherever he went, who had a luminous word for everyone. With three Afghan colleagues, he had driven out along the ghostly trail that can scarcely be called a road, which winds northward from Kandahar to Tirin Kot, the capital of Urozgan Province.

Urozgan was a complicated place. In the hands of a grizzled governor with one milky eye and the manners of an aging lion, uncouth and rapacious and devoted to President Karzai, it was the base from which Karzai had launched his campaign to pry the hidebound southern Pashtuns away from the Taliban. And yet this same Urozgan was where many of the Taliban had come from. In the conservative south, it was the most isolated and backward province. Hardly any aid organizations worked there.

The day after Ricardo's death in that godforsaken place, I had another appointment with Akrem, at his house. I got there just as the U.S. State Department's representative in Kandahar was arriving. I invited him in with me. He was visibly shaken—he had seen Ricardo's body, and it had hit home.

He wanted the police chief's opinion: Didn't he think that people loyal to the old extremist *Jihad* commander Gulbuddin Hikmatyar had done the murder, and wasn't it likely that . . . And the rattled U.S. official launched into an involved exposition of his own theories about the event and the light it shed on the nature of what was beginning to be termed the "insurgency." At last he asked Akrem, "So, what do we do?"

Such a speech could only draw the most general kind of response, and Akrem obliged—keeping close to the terms of the question he had been asked out of native caution. The presence of the official's interpreter, a Shirzai crony, hardly encouraged frank discussion either. Akrem laid out the elements necessary in his view for the proper governance of the Afghan south: clear job descriptions for administrative departments and security forces, direct supervision by the central government, fair distribution of employment and reconstruction benefits across the various tribes, and so on. It was a policy speech, and it was sensible; it seemed to satisfy the State Department official, who left in a rather distracted rush. He might have been bucked up by these abstractions, I realized as he made his way out, but he had not learned anything very concrete.

A reporter's habits come in handy: my questions formed themselves. How many cars? What terrain? How many fighters? Who were they? And the picture took shape under the precise brushstrokes of Akrem's answers.

Insurgents had trickled across the border in groups—taking ancient footpaths across the deserted frontier, or walking brazenly through at Chaman, where complicit Pakistani guards waved them past—then gathering, maybe more than a hundred strong, in northern Kandahar Province. Ambush sites are abundant there, and the assassins had selected a good one. At the very fringes of the jurisdictions of Kandahar and Urozgan, a place where patrols are rare, the road wedges its way between two towering chunks of rock. The Taliban deployed above, some forty fighters on each side of the road. They only had to put two men down there, aiming guns at drivers.

The fighters stopped several local cars and ordered them aside. Then a two-vehicle convoy appeared—white late-model Toyota Land Cruisers, the ICRC logo painted on in red, oversized antennas flexing skyward from the prow of each. Ricardo and three "local national" staff members were aboard.

Akrem recited witnesses' descriptions: how one of the militants had stepped away with his satellite phone. "We have three Afghans, one foreigner," he was heard to ask. "Do you want four bodies or one?" The answer came back. He smacked the fat antenna back into his sat-phone with the palm of his hand, and signed to his men to stand Ricardo up against the side of his car and shoot him. When the Taliban set the car ablaze, the ICRC's Afghan staff begged to be allowed to take the body out of reach. No wonder the sight of it had unsettled that State Department guy.

By the time I left Akrem's house a half hour later, I had details down to the names of the two villages where the Taliban had spent the night. And I was angry, because this thing could have been prevented.

Ricardo's execution was no vague hint, like those harmless explosions we had become used to. The killers were notorious former Taliban. They had deployed into the area in insolent platoons. They had selected Ricardo, the first foreigner to arrive, ignoring other potential victims. They had pushed him up against his car and emptied their guns into him, and they had let his body burn.

The impact on Kandahar's small international community was like an electric shock. After drawing together for a moment to grieve, lining their cars up in a cortege to bear Ricardo's body to the airport, the foreigners sent up a yell. More offices closed, agencies "suspended operations"; employees were evacuated to Kabul.

I felt at the time—and I still do, to some degree—that the clamor was a bit excessive. An objective comparison of conditions in Afghanistan with those in any other recent conflict or postconflict situation came out in Afghanistan's favor. I remember trading assessments with a former member of the British Special Air Service, converted in his retirement to protection work for war correspondents. Bosnia in 1996 was far more dangerous than Afghanistan was now, he judged (and then treated me to the details of his only bit of real work so far: patching up a hole in the BBC crew's cook, who had been stabbed by a jealous colleague).

I had to agree. It is not that I deliberately discounted the value of Ricardo's life. Had I known him personally, had he been my friend, I might well have felt differently. But I did not know him, and I was left with the bare count. In more than a year, in the place whose very name had become a synonym for anti-Western fanaticism, one single foreigner was dead.

So why such panic? The international humanitarian organizations, I concluded, were committing an amalgam. They were harnessing the issue of security to another debate entirely.

That debate had to do with the way the United States was behaving abroad. Most foreign humanitarian workers in Afghanistan were not American. Most of them came from countries and segments of the population that were, rightly or wrongly, furious at America's foreign policy. It was not just the recent invasion of Iraq, which drew unanimous—and, as it proved, well-founded—criticism from every country on earth, but what had come before Iraq as well. The Kyoto Protocol on climate change, the U.S. attitude amounted to saying, "Because we do not wish to reduce our standard of living, you will breathe polluted air." The Land Mine Treaty, which had helped reap a Nobel Peace Prize and which the United States refused to consider ratifying. The International Criminal Court, aimed at curbing war crimes, which the United States had sought to undermine. The United States seemed to be sticking out its tongue at the rest of the world, and the rest of the world had no leverage to respond.

September 11 had prompted people all across Europe to drop these concerns in sympathy. And now it seemed that the United States was taking advantage of that sympathy to push its agenda down their throats. For international aid workers in Afghanistan, the only available target upon which to vent their frustration was the U.S. presence there.

And so humanitarian workers, Europeans as well as many Americans, opposed this presence far more vocally than Afghans did. They said it was the U.S. troops who endangered their lives, since the U.S. troops were doing reconstruction, and "insurgents" could not distinguish between soldiers and aid workers. In the context of an argument that was really over U.S. policy and the U.S. presence in Afghanistan as a political issue, inflating the danger to aid workers was a way of reinforcing their case.

I think my colleagues' arguments were wrong. I think the presence of U.S. troops in Afghanistan made all of us safer. The expatriates, I believe, misunderstood the nature of violence in Afghanistan. Afghanistan is a place where mutually assured destruction remains a viable doctrine. It is a culture of retribution. I learned this back when I was reporting, and I sensed the importance of having that young fighter with me on the road to Kandahar. Not because he could actively protect me with the Kalashnikov he held between his knees, but because his presence silently threatened the vengeance of his tribe should any harm befall me. Walls and barbed wire, I had learned, are not all that significant in Afghanistan, when it comes down to it. Preventing your own murder—once someone has resolved to commit it—would be almost impossible. But if you are seen to belong to a recognized group, a family or tribe that might retaliate, your chances of survival increase. The way to stay safe in Kandahar was to suggest the certainty of violent revenge should you be killed or dishonored, so as to deter attack before it is undertaken.

That is, to advertise your affiliations.

For this reason I felt, in my own case certainly and to some degree for the rest of the foreigners, that being confused in Afghans' minds with the Americans actually improved our chances of survival. I took some elementary precautions: I kept a Kalashnikov beside my bed. I varied my times and my routes, and I rolled up my windows. But I was not troubled that Afghans saw me driving on and off the U.S. base.

There was something deeper to the humanitarians' confusion, however.

I am beginning to believe that the international humanitarian community failed to perceive a transformation that was taking place in the world around it, which profoundly altered its status.

Aid workers took their own good intentions for granted, and were used to beneficiaries doing the same, more or less. Arriving on the heels of an earthquake or a tidal wave with their stretchers and rehydration salts and their kits for putting up temporary shelter, or spending a year in an African village improving an irrigation system, they were siphoning off some of their rich countries' surplus to alleviate pain in the Third World. They could count on gratitude, even if it was grudging or muddied by cynicism.

In the internal conflicts that shaped humanitarian action in the 1990s— Somalia, the Balkans, Rwanda—the aid workers' very outsider status, and their neutralist credo, was their force. Only a foreigner, it seemed, could be trusted by the different parties. Only a foreigner could shuttle between the factions, ministering to victims on all sides. And so the aid workers flaunted their foreignness, and clung to their neutrality—in spite of its moral ambiguity in some contexts. This neutrality was both their power and their safe-conduct across the front lines. Aid workers were harassed; occasionally they were used as bargaining chips. But when they got killed, it was usually by accident: they had misjudged the direction of an offensive and been caught in the shelling.

This self-image still dominates in the international humanitarian community. Aid workers have trouble accepting that they are now in the crosshairs themselves. When one of them is killed deliberately, the loss sparks shocked hurt feelings as well as grief. For the unconscious belief persists: If humanitarian workers are being targeted, there must be some mistake.

Afghanistan, regarded through the old prism, would seem to be a conflict between the United States on the one hand and some constellation of Muslim groups on the other. In line with their traditional role, aid workers wanted their neutrality recognized so they could cross the front lines as usual. But it wasn't working. Something was wrong. Ricardo had been killed.

What must be confusing things, the humanitarians decided, was the behavior of the Americans. It was muddying aid workers' white-painted neutrality. In other words, if Ricardo was killed, it must be because he was mistaken, in some way, for an American.

I think this analysis is wrong. I believe this conflict is different. This is a struggle between parties—on both sides—working to precipitate that "clash of civilizations" between Islam and the West. To Muslim parties to this conflict—Al-Qaeda or a few leading Taliban—there *is* no difference between an American soldier and Ricardo. No matter how nuanced the aid workers' specific views might be, no matter how opposed to U.S. policy, they cannot be outside this conflict.

If anything, they are more threatening to Al-Qaeda's goals than Washington hard-liners. For Western crusaders and their with-us-or-against-us rhetoric force Muslims to choose sides, and most choose the opposing camp—just what Al-Qaeda wants. A Ricardo, by contrast, with his hand out like a bridge, increases understanding, believes in coexistence, offers human dignities to the people he helps without stripping others away. He appeals to the Muslims he is assisting in ways that allow them to approach and consider. Ricardo's death was no mistake. He was the militants' principal foe.

My reasoning has been confirmed to some degree by the fact that the attacks against foreign civilians were not visited disproportionately upon Americans. On the contrary, those organizations that made the most elaborate show of their neutrality and their opposition to the U.S. government, like Ricardo's International Committee of the Red Cross or Paris-based Doctors Without Borders, seemed to be taking the worst hits.

By pulling out when struck, groups like this relinquish the new and vital role that is beckoning—to take on the belligerents on both sides, by obstinately forging links, eroding ignorance, rebuilding bridges.

This is a combat, I believe, that is worth taking risks for.

Ricardo's murder did not make me panic; it made me mad. The inquiries into its circumstances that Akrem and I conducted in tandem proved more than anything to date the cynicism of Governor Shirzai. He was playing for the new Afghanistan, getting plenty of money for it, and playing against it too.

The militants who killed Ricardo, according to Akrem's information, included some of his own Alokozai tribesmen—that is how he had managed to land an informant. But they were mostly Barakzais, members of the governor's tribe. Natives of the villages up there by the Urozgan Province line, they had run to Pakistan with the fleeing Taliban. This was their first time back.

It is not that I suspected Governor Shirzai of active collaboration in the killing just because the perpetrators were Barakzais. It was that it simply did not seem possible for him to be unaware that some kind of attack was coming and, the way it looked to me, he chose not to thwart it.

Contrary to popular assumption in the West, the very loneliness of the Afghan countryside makes it harder, not easier, to hide in its wilds: navigable trails across the cragged wasteland are scarce and locals know them intimately, lovingly. No stranger can pass unseen, unknown, unbidden, unprotected. Given the tribal affiliations with Shirzai's Barakzais, the size of the infiltration, and given the efficient Afghan grapevine, Shirzai must have been alerted to the militants' arrival. Even I knew about the infiltration, in a way, since I had heard about their presence that afternoon in Akrem's office.

I soon found out my hunch was right. An army officer loyal to the Karzais had received a call from a colleague up in that wild district, saying that a large group of armed men had moved in. The Karzai loyalist had taken the information to Governor Shirzai, urging action. "We'll see about it next week," the governor had replied.

But next week was too late.

Shirzai's behavior after Ricardo's execution rang an equally false note against the tuning fork tempering inside me. He took to the airwaves denouncing the insurgents, swearing he would root out all Taliban from government office—as though the personal rivals he was referring to had anything to do with this event. But it was not till the next day that he moved an armed force to the zone, less than three hours' drive from Kandahar. In Afghanistan, that kind of body language signified safe conduct for the insurgents.

U.S. officials, meanwhile, snatched at the declarations Shirzai pronounced for their benefit, parsing them for meaning like a poem in school, but never holding them up for comparison with his actions. Through several discussions at the airport and with contacts in Kabul, I learned what the State Department representative was writing to his hierarchy; I fired off a note of my own to counter his. To me, the event and the governor's handling of it were the clearest proof to date that Shirzai was working for—and satisfying—two masters with contradictory agendas: the United States and Pakistan. He was a man with two kites in the air.

I was at a loss to understand why U.S. officials could not see this. More broadly, I was at a loss to understand why American decision makers could not see how suicidally contradictory their alliance with Pakistan was.

To us on the ground, it was obvious that the resurgent Taliban who had killed Ricardo, these "insurgents" whom U.S. soldiers were fighting and getting killed by, did not represent an indigenous Afghan movement rooted in local ideology. Afghans, for one thing, were vaccinated against ideology by now, having lived through three ideologically inspired revolutions and a civil war in twenty-five years, and having had untold suffering inflicted on them at each turn. Afghans, according to every one of them I had spoken with in town or in the countryside, wanted a government that functioned, whatever its stripes.

And so, in the sense of a popular indigenous movement of opposition to the new government in Afghanistan, the "insurgency" was not one. It was a nuisance deliberately stirred up across the border. This was evident to us in Kandahar because no effort was made to hide the fact in Pakistan. Taliban, advertising their affiliation by way of their dress or their explicit self-identification, were given privileged treatment at the border in Chaman; they paraded around Quetta; they carried guns and weapons-authorization cards issued by the Pakistani government; their offices and lodgings were located in a well-known Quetta neighborhood, previously provided to the anti-Soviet mujahideen. These insurgents were not squirreling themselves away in warrens in Afghan mountains or the supposedly uncontrolled tribal areas of northern Pakistan, as the Pakistani government artfully persuaded the West. They were manufactured and maintained, housed, trained, and equipped by stubborn, shortsighted officials in that very Pakistani government. Our allies.

By so doing, these Pakistani officials were merely persevering in an established policy. For the past three decades, Pakistan had been manipulating religious extremism to further its regional agenda in south Asia. During the Soviet invasion, the Pakistani government cultivated the most ideologically extremist Afghan faction, Gulbuddin Hikmatyar's group.[1] When it failed to gain control of Afghanistan after the Soviet withdrawal, the Pakistani government largely ginned up the Taliban "movement," pressing into service ambitious petty commanders from the anti-Soviet period and uprooted, *madrassa*-inculcated youth from the refugee camps.

Similar factions had been employed to keep alive Pakistani claims to Kashmir, a paradise in the Himalayan Mountains over which India and Pakistan were in a custody dispute: four wars since independence from the British in 1947. Pakistani troops, under the man who now ran the country, General Pervez Musharraf, had mixed with and even dressed up as fundamentalist militants to launch an attack on Indian territory in Kashmir in 1999.[2]

However, there is an important distinction that I began to discern as I pored over this issue during those early months of 2003. It is a distinction between global agendas and local ones. Pakistani officials' support for and manipulation of extremist factions seemed to be essentially local and tactical—the manipulation of religious ideology for ends that were not fundamentally ideological. Some of these officials must have been moved on a personal level by international holy war convictions. The government certainly tapped into the vocabulary of those convictions in order to win recruits. But in substance, it did not appear to me that Islamabad was embarked on an Al-Qaeda–style global *jihadi* movement. Pakistani officials' aim was not to bring the world under an Islamist government or even to cut ties with the West; rather, their goals were consistently regional and temporal—maintaining an upper hand in the regional balance of power, especially vis-à-vis India. Unfortunately, the Pakistani people were paying for these goals with their long-term futures, for, by instrumentalizing Islamist extremism, their government was deliberately wallowing in the forces of violence and regression.

It is this distinction between global and local agendas that explains how Pakistan has been able to play Washington so deftly since the Taliban demise. Every few months, the Pakistani government has caught and returned over an Al-Qaeda figure, as though throwing the United States a bone, while continuing to abet the Taliban insurgents who are aiming rocket launchers at U.S. soldiers, aid workers, and loyal Afghans inside Afghanistan.

Recent history helps explain the paradox of the contrasting treatment meted out to Taliban and Al-Qaeda leaders—who are ostensibly, though not actually, part of the same overall movement.

When, a few years after the Soviet withdrawal, Washington and Moscow agreed to stop financing opposing factions in what had by then degenerated into a savagely vengeful Afghan civil war—the "*mujahideen* nights"[3]—Pakistan was abruptly deprived of a gush of U.S. taxpayer dollars. It had to look elsewhere for money for the protégés it was still backing in the fight to take over Afghanistan: first Gulbuddin Hikmatyar, and then, when he failed to gain power, the Taliban. Saudi Arabia had matched U.S. grants to the Afghan anti-Soviet resistance for years. And when Washington and Moscow stopped funding the civil war, Saudi Arabia stayed the course.

The Pakistani government must have been grateful, for conservative Saudis, inside and outside government, were eager to put their piety on display. Hoping to make up or cover up for a certain contradiction between their strict precepts and their occasionally debauched behavior, they tended to support the same extremist groups that Pakistan did.

In 1994, the Taliban, with overwhelming Pakistani support and involvement, swept across the Afghan south. But they had a more difficult time crossing the invisible ethnic line that divides Afghanistan just below Kabul. There the front line ground to a halt, amid bloody fighting. And so when, in 1997, a rich, influential, and seasoned Saudi individual named

Usama bin Laden offered to come back to Afghanistan, where he had fought against the Soviets, when he offered to bring the threads of a network he had been building, along with money and veteran fighters and the know-how to train more and the beginnings of a worldwide charismatic following, the Pakistani government was apparently happy to have him come and quickly throw his weight behind the Taliban's effort to conquer the rest of the country.[4] Given Pakistan's overwhelming interest in what went on in Afghanistan, it is inconceivable that Usama bin Laden could have set himself up there without Pakistani approval.

But his agenda diverged from that of Islamabad. His focus was global, not local. And his was a totalitarian ideology. While detailing fighters to the Afghan front and Kashmir, Usama bin Laden was also setting about the job of provoking world war. Eventually, that agenda hijacked the Taliban movement. Kandaharis began experiencing Arabs as their rulers, instead of the local mullahs they thought they had bargained for. And Afghanistan was transformed into a country-sized staging ground for terrorist actions against the West.

The culmination of this progression was 9/11 and the U.S. reaction to the attacks. Because of what its Arab guests had done, the Pakistani government found itself, overnight, expelled from ownership by sometimes prickly proxy of about 90 percent of Afghanistan. Now Pakistan was a reviled refugee, driven out, like all of those miserable Afghan families.[5] All because of Al-Qaeda.

My own guess is that the Pakistani government did not waste a lot of love on Al-Qaeda operatives after 9/11. And so, in the post-Taliban calculus, Pakistan was not protecting Al-Qaeda operatives any more. While I was waiting on the border in Chaman to cross into Afghanistan back in December of 2001, I heard about dozens of Arabs who were being harbored in Pakistan. Even then I had the feeling that they were a kind of bank account, money squirreled away to be exchanged later for Washington's indulgence.

And sure enough, in the years following the Taliban defeat, Islamabad has captured and turned over a leading Al-Qaeda member at the steady rate of one every three to four months. Interestingly, these terrorist masterminds have usually been arrested in major cities, and not in the wild "tribal areas" where the Pakistani army stages highly publicized military operations against anti-American militants.

Meanwhile, Pakistan has hardly captured or turned over a single leading member of the Taliban regime, though they display themselves openly in Quetta and meet to plan their activities there. On the contrary, Pakistan has continued to provide former Taliban with logistical and material support, to tolerate the training camps that operate in plain sight, to provide "former" Pakistani army officers to teach there, and to offer insurgents safe passage back and forth across the Afghan border.

No one involved even bothers to hide these things. That same spring, when I went to visit Mahmad Anwar in Chaman, he wanted me to stay the night so he could show me the distributions of automatic weapons, motorcycles, and cash at a *madrassa,* or religious school, around the corner from his house. At the camp near the border, due north of Chaman, where Akrem landed an informant, the trainers were a Pakistani army colonel and two majors. Akrem gave me their names. The curriculum included such subjects as constructing explosives from improvised materials and how to plan and carry out the assassination of public figures.

The Pakistani ploy of buying Washington off with well-timed deliveries of Al-Qaeda operatives while continuing to support the Taliban worked quite effectively. I remember at the U.S. embassy once, I was providing details on a training camp on the road from Quetta to Karachi, and on a top Taliban official who was swaggering around Quetta. I had his license plate number—an ISI plate—and the addresses of his two government-provided safe houses.

The U.S. official groaned. "I know, I know, Sarah. But there's not a thing we can do about it. Pakistan just gave us Khalid Sheikh Muhammad."

And so U.S. troops fighting resurgent Taliban found themselves in the ironic position of battling foes sent against them by a country that was supposed to be their ally. Indeed, when Washington awarded $3.5 billion to Pakistan in the summer of 2003, American troops following the news on TVs in their plywood hooches had every reason to assume that a good chunk of that U.S. taxpayer money would be spent on the very Taliban who were attacking them. In other words, Washington was actually supporting the terrorists it claimed to be waging war upon. The war on terror was a charade.

When I brought these issues up with U.S. soldiers, they tended to react strongly: "If it was to invade Pakistan, I'd sign up for another rotation," one of them told me. "We all feel that way," shrugged a military police officer, who had kindly let me sit in the sandbagged bunker behind Gate 2 one sizzling afternoon. "The Pakistani border is just an imaginary line keeping us from doing our job."

CHAPTER 22

MONGOL CONQUESTS
AND REBIRTH

> While Genghis Khan was waiting, Bala crossed the River Shin and pursued Jalaldin-Soltan and Qan Melik to the land of the Hindus. There he lost them and was unable to find them again though he searched right into the heart of the land of the Hindus.
>
> —*The Secret History of the Mongols*[1]

THOSE LINES WERE written in the thirteenth century, but when I read them, I couldn't help thinking that the action they depict sounded a lot like what U.S. soldiers were doing in Afghanistan: chasing an elusive foe to the border with "the land of the Hindus"—read, nowadays, Pakistan—and losing him. The operative difference being that U.S. soldiers were not allowed to "search into the heart of the land of the Hindus." They had to stop at the border.

It turns out that the American soldiers who spent years hunting Al-Qaeda and Taliban holdouts in Afghanistan were respecting an old tradition. The theme of conquering army hunting vanquished foe through desert, dale, and mountain vale is a recurring one in Central Asian history. An examination of some of these quests debunks a famous myth: that Afghanistan has never been conquered. The fact is that the lands of Afghanistan have been repeatedly invaded, and conquered, during their long history. The fact is, indeed, that conquest—devastating, waste-laying conquest—has come to define the character of these lands perhaps as much as stubborn independence has. And the *yaghestan* principle, while often successful in stymieing would-be invaders, has just as often constituted the fatal chink in Afghanistan's bulwark: allowing those invaders in.

The most famous chase of a defeated local leader across Central Asia is one I have reveled in since adolescence, when I discovered a riveting historical novel by Mary Renault called *The Persian Boy*. It tells the story of Alexander the Great, who, in the early 330s B.C., pursued the shah of Persia and then his would-be successor well beyond the confines of the Greeks' known world, into the heart of Central Asia.

Back then the Persian Empire covered all of today's Iraq and stretched beyond it to the shores of the Mediterranean. Alexander's original goal was to retrieve some Greek city-states in modern Turkey, Syria, and Israel/ Palestine, which had been conquered by the Persians.

The ambitious young Macedonian first did battle with Persia's king of kings, Darius III, at the northeast corner of the Mediterranean, where the coast of modern Turkey meets the top of Syria. The shah deployed his forces in a narrow defile, where his serried contingents were unable to maneuver to advantage.

Alexander, mounted on his beloved and now rather elderly steed Bucephalas, threw himself at the Persian royal bodyguard and the tall, gem-studded monarch in its midst. Darius, to his eternal shame, turned and fled. Like a drowning man shedding sodden clothes and shoes, he cast off accoutrements, cumbersome chariot, royal weapons, and robe of state as he leaped to the back of an unharnessed horse and galloped for his life.

Alexander turned back from the chase with the trophies but not the king, and discovered at the Persian camp what kind of style Darius traveled in. The shah had abandoned sumptuous tents and furnishings, harem, even his mother to the Greeks. A filial friendship was born between Alexander the Great and the Persian queen mother.[2]

After a detour to Egypt, Alexander headed back north and east across modern Syria and Iraq. The Greeks fought Darius and beat him again, not far from Mosul. Deployed in the left wing of the Persian army, behind the elephants and to their left, was a small cavalry contingent from Kandahar.[3]

According to one account, Alexander sacrificed to Fear ahead of the fight that morning.[4] Apparently, Fear heard him: again Darius turned and ran. The Greeks caught up with him just south of the Caspian Sea. They found his body, that is. Some nobles had tied him up and thrown him in a cart, then stabbed him and fled.

One of those nobles tried to set himself up as king of kings in his murdered kinsman's place. He headed for the wild east, rallied the tribes, took a shah's name, and began wearing the Persian cap of royal office.

It was to pursue and punish this regicide that Alexander persuaded his army, already so far from home, not to turn back toward Macedon, but to push yet farther eastward into lands that were well off the map. The Macedonian army was a democratic affair, with major decisions decided by general assembly. So it was indeed a matter of persuasion on Alexander's part, not force. It is hard to imagine what kind of charisma he must have had to move his men to follow him to the back of beyond.

They chased the regicide across Persia, detoured southward to Herat on modern Afghanistan's border with Iran. By autumn of 330 B.C., Alexander's army was encamped in today's Farah, roughly halfway between Herat and Kandahar. Then, passing by Zaranj and the home counties of those Persian folk heroes Zal and Garshasp and Rustam, the Greeks turned eastward along the mighty Helmand River. The winter, passed in those warm regions where the zunbils of Zabulistan spent their winters almost a thousand years later, was a delight. A "peaceful tribe"[5] provisioned the army and received reward. And, with no battle noted, Alexander founded another one of his Alexandrias there, Alexandria in Arachosia, on the approximate site of modern Kandahar. It was one of many Greek colonies he was to leave behind to administer the vast new empire he was building.

It took a lot more chasing before Alexander finally caught up with Darius's assassin. By sheer force of will he hauled his army over the towering and snow-drifted Hindu Kush Mountains north of Kabul, later in the year than he should have dreamed of trying it. He spent five days crossing the Oxus River, now Afghanistan's northern boundary with Uzbekistan, much the way Afghans do today: on rafts made of inflated animal hides. His soldiers finally put a collar around the neck of the regicide not far from modern Samarqand.

That was a city with an illustrious future ahead of it.[6]

Just short of fifteen hundred years later, in the early A.D. 1200s, Samarqand was a flourishing commercial town, polyglot, its people sporting the fabulous dress of a dozen countries, eating foods that revolted each other. Samarqand was a key halt along the silk route, plied by caravans with their multicolored bales of goods headed from China westward to the Mediterranean. The capital of a small steppe principality, the town enjoyed great prestige. "It was by common consent the most delectable of the paradises of this world among the Four Edens," wrote the historian Ata Malik Juvayni in the 1250s, "a country whose stones are jewels, whose soil is musk and whose rainwater is strong wine."[7]

UNESCO, the United Nations Educational Scientific and Cultural Organization, has a publications division. It has seen fit to put out a translation of the above-quoted, absolutely crucial source for the Mongol conquests, one of the most traumatizing events ever to occur on earth. The book is available in paperback; it can be ordered on the Internet.

Here is what propelled me to do that. The Mongols swept across Central Asia in the 1220s like a tidal wave. Nothing stood in their way. They killed people in the hundreds of thousands, pushed down trees and uprooted fields, sacked magnificent cities. And on the wreckage they founded the largest contiguous empire in human history, spreading from China all the way across Asia to the Mediterranean and Eastern Europe. The Mongol conquests had an unimaginable impact on the collective psychology of an entire continent, one that has lasted until today. And Afghanistan—Kandahar—was in the Mongols' way. I just had to know how Kandahar had fared. How had the conquest that defines the very idea of conquest in the human imagination treated Kandahar?

I did my now-familiar trawl in the library. I took out five books on the Mongols, photocopied them, and returned them the next day. The later arrival of that UNESCO primary source added priceless details to what I first read.

When the Mongols under Genghis Khan—the greatest military genius since Alexander—erupted onto the plain before Samarqand in 1220, they enjoyed a military superiority every bit as dramatic as that of the Soviets over the Afghans in the 1980s or the United States over the Taliban in 2001.

Their first advantage was speed. The Mongols on their shaggy ponies could race across territory with unimaginable swiftness because, unlike any army of the day, they traveled unencumbered. They would not even

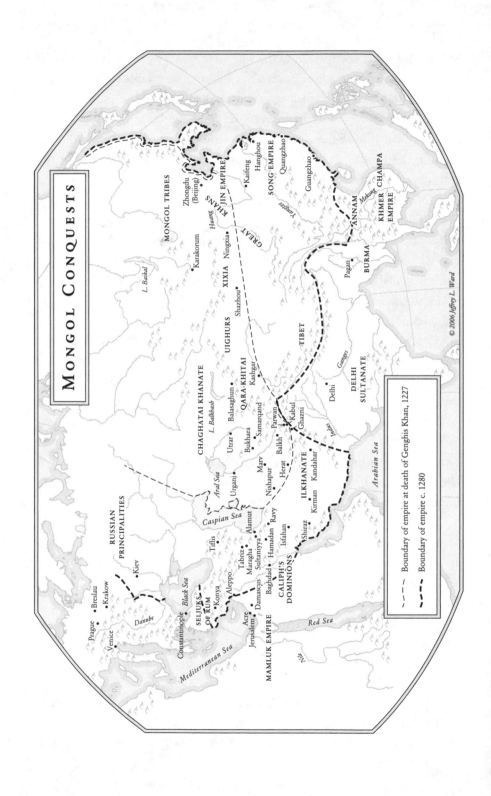

MONGOL CONQUESTS

MONGOL TRIBES

Zhongdu (Beijing)
Karakorum
L. Baikal

JIN EMPIRE
Kaifeng
Hanghou
SONG EMPIRE
Quangzhao
Guangzhao

CHAMPA EMPIRE
ANNAM
KHMER EMPIRE

GREAT KHANS

XIXIA
Ningxia
Shazhou
Huang

Yangtze
Mekong

BURMA
Pagan

UIGHURS

QARA-KHITAI
Kashgar
Samarqand
Parwan
Kabul
Ghazni

TIBET

DELHI SULTANATE
Delhi
Ganges

CHAGHATAI KHANATE
L. Balkhash
Balasaghun
Utrar
Bukhara

Marv
Urganj
Herat
Balkh
Kandahar
ILKHANATE
Kirman
Nishapur
Ravy
Alamut
Hamadan
Isfahan
Shiraz

Jaxtus
Arabian Sea

Aral Sea
Caspian Sea

RUSSIAN PRINCIPALITIES
Kiev
Tiflis
Tabriz
Maragha
Sultaniyya
Baghdad
CALIPH'S DOMINIONS

Prague
Breslau
Krakow
Venice
Danube
Black Sea
Constantinople
SELJUKS OF RUM
Konya
Aleppo
Damascus
Acre
Jerusalem
MAMLUK EMPIRE
Red Sea
Nile
Mediterranean Sea

© 2006 Jeffrey L. Ward

– – – Boundary of empire at death of Genghis Khan, 1227

▬ ▬ ▬ Boundary of empire c. 1280

carry food, hunting along the way instead and crossing deserts in winter so they could graze their ponies on shoots of dew-fed grass. The Mongols carried no siege engines, preferring to load much lighter engineers, who could build what they needed on the battlefield. They wore tough but flexible rawhide armor, the contemporary equivalent of a bulletproof vest.[8] Practically born on horseback, the Mongols could shoot their arrows while hanging sideways or backward off their mounts. They perfected the old steppe ruse of the feigned retreat, drawing an overconfident foe into a cul-de-sac and then falling on him from all sides.

Apart from these advantages, which grew almost naturally out of the Mongols' native environment, Genghis Khan's genius added others. Like the leaders of the early Muslim Arabs six hundred years before, he had learned that tribalism hampered conquest. Genghis Khan abolished tribes and reorganized his army on a decimal principle. The Mongol army was the most disciplined fighting force the world had ever seen.[9]

Like Alexander, Genghis Khan loved surprise. When, to avenge a grievous insult, he made up his mind at the age of sixty to go out west to Persia and conquer the shah, Genghis Khan did not take the straight road traveled by the silk merchants. He opened up a longer route on a northern arc—fully two thousand miles of rugged mountain and Kyzyl Qum Desert that *no one* crossed. Appearing impossibly at the gates of Samarqand's neighboring city Bukhara in March of 1220, Genghis Khan strewed panic.

The pages of Juvayni and other Persian-speaking chroniclers of these events indicate what a tremendous clash of cultures then transpired. Islam in those days, though politically chaotic, was a deeply learned, cultivated society—much more so than contemporary Europe. Of Bukhara, Juvayni writes, "Its environs were adorned with the bright light of doctors and jurists and its surroundings embellished with the rarest of high attainments. Since ancient times it has in every age been the place of assembly of the great scholars."[10] Among the horrors that followed in the Mongol sack, the destruction of Bukhara's library was the most painful to these authors: "And they brought the cases in which the Korans were kept out into the courtyard of the mosque, where they cast the Korans right and left and turned the cases into mangers for their horses."[11]

The Mongols at that stage had no use for book learning. They had little use for cities. Bukhara, like the others, they methodically destroyed.

What they did have use for was fodder, which is why they cut up a lot of cultivation and let grassland reconquer the Persians' tilled fields. There was a certain logic to their treatment of Bukhara's books, though, as systematic destruction of cultural objects with no military value, punishable in international tribunals today, it was shocking even then. The Muslims did not understand that by allowing the learned jurists to feed their horses, the Mongols were ritually accepting their submission, sparing them death, and promising them future protection.[12]

Like Alexander, Genghis Khan invoked the animus of fear to aid his conquests. Indeed, he consciously cultivated fear. The Mongols' tactics were designed to terrorize the population into submission.

When he did not massacre the entire population of a conquered place, Genghis Khan would execute the fighting men, after emptying the city so his people could loot it more efficiently. He would allot a portion of the vanquished men to each of his commanders of a thousand for killing. The bones of the dead would be heaped up to frighten travelers, as attested to in another contemporary chronicle by a witness who rode past such a macabre hill: "We supposed that that white eminence was perhaps a hill of snow, but the people of that part replied, 'The whole of it is the bones of men slain.' [Further on,] the ground became so greasy and dark from human fat that it was necessary for us to advance another three stages on that same road until we came to dry ground again."[13] Three full days wading through human blood.

Craftsmen, who might be valuable in equipping the Mongol army, were shared out among its divisions. The Mongols organized most of the other civilian males into "levies," whose duty was to take the lead in assaulting the next city.[14]

It was this kind of army, ghoulishly swelled with conscripted local folk, that took the glorious city of Samarqand. "So many men, both Mongols and levies, were assembled together that their numbers exceeded those of the sand of the desert or drops of rain."[15] Petrified Samarqand swung open its gates, and "the Mongols then entered and that day busied themselves with the destruction of the town and its outworks." Barely glancing up as night fell, the Mongols "lit torches and continued their work until the walls were level with the streets and there was everywhere free passage for horse and foot."[16]

Even before this graphic demonstration of what the Mongols were capable of, their enemy, the ruler of eastern Persia, was terrified. "The control of firmness having slipped from his hands and the attraction of constancy having been replaced by that of flight,"[17] Sultan Muhammad Khwarazmshah had left about a hundred thousand men to garrison doomed Samarqand, and had run away.

The Mongol pursuit of this Muhammad Khwarazmshah to the shores of the Caspian Sea was remarkably similar to Alexander's pursuit of Darius III to the shores of that same sea. The principal difference being that the Mongols chased Sultan Muhammad *westward* to the Caspian, whereas fleeing Darius had led Alexander's army to the east.

Like Darius III, Muhammad Khwarazmshah is mostly remembered for his fear. The Persian chronicles practically wring their hands at it. Juvayni writes that fear had gained such a hold on the sultan that all he wished for was a hole in the ground to hide in. According to another local historian named Juzjani, who fought the Mongols himself for several years in the mountains north of Kandahar, "Fear and dread of them took possession of Sultan Muhammad's heart and mind. . . . This was one of the causes of the miseries and troubles which befell the people of Islam."[18]

Abandoning treasure and "veiled womenfolk"[19] in his final breakneck flight, just like Darius, he made for the mountains south of the Caspian Sea—on foot, according to one account. Then he rode in a boat to one of the tiny islands that dust the coast—and died there, maybe of an ulcer.[20]

So far so good.

But in all the history books I had photocopied to bone up on this background, I had not found a single reference to Kandahar. I tried looking in the indexes under the initial Q, the way the Persians say it. Nothing.

This time, I resorted to a shortcut. I started asking people. I penned a letter to the illustrious C. E. Bosworth in England. "I can find no mention of Genghis Khan ever being anywhere near Kandahar," came his answer in the post. My college Arabic teacher, who is also an expert in Persian and Turkish, was my next target. Offhand, he could not think of any references to Kandahar until Babur's time, 1500. The author of one of the books I had just read kindly trawled the Mongol sources for me, with no more success.

This was fun. I felt like a member of a scholarly community. Everyone wanted to help. But still, nothing on the Mongols in Kandahar. It was ridiculous. The Mongols had swept across an entire continent but had left no trace in Kandahar? Kandahar was the single house left standing on the metaphorical beach after the tidal wave had ripped past? That could not be possible. And so I sent off to UNESCO for Juvayni, to see if my obsessiveness could extract something from his account.

And I found it. An epic story, a story of a fantastic victory against the invincible Mongols, a victory that was brought to naught by the Afghans' fatal flaw: *yaghestan*.

The Mongols' manhunt, like Alexander's after the murder of Darius, did not end at the ignominious death of Sultan Muhammad. The sultan was survived by a rather more distinguished son, whose name is one of the few that even Mongol historians bothered to record: Sultan Jalal ad-Din. For several more years, Jalal ad-Din made the Mongols chase him.

Young Jalal ad-Din outshone his father even while he was alive. When Sultan Muhammad was paralyzed in one of his worst fits of dithering and asked his nobles what to do, the prince spoke up: "My advice is that we should, as much as possible, gather the armies together and advance against them. And if the Sultan have no heart for this, let him proceed to Iraq and hand over the armies to me, so that I may . . . join battle, and smite them like a stone against a clay pitcher."[21] Even if he lost, the young prince argued, at least he would have saved the honor of the Khwarazmshahi house.[22]

But his father would not hear sense. With a filial devotion rare in those days, the disappointed Jalal ad-Din attended his father all the way to his death by the Caspian Sea. Then the new young sultan rushed back to the lands his father had awarded him five years earlier: the future Afghanistan. Jalal ad-Din was going to rally his subjects to fight against the Mongols.

But the *yaghestan* principle was operating in that unruly land. And this time, as events were to prove disastrously, it was not at all adapted to the occasion.

For decades the Khwarazmshahs had been duking it out with a line of local rulers based north of Kandahar and east of Herat who made their rude capital in the mountains of that region near modern Urozgan known as Ghor. These Ghurids spoke a weird dialect, very different from the Persian around them. It could possibly have been Pashtu.[23] In 1205 the line petered out. By 1215 Sultan Muhammad Khwarazmshah was in possession of their land and gave it to his son Jalal ad–Din.

When the Mongols appeared before Samarqand just five years later, the scars of this long rivalry between the two competing dynasties were still painful to the touch.

Jalal ad–Din appointed a cousin of his as governor of Herat. And while he was busy with his father on the Caspian Sea, this cousin moved to rally resistance to the Mongols. With a great army, he set out from Herat for the town of Ghazni in the way you still have to go: not as the crow flies, over the trackless mountains of Ghor, but by the longer, easier route, down and around via Kandahar.

These days, there is a second gate on the east side of town, where caparisoned trucks wait in line to pay their tolls. They have come down the seamed cement road from Herat. Some will drive on out to Pakistan, but many will round Kandahar and head back upward to Ghazni and Kabul. When these car-killing highways were finally about to be repaved in 2003, the project was dubbed the Ring Road.

Cousin Khan Malik[24] of Herat passed through Kandahar along this route and arrived with his cavalry outside Ghazni. He politely sent ahead and asked the governor there (whose name was Muhammad Donkeyskin) to assign some pastureland for his army's horses. For, he wrote, they should join forces, what with the Mongols abroad. But Donkeyskin was a member of the Ghurid house, and Cousin Khan Malik was a Khwarazmshahi. The old rivalry still smoldered. "We cannot live together," Donkeyskin snapped. "The Sultan has assigned fiefs and pasturage to everybody. Let each remain in his own place and see what happens."[25] *Yaghestan* was operating full tilt.

At such insubordination, Khan Malik's allies in the town murdered Donkeyskin. They did the deed in a garden where they had invited him to enjoy a meal. Cushions would have been laid out on rich carpets under fruit trees, as I have often sat drinking tea and eating almonds in Kandahar. Perhaps musicians played for the guests, as they did for the mythical king Jamshid when he arrived in Zabulistan. Perhaps Donkeyskin's blood mixed with the ruby syrup of pomegranate seeds that flavored the rich dishes of meat.

In any case, Khan Malik entered Ghazni and arrayed his forces around the city. The assassination was no doubt necessary, but it piled fresh blood feud on top of the *yaghestan* principle as the Muslims prepared to confront the unbeatable Mongols.

The Mongols were also after Cousin Khan Malik by this time. Genghis Khan had sent out a hunting party. Just missing him in Herat, the several thousand mounted archers pushed on through Kandahar toward Ghazni.

Interestingly, in neither the principle Persian sources nor the Mongol ones is there any record of a fight at Kandahar during these various comings and goings. It seems the town was serving its age-old purpose: as a road. I wonder if its people then, as now, collected tolls.

Who these people were, exactly, is not so easy to determine, for the chronicles only mention important characters, making human history into a kind of soap opera, concerned exclusively with the humors and doings of the great, as though all the world were their living room. But it is likely that the people of Kandahar at that point were what contemporary records refer to as Tajiks. The word did not carry the specific connotation it does today, of kinship with the people of Tajikistan. Back then the label was much looser, meaning local Persian-speaking settled folk. They probably cultivated almond and pomegranate trees as Kandaharis do today, and trained the spring shoots of their vines along the baked-mud walls they mounded up to support them. Kandahar has been famous for its grapes for millennia.

Waiting for Jalal ad-Din to join him in Ghazni, Cousin Khan Malik raised a good-sized army, according to the Persian version of events. Scouts for the Mongol troop galloped up to the city walls on his heels, took a look, and . . . turned around and fled. It was a genuine retreat, not one of those patented feigned ones. Khan Malik sallied forth from Ghazni and beat the Mongol contingent all the way down to Kandahar. Then he turned back for Ghazni while the Mongols drifted up via Herat to rejoin the bulk of their army bivouacked with Genghis Khan in the north.

And so Kandahar bore witness to that very rare thing: a Mongol defeat.[26]

I found another version of this story later. It was in a biography of Jalal ad-Din written by his own court secretary. I had to call that one up from my library's "depository," a grim warehouse located across town from the main building. The back cover of the book was virgin. No one had ever checked it out. The text is, surprisingly, in Arabic, not Persian. This meant that—with some work—I could read it myself. I secured a dictionary, and started laboring through the text, coaxing my creaky Arabic into gear.

According to this rendition, the Mongols *were* besieging Kandahar after all. There it was, right on the page, the name of the town spelled with a Q, not the Pashtu K. I wondered why it had taken such a hunt to find this out. Jalal ad-Din was on his way from his father's grave to Ghazni, and he met up with Khan Malik right outside Kandahar. According to Jalal ad-Din's secretary:

> The two joined together, and decided to attack the Tatars, who were be-siegeing the fortress of Kandahar. And the two pounced on them. And the Enemies of God were downcast. They did not understand how the princes had managed to lie in wait for them, and how the troops of horsemen had closed in on them from all sides. They had counted on [their enemies, like] doe gazelles, running away, unable to withstand them. They had assumed the sharp ends of their enemies' spears would be idle and ineffectual. Until, when they saw [the lance points] thirsting to slaughter them, parched for [the blood of] their chests, they leaped astride their horses' backs in flight. None escaped except an insignificant number, who informed Genghis Khan of what had befallen his soldiers.[27]

Now that was *really* a story—an actual pitched battle, Mongols against Muslims, and the Mongols lost. If real, such a defeat would have been se-vere humiliation for the Mongols; it would have meant their spell was bro-ken. And, according to this source, it happened right there in Kandahar.

The various accounts agree on the next scene in the drama: Jalal ad-Din and Cousin Khan Malik, rallying the anti-Mongol forces in Ghazni to stand against the main body of the Mongol troops. The two princes were lionized. They represented the people's very last hope against the destruc-tion of their civilization. A vast host flocked to their standards, with "bands of soldiers and tribesmen approaching from every side."[28] Jalal ad-Din had been sending letters out right and left, calling fighters in to join.[29]

The historian Juvayni waxes poetic to capture the moment, quoting lib-erally from that Persian epic poem, the *Shahnama*. Juzjani, who was nearby at the time, is less flowery: "Numerous troops joined them, consisting of

Turkmen, Ghuris, Tajiks [local Persians], Khalaj [perhaps the ancestors of the Ghiljais], and Ghuz, and a great army collected."[30] Jalal ad-Din's secretary estimates the total number at 60,000.

The troops would have been spread out across Ghazni's broad valley, washing themselves and watering their horses in the icy river, in the shadow of the chain of mountains that parallels the road, painted a white perfect beyond description by a recent fall of snow. I have seen those mountains once that way. Each contingent would have camped apart under its own commander, but exchanges and sales—of weapons, leather straps, beasts of burden—must have had the men eyeing each other cannily and arguing in a practiced theater.

As they welcomed their arriving comrades and waited for more, they may have let off steam with a bout of that famous warlike Afghan version of polo, or whiled away more peaceful hours playing chess. Most of the fighters would have spoken Persian, but many spoke Turkish. Sunset prayers must have been a moving sight, with several tens of thousands of mismatched toughs bowing in unison over their shawls, as the sun buried itself behind the mountains.

Jalal ad-Din took this force north, doing what no one else in those parts had ever dreamed of: He turned the tables. He went hunting for Genghis Khan.

The only record the Mongols kept about these years is *The Secret History*. Of the battle that followed, north of Kabul, it notes laconically: "Jalaldin Soltan and Qan Melik moved against Chinggis Qa'an. Shigi Qutuqu went as vanguard before Chinggis Qa'an. Jalaldin Soltan and Qan Melik fought with Shigi Qutuqu. They defeated Shigi Qutuqu.[31]

Juvayni's proud retelling is rather more vivid:

Repeated reinforcements were sent from the center and left wing until they drove the Mongol army back to their base. In all these charges many were killed on either side, there was much hand-to-hand fighting and unending recourse to both guile and force and none would show his back to the foe. Finally, when the bowl of the horizon was red with the blood of sunset glow, either side encamped at its base; and the Mongols ordered every horseman to set up an image on his spare horse.

This ruse was designed to trick the Muslims into thinking the Mongol army had been vastly reinforced.[32] But Jalal ad-Din was not intimidated. The next day he joined battle again. The Mongols charged his left wing, but the Muslims staved them off. Some Ghurids under a commander named Ighraq mounted the successful defense.

> Ighraq's men held firm and let fly with their bows, and held the Mongols in check. And when the Mongols withdrew from that attack and made for their base, the Sultan commanded the drums to be beaten, and the whole army mounted horse and made a general charge and put the Mongol army to flight.[33]

The battle was a rout. Jalal ad-Din had cleaned up the Mongols.

It was *yaghestan* that defeated Jalal ad-Din.

After their victory, the Muslims gleefully set to looting the Mongols' camp. "A quarrel arose respecting the booty," Juzjani notes. As usual, Juvayni provides the telling details. The fight was over a horse, he says, one of the Mongols' indefatigable ponies. A commander hit Ighraq over the head with a whip—Ighraq, who had brilliantly held the left wing against the Mongol assault. Unsure how to handle the dissention in his disparate troop, Sultan Jalal ad-Din meted out no punishment. Ighraq stormed off, withdrawing his men from the Muslim army.[34]

Wait a second. I interrupted my reading of the tale. This was sounding familiar; I couldn't quite tell how. I searched back, finally spooling up from my memory a line from an ancient poem.

> Rage—Goddess, sing the rage of Peleus' son Achilles
> murderous, doomed, that cost the Greeks loss on bitter loss,
> hurling down to the house of Death so many sturdy souls . . .
>
> Among the Gods, who brought this quarrel on?[35]

Again, I realized, the parallel is Greek. From Homer's *Iliad*.

The fabled quarrel between Achilles and his king Agamemnon beneath the walls of Troy was over booty too, a girl, Achilles' rightful share.

Agamemnon would not give her up. Furious, Achilles withdrew to his tent, pulling his troops out of the war and almost dooming the Greeks.

A closer look at the events helps explain his behavior, and sheds some light on the even darker fate of the unhappy Muslims so many centuries later. The principle at stake in both cases is honor, a taproot of both societies.

Greek officers, writes Jonathan Shay in his stunning analysis of post-traumatic stress disorder, *Achilles in Vietnam,* went into battle in pursuit of honor. "Honor," Shay points out, "was embodied in its valuable tokens," such as Achilles' girl Briseis or that sturdy Mongol horse that Ighraq wanted so badly. It was for honor that men would risk their lives, Shay argues, and "the material goods that symbolized honor were not per se what made them face *'a thousand shapes of death.'* It is easy for us to caricature ancient warriors as simple brigands or booty-hunters motivated by greed, but this is almost certainly a misunderstanding."[36]

Thus explained, Ighraq's huff is a little easier to understand. Getting smacked in the face with a riding whip, after he had preserved the Muslim line from the invincible Mongols, was a breach of honor he could not bear. No amount of "reasoning" on Jalal ad-Din's part could bring him back to the army.

The result of Ighraq's rage was even more devastating for the Muslims than Achilles' wrath had been for the Greeks—for they did end up taking Troy. The Muslim defense against the Mongols crumbled. "The Sultan's strength was broken by Ighraq's defection," writes Juvayni, "and the highway of honor and success was closed to him."[37]

The weakened Jalal ad-Din knew he could not possibly hold his own against the Mongols now, so he withdrew to Ghazni. This time Genghis Khan went after him in person. Sultan Jalal ad-Din made for the Indus River, the border with the "land of the Hindus." He hoped to cross it and rebuild his fragmented army on the other side, but the lightning Mongols were too quick. Genghis Khan caught up with him at the river's edge, and another epic battle was fought. Jalal ad-Din, Juvayni says, was "left between water and fire": the Indus River at his back and the Mongols in front of him.

The dashing sultan fought hard, but he was going to lose. At last, he called for his spare horse, jumped astride and, shouting a war cry, spurred it forward into the Mongol front—charging like a crazy man, forcing the Mongols back inch by inch. Then, dropping his shield, Jalal ad-Din spun his horse around in the few yards of space he had just cleared and urged it, in a flying leap, off the bank and into the Indus River, some thirty feet below.

Juvayni has Genghis Khan so astonished at this feat that he rides to the riverbank and remains fixed there, watching Jalal ad-Din strike off for the farther shore. When some of the Mongols want to jump in the water after him, Genghis Khan stops them, with an immortal line: "Such sons should a father have."[38]

A lot of the Muslims were killed in this action, their blood turning the Indus a proverbial red. Cousin Khan Malik broke away and tried to escape northward to Peshawar, but a Mongol detachment cut him off and killed him. Eventually, Ghengis Khan did order one of his generals, Bala, to take a detachment and ford the river to resume the chase for Jalal ad-Din.

> While Chinggis Qa'an was waiting for him, Bala crossed the River Shin [Indus] and pursued Jalaldin-Soltan and Qan Melik to the land of the Hindus. There he lost them and was unable to find them again though he searched right into the heart of the land of the Hindus.[39]

In fact, the Mongols did not get anywhere near the heart of India. Men and ponies, so tough in the harsh climate of their windswept steppes, could not withstand India's humid heat. Jalal ad-Din got away. But he never was able to regroup. Though some of the old Ghurid fortresses in the central Afghan mountains held out for years—the historian Juzjani battling away in one of them—nothing further barred the Mongols from establishing their empire. It stretched from Hungary in the west all the way across China. And it changed the world.

It is difficult to convey what the impact of the Mongol conquests must have been, for nothing like them has taken place in modern history. For the sheer psychological effect, think back to September 11. Remember how you felt as you watched those buildings collapse, or smelled the cinder in the air. Now imagine it was not two buildings but all of Manhattan that was razed to the ground, with just such scientific precision, "till the walls were level with the streets." And imagine the whole population of New York being driven outside the city like a herd of animals by wild-looking men, frightening savages to your eyes, and then butchered, systematically.

All of Central Asia's fabled cities suffered this: Merv, Bukhara, Herat, Samarqand. It took these places half a century to begin to recover. Some never did, their remaining populations scattering to nearby villages, sand or grassland eating up their ruined walls. In volleys of lengthy footnotes, scholars skirmish now about their likely locations. What the impact on their people must have been is beyond imagining. I wonder how many went mad.

Very slowly, some cities did return to glory. Very slowly, the great Central Asian culture sprouted again from its roots, like a field after a forest fire. The father of historian Juvayni won service with Genghis Khan's son and first successor, becoming the finance minister for all of Persia. A generation later, Juvayni himself got a job with Genghis Khan's grandson Hulagu, ruler of the Persian part of the empire. Hulagu eventually appointed Juvayni governor of Iraq. The historian ordered much reconstruction, rebuilding cities and digging new canals.

Like Alexander the Great, in other words, the Mongols used locals to administer their conquered territories. Like Alexander, the Mongols learned from these locals, adopting their ways. Hulagu Khan revived the flourishing and original Muslim research in mathematics and astronomy. Along with administering provinces, Juvayni wrote his history. The *juris doctors* launched into their debates again, and the Persian poets began to sing again.

Another useful, if schematic, way to think of the Mongol conquests is, indeed, as a tidal wave. Like a tidal wave, the gigantic force of these conquests hurled people, belongings, animals, and ideas far and wide in front of them. After fighting Mongol besiegers from inside a cragged central Afghan fortress for four years, the more sober-styled historian quoted above, Juzjani, moved down to India along with much of the population of modern Afghanistan. There the floodtide of refugees laid the foundations of Muslim culture in the subcontinent.

As a tidal wave does, the Mongol conquests left everything topsy-turvy, jumbled, and mixed up in their wake.

Kandahar, for example, settled back into its age-old frontier role, marking the boundary between the Mongol empire and India to its south. And
it seems that the Mongol and Turkic troops who continued fighting on this
Indian front began marrying in with the Hindu girls they brought back as
booty. The result was a new group called the Qara'una. "What seems to
have most struck the Iranian historians writing in the time of Hulagu,"
writes the expert on this group, scholar Jean Aubin, "was the Qara'una's
lack of discipline."[40] *Yaghestan*—what a surprise. And so the Kandaharis'
Persian blood was becoming mixed as Turkic people, Indians, mountain
Ghurids, and some "Afghans" began settling in the oasis.

While all of this was slowly shaking out, it happened all over again.
Consciously imitating Genghis Khan, Tamerlane, a tribesman born near
Samarqand, conquered all of Central Asia in the fourteenth century.[41]

In 1383, and it is well known this time, Tamerlane besieged and captured Kandahar, and pulled down its defensive wall. He smashed up the old
citadel of Zaranj too, that oasis about four hundred miles west of Kandahar that had been the early Muslim Arabs' garrison town. And just as
Genghis Khan would have done, Tamerlane systematically tore up the
complex irrigation system between the two cities. Time out of mind, it
had spread the water from the great Helmand River out across that sullen
land, making a garden of it.[42]

Ever since then, the place has been a desert. On maps today it is called
Rigistan, "Sandland." In the 1970s, Americans dug some new canals near
the ancient town of Bost. The invading Soviets had deliberately mined the
sluice gates on these canals, seeking—as Genghis Khan and Tamerlane
had—to ruin local agriculture. In 2002, one of the policy papers we did
at Afghans for Civil Society was an assessment of the socioeconomic impact of repairing one of those canals.

Tamerlane's son Shah-Rukh moved his palace from the old Central
Asian capital of Samarqand to Herat, northwest around the Ring Road
from Kandahar. There, under his patronage and that of his successors, Persian painting reached its pinnacle. Artists, turning mere paper into gem-
encrusted cloth-of-gold with the points of their pens, weaving into their
landscapes Chinese forms that came westward in the Mongols' wake, il-
lustrated copies of the famous epic poems. One of their favorites was the

eleventh-century *Shahnama,* or Book of Kings, which, wishfully, sang the Persian heroes' exploits against the Turanians of Central Asia.

Though in real life the Persians lost the fight, they also won. For, like Alexander and the Arabs, the Mongols ultimately came around to Persian culture. Like the legendary phoenix that Herati artists painted into their books of verse, Persia rose flourishing again and again from the ashes.

Perhaps there is hope in this for Afghanistan.

CHAPTER 23

FIGHTING WITH THE PEN

IN THE SPRING OF 2003, I was still clinging to the hope. I still thought that somehow, if I just worked hard enough, if I redoubled my activity, argued more persuasively, forced the messages through to people who counted, I could help shake something loose on the warlord issue. I wore out the road to Kabul, explaining Gul Agha Shirzai's cynical and dangerous behavior to U.S. and Afghan officials. My favorite interlocutor was the constructive and ever-cheerful senior diplomat Bill Taylor, at the U.S. embassy. From our startingly frank exchanges, from what Qayum and President Karzai's chief of staff were saying, it was evident that the pressure was rising, slowly, to remove some of the worst offenders.

Too slowly for my liking.

One day in April I found myself in the departure "lounge" of the Kabul airport, which looked something like the bar scene from *Star Wars,* outlandishly garbed foreigners sticking out like visitors from an alien planetary system among the Afghans, whose regions of origin were gaudily proclaimed by their disparate headgear. I was awaiting the UN flight back to Kandahar. Behind me in line was a beanpole, her potentially unruly hair cropped in a severe 1930s bob, called April. April Witt.

She was a *Washington Post* correspondent, fresh off the national desk. Most of her professional experience had consisted of holing herself up with stacks of financial documents during drawn-out investigations into white-collar crime. She might spend nine months on a single story, she told me.

She had hardly ever reported overseas, but there she was, barely three days in country, heading to Kandahar because she was sure that was where the story was.

I liked this April Witt immediately.

ICRC water engineer Ricardo Munguia had just been murdered. For the entire flight April pumped me for the context, forcing me to crane around to maintain eye contact, since there was just one seat to a row in those tiny planes. Not that it took a huge effort to get me going. I was still boiling over about the assassination. I was still dumbfounded by Gul Agha Shirzai's response. I was struggling to contain a head of steam, as though truth has a force of its own: if I could just communicate it, get it exposed, it would automatically bring about the right decisions. I had to keep slowing myself down and backtracking to make sure April was with me.

I remember her echoing, with an effort to hide her dubious tone, "Warlordism actually *encourages* terrorism . . . ? Close that loop for me." I took a breath, and spelled it out.

My basic point was that our friends the Afghan warlords were profiting from terrorism. It provided employment for their trigger-happy acolytes, as well as ample opportunity to plunder their countrymen. And in Shirzai's case, it allowed him to exploit the contradictory relationship between Pakistan and the United States. The Kandahar governor was aware, as U.S. decision makers apparently were not, of how different Islamabad's agenda was from Washington's. Simpleminded he may have been, but he had figured out that his old friends, the Pakistanis, were running circles around his new friends, the Americans. And he saw how he could stay in favor with both by acceding to just enough of their demands to keep them on a string. Warlordism encouraged terrorism because a warlord like Gul Agha Shirzai had a material interest in maintaining at least some terrorism so that the Americans would continue to "need" him, and because it drove the harried rural population into the arms of the terrorists out of exasperation or powerlessness.

When we touched down in Kandahar, I packed April off to see Zabit Akrem. She and I chatted a few more times—I remember having her over for dinner and introducing her to Mullah Omar's cow. But she was basically on her own. And she wrote a bombshell.

AFGHAN GOVERNOR STRAINS TO SHED WARLORD IMAGE, it was headlined.[1]

According to the article, Gul Agha Shirzai topped a short list of provincial governors whom members of the Karzai administration wanted removed. April had extracted some remarkably daring quotes from Kabul celebrities whom she interviewed on her return from Kandahar: "The reason they want to replace him," Shirzai's long-term aide and now the minister for urban development told her, "is because he is still—with all his delicate qualities—considered a warlord." April caught the minister's smile as he added: "He is trying to conform to the rule of law. He's not 100 percent successful . . . sometimes he himself breaks it."

This was absolutely unheard-of gumption for Afghanistan. Especially in someone who had worked side by side with Gul Agha for almost a decade. Everyone was talking about it. I was aware that this minister's name was in the ring as a possible replacement for Shirzai. The decision must have been all but made, I exulted, and this was his bid for the job. The rat.

I was quoted in the article too, with the Akokolacha story. Ahmad Wali Karzai was in there, making a mild point about the distance between government and the people. Akrem complained about nonpayment of his policemen, and jokingly threatened to wrap Shirzai up and deliver him back to his pals the Americans at the airport.

Thus was our private alliance aired in public.

April got Shirzai's factotum Khalid Pashtoon to admit that customs revenues, in the amount of several million dollars a month, never made it to Kabul. And Ali Jalali, the jolly, rotund Afghan interior minister, said he had told U.S. officials—Qayum Karzai's words almost verbatim—"that in many cases their short-term military goals might undermine their long-term political priorities."

Then there were the glinting gems that April deftly inserted into the setting of her article. For example: Gul Agha "no longer blows his nose on the tail of his turban in front of visitors. . . ." When I first read the piece, I was disappointed that it did not quite "close the loop" between warlordism and terrorism as I had done for April on the plane. But I soon realized that her subtle but dastardly humor was every bit as effective as a policy rant would have been.

Meanwhile, April's questions on the flight had refined my own thinking. If she had needed me to close the loop, then maybe others did too.

I decided the time was ripe for another Letter to Washington, one of the occasional reflections on the situation in Kandahar that I wrote up every few months when the situation seemed to warrant it. Expressly advertised as my personal views, not those of Afghans for Civil Society, they were sent out to contacts in the U.S. Congress or the executive branch with an interest in Afghanistan.

"Terrorism and Warlordism, Closing the Loop," I quoted April.

I took aim at a widely accepted thesis, which I had heard over and over again from U.S. and Afghan officials, journalists, and humanitarian personnel as a justification for the passive policy toward the warlords. The theory went like this: as unsavory as they are, the warlords provide security as well as reinforcements we need in the fight against terrorists. The truth, I argued in this Letter to Washington, was the reverse. Warlords like Shirzai were actually the source of *in*security. Their economic and political interests were bound up in lawlessness and ongoing extremist activity, which guaranteed their continued—fantastically beneficial—alliance with U.S. forces. Therefore, I wrote, though warlords might gamely gird up and sally forth with the Americans on their anti-Taliban raids, they had no intention of completely eradicating the insurgents. Shirzai's delayed operation against those who had killed Ricardo proved my point.

These warlords are old hands, I suggested, practiced in the skill of playing one foreign patron off against another. Nothing they did or said was to be taken at face value. Think of Gul Agha Shirzai as operating a valve, I directed my readers, carefully regulating the flow of extremism, but never fully cutting it off.

Then came the matter of who Shirzai's other patron was. I decided to forgo the customary euphemisms and circumlocutions, and finally tackle this biggest and most incomprehensible riddle of U.S. foreign policy.

"How Pakistan Is Playing the United States to Its Benefit" read my next heading.

I began by noting the remarkable consistency in Pakistani strategy regarding Afghanistan over the past thirty years, namely, the use of religious extremists to gain control of the country or at least to provoke instability.

Despite some cosmetic changes since 9/11, I argued, there is no reason to believe that that strategy has significantly altered.

So why, again and again, has U.S. policy come down in favor of Pakistan and its agenda? Largely because of Pakistani skill in exploiting U.S. inattention, I wrote. And I spelled out the current equation as I saw it:

- Despite the proven danger and destructiveness of this policy to Pakistan itself, Pakistan is still using extremism as a tool to further its regional agenda. . . .
- Pakistan's agenda is exclusively regional and tactical. The Pakistani government is not part of a Bin Ladin–style Islamist International.
- Therefore, Pakistan has no interest in Al-Qaeda members. In fact, Pakistan regards Al-Qaeda with distaste because Al-Qaeda has an agenda of its own.
- The raw material Pakistan likes to work with is former Taliban or Hizb-i-Islami members who, lacking a deeply rooted independent ideology, are more easily manipulated.
- U.S. attention, by contrast, is riveted on Al-Qaeda. (And is now being distracted away from Pakistan by the focus on Iraq.) American policy makers don't care much about former Taliban or what they might be up to.

I concluded that, given Gul Agha Shirzai's close links to Islamabad, to which he openly admitted and which were demonstrated by the frequent presence of Pakistani military personnel in his office and his regular trips to Islamabad, it was perfectly conceivable that he had received a Pakistani directive to delay action against the insurgents who had blown away Ricardo. I had no direct proof of this, and I indicated as much. But it fit the pattern.

When, on occasion, my Afghan friends wanted to offer up some praise for the latest "revolution," as they still called the U.S.-backed regime, there was a phrase they were always using. Afghans, they told me, weren't fighting with guns so much anymore. They were fighting with the pen.

Well, I was trying.

We did not have an Internet connection at ACS yet. An Internet café had opened in town, its computers blanketed behind heavy velvet curtains in private booths. You wanted to wash your hands after touching the keys. This revolting place adjoined the office of the governor's hachet man, Khalid Pashtoon, and was run, quite manifestly, by the Pakistani intelligence agency. The look and behavior of the Pakistanis who staffed it made that much clear. As did corroboration I received later from the Indian consul, who, to his horror, had had some e-mails read. I did not care to offer up this particular missive to its scrutiny, so I asked a friend out at the U.S. base if he could send it to Qayum and my sister Eve in the Boston office, as well as to the trusted diplomat Bill Taylor at the U.S. embassy in Kabul. He said he'd be glad to.

First thing in the morning, two days later, my cell phone fluted out its ring, a long note then descending minor thirds. It was my friend on the base. "Sarah," he chirped gaily. "You need to come to the base." I tried to find out why, but he wasn't telling. Belying the sunny tone he had adopted for the benefit of any third parties on the line, he insisted: "You just need to get out here, right away."

I clambered into the black Land Cruiser. He met me at Gate 2. For once he was right on time. To my surprise, we weren't going to his office or his messy hooch. We were going to drive around the base for a while, crawling at the ten-mile-per-hour speed limit so he could explain in private.

Even so, his voice was hushed. My missive, the one he just sent out for me, had been intercepted.

I should have known. Electronic surveillance is activated by keywords. If one or more preset word is detected in a communication, it triggers closer inspection. My Letter to Washington, as another officer joked to me later, contained about nine keywords a line. The whole thing had been pulled down verbatim.

Well, that's not so terrible, is it?

I had written the thing with the hope that U.S. policy makers would see it and take it to heart. I supposed this was as good a way as any to get their attention.

But my friend wasn't done yet.

The signals intelligence people, he told me, had photocopied my letter and passed a copy over to the Special Forces shop. An officer there had dropped it off on the desk of the man assigned to liaison with Governor Shirzai's brother Razziq. The SF trooper was to show my letter to Razziq Shirzai, discuss it, and find out who had written it.

I blenched. That, in this region, could be a death sentence.

But my friend, bless him, had thrown himself into the line of fire. He just happened to know the SF officer in question. He just happened to have overheard.

"You can't do that!" he had cut in. "You can't go over there with that letter. That's an American citizen. She could get killed if you show that thing to Shirzai." Argument had ensued. The intelligence people had claimed they'd obtained the letter from an open source. My friend knew otherwise. He informed me that no document obtained by means of electronic interception may be reproduced on an open copying machine, or left out on a desk in everyone's line of sight. It is automatically classified. The breach was pretty serious.

A storm front had rolled through Kandahar Airfield's high command. Arguments and recriminations were hurled about all day, my friend told me, though eventually his point was taken. Still, he had made the extra effort to join the Special Forces trooper at dinner at Shirzai's compound that night. He wanted to ensure that, under the influence of ready alcohol and hail good-fellowship, the SF guy did not come across with my letter after all.

I was stunned. Not just at the danger I had narrowly escaped, but at the U.S. Army's rank stupidity. I simply could not believe they would be so cavalier with another American's safety or so wasteful of potential resources in an environment where they had so few to draw upon. Surely an American citizen who lived in Kandahar, was conversant with its culture and cast of characters, and was willing to talk about them—unlike any other aid worker there—had to be worth something. I was aware that the conclusions I drew were not to everyone's taste. But why recklessly jeopardize a potential source?

My friend suggested I meet the trooper who had been ordered to show Razziq Shirzai my letter.

So the next day I found myself near the traffic island between Razziq's compound and Gate 2, in the shade of the one scraggly tree in sight, sitting on a slanted chunk of cement with a rusted metal eye sticking up from its surface, beside a heavy-set, sandy-haired member of the U.S. Special Forces.

I fell instinctively into another habit from my reporting days: don't contradict the man; let him say it all the way out; be shocked on your own time, not in his face. Because what the trooper was telling me surpassed my worst nightmares about how entangled the U.S. Army was in Shirzai's web.

"The military is very pleased with him," the officer was saying. Personally, he found him "the most helpful governor in Afghanistan." His dealings with Shirzai were nothing but positive: every time he'd "asked for stuff, it's happened."

The officer described a friendship that was thickened over frequent dinners at Razziq's compound, where the Afghan and American comrades in arms would sprawl out in front of DVDs, beers in hand. (This in Afghanistan, where alcohol is not just illegal but severely taboo.) Ahmad Wali Karzai, by contrast, with his formal elegance, irritated the officer. He was too "stuck up."

That such an exclusive relationship with a single local player, in treacherous Afghanistan, makes the army vulnerable to manipulation apparently never crossed this officer's mind. It seemed to be with pride that he confirmed the extent of Shirzai's monopoly: "everything that happens in this province goes through the governor," he proclaimed. "We don't trust the others."

I was stunned. And I shakily tried to convince myself this was just an SF view, particular to that very particular unit in the U.S. Army, or maybe just to this individual officer.

I glanced up. One of the fighters in Shirzai's unit was eyeing us curiously, but did not dare approach. Abdullah had the front seat tipped back and was dozing, or seeming to. What a wild combination of casual and cloak-and-dagger this is, I caught myself smiling—the latter sensation intensifying when I noticed a white UN vehicle idling on the far side of the traffic island. Inside was Talatbeg Mazadykov, head of the UN mission in Kandahar, and the image of a former KGB agent if there ever was one, with his perfect Pashtu acquired by way of a PhD in Pashtu *literature,* no less, before the fall of the Berlin Wall, and his frequent visits to the Taliban leadership in Pakistan. He was observing us: the unclassifiable American female and a Special Forces officer, heads bent in quiet conversation in a spot where no one could get near them to eavesdrop.

The officer and I began discussing the recent murder of two of his Special Forces comrades in Helmand Province, to the west of Kandahar. Coming on the heels of the ICRC execution, this brazen ambush of a U.S. military convoy had added to everyone's conviction about a growing and increasingly lethal insurgency in southern Afghanistan.

The SF officer was fighting mad about it. He and his buddies were positive the governor of Helmand Province was behind the attack. They had asked permission from their hierarchy to take the governor out, but they hadn't gotten the green light yet. "Pretty much all the bad stuff that happens here is coming in from Helmand," the officer assured me.

My breath came short. *Is coming in from Helmand? That backwater? What about Pakistan?*

The notion that Helmand governor Shir Mahmad killed the U.S. soldiers was preposterous. Smooth Shir Mahmad, with his weirdly sexy kohl-lined eyes and his Taliban turban, the son of a mullah (the man who had introduced wide-scale opium cultivation into southern Afghanistan), was reputedly a drug dealer and certainly nobody's saint. But he was a Karzai ally and would not raise a finger against a U.S. soldier.

"Really?" I asked the SF officer, willing my eyes to look interested and impressed, nothing more. "How do you guys know?"

"We've got some intercepts," he confided. "The governor giving the order."

I visualized telephone protocol in Afghanistan. No important person ever carries his own phone. A trusty holds it, or, in the case of the fold-out satellite phones the size of a laptop computer, rushes over to pick up incoming calls. And possibly, if he is alone, makes a few calls of his own. Even if Special Forces had a telltale call coming from the governor's phone, that did not necessarily mean the governor made it.

"So, um, what kind of a voiceprint can you guys get for a satellite call?"

"Well, actually," the officer conceded with a little grin, "our voiceprints are more like three guys sitting around a room saying, 'Yep, that sounds like him.' "

My heart skipped another beat. On the basis of "yep, that sounds like him," these men wanted to assassinate the governor of Helmand Province?

I thought back to the amazing piece of information Akrem had shared with me over the plates of pomegranate seeds at our very first meeting in my compound: that U.S. Special Forces in Helmand were bunking with a well-known acolyte of the extremist faction leader Gulbuddin Hikmatyar. Hikmatyar himself was in hiding, but his people had stepped up their activity again, in loose alliance with former Taliban. On an introduction made by Shirzai, the Special Forces had bedded down with a Hikmatyar loyalist.

It seemed unnecessary to look much further for the people who might have arranged the killing of the two officers than the Americans' own hosts.

"So where are you guys getting most of your intelligence from?" I asked.

"It's almost all from Shirzai. He's great. He's got sources everywhere."

I'll bet he does. And he was currently feuding with the neighboring governors because he was trying to set himself up as a kind of superprefect, or overlord of the whole south.

With little exertion, I grasped, Shirzai had, with his carefully planted "information," wound the U.S. Special Forces right around his finger. By blaming Helmand governor Shir Mahmad for insurgent activities in the region, he was achieving two objectives at once: shielding his patron Pakistan and channeling U.S. wrath against his rival.

But the kicker was still to come.

"He really dictates to President Karzai," the officer was saying. "In fact, if Karzai doesn't win the election next year, the U.S. military won't be that sorry. A lot of us would be happy to see Shirzai as president instead."

For the first time since my arrival in Afghanistan, an icy surge of panic spiked through me. My racing mind tried to imagine the scenario. What would it mean for the province, the country? What it would mean for me, personally? Surely this could not be right. Surely this guy was speaking for himself. Because if this represented the position of the U.S. military, then the entire Afghan equation was disastrously transformed. Somehow, I had to find out.

I spent the next couple of days in shock. A call came from Bill Taylor, the dapper diplomat at the U.S. embassy.

Bill was technically in charge of donor assistance to Afghanistan, but his conversations with me would invariably stray wide of that patch. We

would sit at the end of a long, dour table in a 1960s conference room be-
hind a combination-lock door on the embassy's second floor, and plunge
right in: How can we get more Pashtuns to enlist in the national army?
Can I think of any candidates for the job of corps commander? (I suggested
Akrem. President Karzai offered him the job, but he refused as long as
Shirzai remained in Kandahar.) Did I think the election scheduled for
June 2004 should be delayed? Should it be organized as a Western-style
one-man, one-vote contest or more like the *Loya Jirga*? I relished these
chats, the substantiveness of them, the sense that my reflections might actually be folded into whatever mix it was that produced U.S. policy. Slender, well-turned-out Bill was an unwaveringly charming workaholic;
unflappable, enthusiastic, and engaged, his oddly stubby fingers reaching for
a minuscule notebook to jot down our thoughts when we got into the
thick of things. His rank was ambassadorial, and I always thought of him
as a coambassador, standing shoulder to shoulder with Ambassador Robert
Finn. Instinctively, I trusted Bill enough to forward him my Letters to
Washington unexpurgated, in the same batch that went out to Qayum for
comment or censorship.

"I read your Letter," Bill told me on the phone. "It was great."

"Oh, good," I answered. "Did you hear what happened to it?"

He had not, and I told him the whole story.

There is something else that having this team at the embassy meant to
me on a personal level. For a brief moment, they made me feel part of the
American family. I felt that someone was there, that someone cared enough
to watch out for me, in case I did manage to get into a serious bind. Bill's
reaction to my tale cemented that feeling. As soon as he hung up, he convened a crisis meeting with the ambassador, the chargé d'affaires, and the
political affairs first secretary to discuss the unbelievable cock-up on the
base. Bill called me back shortly afterward and told me they wanted me to
go up to Kabul and camp out at the embassy for a while, because it was
just too dangerous for me in Kandahar.

There was no way to convey to him, in mere words, my gratitude.

It was not that I lived in any real consciousness of fear in Kandahar. And
Lord knows my mother's worry, and my sister Eve's worry, which would
flare up like a sunburst in response to nothing more or less concrete than
her own urgent intuition, was enough worry to have to keep at bay. In

Kandahar, I had Ahmad Wali Karzai. It was largely thanks to him, I knew, that I stayed safe. If I wanted guards, I could ask him for them; I could sleep in his house if I needed to; I knew that. Even more powerful was the invisible force field of deterrence flung about me by the public notoriety of his protection, as well as the suggested protection of the Americans. And yet I wasn't a Karzai, either. I never knew what Ahmad Wali really thought of me, who he thought I was.

Perhaps it came down to this: a feeling of belonging that a part of me hungered for. Ten years reporting from Paris, accepted by the French, though frequently the target of jibes, never denying my Americaness but distancing myself at every opportunity from U.S. policies and attitudes that, viewed from across the Atlantic, were next to inexplicable; coming over time to understand that I would never again reside in the country of my birth; not becoming French, of course—you can't—but not really American anymore, either. And then in Kandahar, even worse: not being part of the community of foreign humanitarian workers because their careerism and disdain for Afghanistan, their Thursday night drinking parties with no Afghans allowed, repelled me, and because I, too close to the Afghans and too close to the U.S. military, repelled them; held at arm's length by that same military because I was a former-reporter and a humanitarian worker; and not, of course, being Afghan, viewed by Afghans as a curiosity for my maverick style, but mostly as a potential, and temporary, source of material gain, nothing more human.

In other words, I was alone, fighting a war of my own invention, for what sometimes felt like the future of the world.

My boss, Qayum, the closest I thought I had to a comrade in arms, the man, if there was one, to whom I had utterly devoted myself, hurt me more than I knew in his absentminded indifference to my welfare. The fact was, whether I experienced the emotion of fear or not, Kandahar was a dangerous place. And I was very exposed. Qayum, bounced around like a badminton birdie among the exigencies of his three restaurants in Baltimore, the momentous requirements of governing the newly fledged Afghanistan alongside his kid brother the president, the sunroom he wanted to build onto the side of his house in the suburbs, and the silent rage of his beloved daughter at his extended absences, stayed up there in the ether, where he was most comfortable. He lived, for someone of his rank, an extraordinarily austere life. Still, he rarely made it down to Kandahar, and he never made it down to the Kandahar I inhabited. I remember pulling up to his Kabul house one night around nine-thirty, close to curfew, after more than fifteen hours on that appalling road. It was a trip, so far as I knew, that no other foreigner had ever taken. Qayum looked up from CNN on his satellite TV: "Hello!" he said warmly. "Did you come alone?" *Alone? Are you kidding?* The risks I took just never registered.

All of this was why Bill Taylor's invitation to stay at the embassy moved me more than he would ever know.

"Thank you so much, Bill," I answered him, from my perch on the back steps where cell phone reception was good, and I could watch the cows at tether and the antics of Wooly the Sheep. "But I think I'm OK. The letter never did get to Razziq Shirzai. An alert lieutenant kept that from happening."

"Oh, I see," Bill said. "All right . . ."

I assured him I was on my way up to Kabul before long anyway, and not to worry.

"Listen, Sarah," Bill pursued. "Would you mind if I passed your letter along to General McNeill, the commander of Coalition forces?" Dan Mc-Neill, Bill thought, ought to hear what had happened on the base, and maybe the whole flap could provide an opening to transmit some of my views. For, mirroring the great divide between the two bureaucracies in Washington, a chasm had opened up between U.S. civilian and military leadership in Afghanistan. Bill accorded McNeill a pinch of praise to reassure me. He'd talked to him a few times, he said, and McNeill did not seem "too unreasonable."

For me, the sentence—and the tone in which it is uttered—served as an abrupt initiation into the devastating rift between the Defense Department and the State Department in their supposedly joint conduct of U.S. foreign policy—far more telling than what was filtering out to me from media coverage back in the States. Bill Taylor was equivalent to the highest-ranking U.S. official in Afghanistan. And he had only spoken to the general in command of U.S. troops "a few times"? Bill's tone of voice was just as eloquent as his words. It assumed a kind of comradeship between us— fellow humans, the implication was—as we contemplated the specimen of some other species. State Department civilians found McNeill almost impossible to work with. They said he ran his show in Afghanistan as though they did not exist.

For my part, I could not have wished for a higher-value target, short of Defense Secretary Donald Rumsfeld himself. I said, by all means, send the letter to General McNeill.

A few days passed and I got another call from Bill. "General McNeill wants to see you." I later found out how it had gone, McNeill's response to my letter, a rant: "What does she think, we believe Shirzai? We trust the guy? A guy who's got a used-car salesman with a bad toupee for a side-kick? Does she think we trust *any* of them? But what's the alternative? And what about her, in with the Karzais? I can think of one of them who's mak-ing a whole pile of money out of our presence in Kandahar . . ." And on and on in this vein till the very end, when he suddenly asked: "When can I see her?"

I took the next plane to Kabul.

We met at the embassy, attended by a note taker named Tim. On his lapel, General McNeill wore a stickpin from Harvard's Kennedy School of Government. That was his silent handshake across the divide, his signal that we belong to the same species after all.

I have never been especially adept at the unspoken; I always insist on spelling things ponderously out. So I reached for the much more unwieldy tool of words. "General," I ventured, "before I say anything else, I want you to understand that I am with you. I consider myself to be on your team. I'm not allergic to men in uniform. If I sound harsh, it's a harshness that comes from disappointment, not knee-jerk opposition. Almost the way I'd be harsh with my own family."

McNeill seemed to take this in.

I was burning to know if what the Special Forces officer told me out at Kandahar Airfield represented the position of the U.S. Army. McNeill, with a hint of a grimace, remarked that he had been having "some trou-ble" with that Special Forces team, and would be glad to see the back of them. From his response, it seemed clear that the SF soldier was speaking substantially for himself regarding the myriad virutes of Gul Agha Shirzai.

A bit reassured, I pounced on what seemed to be the most immediate fire to put out: Helmand.

"Governor Shir Mahmad did not order the assassination of those two troopers," I told McNeill, "there's just no way." General McNeill confirmed that he had aborted the Special Forces plan. He had ordered SF not to move on the governor, he told me, a spark of self-satisfaction in his voice.

Picking up on the tone, I suddenly glimpsed another divide between Americans, this one within the U.S. military itself. General McNeill was supreme commander of Coalition troops in Afghanistan. And yet Special Forces, the outfit that was conducting the greatest proportion of combat operations, did not answer directly to him. Special Forces, cohabiting with regular army troops on the U.S. bases at Baghram and Kandahar, roaming about bearded and grubby in the Afghan countryside, had its own separate chain of command, and answered to its own chief in Fort Bragg, North Carolina.

So. Here's another factor thwarting the coordination of U.S. policy in Afghanistan. I sighed. Though General McNeill did not say so explicitly, he made it plain that he shared my frustration.

The subject of Gul Agha Shirzai was, of course, the elephant splashing water on its back in the middle of our conversation. McNeill was clear. "We are here to support President Karzai. Shirzai is President Karzai's governor, and so long as he is President Karzai's governor, we will support him." I launched into my argument that intermediate steps existed between removing Shirzai and writing him a blank check.

I pointed out, for example, that Kandahar has legitimate security forces: the army and the police. These forces had legal status under the 1964 constitution, which was supposed to be governing Afghanistan until a new one was written. In Kandahar, President Karzai deliberately took these legitimate security forces out of Shirzai's hands and placed them under someone else's command. Shirzai, by setting up his own private militias that now compete with these forces, was actually engaged in an act of rebellion. Collaborating so closely with his illegal militias, the U.S. military was not working *for* the central government, but *against* it. "Those militias should be disarmed," I said.

I had had this conversation with military intelligence officers in Kandahar, and they had vehemently agreed. They had even worked up an operational plan for doing the job, which fell under the disarmament and demobilization mandate of the international community. But I could tell from General McNeill's expression that no such vigorous action was in the cards.

On the other hand, past the party line, he did display undisguised distaste for the caliber of most Afghan government officials. An opinion he let slip late in our discussion indicated—so starkly as to give me a jolt—that he included the Karzais with the rest.

The conversation went on, for a long time. I offered McNeill several openings to wrap it up politely, but he did not, circling instead from policy to personal antecedents and back around to policy. Finally he told me he wanted me to see his commander in Kandahar, a Colonel John Campbell. "A very competent youngster," McNeill styled him, a man he said he himself would be proud to serve under, very smart. "Don't get me wrong," he hastened to add, "he's a warrior. But he is intelligent. A good conversationalist."

Army style, McNeill made it happen. Within days of my return to Kandahar, I had an appointment to see the base commander. I was bringing my Ghiljai elders out for a meet-and-greet with a Civil Affairs captain, so we decided to make a day of it.

Colonel Campbell proved to be every bit of what McNeill had promised. At first, our conversation was a little more awkward than the channel that had miraculously opened with the general. Maybe the fact that I had been forced on Campbell from on high put his back up. Maybe he was embarrassed that the Letter to Washington snafu had happened on his watch. He had read it, of course, so he knew where I was coming from.

We quickly abandoned territory-marking preliminaries, however, in favor of a remarkable frankness. Campbell, his hair shaved to the length and consistency of peach fuzz, his arched eyebrows expressing most of his reactions, was listening. His questions were direct. In reply, I was more detailed about the ways in which the exclusive U.S. relationship with Shirzai and his gang undermined the central government and undermined what the colonel was trying to accomplish in southern Afghanistan.

Campbell absorbed my points. And he turned and quietly asked the Civil Affairs captain sitting in on the meeting: "How did we let this happen?"

He turned back to me. "Tell me three things I can do, right now, to make things better." I found five on the tip of my tongue. The first was to open up a direct channel with Akrem.

"Provide training for the Kandahar police force," I said. Akrem had been begging for this kind of help for months. I had spent time with him, drawing up an organization chart of his department, listing the most-needed skills. "My men are fighters," he would say; "they don't know how to conduct criminal investigations—they don't know how to direct traffic, for that matter. They need to be trained in the ways of a civilian institution of law and order."

Here was an irony. Long before I had met Akrem, back in the first months of 2002, before I had even returned to Afghanistan to live, I had entertained a fantasy. I wanted to get U.S. cops to train their Kandahari counterparts. I wanted to make a symbol out of it. I thought: what if we get the New York City Police Department, the NYPD, to adopt the Kandahar police department. What if those heroic New York City cops came to the very place where the 9/11 attack was planned, and waded in and helped forge their counterparts into the police force of a new, democratic Afghanistan. What a phenomenal way to build a bridge out of the rubble of September 11. But the enormity of it daunted me. I did not know anyone in New York municipal government. I did not know whom to approach. Besides, in the postwar division of labor, the United States had been assigned the Afghan National Army to nurture, and Germany was put in charge of the police. A full year later, nothing had happened. Desperate, Akrem had set up a training facility himself, till he ran out of money. By now, with still no Germans in sight, there seemed to be no reason why the U.S. Army should not step into the void.

Idea number two for Colonel Campbell was for him to break his exclusive bonds with Governor Shirzai's private militia. Diversify, I told him. Work with other Afghan units. Even if, as seemed to be the case, constructive, reliable commanders were scarce in the regular forces, the United States would be less vulnerable to manipulation.

I told him to stop systematically turning low-level suspected insurgents over to Gul Agha's forces, since that gave them an incentive to point the Americans toward their personal opponents, calling them Taliban. I told the colonel to start meeting with tribal elders, for they were the leaders respected by the community. Finally, I advised him to work to target reconstruction contracts so as to benefit a cross section of the population.

When I was done, Colonel Campbell leaned back and looked at me, levelly. "We make mistakes," he said. "But I think you will see that we also have a procedure for trying to catch and correct them."

It was a fair point. What civilian NGO has postoperation assessment built into its mode of functioning? Of course, the military did not always get it right. Defensiveness in the glare of the media's occasionally harsh light, or impunity in its absence, left grave faults to grow, fester, and metastasize. The treatment of prisoners in Afghanistan as well as in Iraq is an egregious case in point. Still, the procedure does exist and compared not so badly to the ways of self-righteous humanitarians, myself included, who use the angelic nature of their self-sacrifice to cover everything from excessive salaries to an utter lack of accountability, as they mount the steps, measured off in one-year assignments, of their careers in the burgeoning aid industry.

Colonel Campbell was as good as his word. He told the Civil Affairs captain, a Niagara Falls police officer in civilian life, to get together with Akrem and see about designing a training program. The captain did so, though nothing ever came of it; he was more interested in the intelligence-gathering opportunities the relationship offered. Campbell asked me to draw up a chart depicting the main tribes in the region. To my dumbfounded amazement, there was no such information available to the U.S. army in Kandahar—almost a year and a half after its arrival there.

Hearing that I had arranged for a group of elders to come onto the base that very day, Colonel Campbell suggested that maybe he should stop by. He did so, at perhaps the most surreally awkward moment of a meeting that had kicked off a bit awkwardly anyway. The Civil Affairs captain had arrayed Formica tables with foldout metal legs in a U around a makeshift conference room—partitioned off in plywood from the main terminal building, which, despite some blackened spots left over from the anti–Al-Qaeda bombing, housed most of the army's offices. It was lunchtime, and in deference to the notion that Afghans might eat at lunchtime, the captain had placed cardboard trays of raisins and blueberry muffins and stacks of packaged PowerBars at intervals around the tables. Fifteen venerable

Ghiljai elders considered this unhabitual arrangement, and gamely found places upon folding metal chairs arranged around the tables.

The captain had made the effort to avoid Shirzai's interpreters, bringing a middle-aged Afghan American instead, who proved to be both not too bright and a native of eastern Afghanistan, so the elders' broad Kandahar accent was a trial for him.

The captain's attempt at a fulsome greeting completed, and the response of the group's president underway, an odd noise began emanating from one of my favorite elders, Tukhi, with his wide, solemn eyes and enormous beard. It was a kind of moaning sound, punctuated by ragged breaths. Then he collapsed.

We had just gotten him laid out on the ground when Colonel Campbell arrived, for once absolutely ignored upon his appearance in a room. He quickly sized up the situation and brought order to the frightened pandemonium, commanding the two soldiers who had arrived with a stretcher to stop gawking and get a move on, and reassuring the elders that he had some "pretty good docs here" who would get their friend "back in shape."

Then he took over the meeting, running it with dignity, patience, and natural grace. "What you're telling me," he said after carefully hearing the elders out, "is that because the U.S. troops are working so closely with one tribe, the rest of the Afghans are losing faith in them. Is that it?" He said he wished he had held this meeting earlier.

It proved to be the first of several that Colonel Campbell would convene with Kandahar-area elders.

The episode helped me reach another realization about the role of the U.S. military in places like Afghanistan. Two issues regarding the U.S. military presence are being confounded in the minds of many Westerners, I suddenly perceived, and they need to be disentangled. One is a theoretical question, a subject that requires serious deliberation and debate inside the United States. That question is, do we, as American citizens, wish to have the bulk of our foreign policy conducted by the Department of Defense? It is a crucial question for us as a nation, and it ought to be explicitly addressed and pronounced upon in the United States.[2]

But how to interact with U.S. troops in theater is, at least for me as an American, a separate issue. For on the ground in Afghanistan, the Department of Defense *was* conducting the bulk of our foreign policy. Concretely, the sheer numbers made this truth incontrovertible. Upward of 5,000 U.S. soldiers were stationed in Kandahar. And one State Department representative. Even the newly constituted U.S. embassy, graced by the likes of Bill Taylor, could hardly make an impression next to the massive footprint of the U.S. military. For all intents and purposes, U.S. foreign policy was in the army's hands. And no amount of hostility directed by civilians at soldiers on the ground was going to change that.

There was just one problem. Whoever it was in Washington who had decided upon this state of affairs or allowed it to evolve, had neglected to inform the U.S. Army. Men like Colonel Campbell were trained in the skills of enemy engagement, battlefield tactics, military planning—not in politics and diplomacy. And they were being expected to do a job that had not even been properly defined for them. This was why so many of their decisions, like the empowerment of men like Gul Agha Shirzai, were ill adapted to the peacetime nation-building dimension of the U.S. mission in Afghanistan.

Arguably, a Colonel Campbell should have caught on a little more quickly, but now that he had, now that he was grasping the true dimensions and potential import of his mission, he was struggling to catch up.

When, about six months later, in December 2003, I found myself sitting opposite another colonel, Richard Pedersen, in his office at Schofield Barracks in Hawaii, I made this point explicitly. "I'm not sure this is what you signed up for, Colonel, but you're the one who's going to be running U.S. foreign policy out there. And you had better prepare yourself for it."

"I don't like it," he answered, "but I think you're right."

Pedersen's unit, Bronco Brigade, Twenty-fifth Light Infantry Division, was on its way to Kandahar, and I had been flown out to brief its officers. I was at Schofield Barracks for three days, and could not have asked for a more attentive reception. I must have spent fully eight hours closeted with the colonel, who liked to learn orally, interacting with someone. His penetrating, rapid-fire questions led us all over the map that we had dug up and spread out on his desk. He introduced my talks to two successive groups of officers, seated at dozens of round tables after lunch at the base club, throwing a mantle of benediction over me with his generous words. I was a soldier too, he told his troops, working out there in Kandahar "without benefit of five thousand of her closest friends for protection." I spent a lot of time with the division Civil Affairs team. And I drew up a longer and more complete version of the chart of the local tribes I had drafted for Colonel Campbell back in Kandahar.

The only thing that bothered me about this whole experience was that it had come about entirely by accident. A friend from my days in the Balkans was enrolled at the School for Advanced Military Studies at Fort Leavenworth, Kansas, and had suggested me as a guest speaker. I was suddenly battling my worst stage fright since that original talk at First Parish Church in Concord, standing in front of a roomful of men in uniform. Concord citizens were my people, but I had no idea how what I had to say would go over with army majors.

Past a cold, slightly halting start, the talk went great. It appeared that previous guest speakers, general officers as a rule, had rarely given it to them so straight.

One member of the audience was from the Twenty-fifth Infantry Division, and made the contact with battalion HQ out in Hawaii—ending his e-mail to Schofield Barracks with terms of praise I would never have imagined reaping: "She's like no journalist you've ever seen," he enthused. "She's a hawk!"

My point is this: I wound up briefing the Twenty-fifth by way of a coincidence. No concerted effort was being made to educate the army about the radically new duties that had been thrust upon it. With $178 billion in defense authorizations for 2004, almost nothing was earmarked for the acquisition of knowledge about the place where the troops would be investing the next year of their lives—about its languages, its history or culture, about what was currently at stake there. None of the GIs I talked to out at the base in Kandahar had received such training.

It is not that I, personally, knew so much. But, given the hybrid nature of the mission the army was now being asked to perform, the type of information and experience possessed by maybe a dozen people who had recently spent real time on the ground in Afghanistan had a new value. It seemed to me that such learning should be actively sought out, not just encountered by accident. It should be paid for, just as the latest in weapons technology is paid for. It seemed to me that as long as the Defense Department is conducting U.S. foreign policy, officers should be taught about the foreign land upon which their actions will have such a lasting impact.

Two months after the Twenty-fifth Infantry Division arrived in Kandahar, in the spring of 2004, I received an e-mail message from a highly competent female Civil Affairs sergeant named Heather. She had been tasked by high command to gather some material on local tribes and wondered if I could help. I had to laugh. I forwarded to her the crib sheet I had written up in Hawaii six months before. Heather sent it to Colonel Pedersen, verbatim. He commended her, giving no sign of ever having seen it before.

When I had my first long chat with him, I found that he had spent the two months since his arrival in Kandahar closeted almost exclusively with the new governor—not Shirzai by then, but Shirzai's close friend, the former minister of urban development, Yusuf Pashtun.

I suggested a few tribal elders whom Pedersen should really meet with for contrast. In the absence of Zabit Akrem and Ahmad Wali, who were both out of town, Akrem's elder, former crack anti–Soviet commander Mullah Naqib, was an obvious pick—Mullah Naqib, who had been a direct contact of the CIA during the anti–Soviet *Jihad;* Mullah Naqib, who had shot down three Soviet helicopters with U.S.-supplied Stinger missiles and who had actually returned the unused ones after the war was over; Mullah Naqib, who was appointed governor of Kandahar after the Taliban surrendered, but got shouldered out of the way; Mullah Naqib, the owner, for all intents and purposes, of Arghandab district, and the acknowledged leader of swathes of population all through the districts that counted militarily: Ma'rouf, Arghestan, Maywand.

Pedersen had never heard of him. There was no information on him available in any database. The U.S. Army, I discovered to my disbelief, had no institutional memory at all.

It has caused me to wonder ever since: how is it that an organization as rich in capacities and resources as the U.S. government can so neglect the fundamental task of learning?

Afghans don't believe in incompetence. When I would argue its preponderant weight in any given outcome, they always waved my words away, reaching instead for a theory, a tale of conspiracy or alliance, to explain U.S. actions. Akrem alone seemed intuitively to understand. I asked him one day how it had felt, back when the Taliban had finally fallen, to have to obey Mullah Naqib's command of nonviolence, to be forced to allow Gul Agha Shirzai to seize control of Kandahar.

Akrem surprised me: "We were overjoyed," he answered. Then he explained. "We thought the Americans had a plan, that their support for Shirzai was part of a plan. We thought they were going to lay the foundations of a good government, a government that would be inclusive, acceptable to all the tribes."

In the beginning, Akrem assured me, such a proactive form of nation building would have been easy for the Americans to pull off. "The people were so fearful. They were fearful of the Taliban, and they were just plain fearful because there was no courage left to them. Anything the Americans did would have been accepted."

But slowly, said Akrem, the unruly Afghans roused themselves and began to examine the situation. "Gradually the people realized that there was nothing there. And they became rebellious. They realized the Americans had no plan at all—not for the government of Kandahar, not for Gul Agha Shirzai, not for anything. And they realized that President Karzai had no plan either, no *idea.*" Akrem used the English word to give the notion weight. "And now," he concluded, "the government of Afghanistan is a government in name only."

CHAPTER 24

MISFIRE

SPRING 2003

I CONFESS. I had a further reason for rushing to Kabul to meet Coalition commander Dan McNeill that April of 2003. I wasn't going merely to satisfy his curiosity and to expound my theories, yet again.

Two long months had passed since Qayum and I had written up that plan: How to Fire a Warlord in Eight Easy Steps. The real reason I went to Kabul was that I wanted to lay it on the general. I wanted to gauge his reaction. I wanted to see if he would in fact be willing to play the part we had assigned to him.

The plan provided for consultations between President Karzai and U.S. military officials. And it assumed that the U.S. military, so consulted, would help. I was pretty sure the United States would indeed provide such assistance to the president, if properly looped in. But I did not exactly *know* it. A one-on-one with General McNeill was my chance to find out.

For, nothing was advancing. American and Afghan officials were still locked in their spellbound waltz, dancing around each other.

Out of patience with the reticence in official quarters, I took it into my head to do the parties' turkey talking for them. I answered to nobody, so my actions could not really spark a diplomatic incident, or get me fired or anything.

"General," I waded in, "a hypothetical. Let's say President Karzai wanted to dismiss one of these warlords—Governor Shirzai, just as an example. And let's say he approached you on it, asking for your help. Let's say he had some very specific tactical support he needed—not open-ended green-on-green kind of help, but some specifics. Park a couple of tanks by Razziq Shirzai's compound in the no-man's-land between Gate 1 and Gate 2 at KAF, for example. Or step up the patrols you already run along the border by Spin Boldak. What would you tell him? Could you do it?"

General McNeill did not say yes—exactly. His answer was more roundabout than that. I was putting him on the spot, and there was that note taker named Tim. What McNeill said, in substance, was that his mission was to pursue and catch members of the Al-Qaeda network and to create a safe and secure environment for rebuilding Afghanistan. And that—while he had to be careful not to attract too much attention—if he stayed below the radar operated by his superiors at Central Command, there was a lot he could manage to do within an imaginative interpretation of this mission.

It was all I needed. I *knew* the Americans would come through if asked the right way. I communicated as much to Karzai's chief of staff.

I was elated. I had closed the loop.

And then . . . I had to leave. It was almost physically painful. I was being ripped up by the roots just when everything was finally starting to happen. April Witt's article was still setting off time-release explosions like a fire in a munitions warehouse. I had McNeill's expression of concrete support. My Ghiljais had been received in Kabul and on the base in Kandahar. The base commander was alert and listening. And finally, a direct channel was opened up for Akrem. The pot was nearing the boil, and damned if I wasn't required, by previous engagement, to go back to the United States.

Anyway, I had hepatitis. In fact, I could not sit upright long enough to attend a children's workshop we were hosting at ACS. When I arrived at the airport in Dubai, I had been peeing yellow for two days. I looked in the stainless steel ladies' room mirror and was impressed with my tan. "Mom," I said on the phone. I would never have called her from an airport; I must have been worried. "If you take vitamins, does your pee turn yellow?" I could hear my sister Eve's voice in the background. A pause. "You've got jaundice, dear," my mother answered evenly. "Sounds like hepatitis."

You're supposed to be laid up for weeks with hepatitis. I had to talk at the Harvard Kennedy School of Government three days after I made it to

Boston. In a major concession, I spent two of those days in bed, before launching into the most suicidally frenetic U.S. visit I have ever survived.

At ACS-Boston we had hired a publicist. It was kind of second best to throwing ourselves into intensive fund-raising, which no one much enjoyed. Sue Dorfman was a short, tough, big-hearted broad who did her job well, meaning she booked me solid.

Harvard's Kennedy School kicked things off. It was their Forum series—heads of state had preceded me at that podium. It was just about in my front yard, thank goodness, so I was not too intimidated. I had to cling to the lectern to stay standing. I remember it as not one of my most stellar efforts, but it seemed to go down OK. I received a kind letter afterward from the Forum director.

Then it was editorial meetings with newspapers—the *Boston Globe,* the *Christian Science Monitor,* the *New York Times,* the *Washington Post—* contacts with such glittering potential partners as Physicians for Human Rights, radio interviews, naturally, and a few on TV, a visit with our beloved supporters in Lincoln and Concord, school trips to see kids who were interested in joining our sister-school program or who had already collected boxes of pencils and notebooks, meetings at the Pentagon and with congressmen . . .

And all of this for what? What was the objective? Consciousness-raising about Afghanistan? About Afghans for Civil Society? Grandstanding?

And I saw how this publicity stuff can take on a life of its own—how easy it is, even with good intentions, to get caught up in it. One becomes confused. Appointments are felt as obligations. A responsible girl does not miss them, and so she shows up—and performs. I remembered Bill Taylor telling me at the U.S. embassy in Kabul once, how impressed certain people were that I had chosen to drop a life at National Public Radio that offered a lot of public exposure, celebrity even, to work more discreetly and concretely behind the scenes. Well, what was Bill thinking now, I wondered. The loss of his respect was a painful price for admission to this circus. I tried to assuage my conscience with the thought that we were focusing some attention on the key issues in Afghanistan. We did get a few editorials into big newspapers.

One day, the road show was leaving for Washington. Eve had decided to stay behind. My support group consisted of our administrator, Ayse

Yildiz, a funny and unflappable Turkish American artist who once death-lessly remarked: "Here we are, a bunch of kids from dysfunctional fami-lies, working at a dysfunctional organization, trying to fix a dysfunctional country"; and Amir Soltani, originally from Iran, penetratingly intelligent and as sensitive as fine crystal. Revolutions aside, Amir and I had discov-ered the first day we met that we had lived almost identical lives. He was irreplaceable solace and goad to thought during a tumultuous and soul-searing time.

We were late. We were running through the airport in Providence, Rhode Island. We weren't fast enough: we missed our cheap flight on Southwest by just over three minutes. We looked at each other, catching our breath. Amir and Ayse could take the next Southwest plane. I had to speak at the National Press Club Newsmakers series at two o'clock that afternoon. I would have to find another carrier. We bought a $400 United ticket to Reagan National. Next crisis: I had checked my damned bag. A first. And, another first, I had followed my mother's advice to wear some-thing "comfortable" to travel in—read slovenly. I was going to have to buy some togs the second I hit the ground. There was a Banana Republic right around the corner from the National Press Club, praise the Lord. Never have I been so efficient. Light wool slacks, an appetizing brown herring-bone, a bit too flared at the bottom for my absolute taste, but hey. Thirty-five bucks. Shopping bag dangling from my elbow, I rode up in the elevator and, introductions barely complete, asked the Newsmakers moderator to show me the ladies' room. And I emerged, like Cinderella, presentable.

Despite the prestige that Sue Dorfman had drummed into my head, I knew this talk was not a really big deal. I used to be a journalist. No re-porter with anything to do goes out to a lecture in the middle of the af-ternoon, and then writes about it. I was not the least surprised to see only about fifteen people sprinkled through the auditorium. And so I prepared to let loose. My Letter to Washington about the warlords and terrorism and the role of Pakistan was more than a month old. As is so often the case with epiphanies, everything in it seemed self-evident now. I was wound up like a toy mouse. And no one, I thought, was listening.

I put absolutely everything out there, my tirade only interrupted by Amir and Ayse, who came in halfway through, lugging our suitcases, try-ing to clamber discreetly into seats in the back. I was on about warlordism being the source of insecurity in Afghanistan, warlordism and terrorism linked hand in hand, Gul Agha Shirzai answering to both Pakistan and the United States, Pakistan's double game—the works. I got encouraging looks from a Voice of America delegation sitting in the front row, whose elderly team leader alternated between nodding in energetic agreement and falling asleep.

Later that evening I found out, ice water drenching my back, that VOA had made an eight-and-a-half-minute story out of my talk. I used to be a radio reporter, and I know: eight and a half minutes lasts approximately as long as the Jurassic Age. The thing was broadcast in Persian and Pashtu in, of course, Afghanistan. I called up VOA and asked nonchalantly what they had used. "Oh, the stuff about the Kandahar-to-Kabul highway," they replied comfortingly. Right.

Someone told me during those frenetic days, on the phone from Kandahar, that Gul Agha Shirzai had actually gone to President Karzai to complain about me. I thought it was a joke.

Meanwhile, it did seem that at long last some of the warlord governors were on the verge of being fired. In telephone conversations, Qayum changed his focus away from Shirzai and toward the defense minister, a much bigger fish. When I asked why, Qayum told me Shirzai was a "done deal." I got confirmation from my friend Roy Gutman, an illustrious former *Newsday* and *Newsweek* reporter with whom I had mightily enjoyed working in Bosnia and Serbia. Roy said that on a flight back from Kabul, he had talked to the U.S. special envoy, who had told him Shirzai's replacement was already chosen.

I learned that preparations were under way for a big governors' meeting in Kabul. They were being summoned, a round dozen of them. They were going to get the riot act, maybe several of them the ax. I started hopping up and down. There was no way I was going to miss this. I called in to President Karzai's chief of staff every day, ready to change my airplane ticket and race back for the show. It was happening. Everything was moving in the right direction.

Then, suddenly, on the phone one day, the chief of staff's tone of voice was not the same. "Uh, I don't know, Sarah," he said. "I don't know if it's going to work. The Americans are backsliding."

It was not possible. General McNeill had *promised* me. How could he be backsliding? But the chief of staff could not be cajoled out of his disappointment: it seemed that the U.S. invasion of Iraq a few months back was having an impact on people's enthusiasm. The Americans just did not want to take risks that might tie down troops in Afghanistan. Iraq was the main concern.

I needed a second opinion. I e-mailed General McNeill. I was trying to make travel plans, I told him. Were there any fireworks upcoming in Kabul that I might not want to miss?

The general wrote back: "Enjoy the spring flowers in Harvard Yard."

That, to my dismay, sounded like a signal. "I copy," I sent back. And I stayed in Boston.

Sure enough, the governors' meeting was a bust. Twelve notorious warlords gathered in Kabul, and President Karzai kept them there. I held my breath. Karzai made a thundering speech at the Supreme Court, threatening to resign, to bring down the government and call a new *Loya Jirga*, if they would not change their ways.

I knew the market value of this kind of threat, and I suspected the governors did too. On May 20, 2003, they signed a solemn oath to President Karzai. From now on, they vowed, they would send every bit of the money they were collecting in customs dues up to Kabul. They would obey Karzai's orders on the double, and they would refrain from pulling knives and guns on one another. Gul Agha Shirzai had been the first to leap to his feet and swear fealty. He boasted that he was making more than a million dollars a day in customs. From now on, all of it was Karzai's. Cross his heart.

Karzai's chief of staff tried to put a good a face on things: "They agreed to send every penny to Kabul," he told April Witt for her story in the *Washington Post*. "When the president submitted the list of requirements, all of them said they would comply with no objections at all."[1]

Well, of course they would *say* that, I thought. This is Afghanistan.

Many intelligent observers were impressed, however. *New York Times* correspondent Carlotta Gall described Karzai's "new firmness,"[2] and several foreign friends of mine in Kabul applauded. April was a bit more circumspect: "If honored," she emphasized in her article, the pledge would bring many benefits. "But the agreement has no enforcement provision, and it remains to be seen whether it will have any effect on the warlords and provincial authorities throughout Afghanistan, who routinely act with independence and impunity."[3]

As for me, aware of what had really been in the works, I knew what a climbdown this result was.

The first thing I wanted to do when I arrived back in Kabul was to find out what had gone wrong. I made the rounds. The U.S. embassy, President Karzai's chief of staff, and Interior Minister Jalali were my chief sources.

Their stories, of course, diverged. "They ganged up on us," complained Jalali of the Americans. "They told us everything short of 'Don't do it,' spelled out in capital letters."

Karzai's chief of staff described U.S. civilian and military brass, several of whom had flown in from Washington, virtually lining up outside President Karzai's office to deliver messages like: "Have you thought through all the implications of this?" "Our troops are tied up in Iraq now." "This just isn't the time."

Faced with such explicit reservations, there was no way the Afghans could go ahead, the chief of staff told me.

At the U.S. embassy, I got a slightly different picture. Zalmai Khalilzad, Washington's special envoy and later U.S. ambassador to Afghanistan, had asked President Karzai to detail his plans. "There's checkers," Khalilzad had reportedly told Karzai, "and there's chess. When you play chess, you calculate your moves, two or three in advance." The Americans, it seemed, had suggested some scenarios that might transpire if the warlords were fired. And they had asked Afghan officials to think about them: "What if . . . ? Or if . . . ? Or if . . . ?" And the Afghans' response had been a little vague.

With nothing specific to counter Khalilzad's contingencies, the Afghans appeared to be presuming U.S. troops would bail them out if things went wrong. They seemed to be taking American help for granted. This was just the kind of attitude that would give a General McNeill indigestion.

The embassy told me the Afghans had pondered these discussions and had come back "spooked," saying: "Maybe it's not such a great idea after all." I suspected something closer to petulant deflation on the Afghans' part, a perhaps slightly relieved resignation together with an aggrieved sense that their suspicions had been right all along: the Americans were not going to back them up.

I brought the U.S. descriptions of poor Afghan planning to President Karzai's chief of staff. He shrugged. "He doesn't think that way. The president doesn't do detailed contingency planning. He just knows when something is going to work."

It was the tuning fork. He probably did "just know" the move would work, with his finely honed intuition. But I was beyond irritated. Let him *pretend* to plan, I fumed to myself, enough to calm down the Americans anyway. I mean, gee. Hadn't we described exactly how to do it in our eight-point plan? Had he forgotten to read it or something?

As for the Americans, if their protestations of support for Karzai were in good faith, I wondered why they didn't offer to *help* with the planning process? Why didn't they put their chess-playing experience at his disposal, once it was clear that he really did want to rid his country of the warlords?

Both sides, I concluded, had blinked.

The Afghan proposal had been to fire half a dozen warlords: along with Gul Agha Shirzai, Isma'il Khan in Herat—perhaps the mightiest of all and backed openly by Iran—the double-crossing Uzbek general Abd ar-Rashid Dostum, who had the very worst record from the "*mujahideen* nights" and was currently duking it out in beautiful Mazar-i-Sherif with another thug called Ustaz Ata, and a couple more for good measure. In fairness, I could imagine the cautious Americans breaking out in a cold sweat at the prospect of such a hecatomb.

"Well, what about just Governor Shirzai?" I asked at the embassy. The answer came back that this would have been acceptable to Washington. "We were ready to do that. He was easy." It was the Afghans, it seemed, who were playing for broke.

I went back to my friends in the Afghan government to get this confirmed. "That's right," one of them conceded, "we couldn't have fired only Gul Agha. Pakistan would have been against it." I almost passed out. *Pakistan?* Who's Pakistan? What does Pakistan have to do with this?

It was the beginning of my slow realization that Pakistan might have quite a lot to do with such matters. For whatever reason—fear, painful re-

alism, or complicity—the very summit of Afghan government was relin-
quishing a good deal of sovereignty to its neighbor to the south. To this
day, I have not fully worked out why.

For his part, Interior Minister Jalali proudly declared that he himself had
argued against removing only Shirzai. "He hardly matters," Jalali told me.
"And it didn't seem fair, really, since it was Shirzai who stood up at the governors' meeting and said he would turn over his customs money to Kabul.
It didn't seem right to punish him." *And you believed him?* I saw that Shirzai's
teddy bear routine was working on Jalali—the Afghan who had spent so
much time in America that he had forgotten the wiles of his own people.

Then I remembered that someone at the embassy had used the exact
same word to describe Shirzai's relationship with President Karzai. Karzai,
it seemed, felt a kind of fondness for the Kandahar governor. He was like
a teddy bear that President Karzai would be lonely without.

What a long way we had come since December 2001, when Karzai had
worked shrewdly to contain Shirzai's power in Kandahar after the Americans had imposed him as governor.

As though all of these discoveries were not demoralizing enough, Interior Minister Jalali landed one more blow. "I'm going to fire your friend,"
he declared.

"What?"

"Zabit Akrem, the police chief. I'm going to dismiss him this week."

"What?" I gasped again. "You're kidding me, aren't you? Why?"

"He's cor-*rupt,*" said Jalali, practically rolling the "r."

It was simply beyond my fathoming anything anymore. Here was the
one Afghan official who seemed *not* to be corrupt. The one bent on doing
his job. I suspected Akrem wasn't perfect: his wife was cloistered, and I had
heard something about a house he was building in Kandahar, suspiciously
large. Sometimes I hid my own enthusiasm for him because in Afghanistan,
they were all rotten, weren't they? It was naïve to think well of anyone,
right? And yet Akrem had never disappointed me. On the contrary.

I began begging. "Please, Ali, don't do that. I am telling you, he is the
president's most loyal supporter in Kandahar. He's a good official. If you
do it, not only will you have left Gul Agha in place, you'll have rewarded
him. You'll have infinitely strengthened him. You can't fire Zabit Akrem

and leave Gul Agha. And besides if you do it, the Alokozais will be furious; you'll lose the whole tribe."

I felt like one of those petitioners, kissing my eyes in entreaty.

As a kindness to me, Jalali put it, he would stay execution till he went
down to Kandahar in a few days and took stock of the situation himself.
I slumped back on his couch, exhausted. I felt as though I had been hauling on the arm of a man with a gun—hauling his arm upward, to keep
him from shooting his own foot.

It was time to go home to Kandahar.

CHAPTER 25

ROUND THREE

IN KANDAHAR, THE first order of business seemed fairly clear: I had to have a face-to-face with Governor Gul Agha Shirzai.

I had been receiving fresh reports about how incensed he was. He really did complain to President Karzai about me. The president's younger brother Ahmad Wali, who had witnessed the scene at the Palace, had driven over to our compound in my absence and regaled my staff with the story.

Shirzai had actually threatened to quit if I remained in Kandahar. Interior Minister Jalali filled in the details for me later; he had been there too: "That *nar-shizai!*" Shirzai had fulminated to President Karzai—using a gutter term that means something like "mannish woman." "So long as she's in my province, I can't work! I want to resign!"

"Nar-shizai! Jalali cackled. *"Nar-shizai!"* He was in stitches.

Well, shoot, I thought. Why didn't the president go ahead and let Shirzai resign? That would have solved several problems.

But it seemed President Karzai was not amused. Everyone knew I was connected with the Karzai family. What was I doing giving all those interviews in the United States? People would think I was speaking for him, that my pronouncements were his indirect way of passing a message—that he had put me up to it. That was a fair enough critique. Not that it would shut me up any.

The governor was not home, so I pushed on to pay my respects to

Ahmad Wali Karzai. He was pumping away on an exercise bike. One can't exactly go out for a jog in Kandahar, especially if one is the president's brother.

"No, Sarah. Don't go over there," Ahmad Wali gasped. "He's really mad." He said Shirzai had told the president that I was handing out money to get people to oppose his governorship. Typical Gul Agha Shirzai, I thought, declaiming wide-eyed the biggest whopper that came to his mind. *He* was the one who went around distributing handfuls of cash out of his black Land Cruiser. The old fellow who took care of Mullah Omar's cow in our back yard had got lucky the previous week: Shirzai had handed him the equivalent of a hundred dollars.

I left Ahmad Wali to his exercise and went, of course, back to the governor's residence. The soldiers in their U.S. fatigues shoved us roughly back from the gate. The governor's motorcade was about to come out.

Standing my ground as the black cars emerged, I raised a finger in a signal to stop. And I'll be darned: they did.

While an aide fumbled for some money to hand a beggar woman (he fished a blue bill out of his pocket, the locally colossal sum of $10), Gul Agha barreled out of his seat like an angry bear. ". . . do you think you're doing?!" He was in the middle of a sentence when he hit the ground. "Are you doing aid work or politics? Why are you going around—"

"We need to talk," I interrupted. "But not here." There was some kind of delegation from the finance ministry in the car with him, politely refraining from gawking. "Let's meet tomorrow. What time can I come?"

And so we made a date for the next morning at nine o'clock.

I had Engineer Abdullah with me to translate. In the opposite corner, it was just Governor Shirzai and his venom-filled factotum Khalid Pashtoon. The animosity I had long sensed between the two of them crackled in the air, blue-white, as if from a pair of short-circuiting wires. Pashtoon, the nominal subordinate, snapped at his boss two or three times in a tone of such manifest contempt I would have shown him the door right away, had he been my flunky. I wondered what he had on Shirzai for the governor to keep him around.

But I had never seen Shirzai so firm with him. For once, the governor insisted on running the meeting himself, chewing Pashtoon out like a private when he got out of line. It was great fun to watch.

Governor Shirzai had a whole list of questions for me, beginning with the one about my job description. Was I doing humanitarian work in Kandahar, or politics? Well, that was a good one. I asked it myself just about every day.

The governor continued. What had he ever done to me anyway? Was all this a personal vendetta of mine?

That was the cue for the one line I had rehearsed before coming in, the thing I had wanted to explain when I set up the appointment.

"This is nothing personal," I answered. "What I am opposed to is a system, a certain way of governing. I'm not against you as a man. It's just your bad luck, Mr. Governor. If I lived in Herat, I'd be saying all the same things about Isma'il Khan."

Khalid Pashtoon had made notes of practically every word I had uttered in the United States, and he kept himself busy consulting them. Every few minutes he would lob one, like a hand grenade. I had said Shirzai worked for Pakistan and the United States at the same time, he quoted, looking up to see what kind of damage that one would do.

The governor reared back with a bellow: he was the man in all of Afghanistan who worked hardest against Pakistan. "Since my father's time! The Americans called my father the Lion of Afghanistan! And now the Pakistanis are trying to kill me!"

"Is that so," I replied. "Then why does the ISI run the one Internet café in town, which your friend here Khalid Pashtoon recently inaugurated?"

At first Governor Shirzai pretended not to know about the café-cum-listening-post. When I pushed him, he claimed it wasn't really important. "And besides," he added, pausing to contradict his point with a most enlightening proverb:

"If you can't twist their arm, kiss their hand."

It was an Afghan version of If you can't lick 'em, join 'em. And it confirmed what I had known for months: Shirzai was working for Pakistan.

"What a shame, Mr. Governor," I parried back, "that someone of your valiant reputation—the son of the Lion of Afghanistan himself—should have to kiss *anyone's* hand."

Shirzai's memory of his exchange about me with President Karzai diverged characteristically from the other accounts I had heard. In the governor's fantasy, it was Karzai who had offered to expel me from Kandahar, and the big-hearted governor had stayed his hand. "No, no," he described himself urging the president generously, "it's OK; leave her."

He could not resist just one subtle threat. The way I was going on, Shirzai warned me, some people might get upset, and then there was no telling what they might do; there was no controlling them.

Ah, I thought. We're going to play hardball? And I pulled out the pitch that Abdullah had counseled me to absolutely use. "I'm not working for the Americans," I repeated, "but when General McNeill or Colonel Campbell asks me what's going on in Kandahar, I can't tell him a lie. I have to describe things exactly as I see them."

"Name-drop," Abdullah had said. "Name-drop as much as you can, and watch him wilt."

It worked like a charm. Suddenly Gul Agha turned teddy bear. "Why did you have to write that I blow my nose in my turban?" he wondered, truly hurt. I assured him I had written no such thing. I was only quoted in that *Washington Post* article. I had not authored it.

"Well," Governor Shirzai cheered up and said, "listen, you've been here a long time. You're not a foreigner anymore. You're a member of the family now." The change in tone was breathtaking. "If you have any problems with anything I'm doing, come here and talk to me about it. I don't even mind if you write more articles, that's OK; just come to me first."

And then Shirzai came out with his second local proverb, the import of which stayed with me for weeks. "Kill me," the governor said. "But don't put me out in the sun."

Better dead than exposed. It was a notion that cut to the core of the worst cultural clash I confronted in this land I had adopted: its utterly incomprehensible relationship with the truth. Words were not all that important, it seemed, since people lied so systematically. And yet words were terribly important, since they outlasted deeds; so the battles that counted were about getting the last word. I could not make it compute. To me words were precious and weighty—but only in their power to communicate the truth. For the truth, once communicated, was a potent force for good. So I thought.

The governor repeated his kind invitation. "Any time, day or night," he effused, "if you have something to say to me, you come here. If I'm asleep, slap me on the ass and wake me up."

"Thank you, Mr. Governor," I managed. "Thank you so much."

This encounter ushered in about three weeks of truce. A delegation from the National Endowment for Democracy (NED) came to visit from Washington. We needed to talk about an idea Qayum and I had dreamed up for founding a provincewide council of elders—NED might just fund it—and they were checking on a project they had already sponsored: the conversion of our weekly women's discussion group into a more focused examination of the proposed new Afghan constitution. While they were there, the NED folks said, they wanted to meet the governor.

I called him up. "What kind of friend are you?" my erstwhile dueling partner demanded. "I've been sick with a cold for three days and you didn't even come to visit!" So I mixed some echinacea in with a jar of honey and brought it along as a gift.

Shirzai was resolved to make the most of this unexpected U.S. visit. He invited us to join a breakfast he was giving. We took our places at a table groaning with platters—kebabs alongside breakfast pastry. The other chairs around the table groaned with some of the city's top dignitaries: the chief judge, the public prosecutor, and Police Chief Zabit Akrem, among others. In this public setting, Akrem and I played our tacitly agreed charade, pretending polite acquaintance, no more.

I gave the governor-bear his honey, and lapsed into the kind of impudent informality that certain people bring out in me. Shirzai was explaining to the NED people what a democratic fellow he was. Anyone could say anything they wanted in his province. I think I audibly choked back a laugh. "Good," I said. "I've got an article coming out soon." He did not bite.

The brunch was pure enjoyment. It was NED's meeting; I was just along for the ride.

In light of our suddenly friendly truce, I actually decided to make a concession to Governor Shirzai. I was writing an op-ed for the *New York Times,* about warlordism, of course. I decided that this time there was no need to mention Gul Agha by name. It would, it seemed to me, be unnecessarily provocative, and it would not add much substance to what I was trying to say.

I searched my conscience. Was I, too, falling for the teddy bear act?

The op-ed appeared on July 1: "Afghanistan's Future, Lost in the Shuf-

fle." I hammered out my now-familiar refrain: U.S. policy could not succeed in Afghanistan if U.S. officials kept hedging their bets. I did spare the
governor, referring to him only as "the local warlord."

"Why are the Americans helping President Karzai and helping his enemies, the warlords, too?" I quoted puzzled Kandaharis, and concluded:
"The United States should back any future decision to remove the warlord governors."[1]

Governor Shirzai was not taken in by the omission of his name in this
article. He knew exactly who was meant. His riposte came shortly afterward, in the guise of a phone call from the political affairs officer at the
U.S. Embassy, Kurt Amend.

"You have to come to Kabul," he said. "Immediately. There is a really
serious threat out against you. I think your life is in danger." I could feel
his urgency. It was me by name, Kurt was saying, and the details about the
vehicle I drove and my recent activities were really scary.

This was sounding familiar. "Let me check around a little. I'll call you
right back."

I punched the number of a friend in the "intelligence community."
Not a civilian, a military man. He said he'd ask a few questions. Within
half an hour he confirmed my suspicion: there was no "threat matrix" at
the moment against any known group or individual in Kandahar. And it
so happened, I had found out in the meantime, that Governor Shirzai and
Khalid Pashtoon were in Kabul. Beyond any doubt, one of them had
gone to the CIA station, and that was how the "threat" had been relayed
to the embassy.

When, later, I saw the wording of the thing, I found it almost comi-
cal. It referred explicitly to the previous threat, petulantly complaining
that it had had no effect on me at all. I had not lowered my profile one little bit and was still engaging in dangerous behavior, like meeting with
moderate mullahs.

The shared inspiration of the two reports was pretty evident.

I called Kurt and told him not to worry.

And I wasn't worried. Much. But I did feel I had to respond. I felt that
in the Afghan cultural context, so bold a challenge demanded a riposte;
otherwise I would be seen as weak and easy prey. So I asked that friend in
the intelligence community: "Next time you see the governor, would you

mind letting him know that the U.S. military would be pretty displeased if anything should happen to me?"

"I'd enjoy that very much."

I asked Bill Taylor at the embassy to pass on the same message. I did not have to ask Governor Shirzai's boss, Interior Minister Jalali. He did it of his own accord, in public, at a luncheon in Kandahar for his British counterpart, Jack Straw. Minister Jalali called me over to where he stood with Shirzai, leaning against a wall in private conversation.

"How's security?" Jalali asked.

I launched into my spiel about how "security" in Kandahar means different things for Afghans and for foreigners, and how the real security problem here—

"No," the minister interrupted. "How's *your* security?"

"Oh . . . fine," I managed, caught off guard.

"Well, if you ever have any kind of problem at all, here's your man." And the minister poked a finger into Governor Shirzai's inviting belly. "He's responsible for you."

I never received another threat.

CHAPTER 26

FEAR

BUT THEN WE plunged into a truly hair-raising summer. As those dust-caked, bone-dry, hundred-twenty-degree months progressed, I did, at last, become alarmed. I can't put my finger on exactly what did it. Inexplicably, as though I had been brushed by a ghost, my hair stood on end.

With Ricardo Munguia's murder, a line had been crossed. His death was followed by the assassinations just outside Kandahar of two mullahs, religious leaders, who supported the new regime. At a mosque right in town—my favorite one, from Ahmad Shah Durrani's time, whose outlines are rubbed out against the sky in mud plaster—an explosion shattered the joint murmur of prayers, though no one was badly hurt. This time.

Worst of all for me was watching Akrem, one night over tea, count off the deaths on his fingers. He had lost an average of a man a day for a month, in attacks on police posts. Those fighters were his charges. What must it have done to him to watch them die?

We were at my house. He had shucked off his police uniform and was wearing Kandahar civilian clothes: a tunic just the peach-hued side of white, with a charcoal-colored vest over it, and a glimmering gray silk turban around his head. I had my camera. I was trying to lighten the mood by taking pictures. "No, forget about me. Keep talking," I scolded when he posed face front with that stern glower on. Finally I got him, one arm resting on his raised knee, a glass of tea in his hand, the trace of a smile grazing his features.

When I look at that picture now, I am stunned by how young and gentle Akrem looks, two years before his death. His face was not yet hardened and darkened by the trials to come.

But it was a very bad night. We were talking about all the portents raining down on us. Akrem was deflated; there was no other word for it. None of his people wanted to work out in the districts anymore, and he did not know how to ask them to. "Poor Comandan Saab," I remember Abdullah murmuring. "They will break his heart." With the world closing in around us, we felt alone, hugging ourselves into a corner of my unmarked compound like beleaguered fugitives.

There had been another ambush on the road to Tirin Kot. A half dozen of the Urozgan governor's men had been shot. A driver for the aid group Mercy Corps had been killed with two others in an attack on a district office in Helmand Province. Whatever it was that was going on had gotten very violent, and Afghans affiliated with the new authorities were taking the brunt.

And yet this litany is a bit deceptive. It was not just an upsurge in the number of incidents that changed the background music, altering its key to ominous. It was the outlines of a progression that suddenly became discernible that summer, the way an image begins to emerge on photographic paper soaking in a chemical bath. Once a jumbled collection of disparate events, the insurgency was resolving itself into a series of inexorably intensifying stages. It was that night that Akrem sketched them out for me, bringing the pattern to light. It was the progression that scared me more than any of its individual parts.

The ballooning fear of ordinary Kandaharis, too, was catching. It was a mixture of breaking-point exasperation with the favoritism and arbitrary violence they continued to suffer at the hands of the governor's thugs— and exasperation with the Americans for not preventing it—and a new concern, voiced for the first time. Kandaharis were afraid they might undergo yet another change of regime: the Taliban might always come back.

That was a first.

Many sentiments found words for the first time that summer. "If things keep on this way," I heard, "people will take up arms against the Americans as they took up arms against the Russians. And *everyone* fought against the Russians. Even doctors and engineers joined the jihad." It seems in-

credible, given how often Westerners drew the comparison, and how afraid
Washington was of following in Moscow's footsteps, but that was the first
time I heard an Afghan mention the United States and the Soviet Union
in the same breath.

It was the first time that women told me, with regret, that they would
rather I did not come to their homes. People were beginning to take precautions, to avoid marking themselves out from the conservative norm.
They were beginning to hedge their bets.

In deference to the women's unease, I took to wearing not exactly a
burqa—I tried on half a dozen for size and Abdullah, with his wickedly accurate sense of lampoon, informed me that I looked like a telephone
pole—but a head-to-toe black wraparound garment typically worn by
wizened crones. I still looked quite a bit like a telephone pole.

The men's fear got to me just as much, because it contrasted so
poignantly with the hard-boiled image they liked to project. One of
Ahmad Wali Karzai's bodyguards bought a car. His explanation was: "We're
all going to get killed soon anyway, so I may as well live it up till then."

Many people I knew who were aligned with the Pax Americana began
wondering out loud where they would be able to run this time. "We can't
go to Pakistan; we can't go to Iran," Abdullah blurted out shakily one
evening. "Everyone will kill us."

For Akrem, the menace was growing precise. This was when that messenger brought him a threat, from a notorious ISI colonel in Pakistan, a
former classmate of Pakistani President General Pervez Musharraf. The
message was a bit cryptic, phrased almost like a charade. "When you become a refugee this time, where will you run?" the man recited his mem-
orized question to Akrem. Another line: "The ground you are standing on
will soon be Pakistan." And a few more provocations in this vein.

Akrem wondered if he might send a message back to the ISI colonel.
"I am a student of history," he parried the second barb. "And history tells
me that Afghanistan has existed for a thousand years, but Pakistan for only
fifty-six. I think that we will outlast you." To the first question he replied:
"My next refuge, should I need one, will be the graveyard."

I was distraught. It had been months since our first meeting, when he
had had news of Pakistani army officers ordering Shirzai: "Make problems
for Zabit Akrem. Kill him." And here we were still? No further along?

There were vaguer and more primitive portents. A dust storm, which lasted almost a week. The sky descended, weighing down on our shoulders. The air turned to mustard. It lashed us. It wasn't the wind, day and night, it was the whole universe, blowing. The mulberry tree in our yard was lost to us. Big trees on the streets, when they swam forward through the muddy air, were bent over, begging with outstretched leaves. Dust—not particles, just an opaqueness—would sift inside the house. By the end of a day it would relinquish the air and be transformed into a solid, settling, covering the white stone floor and drifted up against the walls in little snow banks of brown powder.

Women started remembering the last storm like it: when Prime Minister Daoud Khan was murdered in 1974. It was weather for revolutions, the women said.

To make everything worse, my fight with Interior Minister Jalali over Akrem's job was not finished.

I didn't have the heart to repeat the terminology of this battle to Akrem, or tell him of its intensity. He was dealing with enough disillusion as it was.

Each week, it seemed, the ax was going to fall. I pleaded. I parried. I argued. I raged silently and not so silently. I demanded proof of Jalali's assertions that Akrem was corrupt. Once, the minister showed me a letter, supposedly from the pen of a Taliban insurgent, denouncing evil deeds by Akrem's men.

An anonymous letter? Anyone with any agenda could have written it!

"You only see things on the surface," Jalali snapped another time, exasperated. "I know what's going on beneath."

I *lived* in Kandahar. What could Jalali possibly see that I couldn't?

I knew, at best, I was helping delay the inevitable. It added to my sense of encroaching doom. If the Afghan government I supported couldn't even get this right, the whole venture must be hopeless.

The clammy ghost had dragged its finger across my skin, leaving me almost trembling with nerves, when I was invited out to the U.S. base for a meeting with the individual known as the PolAd—the political adviser to the commander of Coalition forces in Afghanistan. This was the civilian whom many military men believed really called the shots when it came to strategic decisions in Afghanistan, the one who, when the generals did something stupid, had made them do it.

I do not remember much about that meeting. I remember the one right afterward, with a different man. It was dressed up as just a casual get-together with a high-ranking officer who had accompanied the PolAd down from the Baghram base near Kabul.

Not until we sat down did this colonel tell me I was the main reason he had made the trip. He wanted, it came out, to make a deal. "If I were to ask you to take a vacation for a little while, would you do it?" His reasoning was deliberately unsentimental. "I don't know you, so I can't pretend it would be a personal blow to me if you got killed. But it would set back the work we are trying to do here by about a year."

I knew exactly what he meant. After Ricardo's death, if another international aid worker were assassinated, just about every foreigner in Kandahar, UN included, would pack up and lock up. Head offices would review all the projects they had scheduled for the Afghan south. Dozens of Afghans would be put out of work. It would be a mess. And it would look very bad. The officer explained he wasn't telling me to leave right then; he was trying to open up a communications link, in case such a time did come later.

I liked his directness—and I returned it. Before agreeing, I said, I would have to be sure that he would not become an inadvertent channel for people who merely found me inconvenient—Governor Shirzai, for instance, not to mention Americans who might not like my style. Shirzai had learned how to exploit the Americans' blind faith in his judgment, and their knee-jerk sensitivity to anything that could be described as a terrorist threat, to neutralize people he didn't care for. I alluded to the way the CIA had passed along, without scrutiny, news of an "active terrorist cell" planning to kill me.

The officer followed my gist, and provided some precise assurances that he would not let himself be so used. As the conversation continued, I found that what I really liked about him was the courage of his frankness.

He told me flat out that the recently launched war in Iraq had stretched military resources in Afghanistan beyond their capacities. "We simply don't have the men to do the job here," he said. After the first wartime rotation in 2001, the B team had been sent in to relieve the troops in Afghanistan; but now the B and C teams were tied up in Iraq, and the United States was dredging the bench for something like the D team to cover in

Afghanistan. "There are reservists doing military intelligence here," he said, without further elaboration as to the absurdity of this, given Afghanistan's ongoing strategic importance to U.S. national security. His opinion was evident in the tone of his voice.

Drawing a pie chart on a scrap of paper, the officer explained the doctrine of military deployments. It jibed with what I had learned in the Balkans. "Normally, a government wants about a third of its active-duty troops deployed in theater," he shaded in part of the pie, "a third resting up from deployment, and a third training to go back out. Right now . . . ?" He looked up, locked my eyes. "The United States has fully two thirds of its soldiers on active deployment overseas."

The colonel indicated that he thought the focus of U.S. military attention in Afghanistan was misdirected.

Steady fighting—skirmishing, mortar rounds, night raids—had kept U.S. troops busy since spring at a string of firebases along the Pakistani border in eastern Afghanistan. These almost daily firefights hardly penetrated our consciousness in Kandahar, for the details were kept shrouded and the stakes seemed minimal. No one lived out in that wild border country. The U.S. troops there were not protecting any Afghans. And most of the serious incursions by militants were happening farther south, in Zabul Province. The U.S. outposts up by Gardez seemed to serve little purpose other than to mark the border. News of the skirmishing out there seemed of no more consequence to us in Kandahar than the distant sound of yelping from a dogfight. But this was where most U.S. military attention was focused that spring, because there was "contact."

The officer agreed with my unvoiced sense of priorities. "Gardez and all that stuff on the border?" he said. "That's a distraction." The real battleground of this conflict, he believed, was in Kandahar. I could discern memories of Vietnam between the lines of his prediction: "Here, we won't know it till they're all around. We'll realize what's going on when we can't find workers to come out to the base anymore, when we can't buy vegetables in the market."

And I suddenly glimpsed a nightmare scenario.

I had never believed the September 11 terrorist attacks were designed "merely" to cause the death of three thousand Americans. The point of those attacks, as their breathtaking symbolism indicated, went far beyond.

It was to help bring to fruition some version of the "clash of civilizations." Those attacks were an effort to force people—Muslims as well as Westerners—to withdraw from contact and exchange with each other, and to acquiesce to oppressive policies at home and bloody ones abroad that they might not really approve of, because the situation seemed to warrant them, and because the other side no longer seemed to be composed of human beings.

Al-Qaeda strategists had to know that Washington would retaliate for 9/11 by engaging in Afghanistan. And they had to assume that once involved in that intractable land, chances were high that the United States would make mistakes, just as the British and the Soviets had. And those mistakes might just bring the longed-for war closer. Especially since some U.S. strategists seemed to be promoting a similar agenda from the opposite side.

As I listened to this canny officer, with the backbeat of my Afghan friends' mounting frustration thudding in my ears, the parts of this scenario suddenly meshed for me, and I understood how it could play out.

What if villagers, driven to distraction by the arbitrary violence the warlords were wreaking—the extortions and the arbitrary searches, aimed more at looting than finding weapons or opium, the fingering of tribal enemies as Taliban, the monopolizing of foreign subsidy—what if villagers, sick of all of this, began conniving with the Taliban militants who passed through their territory or who set up ambushes on their roads? What if villagers began giving the militants food at night, or letting them use their houses, or even lending them their sons? These isolated villagers might do that because they had no choice when the armed insurgents were demanding their help at gunpoint. Or they might do it because the Taliban did not seem much worse than the current alternative, the gunmen who preyed on them under cover of U.S. army fatigues. What would happen then? Would the United States begin bombing those Afghan villages? And then what? Would the Afghan people pull out of this latest experiment in nationhood? Would they revolt? Would my friends' warnings be fulfilled, and even doctors and engineers take up arms against the Americans, the way they had against the Soviets?

I arrived at that meeting shaken. I left it almost paralyzed with fear.

It was in this condition—I can't quite remember on precisely which

July day—that I made another trip to Kabul. I was at Qayum's house in the leafy Wazir Akbar Khan neighborhood, resonating with the menace of Kandahar, unable to adjust. Qayum invited me to join him for dinner at Interior Minister Jalali's place a few streets over.

Jalali was a former colleague of mine, of sorts. He used to run the Persian and Pashtu service of the U.S. government–funded shortwave radio service, Voice of America. In the distant past he had served as an army officer. Jalali was a member of the Afghan American mafia Qayum had corralled into accepting cabinet positions in the fledgling Afghan government. He was inordinately kind to me, absorbing my impertinent humor like a soft punching bag, top cabinet minister though he was. He took to addressing me as Kid, in our e-mail exchanges. I would write back to GU, for "grown-up."

Jalali was trying, against difficult odds, to bring some professionalism to his ministry. But he had been away from Afghanistan for a long time, and his decisions often smacked more of wishful thinking than of savvy solutions turning local conditions to advantage. Jalali was gravely out of touch, and he was about to waste Akrem, and that night, I had run out of patience for it.

Just the scene, when we entered the house, almost made me bolt. I was up from Kandahar, where the food we ate seemed to be extracted from the parched ground with the same painful travail as an impacted molar. Jalali's tables buckled under the spread. There were five large oval platters heaped with meat. In one of them, the meat was liver. Without at first realizing what I was about, I caught myself scanning the size and number of the pieces, engaged in a rough estimate: how many sheep had gone into that plate of glistening morsels? There was an array of succulent vegetables, the sweet, light-green squash that is cooked down unctuously, plates of fresh tomatoes and cucumbers and herbs, and, on each coffee table, several bowls filled with sweetmeats: almonds crystallized with sugar and orange blossom water; cashew nuts, almost unheard of in Afghanistan; and the very best raisins, two sorts.

To consume this gargantuan feast, we were seven. Jalali and his wife, a tiny pistol of a lady, on her first visit from the United States since the Taliban collapse, dressed, the way I did in Kandahar, in an embroidered man's tunic. I registered, with gratitude, a current of sisterhood. There was Jalali's housemate, the deputy defense minister, revoltingly overweight. He would sit silently inside his rolls of fat, looking out like a malevolent Buddha. His wife was a Walt Disney witch, long fingernails filed to a tapering point and daubed with silver polish, face like a Venetian mask. There was another man, positively normal in this company, and Qayum, and me, Cassandra.

I went on and on that night. I lectured them about the warlords, about Pakistan, about the mounting danger, telling Qayum and Jalali they didn't know what they were talking about.

That one drew an uncharacteristically harsh retort from Qayum: "After a year and a half here, you think you know more about Afghanistan than we do?"

I did. Kandahar was burning, and they were enjoying their meal in a shaded back garden, oblivious. When they tried to jolly me out of it, their smug condescension only infuriated me more.

There was one piece of business I had to conduct with Jalali. Akrem's police force had gone unpaid for months. I had told the minister about this on an earlier visit to Kabul. The central government, I learned then, had been transferring the money to Governor Shirzai for distribution, but Governor Shirzai, naturally, was not passing it along to Akrem. Even that equation was a little theoretical, it emerged. Despite his promises at the big governors' meeting that May, Shirzai was still keeping customs revenues for himself. So in retaliation the central government was sending little if any money to Kandahar. Shirzai was not the one who suffered. He made sure *his* private militiamen got paid out of the customs dues. It was Akrem who, starved of public funds, could cover the cigarettes his men smoked only thanks to contacts in the Alokozai business community. Akrem, and his police force, was living on donations again.

I spelled all this out in front of the assembled company. I was stunned that Jalali didn't understand why, given the context in Kandahar, the riches Shirzai was robbing from the Afghan state and people would never make it to the police department.

When we returned home, Qayum gave me a dressing down. Jalali was my elder, and he was a minister, for God's sake. It was unforgivable for me to behave that way in public. And another thing: hadn't he told me not to breathe a word about Pakistan in front of the deputy defense minister?

Oh? Did Pakistan control officials so high up? Even Qayum was cowed?

The next day, I phoned Jalali to apologize. He accepted, gamely telling me to keep it up, he liked it. That afternoon, he called me back: he had checked the records; I was right; he would be sending the police salaries to Kandahar.

I sat in on the distribution of some of the money. To my surprise, Akrem was not even present. He directed me to his finance department in a different building, and got on with the business he was attending to. I had assumed that he, like any other Afghan official, would want to bask in the glow that day, taking personal credit for the arrival of the money.

I did not know Akrem well enough yet.

Anyway, it did not matter much. I was about to lose the war over his future that I had been waging with Jalali all summer long.

CHAPTER 27

THE PROMOTION OF VICE
AND THE PUNISHMENT
OF VIRTUE

AUGUST 2003

AKREM WAS ON the phone. It was August 13, nearly noon. He had received a summons from the ministry; he had to go to Kabul. His voice was flat. He was calling because he wondered if I would mind checking if there was a flight on one of the planes that catered to humanitarians. The U.S. Army still occupied Kandahar's civilian airport, and he could only fly if I got him a seat.

Oh no. I knew what this meant. And I couldn't keep the knowledge out of my voice. "Oh, Comandan Saab . . . " I stammered. He was silent. "Of course. I'll call you right back."

"*Salamat wosai,*" he thanked me gently. He knew what it meant too.

I looked at my watch. I knew there was no way, but I called the UN and the subsidized humanitarian airline anyway. If Akrem had to go by road, he would be driving all night. The thought of it, in my alarmed state, terrified me.

I remember exchanging a couple of calls back and forth with him, asking what time he had been ordered to report, and waiting while he checked with the ministry. Ten tomorrow morning, came the answer. That settled it. There were no more flights that day, and the next day's UN plane would get him there too late. He had no choice but to take that road. It seemed unfair. Governor Shirzai had been called to Kabul too; he had flown up that morning. Jalali could have had the courtesy to give Akrem the same prior notice.

"Call me when you leave," was all I could say.

He did, his voice reaching me as if through water from his satellite phone, some ways outside Kandahar. It was around 5:00 P.M. I had never set off for Kabul later than dawn.

The next morning, I started calling him as soon as I woke up. I couldn't get him. I called some more. I imagined him meeting with the president, his phone turned off. I imagined a lot of things.

Finally, in the early afternoon, I found out what had happened. It wasn't as bad as some of the things I had conjured up, but it was pretty bad.

On that impossible road, with the sine curves and the ruts carved into the hardened clay and the desert floor on either side split open by dry river beds, his bodyguards' truck had tipped into a ravine. Fighters sit on benches fitted into the open backs of those trucks. One man was killed; another—slight, with a pointy face—suffered a compound fracture of the femur; and another whom I came to know later, who looks like a Mexican out of a television Western with his drooping mustaches and crossed bandoliers, broke his shin. There must have been a lot of other wrenches and bruises; I didn't hear about them. Akrem had worked through the night at the crumpled wreck, calling for a car to carry the body back to Kandahar, and then rushing on to Kabul and the Emergency Hospital near Qayum's house.

And so Zabit Akrem arrived in the Afghan capital, his mind otherwise occupied, after his dismissal had been broadcast on the radio and TV.

He and Governor Shirzai had both been removed. Shirzai was promoted to run the ministry of urban development. As had been suggested months earlier, his longtime confidante, Yusuf Pashtun—that same cabinet minister whom April Witt had quoted in her naughty article—was sent down to Kandahar to take over the governorship. And there was no job for Zabit Akrem.

Why had I bothered meddling? Shirzai was now promoted. He was replaced in Kandahar by a fellow tribesman and intimate, a man who had served him faithfully for the past decade, only leaving his side when President Karzai had appointed him minister. Now, deprived of Akrem, Kandahar was at the complete mercy of Shirzai's mafia. And the new governor, according to three separate sources, was not just some Pakistani sidekick, he was a close interlocutor of the intelligence agency, the ISI.

My shocked and self-lacerating reverie was interrupted by a call from Dubai. It was my boss, Qayum Karzai, on his way to the United States. In other words, I suddenly realized, he and Jalali had bolted Kabul the minute they announced the shuffle. *Well, well, well. How very brave.*

"So, how's it going down there?" Qayum wanted to know.

These big people—I was picturing it now—the president's older brother and his pal the minister of interior, had been standing on the airplane steps when they fired their warlord. The steps had pulled back and the plane had whisked them off to safety, just in case anything went wrong. I was here in Kandahar, in the line of fire. And they wanted a situation report.

The situation in Kandahar was flat calm, I informed Qayum.

How very odd it was after all that effort. After all the hand-wringing and plan-making and climax and anticlimax, the decision, when it finally came, seemed almost offhand. Far from being consulted or asked for technical support, the Americans had not even been informed.

In any case, the U.S. Afghan mission was back where it had started. Ambassador Finn was gone but not yet replaced, and the whole team I had come to like and rely on—Bill Taylor and Kurt Amend and one or two others—was back in Washington. Colonel Campbell had taken up a new post at the Pentagon. But his unit's rotation in Afghanistan had been extended. The exhausted, homesick, disgruntled soldiers were on automatic pilot, while a three-month interim commander struggled to learn how to pronounce local place-names. There was no one home again in Fortress USA. It was just astonishing. It was as though President Karzai had made his changes in the dead of night, when no one was looking. And disaster had not struck.

Over the next day or two, the significance of this event I had so urgently desired sank in. And I was devastated.

In effect, Shirzai had not been removed at all. His brother remained at the airport in charge of outer rim security, reaping the attendant benefits. A henchman of his and of Pakistan's was now effectively running the police department, so all of the brutal petty commanders still held sway at their checkpoints from Kandahar to the border. Factotum Khalid Pashtoon had swiftly transferred his allegiance to the new governor. My friends the unsavory but sometimes usefully insubordinate Achekzais were being cleared out of their positions on the border. Ties to Pakistan at the top of the provincial administration were even stronger than before. And the best official I had encountered in Afghanistan was unemployed.

Everything, in other words, was the opposite of what was being described in the press, and to and by the international community in Kabul: applause for the arrival of a qualified technocrat to replace the warlord Shirzai.

For two full weeks, I turned the facts over and over in my mind. How could my friends the Karzais possibly be so stupid? How could these mature Afghan government leaders not see the implications of what they had done? A great service to Pakistan and to the cause of corruption in the Afghan south.

And then it hit me: a blow to the gut that left me struggling for air and on the edge of tears for days. Maybe they weren't being stupid. Maybe they had made their move this way on purpose. Maybe they had been conniving all along with the forces they claimed so loudly to be combating.

It was the only thing that made sense.

And I realized something else: the forces at work were more powerful than I could ever get a purchase on. The people I had believed in must be compromised in ways I could never understand. I was going to have to part company with them, I realized—though it would take some time and some sorting out of my deeply conflicted feelings in order finally to disengage.

Somehow, it was the president of the Ghiljai elders' tribal council who continued to host Gul Agha Shirzai's farewell lunch. Bustling with busy energy, he met us at the gate of the hotel he had reserved for the purpose. He showed us to the verandah, where the drivers and bodyguards were seated. Abdullah and I looked at each other. We looked at the French windows opening onto the hall where the guests of honor were arriving. And we made for the windows, pushing through the seated servants.

The whole cast of characters was present. Gul Agha Shirzai was wedged on a couch next to his original rival for the governorship, Mullah Naqib. I greeted Ahmad Wali Karzai and the new governor, Yusuf Pashtun, under his shaggy, glowering eyebrows. And, opposite me at table, next to his weak-faced replacement, sat Zabit Akrem. He didn't speak. He was just murmuring under his breath as he fiercely fingered his string of green stone beads. I later learned that the Ghiljai council president, whose steadfast benefactor Akrem had been, had asked him to leave. Gul Agha Shirzai had threatened not to come if he was there. Akrem was feeling homicidal. He was saying prayers to hold himself back.

The Ghiljai council president, who in private had flung at Shirzai every insult he could conjure, delivered an orgy of praise as a welcome speech.

At the end of the meal, when the guests were collecting in a clot at the door, Shirzai, the freshly appointed minister of housing and urban development, called me over. He called loudly, so everyone would hear.

"Sarah," he said. "I'm giving up warlordism. I'm going to Kabul to be a minister."

"That's good," I replied—still, at that stage, excavating some humor in the thing. "It's my turn. I'm going to be a warlord now."

CHAPTER 28

MAZAR-I-SHERIF

AFTER AKREM'S REMOVAL had been announced and everyone was back in Kandahar, his loyal, hotheaded Alokozai tribesmen thronged to him. "This is an outrage," they would cry, seated in his receiving room. "What should we do?" Akrem would take a breath, then raise a hand to quiet them. "I work for the central government of this country," he would say. "And this is the central government's decision. We have to respect it." He told his men to go back to their barracks and their checkpoints, and to give their obedience to the new chief of police.

I was impressed. In his shoes, I could never have come up with that.

Then Akrem returned to Kabul, to await the pleasure of President Karzai.

I made a several trips up to the capital that fall. Qayum was back from the United States, and we were wrangling about our organization, Afghans for Civil Society.

"What about Mazar-i-Sherif for Zabit Akrem," he put to me, during an early visit. We were sitting in the shade of his verandah, admiring the ripening grapes that dangled from the small arbor.

Mazar-i-Sherif is an absolutely beautiful town, clear across Afghanistan from Kandahar, over the towering Hindu Kush range, part of the central Asian steppe culture beyond it that created the marvel of Samarqand. Mazar-the-Holy is named for its ancient turquoise-tiled mosque sanctuary. During the Taliban war to take over Afghanistan in the late 1990s,

Mazar had been the last major holdout. Battles there, in 1997 and 1998, were the very worst of the war. First the Uzbeks, under their charismatic, double-crossing leader, Rashid Dostum, handed the Taliban their most devastating defeat to date: more than six thousand "religious students" were killed, wounded, or captured, including a harvest of seasoned officers and hundreds of Pakistani "advisers." A year later, the Taliban took their revenge. The killing spree, when they captured cosmopolitan Mazar, went on for two full days. Using local Pashtuns as guides, the Taliban hunted down members of northern ethnic groups for a triple-tap execution: head, heart, and genitals. Prisoners were packed in cargo containers and left out in the desert.[1] Now, with the tables turned again after the Taliban demise, Mazar was taking it out on local Pashtuns.

Mazar? God, no. It's a death sentence. I tried to persuade Qayum out of it.

Confabbing in the living room of the house a friend had loaned Akrem, or in Qayum's patch of garden where I could host him in a bit of style, or over the phone when I was in Kandahar, Akrem and I would size up cities. "Farah is way too small," our chats would go. "What about Herat?" And we would analyze the political situation in Herat. As we went over and over the possibilities, I gradually came to roost on one: Kabul. Zabit Akrem would be the perfect police chief for the Afghan capital. I told Qayum. I told Akrem's boss, Interior Minister Ali Jalali. Jalali laughed at me.

And so we kept configuring. Akrem was doing the same thing with other friends, with his tribal elders in Kandahar, with his family. Always, Mazar wound up on the bottom of the list.

Akrem would speak in these terms, weighing preferences and disadvantages, with me and others close to him. But not with President Karzai when the president summoned him to the Palace. With President Karzai, Akrem played it gruff: "I am a soldier, you are my commander. Where you order me to go, I go."

Once, he invited me to dinner. It was a gesture, a wordless sign of gratitude for my devotion. And it embarrassed me. I knew he didn't have the money.

In Afghanistan, guests of note are invited to occasions along with their friends and retinues. It would never occur to a host to plan for his honored guest in the singular. Akrem planned for a company. The tiny high command of ACS was in Kabul for a showdown with Qayum. Even Amir, our Iranian-born U.S. coordinator, had flown over from Boston. Akrem looked the four of us up and down, and wondered where the rest of my followers were.

He was greeting us at the steps of the Iranian Restaurant, one of the classiest in town. It is built in the round and furnished inside like a tent, tapestries circling the walls. We had a private room with a table eight feet long, covered in food. It seemed like ostentation until I thought for a moment—and I understood that this was just the loudest way Akrem could think of to say thanks.

I don't remember what we discussed that night. I remember Akrem and Amir locking on to each other, pulling their chairs back into a corner after we were done eating, leaning into each other's conversation. Those two deep men found solace in each other. Each had been a refugee—the fact had conditioned their lives—one fleeing to the other's land, Iran, the other away from it. They spoke in Persian, Amir's Iranian accent sounding oddly effeminate to me, Akrem's voice, still clumsy with Pashtu intonations, hewn out of rock.

Akrem and I had time that autumn to indulge in quiet reflection between our sizing up of cities. "Do you think the war on terror is real?" I asked him one October day as we sat on Qayum's back porch.

"Since the fall of communism," Akrem answered thoughtfully, "there has been a void of ideas. Islamic fundamentalism is the only competing ideology facing the West now. And competition is useful. The war on terror is real. But maybe the West is loath to win it totally, to totally eradicate extremism."

Or: "For democracy to work, it has to be implemented by someone who speaks the truth. Now it is implemented by people who say one thing and do another. There has to be a sense of confidence—among villagers, for instance—that they can participate in political decisions. They must feel that what they wish to say about the landlord, about the governor, they can say." Akrem reached for a metaphor. "If you keep a bird in a cage for twenty years and then open the door and say it's free, it may be free, but it doesn't have the courage of flight. There is no one giving the Afghan people that courage."

The time stretched on and on, idly, and still no answer from the Palace.

Once, I asked how his latest meeting with President Karzai had gone. Akrem paused before answering, as he often did.

"There was no meeting," he broke the silence. "I haven't seen him. He won't see me." He looked up, caught my eyes, allowing me to glimpse his embarrassment. "You're the only one I've told this to. I have to lie to my tribesmen when they call me from Kandahar. It's too much shame."

I was beginning to see where this was going, and I was livid. The decision had been made; they were sending him to Mazar. Why did they have to make him twist in the wind?

As for myself, in the wake of the changes in Kandahar, I was thrashing around in a psychological whirlpool, fighting the disillusionment that was pulling me under. On top of the devastating turn Afghan politics had taken and his role in the results Qayum's smoke-and-mirrors management style was getting the best of me. And he kept trying to nudge our organization, ACS, in directions that seemed distinctly sinister. His latest idea, which he had pitched to me as "opening an office in Washington," turned out to consist of setting up a service to collect information on the security situation and the ethnic makeup of the army. I was getting ready to resign.

The only thing that might have held me back was a project we had finally hammered out with the National Endowment for Democracy. It was the idea of organizing a council of elders for Kandahar Province: a training laboratory for parliamentary democracy. The way Qayum and I had conceived it, the council would be made up of community leaders from all the districts, nominated by village elders. There would be three committees: security, reconstruction, and government oversight. The original notion had been that the council would be an alternative and a challenge to Governor Shirzai's autocratic rule.

Since we had first come up with the idea and suggested it to NED, however, things had grown a little trickier. First, Shirzai had gotten a jump on us and set up an official provincial council, presided over by Ahmad Wali Karzai. And now Shirzai had been replaced as governor by Yusuf Pashtun— unassailable because of his impeccable English and his engineering degree from the American University in Beirut. I was not at all convinced, under these new circumstances, that our *shura* idea would work. Still, NED was ready to finance it, to the tune of $80,000. I thought about Akrem. From the beginning, I had wanted him to run this thing.

"Forget this nonsense, Comandan Saab," I begged. "Look at what they're doing to you."

Poor Comandan Saab, they will break his heart. I remembered the prediction. It had come true. They were breaking his heart.

"Why are you sticking with them? Leave it," I urged. "Come and run my *shura.*"

He thought about it. He really considered it. But he kept waiting. I didn't understand. There was something about his stubborn loyalty that did not add up. Surely Zabit Akrem, of all people, wasn't naive?

Finally, in late November, Akrem was appointed chief of police of Mazar-i-Sherif. And at last I understood President Karzai's tactic. After three months' wait in mortified expectation, Mazar, which had been rooted so leadenly at the bottom of all our lists, sounded like paradise.

Akrem left his family in a house near Mullah Naqib's in Kandahar, and departed for Mazar.

As threatened, and after an exchange of angry missives with Qayum, I resigned from ACS at the end of January 2004 and wrenched myself out of the compound with the cows. I had decided to let go of the fantasy of direct democracy building in favor of grassroots economic action. Paralyzed at the thought of being in Kandahar on my own, I forced myself to go through the motions, accomplish all the material acts required to set up a new place for myself in a residential neighborhood. I quickly found myself reveling in the freedom, in my new proximity to ordinary people.

Still, Kandahar without Akrem—and, oddly, without my sparring partner, Gul Agha—was a bit hollow. I felt cut off from its doings, even though I was closer to its population in my new setup.

I would talk to Akrem on the phone every couple of weeks, feeling the distance. He was dealing with a whole new cast of characters, a different situation entirely.

"So how *is* it?" I asked him on his first trip back, when I rushed to meet him in a friend's garden. "What's Mazar like?"

"Sarah," he shook his head with a smile. "It's like here, but ten times more. Here we have the tribes and we have Pakistan. There, it's not just the tribal Pashtuns, but the Pashtuns and the Uzbeks, and the Tajiks and the Hazaras. Even Turkomen! And instead of Pakistan, there's Russia and Iran and China—all of them with a hand in."

And yet Akrem seemed to be swimming, in the sharks' tank they had dispatched him to. He looked healthy. He was alive again.

One day, I was taking a taxi from Kabul to Kandahar. This was another habit of mine unique among internationals. At last the road was paved, and the six-hour drive wasn't so bad. And the $15 taxi fare sure beat $100 on the UN flight. I did take some precautions: I'd have a Palace driver escort me to the station and send me with a driver he knew. Or at least I'd have someone note down the license plate number of the taxi I was taking, and I'd try to ride with other women. On this occasion, there were two women, with children, and a husband. I sat in front.

A few hours into the ride, the driver and the male passenger had struck up conversation. I heard the word *Mazar,* and then *Khakrezwal,* Akrem's last name. I tuned in. My Pashtu was finally becoming serviceable.

"There's this new chief of police," the passenger was saying. "Things are really different now. Security is good. We don't have any problems now."

I butted in: "This Khakrezwal. Who's he to you?" In Pashtu, the question is not quite as rude as it sounds in English. It is a neutral way of finding out what the tribal or blood relationship is between two people.

"He's no one to me," my fellow passenger replied, a little surprised. "We're just Mazaris, that's all, going to visit my wife's family in Kandahar. Mr. Commander Khakrezwal has made things so much better in our town. That's all I was saying."

That was pretty good publicity.

It was some weeks later that I got a call from Akrem. The story that was coming across the weak cell phone connection was impossibly garbled. It seemed that he had been besieged—literally besieged, in the military sense—inside his own police headquarters. The local warlord, Ustaz Ata, wanted him out of his hair, and had drummed up a pretext to intimidate him, I found out later. I think Akrem was telling me he couldn't get men out even to bring in food. Aghast, I called Qayum. "For God's sake, *do* something!"

I was pretty upset.

And yet Mazar was a world away for me, a decor with no depth surrounding Akrem when I heard his voice on the telephone, but substantially invisible to me. I never got up there to visit him, and I hardly made the effort to conjure up a picture, to place him in context, during our chats. And so I could not conceive of what he was going through.

"You have no idea," his young right-hand man told me a year later. "For more than twenty-four hours, looking out our windows at their forces ringed around, we honestly thought we were going to die any minute."

I called a friend at the *New York Times,* asking for the number of another friend, the *Washington Post* correspondent—and, while I was at it, sketching the story. It was emblematic of what was going on with the Afghan central government, I said. Here was its own man, the central government's representative in Mazar, besieged by some local strongman. And no one, not President Karzai, nor the interior minister, nor anyone else in Kabul was lifting a finger.

The *New York Times* article came out two days later.

I was calling Akrem every day. "Do you still not have any food?"

"No, we're OK, we've got food now, thank you. We've come to an agreement about provisioning."

Things seemed to be inching toward normalization. I relaxed a little.

But more than a week later, when I was sure the whole episode was long over, I found out he was still in there, hemmed in by that warlord's militia. I got in my red truck and stormed over to the old warhorse Mullah Naqib's compound. It was early morning; he was still drinking his tea.

"Let's get five hundred Alokozais together, and go up there!" I was only half joking. "The government isn't doing anything, let's us go. We have to. We can't just leave him there!"

Mullah Naqib launched into a patient argument. "Civil war isn't a good thing. We shouldn't fight."

"Let's call him," I said, and punched the number into my cell phone. And the two of us jollied Akrem for a little while with my plan to invade Mazar.

He must have repeated the story half a dozen times afterward in my hearing, only embellishing it a little bit. ". . . and she said, 'I'll bring two hundred American soldiers, you bring two hundred Alokozais, and let's go to Mazar!' "

At length, the population of Mazar-i-Sherif, with some intervention from the U.S. and European military contingents there, ended the siege. Sending delegations to Akrem, and to the foreigners and the government in Kabul, Mazaris conveyed their solid support to Akrem and his men. They said they had confidence in the central government and they had confidence in their police chief; he had pacified the town and they wanted him back.

And thus, as I fully grasped only later, Akrem had performed a miracle. Using his own person as the girders and cables, he had bridged the gap between the two Afghan cities that were the farthest apart, the two cities that hated each other the most bitterly, that had fertilized their vows of eternal enmity with the most gruesomely spilled blood. Akrem had gone to Mazar and done his job. He had patrolled the streets, making them safe for people to travel. He had structured the police department. He had taken no bribes, stolen no land. His Persian improving every day, he had gone to meet community leaders, across all the divides. He had hired Mazaris as bodyguards, enlarging his inner circle to make room for them. Akrem loved Mazar, and Mazar loved him—and loving him, realized: if this man is a Pashtun from Kandahar, perhaps Pashtuns are not so bad after all.

It was a huge step toward turning Afghanistan back into a nation.

But there was a punch line. When it was all over, President Karzai appointed Ustaz Ata, the very warlord who had besieged Akrem, as governor of Mazar's Balkh Province.

I called Akrem. "So. How's your new governor?" I asked sarcastically.

He made a noise.

"You know that book I'm writing?" I asked. "You know what I'm going to call it? *The Promotion of Vice and the Punishment of Virtue.*"

The Taliban religious police, who used to beat women caught outside without a male escort, or men whose beards weren't long enough, were part of the Ministry for the Promotion of Virtue and the Punishment of Vice.

"Woh . . ." Akrem assented with a chuckle, getting the joke immediately. "That's it exactly. The promotion of vice!"

He could laugh. I wondered where he got the resilience from.

By the middle of 2004, it was becoming clear to me that my parting of the ways had not gone far enough. I realized I was going to have to leave

Afghanistan altogether. For a while, anyway. It had been almost three years now—punishing years—and I had to get away for a while. I had to stand back and take stock.

I informed Akrem on the phone, almost as an afterthought, tacked onto another sentence: "*Comandan Saab,* I'm going for a while. Outside." The communicative Pashtu word.

"For how long?" He was used to my trips to the States.

"I don't know . . . six months maybe."

"Six *months?*"

Not long before I left, Akrem was down in Kandahar for a visit. We got together in the private side of his home, for the first and only time. His wife was there: almost as large as he was, intelligent, canny—though kept inside—a true life partner.

"Sarah," Akrem was looking back on his own punishing year. "You were right. I remember what you said so long ago. You told me I should leave government, that this government wasn't what I thought it was. I should have listened to you."

But then he stopped himself and revised. "No . . . it's going to be OK, I think. Mr. Karzai will get better. After the presidential election he'll have legitimacy and he'll improve. You watch."

The vote, Afghanistan's first general election in history, was scheduled for that fall. I could see the confident dream of it in Akrem's face.

"You have to be kidding me," I replied, laughing at his stubborn optimism, my exclamation just a little off-key. During our chats, Akrem had always seemed slightly uncomfortable at my irreverent and sometimes caustic criticism of Karzai. He would agree, in private, when I said Karzai was frightened, or weak, or couldn't tell the difference between his friends and his enemies. He would air his own puzzlement that Karzai seemed incapable of keeping tabs on the people he appointed to office, or of properly defining their job descirptions. But, even now, Akrem seemed to be clinging to his loyalty.

"That's what we said before the first *Loya Jirga,*" I argued, "and he didn't improve. Then we said the second *Loya Jirga* would do the trick. But it didn't. What makes you think this will be different?"

"No, you'll see. This is an election. It will be different."

"Let's bet on it. You know your white wool shawl?"

He'd had that shawl draped over his legs one winter day. To Pashtuns, legs—even when swathed in baggy trousers and calf-length tunics—are vaguely indiscreet, and men often spread their shawls over them when they're sitting down. I took a shine to Akrem's white wool shawl that day. When I was getting ready to leave, he asked if we could take a picture together.

"Of course," I answered. But my hair was uncovered. I guessed he might show the picture to people, so I touched my head with an embarrassed grin, and put out a hand for his shawl. He passed it over, and I slung it around me for the picture. I was hoping he would take the hint and give it to me. He didn't.

"You know that white wool shawl of yours? If Karzai *doesn't* improve, you have to give it to me. If he does improve after the election, I'll give you a pistol. I'll give you a SIG Sauer. I'll get it in through the base."

We shook. We called on his wife to witness the bet.

That shawl is covering my legs now, as I'm writing this.

CHAPTER 29

KABUL

MAY 2005

"OH, ONE MORE thing, Sarah." I was standing up by the phone in Paris.
It was one of my former employees, on the line from Kandahar. "I knew
you'd want to hear this news. Khakrezwal has been moved to Kabul."

"To *Kabul?* As chief of police?"

"That's right!"

I called Akrem. "So! You're in Kabul?" I could hear distraction in his
voice; it must have been bedlam. "Comandan Saab," I released him. "I'm
coming in a few weeks. I'll call you when I get there."

I wrote Interior Minister Jalali an e-mail—the first in over a year:
"Congratulations. You've finally seen the light." With characteristic indulgence, he wrote me back right away, and told everyone about my
"cute note." I started thinking maybe I was going to have to get Akrem
that pistol.

A little more than six months had passed since I'd left Afghanistan. I had
spent the bulk of it writing this book in my apartment in Paris, sitting sideways on my red couch, my legs stretched out the length of it; and at my
mother's place in Boston, taking up one of her bookshelves with my Post-
it encumbered findings from the library, sharing girlish hilarity with her,
and hungered-for companionship, and contemplation of public affairs.

But then I had decided; I was going back. Most of my friends tried to
argue me out of it. "You've done Afghanistan," one commented.

That line would never have worked. It seemed to me that Afghanistan was not something one "did," the way war correspondents in hotel bars had "done" Goma or "done" Iraq. Afghanistan was not a stamp in a passport, not for me. I had always argued the importance of continuity. I had always mourned the precious time that was wasted, the mistakes that were remade, when humanitarian workers or diplomats or military men rotated out after a few months or a year, just when they were beginning to catch on. Afghanistan, I thought, was starving for continuity. If no one else was going to provide it, the least I could do, I felt, was live by my own precept.

But I was not going back to ACS, and I was not going back to politics. I wanted to start something new, something I had been turning over in my mind for several years: making and marketing products that capitalized on Kandahar's fabled fruits—soap, skin-care products, precious oils. I wanted to found a small-scale, artisanal agribusiness.

Amir Soltani, who had been our U.S. coordinator, immediately caught the symbolism. "Soap for Afghanistan," he wrote me in an e-mail. "You still think you can clean the place up."

I was amused, above all, by my conversion to economics. A subject I had refused to take a single course on in college. And now, after three years in Afghanistan, I had become converted to the idea that private enterprise held a key to its recovery. I, pointy-headed Sarah Chayes, was going to start a soap factory.

Predictably, I hit a pocket of panic about a week before my flight.

Paris had not been boring this time; it had been a shuddering relief. For seven months, I had basked in Paris—and in Boston—the way I had basked in the tub my first week home, lemon-oil in the water and lavender soap in my hand. I basked in my friends and my neighbors; I basked in being ignored on the street, in speaking a language I handled competently enough to communicate complex thought. When I needed a break from writing, I took my bicycle on long jaunts around the beautiful city, rediscovering it.

And now I was going to leave again. I was going to exile myself again, plunge into that cauldron again.

Once I was buckled into my seat on the plane headed for Dubai, however, the fear inexplicably dropped away. A Palace driver picked me up at the Kabul airport VIP gate and deposited me on Qayum's street in Wazir Akbar Khan. The temporal telescope slammed shut. I had been there last week, it seemed.

It took me two days to get through to Akrem. *"AH-salaamu alaykum!"* his patented shout of greeting rang across the line. "When did you get here? Why didn't you tell me when you were coming? I wanted to pick you up at the airport!"

Given Afghan protocol, this was preposterous. He was the chief of police.

He kept at it: "Where are you staying? I'll come get you."

"Comandan Saab, don't you dare. Send some men."

And so a green-and-white police truck filled with fighters arrived at my door. Akrem was living on the far side of town, in the lee of the King's Garden, which undulates across the terraced flank of a broad hill. We looked at each other, closed the door, and spread our arms to hug a huge greeting. We were in his room, half filled by a giant bed, tentlike uniforms hanging from a coat tree, pallets for his bodyguards around the floor. "These are my temporary quarters," he told me. He had rented a house across town and was fixing it up, so at last he could bring his family from Kandahar.

And then I remember a kind of swirl. He would call at 8:00 P.M. "Have you eaten?" And I would hurriedly change into something sophisticated; he would send a car, and I would find myself at a wedding, with two hundred men, and me. Or I would arrive late at a dinner table where he was already seated with half a dozen government officials. "This man," he introduced our host on one such night, "is your friend, Sarah. If ever I'm not here in Kabul, go to him." The man looked as if he had eaten a lemon. After dinner, when Akrem was dropping me off, he shook his head, laughing: "Oooh! What a bad man he is. Really bad! The worst of the Northern Alliance."

"You could have told me that," I complained.

Another time I called him from the Interior Ministry, where I had gone to see Jalali. "I'm a few streets away from you," I said. "I guess you're busy."

"No, no, I'm unemployed."

"Yeah, right." I went over to police headquarters. As I walked in, his deputy and four or five others stood up, greeted me, and left the office.

One day he asked me on the phone, "Could you use a car to drive around Kabul?"

It would be a godsend. I was pushing my new project. Potential donors were scattered all over the sprawling city. Akrem sent someone to fetch me, and his chief of staff handed over the keys and registration to a brown Toyota Corolla.

It was like the dinner at that Iranian restaurant. What Akrem was doing was thanking me. What he was saying with this wordless generosity was that he was still there, that unlike many Afghans, he would not discard me now that he had achieved power. He would not forget my loyalty to him during hard times, and now that times had changed, he would return it. I could count on him.

And at last I came to understand part of why he cleaved so unshakably to President Karzai. It was gratitude. Karzai had helped him, back when he was a friendless refugee in Quetta. And there was no way Zabit Akrem could ever be induced to forget that.

His men got into it too. I was *Comandan Saab*'s friend, and honoring me was a way to honor him. They were happy to have trappings to put at my disposal. One night, I was driving home late from his house. The streets were closed after a rocket-propelled grenade attack. One of his men accompanied me to police headquarters, where we had to wait for a truck to escort us the rest of the way. The officers at headquarters gave us a boisterous welcome and insisted on contributing a truck of their own to the convoy. So we roared through the silent streets to Wazir Akbar Khan, my little brown car sandwiched between the two green and white trucks. We pulled up; there was a checkpoint at the end of the street because of Qayum and the offices of a big U.S. engineering company, Louis Berger. "What's the problem?" the guard on the checkpoint asked me, taken aback, as the policemen leaped down from the trucks.

"Nothing!" I laughed. "These are my friends!"

There were just three shadows cast across this celebratory mood. One was that Akrem was absolutely exhausted. I had never seen him like this. His eyes would fade to a glaze in the middle of a conversation, and I would realize he hadn't heard the last two sentences. His heavy head would droop. Kabul was a ponderous responsibility, and he was shouldering it, like Atlas. He was meeting with the commanders of ISAF, the NATO-led peacekeeping force stationed in Kabul, and working out ways to coordinate. He was developing a plan for cleaning up the towns ringed around the capital, where criminals and riffraff would scoot after committing thefts in town. He was trying to professionalize his divisions. He was learning the ways of the different embassies, each meddling in its own fashion, often several in concert. He was constantly switched on, constantly accessible, constantly on the scene. "Yes, come see me tomorrow morning," I heard him tell someone on the phone one evening. "I'm in the office around six. Why don't you come at six-thirty or seven? There won't be too many people then." His days tapered off around nine or ten at night, with a patrol of the empty streets. The bodyguards and his young right-hand man, Shafiullah, were panting. Akrem was having problems with his blood pressure, Shafiullah confided.

Once I asked Akrem if I could go out with them at night. I was still in my dinner clothes, a salmon-colored silk pants suit, gauzy head shawl and heels, when we made for a precinct station on the far side of town. The men consulted maps to get there; they were still finding their bearings. As we arrived, I could tell the visit was unannounced. The half dozen officers on duty rushed to attention. They bustled about Akrem and showed him inside their tiny, leprous station. Manifestly, it was the first time a police chief had ever bothered to visit them. Akrem was pretty horrified at what he saw. While Shafiullah went through the radio check and took down the statistics they were compiling on all the precincts—number of officers, number on duty at night, number and position of checkpoints— Akrem took the time to ask about other things that mattered to these men: Were they safe? Who was on the other side of that wall over there? What was the flow of traffic down this road here, a wide swathe across the map on the wall? Where were the transport trucks coming from? This was a Hazara neighborhood; were there any tensions? Did they have hot water? How was their food? What was that? Rotten meat?

"Next time you get rotten meat with lunch, you send it straight to my office. I'll take it to the logistics department myself!" That was one problem Akrem could solve right away.

The second shadow over my return to Kabul was the discovery that President Karzai had not, in fact, improved. I wasn't going to have to worry about getting that pistol into Afghanistan after all.

When he won the October 2004 presidential election, in one of those moments of overpowering joy—when the people unaccountably, irrationally, threw everything they *knew* to the winds, and waited in line all day to vote—I reserved judgment. Friends, including Kurt Amend, the former embassy political affairs officer, now at the National Security Council, enthused about the new cabinet. I noticed a couple of names I did not care for, but I hesitated to throw cold water. "I'll let you know what I think when I get to Kabul," I told Kurt.

It was worse than I feared. I had discussions late into the night with someone who worked in a ministry. The things described took my breath away: beatings inside the building; the minister locking employees in the bathroom; bricks of cash packed into the minister's SUV. A competent, responsible, dignified man shouldered out of the cabinet by the thugs because he would show them up. That one hit me hard, since I had always fallen back on the vague belief that there were no alternatives to the thugs. But there were; there were good and competent candidates for government jobs and they were being thrown away.

Gul Agha Shirzai had been sent back to Kandahar as governor. The ruins he left behind in Kabul were beyond description. I talked to someone who was struggling over what to tell the World Bank about $50,000 it had allocated for a project in Kabul. Shirzai had sent the money to Kandahar to embellish his father's tomb. And now this person had to come up with receipts to satisfy the World Bank.

In mid-May, anti-American demonstrations broke out. They turned very nasty, with lootings and some deaths. The supposed cause was an article in *Newsweek* magazine reporting that a U.S. guard at the prison camp for terrorist suspects at Guantánamo Bay had flushed a copy of the Koran down a toilet.

But I suspected this was not the real reason for the demonstrations. Proof, for me, was the fact that they had been sparked by "university students." Universities in eastern Afghanistan are packed with Pakistanis. This is utterly illogical, since the worst school in Pakistan is better than the so-called college in Kandahar, where people are taught medicine without benefit of a single anatomy chart, let alone a microscope, and the library is a cramped, locked storeroom. I had always assumed that among these "students" lurked a number of Pakistani intelligence agents.

In the wake of the demonstrations, I realized that the students served another purpose for Pakistan. They were like a giant sleeper cell in Afghanistan, which could be activated to agitate, while affording plausible deniability to the Pakistani government.

Another event had taken place that same week in May, which I thought was the true reason for the demonstrations. President Karzai had announced that Afghanistan was going to enter into a long-term strategic partnership with the United States. In other words, the United States was there to stay, and Pakistan, I suspected, was angry.

I laid my theory on Akrem. I had been down to Kandahar and was back in Kabul for a few days. "You're absolutely right," he said. "Except *all* of Afghanistan's neighbors want the United States out of here, so they're banding together in an alliance of all the old enemies: Pakistan, Iran, Russia, even China. In Kabul, Iran was the busiest with the demonstrations. You want to hear how it went down in Kabul?"

Akrem knew a march was planned. The night before, he had invited several student leaders over to his house for dinner. "I chose Pashtuns," he said. That was one of Akrem's gifts: he knew how to identify Afghanistan's faults and turn them around for the good of the country. He had an intuitive feel for the tribal and ethnic dynamics, but instead of exploiting them to tear the nation apart, he harnessed them to the task of forging it.

"I told them: 'So, you're going to demonstrate tomorrow?' They said they were. 'You're going to carry banners and chant slogans against the central government?' They said they were. I asked: 'But who's the central government?' They thought for a minute. I told them: 'President Karzai is the central government. He's a Pashtun. And the interior minister, and the defense minister, and me. We're the central government. And all of us are Pashtuns. Who are you helping with these demonstrations?' The students thought about it. 'If you're really angry about something,' I said, 'why don't you start right now? Here I am, I'm the central government. Start insulting me, now, like you're going to do tomorrow. Whatever you plan to say then, say it now.'"

The shaken students asked him what he wanted them to do.

"I told them to go to their friends, and explain to them that they were being manipulated. March, by all means. But don't break down buildings. Don't hurt people."

Perhaps Akrem had manipulated those students too. Perhaps he was just a little too delighted to have them "eating out of his hand," as he put it. But he wasn't inspiring them to wreak destruction, like the other manipulators he was up against. In Kabul, the anti-American protest was remarkably small and peaceful.

"The next night, I took those student leaders out to dinner," said Akrem. "With my own money! You would have thought the minister might send me a watch or something to thank me for preventing violence."

It seemed that, even though Karzai and Jalali had seen fit to appoint Akrem to Kabul, they still did not understand his worth. They were still having trouble distinguishing their friends from their enemies.

The third shadow that darkened our mood was the security situation in Kandahar. "Sarah, it's not like when you were here before," Kandaharis living in Kabul would tell me. "You can't go driving around by yourself anymore." When I called down to Kandahar, I heard the same thing. There was a change in atmosphere. Things had gotten ugly.

I told Akrem I was headed out, and double-checked that he absolutely didn't need the little Corolla, that it would be OK if I drove it down there.

"Do you really have to go to Kandahar?" His voice was almost tender. That he even asked signified a lot.

CHAPTER 30

KANDAHAR

I WAS RIGHT about continuity. No one in Kandahar really thought I was coming back. That I did said it all. It mattered not what I was planning to achieve, what project I was working on, what measurable impact it might have. The bare fact that I had come back, that I had left the comfort of my Western country and had come back again to be with them, "in this dust," meant everything to Kandaharis. Ahmad Wali Karzai's retainers practically stood in line to greet me:

"You were away a *long* time! How's your mother, is she well? Your sister? Your friends, great and small, are they doing well?"

A traffic cop posted at an intersection blocked my way across; he pounded on the hood of my red truck: "Daughter of a tyrant! Where have you been?"

And so we renewed our vows, Kandahar and I.

I set about establishing myself. I signed a six-month contract for the place I had rented before, newly painted and twice as expensive. I bought raw cotton from Helmand to fill the velvet mattresses that would furnish the rooms. I haggled in the bazaar over steel bowls and plates, plastic ladles for dipping the watered-down yogurt drink I had learned to love. I bought two gunnysacks of almonds from the relative of a friend, a man from Urozgan who had carried them down to the city to sell. We weighed them out ourselves, a four-and-a-half-kilo stone on one side of the balance to measure the *mans*. We were going to make sweet almond oil for our soaps. I hired loyal Karim away from the Americans, with whom I had found places for my guys, my six-man retinue, when I had left the previous fall. The others would show up around three each afternoon, after quitting time at the base.

On the last day in May, we decided to take a holiday. Hayatullah, the shaggy-haired former bus driver, had an orchard in Arghandab. It is a fantastic place, shaggy as his unruly head, overlooking the mighty Arghandab River, whose shifting bed occupies a great sinuous span of land laid with smoothed river stones, the water slicing channels of changing depth and speed. It was high apricot season, and we were going to Hayatullah's garden to eat fruit. The guys had told the Americans they were sick; all of us were packed into the red truck.

I let Hayatullah drive. The road leaves Kandahar along the bank of a canal, near my old home in the graveyard. Mullah Naqib's house is on the other bank, and the light-blue festival mosque where Kandahar celebrated the end of the Taliban in December 2001. I let my eyes rest on the landscape, my inner eye on the memories. At the last second, I caught sight of a forest-green Land Cruiser coming the other way with a couple other vehicles. I knew that car! Grabbing my cell phone, I dialed up Akrem's number. I got a soldier; I had a hard time hearing him; reception was fading. But I was sure I'd heard "in Kandahar."

Yes! He'd finally made it. Poor Akrem had been trying to get leave for over a month. He had even asked me to intercede with his boss, Interior Minister Jalali, on my last trip to Kabul. His new house was ready, and he had to go to Kandahar to fetch his family.

I had done my routine with Jalali.

"One last thing. It's Khakrezwal."

"*Again?* What *is* it about that man?"

"He needs to go to Kandahar. Would you please give him some vacation?"

"I will, I will. In a few days. I need him here."

"How *many* days exactly? Can he leave the day after tomorrow?"

"Sarah! You haven't changed at all! He can leave in three days. And he can spend five nights away."

"Promise?"

"Promise."

Of course it hadn't been three days, it had been fully two weeks. I told the soldier through the static on the cell phone that I was off to Arghandab and I would call back in a few hours.

It was Akrem who called me, shortly after I returned, grubby from fording the river and clambering among the fruit trees, my pockets stuffed with apricot stones for turning into oil.

"*AH-salaamu alay-kum!*" Irrepressible. He was in that friend's garden across town. I had to come and eat some mulberries.

I told him to give me half an hour to take a shower and get there.

When I arrived, Akrem was seated at a long plastic table set out on the grass. There were plates of apricots and fragrant, chilled mulberries, which he had specially requested from our host, remembering how I loved them. As I sat down, a fresh, mounded plate of them arrived, and a bowl of water for rinsing my fingers. Around the table sat assorted Alokozai elders. I never knew who I would encounter when I went to meet Akrem these days; I should have learned to watch my mouth a little. But I never did. I remember the graybeards smiling at my Pashtu and the frankness of my political humor. As the call to sunset prayer drifted through the air, they all got up to do their devotions, a little apart.

Afterward, the elders stayed seated in the grass at the end of the garden. Only Akrem came back to join me, and his right-hand man, Shafiullah.

I'd had almost no interaction with this young cousin of Akrem's over the years—it was he who had delivered the letter ordering me to leave my house in the graveyard, and I had avoided him ever after. But suddenly he was coming to life for me; our shared affection for Akrem was beginning to forge a kinship. In Kabul I had begged Shafiullah to make him get some exercise.

"So, Sarah," Akrem asked. "What's happening in Kandahar?"

"*Comandan Saab,* I keep telling you. I'm out of politics."

Akrem smiled.

We started discussing the assassination, two days before, of a local mullah, or religious leader. This was a major event. The man had been the head of a provincial council of mullahs, and was an outspoken supporter of the current regime. A distinguished religious scholar, he had debunked the resurgent Taliban's interpretation of Islam in his sermons, staying the course with the fundamentalists, verse for holy verse.

This man had been murdered in downtown Kandahar, on the guarded street that runs between the old governor's palace and the sacred mosque with the relic of the prophet Muhammad. In broad daylight, two men on a motorcycle had ridden up to him, shot him dead, and ridden away.

"What Taliban?" Shafiullah was saying. "The Taliban wouldn't dare!"

"How wouldn't they dare?" I countered. "It doesn't exactly take daring. There's no security in this town. There are no searches. *I* could drive around with a gun in my car; no one would know the difference."

"Agha!" Asma appeared, Akrem's daughter: a little girl now, sparks for eyes framed by a pageboy cut, earrings in her ears. Leaning against his knee, she stood on tiptoes and peered over the edge of the table, reached for a plate of apricots, and then carried it carefully away in two hands.

"His family's been saying that if it was the Taliban, why didn't they kill him in Arghandab or in Malajat, one of those places where they have power? He went to those places every day. Why kill him in the middle of town?"

"But Shafiullah, that's the whole point! They want to make a splash. And what could make more of a splash than nailing him in broad daylight, right in front of his office."

I saw what Shafiullah was driving at, though.

"That street is barred. There are soldiers on the gate. There are fifteen soldiers posted at the entrance to the governor's palace, right next door to the building he was leaving. You're telling me a gun goes off—even if no one is killed—a gun goes off and not one of those soldiers steps out into the street to see what's going on?"

What Shafiullah was saying, and I agreed, was that "the Taliban," as such, as an autonomous movement, did not exist. The "Taliban" were creatures of the Pakistani authorities, and if they had committed murder in Kandahar, they had done so with the connivance of other creatures of the Pakistani authorities who held positions in provincial government.

"Pakistan's strategy," Akrem remarked, "is always the same: to make haste slowly, to take one step forward and ten steps back."

He was right; the proof was before us. Here was the murder of a mullah—and not just any mullah, but the top religious leader of the province, in the middle of town, at one o'clock in the afternoon. This was much worse than what had been going on back in the summer of 2003, when I had been so stricken with foreboding. Mullahs had been killed then too, but little-known ones, out in the districts. This assassination represented a quantum leap. Just as Akrem's mole had predicted before the ambush of that ICRC engineer, two years earlier, the killings had started in the districts; they had slowly circled Kandahar. Now this one had happened right in the heart of town. And we were discussing it calmly. We had been inured. The violence had been carefully dosed, so we needed it in ever-higher levels to register the shock.

"You're right, *Comandan Saab,*" I said. "Do you remember when you infiltrated that training camp two years ago? They were teaching the targeted assassination of public figures, you remember? That's just what you're saying. They were training it back then, and now it's started."

"*Woh* . . ." Akrem assented, in an intake of breath. "Now it's started."

But, my God, I wasn't thinking of him. He was in Kabul. He was chief of the Kabul police. We were impregnable in our garden.

The evening call to prayer threaded the eye of our conversation. Akrem stood up. Our host insisted we stay for dinner. "No, no, we're going home," replied Akrem. He called to his soldiers to "throw those kids in the car." The shouts of his children had edged into the register that indicates the end of the day.

I *think* he wanted me to come with him. This was my difficulty with his elegant manners. I always felt that each of us was silently trying to work out what the other wanted, so we could comply. I *think* he assumed I would join him at his house. But I was imagining his homecoming that day: he had scarcely seen his family in a year and a half. I wanted to give him space. I stuck out my hand. Abruptly, formally, he shook it.

"I'll call you," I said.

And I followed his convoy out the gate. He turned left; I turned right.

CHAPTER 31

INVESTIGATION

JUNE 2005

I WAS UP to my wrists in newly batched soap, mixed from our own sweet almond oil and another—vivid, dark green, pungent with fragrance—that we had extracted with our hand-crank press from anise seeds. The putty-like soap was a pale lime color and smelled like heaven as I wrestled it into some metal sugar bowls we were using for molds. I had tried to tune into the BBC, but I couldn't pick up the signal. In a huge concession, I had handed my little shortwave radio over to Karim, so he could put on some of that vile music he was addicted to—one thing in Kandahar I absolutely detested. Karim twiddled the dial, locked on to the local news.

". . . an explosion . . ." came the announcer's voice, and then a name: "Muhammad Akrem Khakrezwal." That's all I heard. After a stunned second, Karim started a commentary, keeping up for me. It was a suicide bombing, in a mosque in the bazaar. Akrem was killed or wounded, there was no confirmation yet. At least nineteen people were dead.

It felt as though my entire being flew to my eyes as they met and held Karim's. As though, if we could only keep staring at each other, we could make it not be true.

We leaped for the truck. With a competence I had kept under wraps till then, I raced it through the streets, slowing for each traffic bump, turning at the last instant to flow over it at the perfect angle, speeding to the next. At the hospital gates I pushed the truck through a clamoring crowd.

The soldiers let me by. There were about four U.S. Humvees in the circular drive. I rushed up to an officer. "Do you know where the chief is?"

Impassive, without a glance, the American answered, "No."

I waded through another crowd to enter a building. A doctor asked, "Who are you looking for?"

"*Comandan Saab.*"

The doctor looked at me. "*Comandan Saab*'s not here. He's home."

I knew what this meant. I had known all along. This whole trip to the hospital was just pantomime. But I kept it up. I stared into the doctor's eyes, as though my exaggerated surprise could ward it off. The doctor turned away, busy with other distraught people. There was nothing he could do for me.

A colleague of Akrem's was outside; he had on a beautifully embroidered tunic, pale blue. He was on his way to the house too; we could drive together. He just needed to get a stretcher.

"One of those stretchers they put dead people on," Karim defined a word I had never heard. I didn't listen to him. I followed the man's truck around the side of the hospital to the place, Karim explained, where people pick up the bodies of their dead. It was a refrigerated cargo container. Impatient, I went inside, hoping to wrest whatever this stretcher was from someone's hands. There were bits and pieces of people strewn around the floor. But no blood, somehow. I remember two legs, stacked against a wall like firewood. I was less horrified than I dimly thought I should be. I didn't have time. I had to get to Akrem's house—as though there were any reason to hurry anymore.

I left, without Akrem's colleague. I found my way out of the hospital, and sped through town and across the canal.

The radio had lied. There was confirmation. Right here. It was in everyone's faces. It was under his blanket. "There he is, your friend!" Akrem's brother cried, pulling it back.

Then came the vigil on the verandah, and my time in the black van, next to Akrem's lonely body. Mullah Naqib arrived. I had asked people earlier where he was. "In Arghandab," someone had said. "He doesn't know."

"Shouldn't we send someone?" I had asked.

I gripped the grizzled commander's hand as he strode into the schoolyard. "How are you, fine?" he said, mechanically, not seeing me. His eyes were filled with tears. They were running down his face. "But how is it possible? I didn't even know he was here!" I followed Mullah Naqib to the verandah and rejoined the circle on the mattresses. "If I had known he was here, we would have gone to the mosque together!"

The event at the mosque had been a prayer service, a memorial for the very mullah Akrem and I had been talking about the previous night. He was such an important figure that there were two days of services, one at the main mosque that enshrined the Prophet's shroud, and a second that morning, at the old mud-plaster mosque I loved, in the bazaar, which was the mullah's own.

"I couldn't make it yesterday, so I went today," Mullah Naqib was saying. Then he and the bodyguards plunged into the chronology.

"I think you left just as we were arriving," said the black-haired soldier who had been driving Akrem's car. "You were in your white Land Cruiser, right?"

"Yes! How did I miss you? I didn't even recognize your car. I went straight on to Arghandab. If I'd known *Comandan Saab* was in town, I would have waited and gone to the mosque with you."

Mullah Naqib passed over in silence what that would have meant for him. Twenty-two people lay dead right now.

"And, you know, there's something else," he pursued. "When I entered that mosque, I tripped on something. By God, I remember; I said it out loud: 'Why didn't they sweep the ground properly before laying down the carpet?' "

Our tuning forks were ringing out a note. This just did not feel like a suicide bombing.

At the very least, it was not possible to blame it on an Arab. I had seen the remains. How could anyone determine the nationality of one of those darkened hunks of meat in the container at the hospital? And yet, Gul Agha had proclaimed it, within an hour of the explosion. It was a suicide bombing. An Arab had done it. There were documents to prove it.

Documents?

I spoke up. "Look, guys. The governor is never going to investigate this crime. And neither is the deputy chief of police"—a notorious ISI man. "No way they are going to look into this properly."

"That's for sure."

"But we're the police too, right? Why don't we do our own investigation?"

I was surprised at how much urging it took to rouse them. In their place, with what I presumed was their training, I would have been all over it. But they, suddenly, seemed to feel helpless.

I could see that I was going to plunge into things again, into the politics and the hypocrisy. There was no choice. It was the least I could do for Akrem.

After a few moments we stood up and piled into his forest-green Land Cruiser. It was a distraction; it made the bodyguards feel useful, almost as though they were out on a mission again on Akrem's orders. Following in a separate car was an officer from one of the Kabul precincts, the head of criminal investigations. He was very competent, Akrem's friend the businessman assured me. He had a master's degree.

But something about the man made me uncomfortable. "Is he really a friend?" I asked, on our way to the mosque.

"Sarah," replied Shafiullah, "no one is a friend. You'll see. When you don't have power, no one is your friend."

I was not all there; I know it now. Beyond going to the mosque, I'm not sure what I had in mind. But one thing did pierce my haze when we arrived. There was absolutely nothing there. No crime scene tape, no one guarding the site. No investigators taking pictures or picking up objects, no debris, no blood, no nothing. Only, at the back of the courtyard above our heads, by the rooms where the *taliban* lived—the dead mullah's religious students—two municipal employees on the balconies, sweeping up the broken glass. I can't forget the sound.

That was the only sign that something had happened here. I turned about, feeling dizzy.

We were not actually in the mosque; we were inside the compound wall, facing the mosque building some fifteen yards away. There was a small sepulcher beside us, with a tree, and a single course of bricks leading straight ahead, toward the steps to the mosque.

"But where was the bomb?" I asked out loud.

"Over there." A mosque employee, ugly, like Quasimodo, pointed to a place just left of the course of bricks, outside the mosque proper.

It was a patch of dirt, maybe three feet by a foot and a half, studded with some stones, sort of like the road to Kabul before it was paved.

"Was this concrete before, like the rest of the courtyard?" I asked Quasimodo.

"Yes," he answered. "No. Uh . . . there was some construction work. The trucks broke the cement . . ." His voice trailed off.

I was still disoriented. None of this added up. I envied Shafiullah, somehow managing to focus, poking around by the sepulcher and along the compound walls. He came over and showed me something. A ball bearing, a quarter inch in diameter or a little less. There were lots of them. I took it. To be doing something, I walked over to the compound wall, and fitted it into one of the holes that pocked its surface. The investigations officer joined me. "You see? You see how high the splash is? It had to be a suicide bomb."

I didn't know what to say.

I zipped the little ball bearing into my contact lens case and put it in my shoulder bag. We had to go. We were supposed to leave for Khakrez at four.

But a second point was penetrating my consciousness by then. This thing could not have been done by a person in military uniform bending down before Akrem, the way the radio kept repeating. I had seen Akrem's face. It was clean, peaceful, stern. Nothing had hit him from the front.

I did not understand what had happened that morning, but I did know one thing. The governor was lying. Within an hour of the explosion, he had come out with a lie, prefabricated, complete with details plausible enough for the media to pass them along. And just in case anyone might want to test the official story, the scene of the crime had been sanitized. Something was going on.

Two days later, when we were all back from Akrem's burial, Shafiullah wordlessly set about gathering strands of evidence. One night, he came to my house with the bodyguards in tow, including one I didn't know, Landau. He was the round-faced man with the drooping mustache and the bandoliers who had been injured on Akrem's midnight drive to Kabul nearly two years before. He looked so much like a B-movie Mexican that I caught myself asking: "Do you speak Pashtu?"

"Of course," he answered.

Landau's legs were injured. He pulled up his baggy trousers to show me. From the tops of his feet, inside one leg and outside the other, ending where a bit of a bandage was taped to the bottom of his ribcage, were small scabs that matched those ball bearings.

So. The splash wasn't so high after all. It had started at ground level, at the tops of Landau's feet.

"Where were you standing?" I asked him. I flipped back the cover of my notebook and sketched a map of the compound. It was the first of dozens I would draw over the next two weeks. "Here's the wall, and here's the gate to the compound. Here's that little grave; here's the line of bricks. Where were you?"

When Landau's dots on my map got too impressionistic, I made him stand up: "OK. Let's say the edge of this rug is the little course of bricks. You're *Comandan Saab;* I'm Mir Wais. Which direction was Mir Wais facing?"

Mir Wais was another bodyguard. He had been killed.

The bomb, Landau was telling me, exploded after Akrem had said his prayers in the mosque and exited the building proper. The courtyard in front, starting at the course of bricks, was covered in carpeting; there was a tent strung overhead. On the way in, Akrem had left his shoes by the bricks, stepping barefoot onto the carpet and signaling to a couple of bodyguards to remain behind to watch his back. When he emerged from the mosque, Landau was on post at the line of bricks, facing him. He saw it all. He saw Mir Wais approach Akrem with his leather slippers and lay them down—that accounted for the man in uniform. He saw Akrem step into the right shoe, raise his left foot to step into the other, his left arm stretched slightly backward for balance. And then he saw the explosion. "Behind him," Landau emphasized. And that was all he saw. The air was choked with dirt and smoke; his ears were clanging. He was upside down.

"Who was near Comandan Saab?" I pressed him.

"No one. Just us, just the bodyguards and family."

This was starting to make sense. But the image still wasn't precise enough. We went back to the mosque next day and walked it.

"So *Comandan Saab* was here." I was insisting on this, dragging them through it again, obsessively. "Where was Mir Wais? Oh, *here,* to his right, facing *left."* Mir Wais's face had been blown off. "And where was his nephew?" The son of Akrem's brother, our host at Khakrez, one of the other two biers at the burial. Now I was understanding Akrem's brother's confusion, that morning on the stony Khakrez hillside. He had been torn between two graves. "Behind and to the left?" I remembered the boy's wrapped body, face enveloped in a bloody white sack, tied off at the neck.

Another young man was pulling me over toward the compound wall. It was Akrem's cook. He had been the first to reach his body. "He was here." He pointed to a spot beneath the wall, ten feet from where Akrem had been standing and to the right. "He fell on his back," the cook said, recalling how he had tried hopelessly to fix the body. "I was running around and around looking for that arm. I never found it." Akrem's left arm was gone, and the back of his left thigh vaporized. The cook showed me the place on his own leg. "There was nothing in it, just grease; it was held on by the skin."

No wonder his body had looked so small.

The picture was resolving. The bomb would have detonated slightly to Akrem's left; that was why he had been projected rightward, why his left side was injured, and the front of the bodyguard who had brought his shoes and who was standing to his right, watching while he put them on. The back of Akrem's leg had been torn off, but the face of the nephew who was following him toward the gate. The blast must have gone off behind Akrem and in front of the boy.

A suicide bomber between Akrem and his nephew?

There were some other details I needed to check out. An American official had told me the legs I'd seen in the hospital had been found well away from the site, one in a neighboring garden. They had to be the suicide bomber's, he implied. There were even rumors of a head, supposedly retrieved on a roof somewhere. I went back to the hospital and found the old mullah who was keeper of the refrigerated container. Struggling with the horizontal clasp on the heavy hermetic door, he opened it for me. Sure enough, the two legs were still there, shorn off below the knees, veins and sinews curling up from the ends like snapped electrical wires. They were otherwise uninjured. They could not have been projected high into the air and tumbled through branches into a garden. The old mullah confirmed that they had arrived amid the chaos of injured and dead and the other severed body parts. It was terrible; he hadn't had time to pray that whole day long. But no, the mullah told me, no head had been retrieved. It would have come to him.

Over the following days, I questioned three other survivors of the blast, two who had been standing in front of Akrem and one behind. All had seen the same thing.

"The flash came up through the rug," said one older man, who lived among the trees in Arghandab. "He looked so beautiful, I was staring at him." Smiling, the gentleman put out his two fists as though gripping the arms of an armchair, eloquently: "He was nice and big, you know?" *Elephant bodied. Like Rustam.* "He was wearing a white tunic and a black turban, and I couldn't stop looking at him because he was so beautiful. I wanted to go up and congratulate him for being appointed to Kabul. I saw him step into one shoe, and he was about to put on the other when the flash came. Behind him. Through the rug." The man pushed the fingers of one hand up between the thumb and forefinger of the other.

Another bodyguard, very young, still deaf from the blast and limping painfully, flapped his shawl to demonstrate how the rug had lifted.

He had been posted at the row of bricks in front, with Landau. Both were injured. Mir Wais, after putting down the shoes, was standing beside Akrem, with two more bodyguards deployed behind. Those three soldiers were dead. The impressionistic dots on my map were coming into focus. The bodyguards had done their job after all. They had established a close-protection perimeter around Akrem. No unknown person could have penetrated it. This was not a suicide bombing.

I started writing the findings up, reading them out loud to Shafiullah as I went along. What stunned us both was that no one else was doing this. The chief of police of the Afghan capital had been killed and not a single person had interviewed an eyewitness: not the local police, not the commission the interior ministry had sent down to Kandahar, not an American official, not a journalist—neither the Afghan reporters at the radio station I had set up with Qayum Karzai nor any foreigners. Even Carlotta Gall, the seasoned *New York Times* correspondent who made straight for Akrem whenever she visited a city he resided in, contented herself with the official declarations. The site of the blast had been cleaned up within hours; no meaningful forensic examination could have taken place; and the

two legs were still sitting at the hospital, ignored. On the basis of what evidence were these certainties being propounded?

Something else troubled me. The night Akrem's brother had returned
from Khakrez, he had received a visit from Governor Shirzai, accompanied
by the liaison to the investigation team sent down from Kabul, who happened to be Shirzai's tribesmen. The governor had stayed till midnight.
"You shouldn't ask so many questions about this suicide bombing," he had
admonished Akrem's brother. "I'll find the killers and deliver them to you,
I promise. I had information about four Taliban who were planning to do
this thing. Now they're in Helmand Province. I'll get them for you. But
don't keep saying it wasn't a suicide bombing."

"First it was an Arab, and now it's Taliban from Helmand?" exclaimed
Akrem's brother. "He thinks I'm a child."

I was reminded of the assassination of ICRC engineer Ricardo, on the
lonely road to Urozgan. Gul Agha Shirzai had thrown sand in our eyes then
too, storming about Taliban in government, when he had allowed the Taliban who did it to come across the border from Pakistan. This had always
been Shirzai's role in Kandahar: to facilitate activities by the Pakistani ISI
and help cover over the tracks afterward. If Gul Agha Shirzai was lying this
energetically, I thought, if he was trying this hard to keep things hushed
up, then the government of Pakistan had to be involved in this murder.

It fit the pattern.

CHAPTER 32
COVER-UP

JUNE 2005

THERE WAS GOING to be a national memorial service for Zabit Akrem in Kabul, at the main mosque near Qayum Karzai's house. Half the Alokozai tribe was headed up to the capital. I decided to join them. There were some people I needed to explain the truth to. Jalali. The U.S. embassy. President Karzai.

"Comandan Saab, I've left politics!"

The reason this was so important to me was not just that Akrem had been my friend. It was because there were serious policy implications to getting this right. If Akrem had been killed by a suicide bomber, then the culprit was part of some nebulous and undifferentiated "terrorist threat"—was one of those ideological fanatics spawned by Usama bin Laden, who could only be fought in the immediate term by force. A purely military solution was called for. If, on the other hand, a remote-controlled mine, say, had been planted inside that well-guarded mosque, that was different. The assassin had local complicity. Men whom President Karzai and American officials had placed and obstinately maintained in power were responsible. This murder was the direct result of policies that I—and Akrem—had been decrying for the past three years. If, as I suspected, this was a Pakistani job, then a change in U.S. policy toward Pakistan was called for, because it was proof positive that our "ally" Pakistan was working to destroy everything we were working to create in Afghanistan. Left alone, this hidden Pakistani enmity would sooner or later explode in our hands.

And if it was a Pakistani job, then President Karzai finally had to fire those Pakistani intelligence agents who infested his provincial government.

The distinction was crucial. It was terribly important to get this right.

True to form, Interior Minister Jalali agreed to see me immediately. He was devastated. He looked ten years older. After all his jousting with Akrem, it was Jalali who felt in his gut the import of this loss. He wondered how I was doing. I said OK and handed over the document I had drawn up with Shafiullah, launching into my exposition.

Jalali cut me off. "No, no, no . . . it was a suicide." His tone was gentle, that of a rational man trying to pry a grief-stricken relative away from some fantasy about the deceased. "Everyone agrees, Sarah: the local police, the commission I sent down, the FBI; everyone says it was a suicide."

I began making the counterarguments. Jalali's ears pricked a little. "OK, OK," he said. "I'll read your document."

The next stop was the U.S. embassy. I didn't know anyone there anymore; I had been away too long. But I arranged a meeting with the current political affairs officer, and he brought along a couple of FBI agents. I drew my map for them. I passed around the ball bearing.

"I was determined to make doubt triumph over certitude." A line from an Italian crime novel.[1]

They were mildly intrigued. "The thing is," said the chief agent, "we are here in Afghanistan in a supporting role. We have a team in Kandahar, and they made themselves available to Afghan investigators, which meant, essentially, giving them help with forensics. But what I'm saying is, because there were no U.S. citizens killed in that bombing, we couldn't take any . . . initiative. You get me? That understanding is part of the basis for our being here. If there had been an American citizen, on the other hand . . ."

But there was an American citizen. It took me a couple more days to work that out. An in-law of Akrem's, who was visiting from Albany, New York, who had been standing right by Akrem's nephew when the bomb exploded, had been an American citizen. I introduced his son to the FBI team on the base in Kandahar. The Americans had not even looked closely enough to find that out themselves.

The FBI guys at Kandahar Airfield did seem on the ball, though. They were welcoming, energetic, and forthright. They elaborated on the nature of their "conclusion" in favor of the suicide-bombing thesis.

"Look, we couldn't get access to any of the bodies. I mean, you couldn't really call it an investigation as we know it. We couldn't see the bodies; we couldn't get to the scene until two days later. We dug around some, where the blast had broken the ground, but who knows what we were looking at by then."

I was sitting with three agents at an outdoor picnic table on base, with a little wooden roof over it to shade it from the sun. It was the most private place to talk.

"We couldn't interview anyone either, since it's hard for us to get into town. What we did was look at a bunch of photographs that had been taken after the explosion. And there was stuff in those pictures that looked consistent, to us, with a suicide bombing. The legs, for example, blown off at the hip." The agent was on a roll. "Typically, if a suicide bomber has the charge in a vest, or taped around his chest, his limbs are going to be blown off at the joints, because that's the weakest place."

"At the hips?" I interrupted. "But wait a minute. That's not right. Those aren't the right legs."

"Excuse me?"

"The leftover legs that everyone's talking about? They weren't blown off at the hips. I checked them at the hospital last week. They were severed below the knees." I bent over and delivered a karate chop to my own shin.

"Really? See, we were looking at these legs in the picture they showed us, and we just assumed they were the legs in question."

Negative, my index finger waved. "Those ones must have been picked up by a family. The legs that were left in the hospital were shorn off below the knees. I should have taken a picture."

"Was it clean, like?" another agent chimed in. "Cauterized?"

"Like they'd been chopped off with a cleaver and sealed." And I described the curly wires of veins and nerves sprouting from the ends of the legs.

One of the agents glanced at the other: "That sounds kind of like a claymore."

I spoke to other security officials, from other countries. The words *claymore mine* kept leaping to their lips. The expertise of these officers made short work of the other main argument in favor of the suicide bombing theory: the lack of a crater where a bomb would have been laid. "There's a mine called a Jumping Jennie," one officer told me, his Australian twang making a delight of that middle "e." "When it's tripped, it springs about yea high." He held his hand at chest level. "Then it explodes."

That would not have been consistent with those poxlike wounds on Landau's legs, but it gave a notion of the possibilities: a shallow crater did not rule out a remote-controlled bomb.

"Mines are very versatile," said a French Special Forces officer, at a dinner sometime later for the departing U.S. Civil Affairs team in Kandahar. "You can rig a mine to do anything. It's easy to fit it with a remote-controlled detonator."

Claymores. My interlocutors kept coming back to claymores. They weren't very thick, their blast sliced through limbs, and they were usually packed with ball bearings. Surely it was worth consideration?

The FBI agents on base interviewed Landau and the little bodyguard and the gentleman from Arghandab when I brought them out one evening weeks later. They were diligent about it, meeting the witnesses separately, taking notes, backtracking over questions. The agents spent a lot of time. But when I asked one of them afterward, "What do you think the upshot of all this will be?" he took a breath.

"You know," he said. "The problem here is one of mentality. That's the biggest thing we're up against, all the time."

By "here" the FBI agent did not mean "in Afghanistan." He meant where he lived, on base—in the American community in Afghanistan.

"The mentality here is a war-fighting mentality. It's not a criminal investigations mentality. It's like, you don't really have to find out *who* did this, and prove it so it could stand up in a court. The enemy did it. That's the mentality. The enemy did it and we have to kill him. It's like a culture clash between us FBI guys and the rest of them. And so . . . I guess I don't really know what the upshot will be."

This is the mentality that the Pakistani government has so astutely figured out. It is by exploiting this bias that Pakistan has gained free rein to organize, train, equip, and deploy thousands of "Taliban insurgents" in Afghanistan in exchange for turning over a handful of Al-Qaeda members.

By exploiting this mentality, the Pakistani government was able to cling to a policy that will leave not just Afghanistan, but Pakistan too, a dangerous, volatile, hamstrung place for years to come.

Venal provincial officials were catching on too. The suicide-bombing theory that Governor Shirzai had made up out of whole cloth was carefully calculated to continue exploiting this bias.

It was breathtaking, how it worked.

"I don't think the issue of who was killed is as important as the fact that it was a suicide bombing—if that's what it proves to be," the State Department representative in Kandahar told me, as we lolled on overstuffed easy chairs in the Civil Affairs compound that June.

I was speechless. Here was one of the savviest and most experienced U.S. officials currently stationed in Afghanistan, who—past a token acknowledgement that the suicide bombing theory was unproven—was dwelling on how much it impressed him. He had taken the bait.

"See, suicide bombing is pretty common in Chechnya. And there have been reports of Chechens operating around Gardez. This would be the first example of that sort of tactic this far south. It would be really worrisome if Chechens were moving in down here."

Chechens. Members of that far-flung constellation of ineffable terrorist groups. Nothing to do with the realities of the situation in Kandahar. Nothing to do with the poor decisions made by President Karzai and the United States over the past three years.

I was getting nowhere.

My third big meeting in Kabul was with President Karzai. I asked if we could do it alone. Two staff members stood up and left his small office with the tables in a T.

"I've been wanting to see you!" Karzai launched in when they were gone. His voice has a surprisingly rich timber to it. "I saw your article in the *New York Times;* it was excellent."

"I'm glad you liked it." This was an op-ed I had written about the recent anti-American demonstrations. I said that at their root, they had not been about desecration of the Koran; they were fomented by Afghanistan's neighbors in opposition to the "strategic partnership" between Kabul and Washington.

"I was telling exactly this to President Bush," said Karzai, who had been in Washington when the piece came out. "I was speaking quite strongly, and then your article appeared the very next day."

"Oh, good. So I corroborated you."

"Yes, it was very useful. I read your piece about Zabit Akrem too."

That one was a private e-mail that I had sent out to my friends. I had been writing these since I first came to Afghanistan with NPR, one every few months, when there was something to say. This latest one was pretty raw—written the day I came down from the burial at Khakrez. I wondered who had forwarded it to Karzai.

I told him: "Mr. President, you have just lost your best friend."

"I know, I know," President Karzai replied brightly. "We were good buddies, going way back."

"That's not what I mean. I mean professionally. For your government, for your country."

He said something else off the mark. He didn't get it.

"Listen," I pursued. "I've been doing some work on the bombing. There really hasn't been any investigation. I wanted to give you the information I've come up with."

Karzai said he'd love to hear it. I started drawing my sketch-map. "This is the road to Chahar Sou, right? And this is the dirt road next to the mosque . . ." Karzai was from Kandahar; I could refer to the landmarks. I pushed the slip of paper over to him, then leaned over his shoulder to explain the dots: who was standing where when the bomb when off. I told him I was absolutely sure it was a Pakistani job.

"Of course it was!"

We were fellow Kandaharis, communing together. I could hear his tuning fork.

"I don't think Gul Agha did it though. I know him. He's not that kind of person; he's not that clever."

"OK fine, Gul Agha didn't do it himself, personally. But people under him did. He provides the umbrella that allows Pakistan to place its operatives in Kandahar. That's his role. That's always been his role."

"I agree with you."

"So get rid of him," I pleaded. "And the others. You've given these people enough time. Here's what you've been doing: you've been thinking you can buy your enemies, and you've been taking your friends for granted.

But you'll *never* be able to buy your enemies. No matter how much you give them, they'll never change. And meanwhile, you're losing your friends. You've come to the end of that rope. The people can't stand it anymore. Stop dancing with these thugs."

"You're right," President Karzai said. He promised me he would do it.

In Kandahar there were five people, I told him.

"I'll get rid of them."

He promised. I was elated. I was understood.

We moved to other matters. What did I think of Isma'il Khan for interior minister, the president wanted to know. Exhausted Jalali was planning to resign.

Ismail Khan? That warlord?

I paused. "You know who would have been a great interior minister?" I pointed to the sketch-map. "Him."

"You think I wasn't thinking of that?"

Oh. The revelation traversed me. Oh how well this blow had been calculated. It was not just revenge, this murder of Akrem—revenge for his skillful obstruction of Pakistani demolition work. It was a future Afghan interior minister the ISI had just assassinated. I thought another second. I thought about Mazar-i-Sherif, about those Uzbeks in tears up at the graveyard in Khakrez, about the funeral oration in Persian. Akrem was the only person who could unite the country so. He was better at it than Karzai even, for Karzai had begun to alienate his own Pashtuns without really winning over the other ethnic groups. Akrem won people over, and not just with words. Akrem won them over because he did something. He was effective. And he had vision. He had compassion too, but also the decisiveness—harshness even—needed to function in this place. There was no reason Akrem could not have run for president. Mazar would certainly have voted for him, and Kandahar, and Kabul, by the time he had been there for a year. Maybe the next election would have been too soon, but the man had been only forty-six.

The "suicide bombers" in Pakistan were looking ahead, well ahead of the rest of us. This murder had shattered one of the foundation stones of Afghanistan's midterm future—and with it, that of the whole interconnected region.

Nonetheless, I left that meeting on air. At least President Karzai seemed to finally understand. At least Akrem's death would not be for absolutely nothing. It would serve to reverse some of the policies he had fought so hard against. There might be a way forward.

As I drove back to Akrem's former quarters by the King's Garden, I thought of a few more things I wanted to tell the president, just to make sure everything was clear.

I composed one of my letters to him. I hadn't written one in over a year.

"Dear Mr. President:

"I have some further thoughts about steps to be taken in the wake of Khakrezwal's murder . . ."

Six of them, to be precise.

I urged Karzai to use the event as an opportunity. It was the final gift Akrem had given him: a ringing justification for long overdue policy shifts. Just as 9/11 had served as a pretext for major initiatives in the United States, Karzai could explain that Akrem's murder was an event of such magnitude that it obliged him to take extraordinary action in its wake.

But to do so, he would have to treat it as something extraordinary, and not "allow it to be covered over by Afghanistan's drifting dust," as I put it.

I told Karzai to stop playing musical chairs with criminal public officials. Stop allowing the agents of foreign countries free rein in Afghanistan. "To blame Pakistan for Akrem's murder is correct," I wrote, "but not sufficient. You must also blame yourself, Mr. President, for making Pakistan's job easier by maintaining its agents in power in Kandahar."

Then there was the United States. I suggested that Karzai help the United States devise a new policy toward Pakistan. U.S. officials had been bullied into believing that any alternative would be worse: black turbans with their fingers on the button. Washington was paralyzed. I thought that President Karzai, with his unparalleled feel for Pakistan, could suggest different directions for the United States. I reminded him about "most likely/most dangerous" planning and suggested he draw up a policy brief. I'd be happy to help, I added.

Two days later, I delivered this letter to Karzai's chief of staff. The president was sick; he couldn't see me, though he had insisted I check in with him before leaving for Kandahar. The letter, said the chief of staff, would be on his desk as soon as he could sit up to read it. I was back in the game.

But in the end, none of it came to pass.

Blindly, obstinately, in the face of everything Shafiullah and I had brought to light, Kabul officialdom continued to call Akrem's murder a suicide bombing. And I realized: the truth just didn't matter. Another ream of evidence, had we collected it, would not have made a bit of difference. Reality did not matter. Reality was not going to dent this fiction; it was too useful. It shielded the true perpetrators; it absolved Afghan officials of responsibility, incompetence, or even the duty to investigate; and it played to the obsession of the Americans. Shirzai and Karzai had hit upon an explanation that satisfied everyone. My knight, my champion—truth—proved impotent. Quickly, the issue died.

Gul Agha Shirzai was removed from the governorship of Kandahar once more. But he was appointed to Nangrahar, another Pakistani border province whose capital, Jalalabad, commands the only other road connecting the continents across Afghanistan. A strategic place, yet again.

"Let me handle the strategy," President Karzai retorted when I called him on it during a second meeting, over breakfast.

How ironic. I had begun this Afghan journey convinced that Karzai and Shirzai were opposites: white and black, cultivated and doltish, visionary and evil. But here they were, three and a half years on, welded together as solidly as the contradictory elements in the collective character of the Afghans—if there is such a thing.

At that second meeting with President Karzai, over jam and bread and orange juice arrayed on china and white linen, I read off a list of people in Kandahar he simply had to fire—nearly the same list I had sent to Jalali two years before. For nothing had happened yet. President Karzai had promised me when we bent our heads over my sketch map three weeks earlier, but these people were still in place—the people who had killed Zabit Akrem, or allowed him to be killed. I had told the president. He had agreed. He had promised. But except for one, they still held their positions, as if nothing had happened.

Were my list a fly, buzzing over his breakfast table, Karzai would have used the same gesture: "Those are details!" he said, then seemed shocked by my retort:

"You know, most Kandaharis think you're actually allied with the Pakistani government *against* Afghanistan."

"Did you hear that?" he exclaimed to his chief of staff. Then turning back to me: "What is it the people want me to do?"

"*This* is what they want you to do! Take concrete action, don't just talk about it. *Do* something."

But President Karzai steered the conversation back to the theory of America's Pakistan policy. He wanted to show me some satellite photos; he wanted me to expose to America what Pakistan was up to. He was interested in a media campaign. The fault lay elsewhere, not with him. He wiped his lips, scooted out from the table, and cantered off, waving bye-bye to me over his shoulder.

"Do you think he heard me?" I was flopped on the couch in the chief of staff's office.

His voice was dry. "You certainly made your point strongly enough."

It took about two days for the whole experience to sink in. Looking back, I suspect that Karzai's charm offensive, his enthusiastic approval of what I was telling him about Akrem's murder, was aimed mainly at discovering exactly what information I had.

Well, now he knows.

The revolution in me had been swift. It was as though all the changes I had gone through over the course of the past three years had just taken place all over again. For a brief moment, I had believed again. I had seen the manner of Akrem's dying as his final gift. That flash of light that had thrust through the carpet in the mosque had illuminated everything so clearly, I thought. There was no escape from action this time. I only had to reengage, to step forward and point out the incontrovertible facts that the flash had brought to light. Then the truth would work its magic. So I thought.

But I was wrong, again. I had traveled the whole cycle from inspiration and devotion to bitter disillusionment in a few short weeks.

And yet this process had electrified me, even if for a brief moment. The sense it gave me of carrying Akrem's work forward had carried me across that devastating period, and had deposited me—in the company of new friends: Shafiullah, Akrem's younger brother, a new deputy chief of police—back in Kandahar.

When Akrem was killed, I had wondered searchingly if it was not finally time to go. Without him, who was left to fight for? Who was left to support, to contribute my capacities to, such as they were? With him gone, the last rational hope for the future of Afghanistan had been quenched. Of what value could my presence be?

And yet this feeling, acute at first, did not stop to dwell in me. Instead, illogically, what I found myself experiencing was an inarticulate, renewed sense of commitment. I couldn't leave, there was too much to do.

Besides, I loved the place.

I think it was then that I fully understood Akrem's equally illogical commitment. It wasn't that he didn't see the flaws in the Afghan government he served. He saw them in clearer detail than most. But he saw something else too: he understood that, in this specific time and place, this government provided him the framework to keep trying. That was one way he knew to honor his own fallen friends. And they must have been legion—those scraps of cloth on poles in all those graveyards. This Afghan government, flawed as it was, gave Akrem a means to act, and to act his way, on the ground, daubed in the messy reality of it, among the people, helping them concretely, committing faults and trying to rectify—trying.

This isn't much of a conclusion, I know it. It's too abrupt; it's inchoate, unspelled out. It's just the note of a tuning fork. But I am thinking this: I think Akrem understood that it doesn't really matter if there is a chance you will succeed. You have to keep trying. That's what matters. You have to try. You have to give your all.

NOTES

CHAPTER 2: COVERING CRISIS

1. For this term see Samuel Huntington, *The Clash of Civilizations and the Remaking of World Order* (New York: Simon and Schuster, 1999); and for one of many rebuttals, see Roy Mottahedeh, "The Clash of Civilizations: An Islamicist's Critique," in Qureshi and Sells, eds., *The New Crusades: Constructing the Muslim Enemy* (New York: Columbia University Press, 2003).

2. Two examples (orthography as received):

"I'm writing you because this coverage is very upsetting and sad. Specifically the details about the wounded child crying and for that matter all the facts regarding the family members that were killed. I consider myself very liberal and opposed to war and violence but what do you expect to gain from this kind of coverage? What is your reporters motivation? Do you assess the value or damage your reports can cause? The only thing I can compare this to is if we had American reporters in World War II covering the bombing deaths of women and children in Germany. I consider it irresponsible and right wing thinkers may go as far as calling it treason."

"While I am listening to the whimpers of afghany children, the pleas of parents who have lost loved ones due to accidental bombings, or even on purpose bombings . . . What I would like to know, is where are the voices of the US children that no longer have parents because they were disintegrated in the World Trade Center. Where are the voices of the families and loved ones of the five or six thousand people that where anihilated to the point of unidentifiable dust! . . . I am truly getting tired of, and becoming angry; listening to the whimpers and the voices of those who have lost something in Afghanistan. . . . What is the purpose, what is the intent, of broadcasting this information? If NPR must broadcast these reports, then let us be fair, shall we . . . broadcast interviews of the children that have lost their parents in the World Trade Center. Broadcast the interviews of the injured people, the wives of the firefighters whose husbands will no longer be coming home, lives ineffably changed forever. . . . I have had enough and I am one individual that will not listen to Morning Edition for a while. I am embarrassed for the news media of NPR and I am angry that they would use their listening public, who supports them, to be subject to this kind of propaganda for the sake of ratings or some twisted idea that Americans want to hear this! What on earth were you thinking? I think I will listen to a Mozart CD for the rest of the morning."

CHAPTER 3: MOVING IN ON KANDAHAR

1. Tyler Marshall, "Warlord's Politics Could Prove Problematic," *Los Angeles Times,* October 24, 2001, p. A9.

2. A public call office (PCO) is an office where people without phones in their houses can make calls. There is one on just about every street corner in northern Pakistan and Afghanistan.

3. Sarah Chayes, Newscast spot, National Public Radio, November 25, 2001 (from author's text).

4. Ibid., November 28, 2001.

5. Ibid., December 1, 2001 (from author's text).

CHAPTER 4: REPORTING THE LAST DAYS

1. Locally the trademark ghostlike blue garment with its square of mesh in front of the eyes is called a *chadri,* or *bughra.*

CHAPTER 5: THE FALL OF THE TALIBAN

1. See Tyler Marshall and author's NPR spot on November 15: "Today [Pashtun opposition leader Hamid Karzai] called on the Taliban to join a broad-based Afghan government."

CHAPTER 7: TAKING THE CITY BY FORCE

1. See Chayes NPR spots December 8, 9, 2001, and Q&A, *All Things Considered,* December 8, 2001.

2. Bradley Graham and Thomas E. Ricks, "Rumsfeld Says War Far from Over, Tribal Politics and Hunt for Taliban Leaders Pose New Challenges," *Washington Post,* December 8, 2001, p. A-1.

CHAPTER 8: A CHOICE OF ALLIES

1. In a deal with Pakistan, Washington channeled all of its assistance to Afghan resistants through Pakistan's Inter-Services Intelligence agency, the ISI. U.S. officials only began forging direct links to some Afghans a few years into the conflict. (See Steve Coll, *Ghost Wars* [New York: Penguin Press, 2004].) One of them, Mullah Naqib, described to me his secret nighttime meetings with U.S. intelligence agents in Peshawar, Pakistan. When he asked the CIA agents how they had heard of him, they told him that Karzai had suggested his name.

2. My gratitude to Jonathan Shay for his breathtaking work in this field. Please see his *Odysseus in America: Combat Trauma and the Trials of Homecoming* (New York: Scribner, 2002), especially "Pirate Raid: Staying in Combat Mode," pp. 19–34. Note also the habitual lying on the part of people suffering unhealed combat trauma, or retention of the "Army habit of commandeering anything of uncertain ownership," p. 32.

3. For a full exposition of this argument, see Michael Barry, *Le Royaume de l'Insolence* (Paris: Flammarion, 2002).

4. Ibid., p. 235.

5. See George Crile, *Charlie Wilson's War* (New York: Atlantic Monthly Press, 2004).

6. Steve Coll, *Ghost Wars* (New York: Penguin Press, 2004).

7. The use of the masculine pronoun is deliberate. On the attractions of a criminal career to combat veterans, see Shay, *Odysseus,* pp. 26–33.

8. This reputation has held for at least two hundred years. In 1810, Mountstuart Elphinstone, a British envoy to Kabul, wrote: "The Achekzais differ so much from the other Durranis that I have reserved them for a separate description. . . . No traveler can enter their country without being plundered, and they often make nightly expeditions into the lands of their neighbors to steal. Skill in theft, and boldness in robbery, are great qualities among them. . . . Their robberies, however, are never aggravated by murder. . . . They wear their clothes unchanged for months, their beards unclipped, and their hair long and shaggy. . . . Their manners are rough and barbarous, but they are not quarrelsome among themselves. . . . They are not hospitable, they have no mosques, and seldom pray or trouble themselves about religion. . . . All tribes are loud in their complaints against them, and the Durranis will hardly acknowledge them for clansmen." See Elphinstone's *An Account of the Kingdom of Caubul* (Graz: Akademische Druck u. Verlagsanstalt, 1969), pp. 421–22. (Spellings changed for conformity.)

CHAPTER 9: DEALING FOR THE GOVERNORSHIP

1. U.S. officials have repeatedly made the same mistake. When a secretary of defense or a U.S. ambassador, for example, goes to Herat to pay a visit to the virtually independent governor there, a man who regularly flouts the laws of the central government, the American is abased in the eyes of Afghans, and the governor's prestige is immeasurably enhanced.

2. President Karzai told me, when I asked him in mid-2004, that he had wanted to "reconcile the two sides" and that when Mullah Naqib was attacked, he "strongly defended him." This does not jibe with what other participants remember.

3. Roy Gutman, *How We Missed the Story* (forthcoming) (Washington, D.C.: USIP, 2006).

4. Karzai family loyalists, including, the Abdullah, who was living in the same house with Hamid Karzai in Quetta, Pakistan, at the time, confirm his démarche to Mullah Naqib. They also confirm Karzai's intimate involvement with the nascent Taliban movement, including the regular meetings he hosted with its leaders, and the fact that they would enter the house armed. The family's public version of these events is that these were traditional religious leaders acting in good faith to put an end to the civil strife. "We were all fooled," says Hamid's older brother Qayum Karzai. "We all thought they wanted to organize a *Loya Jirga* and bring back the former king." In conversation with me in 2004, President Karzai referred to the Taliban leaders he met with as his "buddies," saying they were "ordinary people" whom he desperately hoped might halt the chaos. He said some months after the Taliban took Kandahar, when his friends among them told him that another faction was getting copious arms from an unknown source, he began to suspect there was more to this Taliban movement than he had thought— that the Pakistani ISI was behind it—and he broke off official relations, "though per-

sonal relations were maintained." Other family members counter that it was impossible not to be aware, from the earliest days, of the ISI role and ambitions in launching the Taliban. And, several noted, this was a cause of bitter disagreement between Hamid Karzai and his father, who opposed any involvement with the nascent Taliban movement. According to U.S. diplomatic documents uncovered by Roy Gutman, Karzai was still identified as Taliban ambassador-designate to the United Nations in late 1996. Cf. John Lee Anderson, "Letter from Afghanistan," *The New Yorker,* January 28, 2002.

CHAPTER 10: KANDAHAR, AFGHAN CAPITAL

1. E.g., Olaf Caroe, *The Pathans* (Karachi: Oxford University Press, 1990) (1st ed., 1958), p. 256.

2. Abdurrahman Khan (amir of Afghanistan, d. 1901), *Mustatab Siraj at-Tawarikh* (Kabul: Kabul Matba' 1331 [H]), p. 10. See also Mahmud al-Huseini al-Munshi (d. c. 1775), *Ta'rikh-i Ahmadshahi* (Moscow: 1974), p. 50.

3. Ganda Singh, *Ahmad Shah Durrani* (Bombay: Asia Publishing House, 1959), p. 29, describes three hundred camels under escort of an Afghan guard. Singh opines that the convoy "had encamped in the city to rest for a few days and to collect five hundred animals for their onward journey."

4. According to some accounts, they were moved there by force, in a form of ethnic cleansing, by Safavi Shah Abbas I. See Laurence Lockhart, *Nadir Shah* (London: Luzac, 1938).

5. See Laurence Lockhart, "The Revolt of the Abdalis," in *The Fall of the Safavi Dynasty and the Afghan Occupation of Persia* (Cambridge: Cambridge University Press, 1958), pp. 95–108.

6. Lockhart, pp. 473–85.

7. On long-distance overland trade, see Rudiger Klein, "Caravan Trade in Safavid Iran," in *Etudes Safavides,* Jean Calmard, ed. (Paris/Teheran: Institute Français de Recherche en Iran, 1993). On the Safavid dynasty, see ibid., Lockhart, and Peter Jackson, Lawrence Lockhart, eds. "The Timurid and Safavid Periods," *Cambridge History of Iran* (Cambridge: Cambridge University Press, 1986), pp. 189–412.

8. Note that Safavi Shah Isma'il assisted Babur in one of his briefly successful efforts to capture Samarqand, which he considered his Timurid birthright. See R. M. Savory, "Safawids," in *Encyclopedia of Islam New Edition* (Leiden: Brill, 1994), VIII: p. 767.

9. Wheeler M. Thackston, *The Baburnama,* trans. Zahiruddin Muhammad Babur, (New York: Modern Library, 2002), p. 254.

10. Ibid., p. 256.

11. Ibid.

12. Klein, p. 310.

13. Ibid., p. 313

14. Michael Barry, *Le Royaume de l'Insolence* (Paris: Flammarion, 2002) (1st ed., 1984), p. 95. Cf. M. Longworth Dames, "Afghanistan: Islamic, to the Rise of the Afghan National State," in *Encyclopedia of Islam,* p. 229.

15. Singh, pp. 11–13; Lockhart, "The Campaign Against the Abdali Afghans," in *The Fall of the Safavi Dynasty,* pp. 321–27; Lockhart, *Nadir Shah,* pp. 31–33, 51–54.

16. Singh, pp. 13, 15; Lockhart, *Nadir Shah,* p. 54, suggests that Nadir Shah's remarkable generosity toward the Abdalis stemmed from a foresightful plan to weld them into a fighting force that would be personally loyal to him, as he did.

17. Singh, pp. 16–17; G. P. Tate, *The Kingdom of Afghanistan* (Karachi: Indus Publications, 1973) (1st ed., 1911), pp. 57–65.

18. Lockhart, "The Reconquest of Kandahar," in *Nadir Shah,* pp. 112–21.

19. Tate, p. 65; Singh, pp. 17–18; Lockhart, *Nadir Shah,* p. 120.

20. Cf. John Keay, *India: A History* (London: Harper, 2000), pp. 385–86.

21. Mahmud al-Huseini al-Munshi, pp. 36, 37; Lockhart, *Nadir Shah,* p. 259.

22. Mahmud al-Huseini al-Munshi, pp. 37–40.

23. Lockhart, *Nadir Shah,* p. 262; p. 332; Singh, pp. 20–22; Tate, pp. 67–8.

24. Caroe, p. 254. Bawdy jokes still current suggest that Ahmad Shah was in fact Nadir Shah's "boy." The practice of older men taking prepubescent males as lovers and openly bestowing favors on them has roots in ancient Greece and Persia. It remains extremely commonplace in southern Afghanistan.

25. Mahmud al-Huseini al-Munshi, pp. 40–42.

26. Singh, p. 18, quoting three primary sources, says Ahmad Shah became "a *bank-bashi,*" or treasury officer, though it is difficult to imagine a horse guard captain also fulfilling this administrative task. Still, it is likely that a man enjoying the personal confidence of the monarch would be aware of the movements of large amounts of revenue.

27. Singh, p. 22, without much clear referencing, writes that the Abdalis did get some of Nadir's treasure, including the royal seal and the Koh-i-Nur diamond. But his description of a chaotic grab for plunder and disintegration of the army does not jibe with his contention that the Abdalis had to flee from "hostile Persians" who surrounded them "on all sides," p. 24.

28. Mahmud al-Huseini al Munshi, pp.45–49.

29. Singh, p. 28, thinks the *jirga* took place much earlier, on the road to Kandahar. But local legend reveres the shrine at Shir Surkh, just outside the modern town.

30. Caroe, p. 255; Singh, p. 25.

31. Personally, I suspect Ahmad Shah of staging some of the scene. Given his possession of the crack troops of half a continent, I question Ahmad Shah's demure pose. The *darwish* remained by his side till death.

32. Singh, p. 33, describes a kind of hybrid between a Persian-style bureaucracy, with "great offices," and a respect for Afghan tribal leadership, in which the chiefs of the various tribes, not just Ahmad Shah's own, were allowed to govern their internal affairs and accorded respect and distinction. See also Abdurrahman Khan, p. 11.

33. Barry, pp. 106, 166, 268, 302.

34. Mahmud al-Huseini al-Munshi, p. 56, expands poetically on Ahmad Shah's generosity with that founding caravan, saying he gave some of the treasure to the heads of the tribes, to the Qizilbashes and the Kabulis, and to everyone else: "*amir wa faqir wa saghir wa kabir wa barna wa pir wa dost wa mawafiq wa manafiq* (commander, beggar, small and great, young and old, friend and ally and hypocrite)."

35. Ibid., and Elphinstone, p. 424.

CHAPTER 12: THE BORDER

1. Peter Hopkirk, *The Great Game: The Struggle for Empire in Central Asia* (New York: Kodansha, 1992); Karl E. Meyer and Shareen Blair Brysac, *Tournament of Shadows: The Great Game and the Race for Empire in Central Asia* (Washington: Counterpoint, 1999).

2. Abd ar-Rahman Khan, *The Life of Abdur Rahman,* Vol. 2, Mir Munshi Sultan Mahomed Khan, ed. (Karachi: Oxford, 1980) (1st ed., 1900), p. 264.

3. Ibid., p. 246.

4. From Martin Ewins, *Afghanistan: A Short History of Its People and Politics* (New York: HarperCollins, 2002).

5. Abd ar-Rahman Khan, Vol. 2, p. 237.

6. See Sir H. Mortimer Durand, "The Amir Abdur Rahman Khan," in *Proceedings of the Central Asian Society,* XVIII (1907), p. 4: "Yakub Khan had resigned his throne, leaving British forces in possession of Kabul and Kandahar, it became necessary to provide for the future government of the country, which we did not want to keep."

7. I owe this analysis, again, to Michael Barry, *Le Royaume de l'Insolence* (Paris: Flammarion, 2002), pp. 161–62.

8. See Waller Ashe, ed., *Personal Records of the Kandahar Campaign by Officers Engaged Therein* (London: David Bogue, 1881), pp. 3–4: "We must remember that its strategic value is very considerable, being the first and only place of any strength, or where supplies in any quantity could be obtained, between Herat and the Indus. . . . The importance of holding can scarcely be overestimated in either a political or a military point of view." See also M. E. Yapp, *Strategies of British India* (Oxford: Clarendon Press, 1980), p. 440; C. Collin Davies, *The Problem of the Norwest Frontier* (Cambridge: Cambridge University Press, 1932), pp. 10–15; and Frank Noyce, *England, India, and Afghanistan* (London: Cambridge University Press, 1902), pp. 117–23. This one is a nearly contemporaneous essay written as part of the requirements for graduation at Cambridge University, and so would reflect establishment opinion of the time.

9. Abd ar-Rahman Khan, Vol. 1, p. 227.

10. Ibid., p. 208.

11. Durand, p. 20.

12. Ibid., p. 5.

13. Ashe, p. 116.

14. Durand, p. 15.

15. Ibid.

16. Ashe, p. 36.

17. Ibid., pp. 29–30.

18, Ibid., p. 2.

19. British Army, Intelligence Branch, *The Second Afghan War, 1878–80* (London: Murray, 1908), pp. 501–2.

20. Ashe, p. 62.

21. Ibid., p. 63.

22. Ibid., p. 56.

23. Ibid., p. 51.

24. Ibid., p. 56; British Army, Intelligence Branch, p. 493.

25. Ashe, p. 86.

26. Ibid., p. 93.

27. Ibid., p. 98.

28. Ibid., p. 152.

29. Barry, p. 172. See the delightfully naive view of this in the 1902 Cambridge University Prize Essay cited above: "It furnished the first occasion for Abdur Rahman to display his loyalty towards the British, and Sir Frederick Roberts's wonderful march from Kabul to Kandahar owed much of its success to the new Amir's vigorous and tactful handling of the tribes which lined the route." Noyce, pp. 118–19.

30. Abd ar-Rahman Khan, Vol. 2, p. 176.

31. Ibid., p. 135.

32. Ibid., p. 135.

33. Durand, p. 15.

34. Ibid., p. 16.

35. "Whether viewed from a perspective of regional economics, ethnography, or basic geography, the line seems illogical." Jeffrey Roberts, *The Origins of Conflict in Afghanistan* (Westport: Praeger, 2003), p. 29. "The new boundary line was not based upon sound topographical data, for, during the process of demarcation, it was discovered that certain places marked on the Durand map did not exist on the actual ground. Many ethnic absurdities were perpetrated." Davies, p. 161. "The result was not altogether satisfactory and the unrest which had been prevalent along the frontier . . . was little, if at all, diminished." Noyce, p. 143.

36. Abd ar-Rahman Khan, Vol. 2, p. 157.

37. "Seeing that every Government was trying to get hold of as much as it possibly could, I also tried to take as much share as possible in these provinces which formerly belonged to Afghanistan and were now under independent chiefs, by making friends with them." Ibid., p. 149.

38. Ibid., p. 159.

CHAPTER 14: PLUNDER AND SUBSIDY

1. Afghans like dogs, and they use them to guard their houses and protect their flocks. But in Islam, dogs and cats are ritually unclean. Muslims perform ablutions before praying and, like urinating on themselves, touching a dog "breaks" the ablution and they have to do it over again before beginning their prayers. This is why "sniffer" dogs can be so distressing to Muslims.

2. For an excellent discussion of PTSD, see Jonathan Shay, *Achilles in Vietnam: Combat Trauma and the Undoing of Character* (New York: Scribner, 1994).

3. See, for example, the following comment of Abdur-Rahman Khan, ruler of Afghanistan from 1880 to 1910, regarding the annual subsidy he received from the British viceroy in India. "The payment of this subsidy does not minimize my dignity: on the contrary, it raises the value of my friendship." Mir Munshi Sultan Mahomed Khan, ed., *The Life of Abdur Rahman, Volume 2* (Karachi: Oxford, 1980), p. 256.

4. See Seymour Hersh, *Chain of Command* (New York: HarperCollins, 2004), p. 188, and George Packer, *The Assassins' Gate* (New York: Farrar Straus and Giroux, 2006), p. 45.

CHAPTER 15: SHOWDOWN WITH SHIRZAI

1. Throughout this entire episode, we were accompanied by a documentary film team, Brian Knappenberger and Anton Gold. They captured every scene I describe on film, and the extremely instructive and visually stunning results were broadcast in 2003 on PBS's *Frontline* as "A House for Hajji Baba," and in a longer version called *Life After War,* on the Discovery Channel. The team's presence not only added joy and sparkle to our lives, but immeasurably enhanced my reflection on the issues that emerged.

2. Sarah Chayes, "Rebuilding Akokolacha, and why America must get more involved—not less—in Afghanistan," *Christian Science Monitor,* December 10, 2002, pp. 12–13.

3. E.g., April Witt, "Afghan Governor Strains to Shed Warlord Image, Gul Agha's Rule in Kandahar Dismays Some in Kabul," *Washington Post,* April 15, 2003, p. A-22.

CHAPTER 17: MILITARY MATTERS

1. This problem eventually came to the attention of the Kandahar base command. In late 2004, I introduced six men as laborers on base—the first and only ones to work there who did not owe alliegance to Shirzai. They were explicitly chosen by base command to serve as a lance-head to begin to break the Shirzais' monopoly. By 2005, the monopoly was significantly weakened, with the Shirzais winning only some 40 percent of contracts on base, down from 80 to 90 percent. The details in this paragraph were communicated to me in private by U.S. Army officers responsible for the relevant contracts. Cf. James Glanz "Audit Describes Misuse of Funds in Iraq Projects," *New York Times,* January 25, 2006, p. A1.

CHAPTER 18: SECURITY

1. Interestingly, the female delegates seem to have been less intimidated than the men. One stepped to the podium and made ringing mention of the warlords' pasts, waving a hand at a nearby neighborhood destroyed by one of the delegates' shelling. One female focus group participant said: "Who cares if they turned the microphones off when we criticized them. We could just shout." See Sarah Chayes "Topak Salaran Basta," Loya Jirge Focus Groups Study, January 2003, available on www.afghansfor-civilsociety.org.

CHAPTER 19: THE COMING OF ISLAM

1. Clifford Edmund Bosworth, *Sistan Under the Arabs, from the Islamic Conquest to the Rise of the Saffarids* (Rome: Istituto Italiano per il Medio ed Estremo Oriente, 1968).

2. Asadi de Tus, *Le Livre de Gerchasp, Volume 1,* Clement Huart, ed., and trans. (Paris: Geuthner, 1926), p. 39. My translation from the French. Of course, no translation out of Persian can begin to do justice to the sound of its poetry, blessed as Persian is with vowels that are both rich and clear, inviting frequent assonance as well as rhyme.

3. Abul Qasim Firdowsi, *The Epic of the Kings,* Reuben Levy, trans. (Chicago: University of Chicago, 1967), p. 15, and for this version of Jamshid's reign, pp. 9–11.

4. For a discussion of the achievements of Islamic Persia, see Richard Frye, *The Golden Age of Persia* (London: Phoenix, 2000) (1st ed., 1975).

5. Approximately.

6. Firdowsi, p. 50.

7. Ibid., pp. 50–52.

8. Jos J. L. Gommans, *The Rise of the Indo-Afghan Empire, c. 1710–1780* (Delhi: Oxford India Paperbacks, 1999); cf. Rudyard Kipling, *Kim*: the character of Mahbub Ali, a Pashtun horse trader, spy, and friend of Kim's, or Kipling's short story "Drey Wara Yow Dee," narrated by another Pashtun horse dealer from Afghanistan.

9. Cf. Mary Renault, *The Nature of Alexander* (New York: Pantheon, 1976), pp. 33–34.

10. Some etymologies of the name Kandahar trace it back to the Persianized version of Alexander. But though there is good reason to believe that Alexandria in Arachosia, one of the cities the Macedonian conqueror left in his wake, was indeed located beside modern Kandahar, archaeologists do not agree upon the exact site of the city. The true origins of the name Kandahar are subject to a similar dispute. See C. E. Bosworth's article on Kandahar in the *Encyclopedia of Islam*.

11. Firdowsi, p. 109.

12. Strabo, *Geography, XV 2:9:* "Alexander took these [lands inhabited by the Aracoti and other tribes, near the Indus] away from the Arians, and established settlements of his own, but Seleucus Nikator gave them to Sandrocottus [Chandragupta] upon terms of intermarriage and of receiving in exchange five hundred elephants." Horace Leonard Jones, trans. (Cambridge, MA: Loeb Classics, Harvard University Press, 1930), p.143.

13. Giovanni Pugliese Carratelli and Giovanni Garbini, "A Bilingual Graeco-Aramaic Edict by Asoka," in *Serie Orientale Roma 29 (1964)* (Rome: IsMEO, 1964).

14. Ibid., p. 60.

15. Ibid., p. 109.

16. For this whole episode, ibid., pp. 195–211.

17. Hugh Kennedy, *The Prophet and the Age of the Caliphates, 2nd ed.* (London: Pearson, 2004), p. 59. See also Marshall G. S. Hodgeson, *The Venture of Islam, Volume 1, the Classical Age of Islam* (Chicago: University of Chicago, 1977) (1st ed., 1974), pp. 197–200.

18. Hodgeson, pp. 208–11.

19. Asadi de Tus, p. 74.

20. Ibid., p. 98.

21. Bosworth, *Sistan,* p. 20. Cf. Frye, pp. 51–52, 92–93.

22. Al-Baladhuri, *Futuh al-Buldan* Part II, Francis Murgotten, trans. (New York: Columbia, 1924), p.144.

23. Bosworth, pp. 34–35.

24. This version of events is quoted from *The History of al-Tabari, Volume XXII, the Marwanid Restoration*, Everett Rowson, trans. (New York: SUNY, 1989), pp. 182–88. In the interest of style, I occasionally change a verb tense or substitute a synonym for a word in the text. Cf. Baladhuri, pp. 150–51.

25. "Their city," in the next sentence, would probably have been the summer cap-

ital, Ghazni, rather than the Kandahar region, since the raid must have been launched during the traditional fighting season, and since only that location would allow for Muslim passage across the vast tracts of land described.

26. Al-Tabari, p. 185; Bosworth, p. 54.

27. Kufa and Basra.

28. This part of the story, from al-Hajjaj's letter to ibn al-Ash'ath's, can be found in at-Tabari, Vol. 22, pp. 188–94. See also Bosworth, pp. 57–59, and Julius Wellhausen, *The Arab Kingdom and Its Fall,* Margaret Weir, trans. (Beirut: Khayats, 1963) (1st ed., 1927), pp. 231–32.

29. Al-Tabari, Vol. 23, p. 4.

30. Ibid., pp. 50–51.

31. For this part of the story, see al-Tabari, Vol. 23, pp. 1–9, 49–53, 77–80; Balad-huri, pp. 151–52 (though his interpretation is rather different); Bosworth, pp. 58–63; and Wellhausen, pp. 232–41.

32. Bosworth, p. 101.

33. Ibid., p. 104. Gardez is the Afghan region where most of the firefights take place between U.S. outposts and "resurgent Taliban."

34. Ibid., 105–21; R. N. Frye, ed., *The Cambridge History of Iran,* Vol. 4, (Cambridge: Cambridge University Press, 1975), pp. 106–14; Theodore Noldeke, *Sketches from Eastern History,* John Sutherland Black, trans. (Beirut: Khayats, 1963), pp. 176–79.

35. *Cambridge History of Iran,* Vol. 4, pp. 111–12.

36. *Saffar* means "coppersmith."

37. *Cambridge History of Iran,* Vol. 4, pp. 129–30, 607–8.

CHAPTER 21: MURDER

1. Steve Coll, *Ghost Wars* (New York: Penguin Press, 2004), pp. 118–19, 121, ff.

2. See, e.g., Owen Benett Jones, *Pakistan: The Eye of the Storm* (New York: Yale, 2002), pp. 100–4.

3. Coll; George Crile, *Charlie Wilson's War* (New York: Grove Atlantic, 2003); Ahmad Rashid, *Taliban* (New Haven: Yale, 2001), p. 184.

4. Rashid, p. 186.

5. See Rashid's chapter 14: "Master or Victim, Pakistan's Afghan War," for telling details about Pakistan's involvement in Taliban-ruled Afghanistan, the limits to Pakistan's overlordship, and the devastating impact on Pakistan's hopes for a healthy development.

CHAPTER 22: MONGOL CONQUESTS AND REBIRTH

1. *The Secret History of the Mongols,* p. 264, a few words cut and brackets removed for clarity. Urgunge Onon, trans. (Richmond, Surrey: Curzon, 2001), p. 255, or the definitive scholarly edition, Igor de Rachewiltz (Leiden: Brill, 2004), p. 195.

2. Mary Renault, *The Nature of Alexander* (London: Pantheon, 1976), pp. 103–5.

3. Guy MacLean Rogers, *Alexander: The Ambiguity of Greatness* (New York: Random House, 2004), pp. 110–11. This book is particularly useful for its clear maps.

4. Renault, p. 134.

5. Ibid., p. 167.

6. For the details of Alexander's campaigns, drawn from a rather limited number of ancient sources, there is an abundance of secondary literature. Apart from Rogers and Renault, cited above, see Mary Renault's fictional version, *The Persian Boy,* narrated by the young Persian eunuch who in fact became Alexander's intimate. It is a dazzling piece of historical reconstruction.

7. Ata-Malik Juvaini, *Genghis Khan, the History of the World-Conqueror,* J. A. Boyle, trans. (Paris: UNESCO, 1997), p. 116. Current standard transliteration puts a "y" in place of the first "i" in the author's last name.

8. See the very detailed description by papal envoy Giovanni di Plano Carpini in 1247. *The Story of the Mongols Whom We Call the Tartars,* Erik Hildinger, trans. (Boston: Brandon Publishing, 1996), p. 72.

9. Almost as much secondary literature exists about the Mongols as about Alexander. For their general description, I have relied principally on Jack Weatherford, *Genghis Khan and the Making of the Modern World* (New York: Crown, 2004). On their battle tactics, see the excellent firsthand account by di Plano Carpini, above.

10. Juvaini, p. 98.

11. Ibid., p. 104.

12. Weatherford, pp. 5–6.

13. Minhaj ad-Din Juzjani, *Tabakat-i Nasiri,* H. G. Raverty, trans. (New Delhi: Oriental Reprint, 1970), p. 966.

14. In the case of Bukhara, its townsmen served these purposes against their own inner fortress, whose "moat had been filled with animate and inanimate, and raised up with levies and Bukharans. . . . Then the people of Bukhara were driven against the citadel. And on either side the furnace of battle was heated." Juvaini, p. 106.

15. Ibid., p. 118.

16. Ibid., p. 120.

17. Ibid., p. 116.

18. Juzjani, p. 270.

19. Ibid., p. 385.

20. Ibid., p. 279, has him "prostrated with a disease of the bowels," which "drove him out of his mind."

21. Juvaini, p. 376.

22. This is just what Giovanni di Plano Carpini advised western Europeans to do twenty-five years later, should the Mongols renew their attack: "If the Christians wish to save themselves, their country and Christianity, they must gather in one body the kings, princes, barons, and rectors of the lands and send the men to fight the Tartars under a single plan," p. 89. In making his argument, according to Juvayni, Prince Jalal ad-Din invoked a rather modern notion of governance. He did not want the people to say that their rulers exacted tax and tribute, "yet in time of need, place us in the jaws of disappointment.," p. 377.

23. The article "Ghurids" in the *Encyclopedia of Islam* by C. E. Bosworth says there is nothing to confirm this surmise. There seems to be nothing to contradict it either.

24. This fellow goes by different names in the various sources: Khan Malik, Amin

Malik, Yamin Malik, Yamin al-Mulk, and so on. I have chosen to use Khan Malik because it is closest to what the Mongols called him, which has credence because they would probably have been writing down what they heard phonetically.

25. Juvaini, p. 461.

26. Ibid., p. 462. Cf. Muhammad ibn Ahmad an-Nasawi, *History of Djalal el-Din Mankobirti, Shah of Khwarazm,* Havez Hamdi, ed. (Cairo: Dar el-Fikr el-Arabi, 1953), pp. 133–34. In French translation: Mohamad en-Nesawi, *Histoire du Sultan Djelal ed-Din Mankobirti, Prince du Kharezm,* O. Houdas, trans. (Paris: Ernest Leroux, 1895), p. 109. Nasawi has Jalal ad-Din and Khan Malik entering Ghazni from this victory at Kandahar together and triumphant. The people of Ghazni, he says, were every bit as thrilled to see the two princes as hungry Muslims are to see the moon that marks the end of Ramadan.

27. Nasawi, Hamdi, ed., pp. 133–34. For the record, here is the complete translation of the incident. I have tried to preserve the Arabic literary style: Genghis Khan was trying to cut Jalal ad-Din off on his way back from his father's burial, "so Jalal ad-Din got serious about fleeing to the outer limits of Bost [near the current Helmand Province capital, Lashkar Gah, about a three-hour drive west across the desert from Kandahar]. He was apprised that Genghis Khan had set himself up in Taloqan [north of Kabul] with a densely gathered troop, soldiers uncountable. And the light of day was darkened for Jalal ad-Din. Both fixedness and flight seemed hard for him, for there was no refuge in store, no security either behind him or in front of him, and his perils persisted. So to Ghazni he embarked, as suddenly as a man who will not remain in place, or who does not tread the earth with sedentary intentions. On his second or third day, he received news that his cousin Amin Malik [aka Khan Malik] . . . had left Herat to get away from the Tatars, and had conceived designs on the province of Sistan [Zaranj], to become its governor. But he was not able to, and he was now returning with roughly 10,000 Turkic horsemen, brave youths like lion cubs, lethal. These were select troops from the Sultan's armies who had escaped the [Mongol] catastrophe with abundant equipment and quantities of provisions. Jalal ad-Din sent word to [his cousin] of his proximity, pressing him to be quick and come. The two joined together, and decided to attack the Tatars who were besieging the fortress of Kandahar. And the two pounced on the Tatars. And the Enemies of God were downcast; they did not know how the princes had laid in wait for them, and how the troops of horsemen had closed in on them from all sides. They had figured that the doe-gazelles would run away from them, unable to stand it, that the business ends of their spears would be idle and ineffectual. Until, when they saw [the lance-points] thirsting to slaughter them, parched for [the blood of] their chests, they mounted the withers of flight. And none of them escaped except an insignificant band, which informed Genghis Khan of what had befallen his soldiers.

28. Ibid., p. 405.

29. An-Nesawi, p. 108.

30. Juzjani, p. 1016.

31. *The Secret History,* p. 257. The text was probably written in 1228, just after Genghis Khan's death, with some later additions. See de Rachewiltz, p. xxxiii. Some believe that this same Shigi Qutuqu is the fellow who wrote *The Secret History,* which would explain with special poignancy its lack of detail here.

32. It was a tactic documented by di Plano Carpini: "When the Tartars are few in numbers they use . . . dummy men . . . so that they may seem more numerous to their adversaries [who] are frightened and confused by this," pp. 75–76. Note that guile has been traditionally seen as just as important to a soldier's craft as bravery and brute force. See Shay, *Odysseus.*

33. For this whole account, see Juvaini, pp. 406–7.

34. Ibid., pp. 407–8. Nasawi's telling is vivid, and it betrays his Ghurid sensibilities: "And the reason [for this separation]," he writes, "was that, after they shattered the Mongols at Parwan, the Turks started shoving [the Ghurids] around regarding what God had showered down on them in the way of booty, in a blameworthy fashion. To the point that, when one of the Turks wrenched a horse from among the Tatars' livestock away from a loyalist of Ighraq's, and the dispute between the two of them grew long, the Turk hit him with a riding whip. And [Ighraq's men's] souls recoiled at this, and their hearts drew back from it. And the arrogant idea of separating [from the army] flew into their heads, when they saw that they could not get a fair division. For, whenever Jalal ad-Din tried to satisfy [Ighraq's men], the Turks would increase in evil and in zealous partisanship, with calamitous deeds. . . . And when Jalal ad-Din was trying with kindness to bring [Ighraq's people] back, and, with leisurely and friendly words to bind them to rejoin, the Turks would bolt away. And it was God's command: [Ighraq's people] separated from the army," pp. 155–56. Note the demonstration of both the *yaghestan* tendency and the tradition of long, drawn-out negotiations to try to thwart it.

35. Homer, *The Iliad,* I:1–9. I have taken from both the Fagles and Fitzgerald translations.

36. Jonathan Shay, *Achilles in Vietnam, Combat Trauma and the Undoing of Character* (New York: Scribner, 1994), pp. 13–14.

37. Juvaini, p. 408.

38. Ibid., pp. 410–11.

39. *The Secret History of the Mongols,* 264.

40. Jean Aubin, "L'ethnogenese des Qaraunas," *Turcica I (1969),* p. 69. My translation from the French.

41. His name was Temur, and he was lamed by an arrow wound in Zaranj. "Leng" means "lame" in Persian, whence the Western "Tamerlane."

42. In the Mongol belief system, rivers were almost sacred, for like mothers, they gave their milk to the land, providing life. In this context, anything that cut up the land, or worse, that interrupted the integrity of rivers, was taboo. So destroying irrigation systems was, for the Mongols, repairing the river and the land by restoring it to its natural condition. (From a private communication with anthropologist Jack Wetherford.)

CHAPTER 23: FIGHTING WITH THE PEN

1. April Witt, "Afghan Governor Strains to Shed Warlord Image. Gul Agha's Rule in Kandahar Dismays Some in Kabul," *Washington Post,* April 15, 2003, p. A22.

2. See Dana Priest, "The Proconsuls: America's Soldier Diplomats: A Four-Star Foreign Policy?" September 28, 2000, p. A1; "An Engagement in 10 Time Zones," Sep-

tember 29, 2000, p. A1; "Standing up to State and Congress," September 30, 2000, p. A1.

CHAPTER 24: MISFIRE

1. April Witt, "Karzai Gets Agreement from Local Leaders," *Washington Post,* May 21, 2003.

2. Carlotta Gall, "Warlords Yield to Afghan Leader, Pledging to Hand Over Funds," *New York Times,* May 21, 2003.

3. Witt.

CHAPTER 25: ROUND THREE

1. Sarah Chayes, "Afghanistan's Future, Lost in the Shuffle," *New York Times,* July 1, 2003.

CHAPTER 28: MAZAR-I-SHERIF

1. Ahmad Rashid, "Mazar-e-Sharif 1997: Massacre in the North," in *Taliban* (New Haven: Yale, 2000), pp. 72–74.

CHAPTER 32: COVER-UP

1. Marcello Fois, *Sempre Caro,* Serge Quadruppani, French trans. (Paris: Seuil, 1999), p. 85.

INDEX